Help Yourself to Advanced French Grammar

NEW EDITION

A grammar reference and workbook
Post-GCSE/A

Thalia Marr
Mireille Ribi

LONGMAN

Pearson Education Limited,
Edinburgh Gate, Harlow,
Essex CM20 2JE, England
and associated companies throughout the world

© Addison Wesley Longman Limited 1998

The right of Thalia Marriott and Mireille Ribière
to be identified as authors of this Work has been
asserted by them in accordance with the Copyright,
Designs and Patents Act of 1988.

ISBN 978-0-582-32945-4

First published 1998
Twelfth impression 2008
Printed in China
SWTC/12

The publisher's policy is to use paper manufactured from sustainable forests.

Help Yourself to French Grammar

Acknowledgements

Our sincere thanks to all the teachers and lecturers who have sent us comments on *Help Yourself to French Grammar*, to Marie-Christine Press, Glasford Rock and Natasha Talyarkhan for their comments on the original manuscript, to Sandrine Belin and Virginia Marriott for their assistance in revising the book and to T J Warner and Catherine and the Mayos for their unwavering support.

Contents

Introduction

Help Yourself to Advanced French Grammar is a French grammar reference and workbook which will enable the student to reach A-Level standard. It is designed for both self-study and class-based learning.

It is intended for all other post-GCSE work including EDEXCEL (BTEC), Institute of Linguists, LCCI and RSA qualifications. It is also used as a grammar revision workbook by students in their first year at university.

Presentation of grammar and vocabulary

The book takes a pragmatic approach to grammar, presenting in plain language the grammatical rules and explanations needed to write correct modern French of a discursive and topical nature. Grammatical terms are kept to a minimum and are always explained.

The vocabulary introduced in the exercises is highly relevant to contemporary French studies, with each chapter presenting a different theme.

Structure of each chapter

The grammar points covered in each chapter follow a carefully worked out progression. Chapters 1–9 reinforce points learned at GCSE, and Chapters 10–24 introduce the more complex points required to raise language to advanced standard.

In Chapters 1–23, the preliminary set of exercises (*Diagnostic*) is designed to identify problem areas and assess the needs of the student. Another set of exercises (*Reinforcement*) follows the grammar explanations: its function is to apply and test newly acquired knowledge. A test (*Revision*) is found at the end of every third chapter. In Chapter 24, there is only one set of exercises (*Practice*) which follows the grammar explanations.

Key to exercises

The key to all the exercises is at the back of the book, printed on perforated pages which can be removed for class use.

Appendices

The appendices include advice on when to use accents, verb tables, a list of **-er** verbs with spelling changes, a list of common verbs and their constructions, a list of common adjectives and their constructions and an English–French vocabulary list.

Advice to students learning on their own

Using the book as a workbook

Before reading the grammar explanations included in each chapter, tackle the *Diagnostic* exercises. These are designed to give you an idea of how much you know about the grammar points presented in the pages that follow.

After correcting your work, read through the grammar explanations carefully. Once you feel that you have understood them, do the *Reinforcement* exercises at the end of the chapter to see how much you have learned. Use the *Revision* tests as an opportunity to revise work done in previous chapters.

The key to the *Reinforcement* and *Revision* sections contains grammar references which refer you back to the relevant grammar explanations so that you can reread them if necessary: for example, 5.8 refers to chapter 5, section 8.

Using the book as a grammar reference

To find out about a particular point of grammar, look up the chapter reference in the *Grammar index* which follows the Appendices on page 211. You can then practise your knowledge by doing the relevant exercises.

Advice on tackling the exercises

1. Before starting each exercise, first read through it carefully. We suggest that you write out the answers in full and check your work carefully for spelling mistakes, agreement of adjectives, verb endings, etc.

2. Then check your answers against the key to the exercise at the back of the book. Learn from any mistakes you make and note down any vocabulary that you did not know.

3. The translation exercises into English (*Version*) and into French (*Thème*) will draw your attention to the differences between the two languages. With *Version*, the titles need not be translated, but you are expected to give a confident and fluent version of the original. With *Thème*, the important thing is to produce correct French using vocabulary from other exercises or from the English–French vocabulary list in the Appendices.

Bon travail !

Mireille Ribière
Thalia Marriott

Vie rurale et vie urbaine

Before looking at the grammar explanations in this chapter, find out what you know by doing the following exercises.

A Many young people today choose to live and work in the country. Insert **du, de la, de l', des** or **au, à la, à l', aux** in the gaps as appropriate.

Ils ont décidé de vivre en zone rurale

1. Après _____ études de droit, Bernard est retourné dans son village natal pour cultiver _____ fruits biologiques et fabriquer _____ confitures.
2. Daniel, qui fabriquait _____ bière pendant ses loisirs, a décidé d'en faire son activité principale. Il s'est rendu _____ Canada et _____ États-Unis pour étudier les nouvelles méthodes de fabrication avant de s'installer _____ campagne.
3. _____ début de l'année, Béatrice a ouvert une auberge dans un petit village situé _____ est d'Avignon. La restauration est l'activité principale _____ auberge mais Béatrice loue également _____ chambres. Elle a mis _____ plats traditionnels au menu et organise _____ cours de cuisine destinés _____ vacanciers.
4. Irène vient _____ banlieue parisienne. Elle a quitté la ville pour créer une entreprise dans un village _____ Nord. Grâce _____ télétravail[1], elle peut travailler à domicile.

B Life is hard for Laurence, a single mother who lives in the suburbs of Paris. Write the verbs in brackets in the present tense.

La vie en banlieue

- *Laurence, vous* (être) *mère célibataire et vous* (assurer) *un emploi[2]. Dites-moi, vous* (devoir) *avoir des journées bien chargées ?*
- Oui, plutôt ! Je *(être)* debout à six heures et je *(réveiller)* les enfants vers sept heures. Pendant qu'ils *(faire)* leur toilette, je *(faire)* un peu de ménage. Je les *(conduire)* ensuite chez ma mère et je *(aller)* prendre mon train. Il me *(falloir)* en général une heure pour arriver à l'agence de voyage où je *(travailler)*. Nous *(ouvrir)* à neuf heures et nous *(finir)* vers six heures.
- *C'est toujours votre mère qui* (s'occuper) *de vos enfants en votre absence ?*
- Oui. Le matin, elle les *(faire)* déjeuner et elle les *(accompagner)* à l'école. A midi, ils *(prendre)* leur repas à la cantine. Le soir, ma mère *(aller)* les chercher à la sortie de l'école et les *(aider)* à faire leurs devoirs. L'été ils *(venir)* parfois m'attendre à la gare. Heureusement que ma mère *(habiter)* tout près et que je *(pouvoir)* compter sur elle !

---

[1] *le télétravail* : teleworking
[2] *assurer un emploi* : to work

How to use le, la, les

See pages 60–61, sections 1–12 and pages 66–68, sections 1–10 for more about ARTICLES

1   **le, la, les** (*the*) are the DEFINITE ARTICLES in French:

	SINGULAR	PLURAL
MASCULINE	**le, l'**	**les**
FEMININE	**la, l'**	**les**

2   **l'** replaces **le** and **la** before a vowel (**a, e, i, o, u, y**) or unaspirated **h**:

l'objet *masc.*   l'heure *fem.*   l'autre femme *fem.*

Note: an UNASPIRATED **h** is treated like a vowel. Some words begin with an ASPIRATED **h** which is treated like a consonant (**p, t**, etc.). Some examples:

UNASPIRATED H	ASPIRATED H
l'histoire (*f.*) *story / history*	la hausse *rise / increase*
l'hôtel (*m.*) *hotel*	le héros *hero*

3   The DEFINITE ARTICLE in French is often used where *the* is omitted in English. Use **le, la, les** in general statements and before names of countries:

Le sport est bon pour **les** jeunes   *Sport is good for young people*
Le Brésil est plus grand que **la** France   *Brazil is bigger than France*

See page 61, section 12 and page 66, section 5 for *in, to* and *from* countries

How to use un, une **and** du, de la, des

4   The other ARTICLES in French are:

	SINGULAR	PLURAL
MASCULINE	**un, du, de l'**	**des**
FEMININE	**une, de la, de l'**	**des**

1. **un** and **une** translate both *a / an* and *one*:

J'ai fait **une** réservation pour **un** mois   *I have made a booking for one month*

2. **du, de la, de l', des** translate *any* and *some*:

Tu as **de la** monnaie ?   *Do you have any change?*
On garde toujours **du** vin à la cave   *We always keep some wine in the cellar*

Note: **du, de la, de l', des** must be used when *any* or *some* may be omitted:

Tu as commandé **du** champagne ?   *Have you ordered (any) champagne?*
Je vais apporter **des** fleurs   *I'm going to take (some) flowers*

3. **du**, **de la**, **de l'**, **des** consist of the preposition **de** (*of* or *from*) + **le**, **la**, **l'**, **les**. They can also mean *from / from the* and *of / of the* and are sometimes the equivalent of *'s* in English:

Il rentre **de l'**aéroport   *He is coming back from the airport*
L'attitude **des** gens changera   *People's attitudes will change*

5   The preposition **à** (*to, at, in*) combines with **le**, **la**, **l'**, **les** as follows:

	SINGULAR	PLURAL
MASCULINE	**au**, **à l'**	**aux**
FEMININE	**à la**, **à l'**	**aux**

J'ai vu ce film **au** cinéma du coin   *I saw this film at the local cinema*
Tu devrais retourner **à l'**hôtel   *You should go back to the hotel*

See page 61, section 12 for **à** before countries

Nouns and their gender

6   A NOUN is the name for a person, place or thing. *student*, *shop* and *books* are all nouns. In French, nouns are either masculine or feminine: this is their GENDER. The ending of many nouns tells you what their gender is:

MASCULINE ENDINGS WITH EXAMPLES			
-acle :	un obst**acle**	**-ème** :	un probl**ème**
-age :	le chôm**age**	**-et** :	un rej**et**
-asme :	le sarc**asme**	**-isme** :	le social**isme**
-eau :	un bat**eau**	**-ment** :	un argu**ment**
-ège :	un coll**ège**	**-tère** :	le mys**tère**

Exceptions: une cage, une image, une page, une plage, la rage, l'eau, la peau

FEMININE ENDINGS WITH EXAMPLES			
-aison :	une r**aison**	**-ière** :	une lum**ière**
-ance :	une tend**ance**	**-sion** :	la ten**sion**
-anse :	la d**anse**	**-tion** :	une fonc**tion**
-ée :	une journ**ée**	**-ude** :	une habit**ude**
-ence :	la pati**ence**	**-ure** :	la cult**ure**
-ense :	la déf**ense**	**-xion** :	une réfle**xion**

Exceptions: le silence, un musée, un lycée, un cimetière

7   The following words are sometimes thought to be feminine but they are MASCULINE. Check their meanings in the dictionary:

le commerce	un échange	un mélange	un régime	un salaire
le contrôle	un ensemble	le mérite	un remède	un scandale
un crime	un espace	un modèle	un reproche	un siècle
le divorce	un groupe	un nombre	un rêve	un signe
un domaine	le luxe	un phénomène	un risque	le style
le doute	le manque	un principe	un rôle	un vote

8   Some nouns referring to people have masculine and feminine forms and some do not.

    1. Some retain their gender whether they refer to men or women.

le bébé *baby*	**la** personne *person*	**le** témoin *witness*
la vedette *star*	**la** victime *victim / casualty*	

    2. Most names for OCCUPATIONS are always masculine, whether they refer to men or women, but some can be masculine or feminine. Examples:

ALWAYS MASCULINE		CAN BE MASCULINE OR FEMININE	
un chauffeur	un professeur	un / une artiste	un / une secrétaire
un médecin	un ingénieur	un / une journaliste	un / une dentiste

    3. Some OCCUPATIONS have different masculine and feminine forms:

-er → -ère	e.g. un infirmier / une infirmière
-ien → -ienne	e.g. un musicien / une musicienne
-teur → -trice	e.g. un directeur / une directrice
-eur → -euse	e.g. un serveur / une serveuse

Plural forms of nouns

9   Nouns are SINGULAR (only one) or PLURAL (more than one). To make a noun PLURAL, add **-s** to the SINGULAR:

    un homme → des homme**s**   une femme → des femme**s**

But note the following plural forms:

nouns ending in **-s**, **-x**, **-z** remain unchanged:
le temps → les temps   la voix → les voix   le gaz → les gaz
nouns ending in **-au** and **-eu** take **-x**:
le drapeau → les drapeau**x**   le jeu → les jeu**x**
ending of most nouns in **-al** and **-ail** becomes **-aux**:
le journal → les journ**aux**   le travail → les trav**aux**

Exceptions: le festival → les festivals, le détail → les détails

Verbs and the present tense

10   A VERB is a word which describes an action: *eat* and *speak* are English verbs.
We recognise French verbs by their INFINITIVE, the form ending in **-er**, **-ir** or **-re**. **parler**, **finir** and **vendre** are the infinitives of regular verbs in French.

11   The use of the French present tense of verbs is similar to the English present. But the words *is / are ... ing* and *do / does ...* have no equivalent.

    Elle **habite** ici   *She **lives** here / She **is living** here*
    Elle n'**habite** pas ici   *She **doesn't live** here*

Here is the PRESENT TENSE of regular verbs **parler**, **finir** and **vendre**:

See also pages 62–63, sections 13–19 for **-er** verbs with spelling changes

je	parle	je	fin**is**	je	vend**s**
tu	parl**es**	tu	fin**is**	tu	vend**s**
il / elle	parle	il / elle	fin**it**	il / elle	vend
nous	parl**ons**	nous	fin**issons**	nous	vend**ons**
vous	parl**ez**	vous	fin**issez**	vous	vend**ez**
ils / elles	parl**ent**	ils / elles	fin**issent**	ils / elles	vend**ent**

Present tense: reflexive verbs

12 REFLEXIVE verbs often describe actions that you do *to yourself*. They are always used with the reflexive pronouns **me / m'**, **te / t'**, **se / s'**, **nous**, **vous**:

se servir *to help oneself*	**s'habiller** *to dress*
je **me** sers	je **m'**habille
tu **te** sers	tu **t'**habilles
il / elle **se** sert	il / elle **s'**habille
nous **nous** servons	nous **nous** habillons
vous **vous** servez	vous **vous** habillez
ils / elles **se** servent	ils / elles **s'**habillent

Note: reflexive pronouns can also be used with other verbs to describe a reciprocal action, that is, something that people do *to each other*:

Ils **s'aiment** beaucoup   *They love each other a lot*
Nous **nous écrivons** des lettres   *We write letters to each other*

Irregular verbs and irregular verb groups

13 Most common verbs are irregular in the present and other tenses! Use the verb tables on pages 160–168.

14 It is useful to know that many irregular verbs belong to verb groups. Check the forms of **conduire**, **craindre**, **ouvrir**, **partir** and **recevoir** in the verb tables and note that many verbs belong to each group:

conduire	construire, détruire, produire, traduire, réduire
craindre	atteindre, contraindre, éteindre, joindre, peindre, plaindre, restreindre
ouvrir	couvrir, découvrir, offrir, souffrir
partir	dormir, mentir, se repentir, sentir, (se) servir, sortir
recevoir	(s')apercevoir, concevoir, décevoir, percevoir

Now that you have studied the grammar explanations on the previous pages, check that you have understood them by doing the following exercises.

A In the following definitions, insert **un** or **une**. Remember that the ending is often a clue to the gender of a word.

1. _____ ville est _____ agglomération urbaine.
2. _____ appartement est _____ logement.
3. _____ immeuble est _____ bâtiment à plusieurs étages.
4. _____ résidence est _____ ensemble d'immeubles luxueux.
5. _____ HLM est _____ habitation à loyer modéré.
6. _____ embouteillage est _____ encombrement de la circulation.

B Write the verbs in brackets in the present tense.

Vous déménagez ?

• *Vous* (compter) *toujours déménager ?*
– Oui, mais on (*ne pas savoir*) où. On ne (*parvenir*) pas à se mettre d'accord sur un endroit ! Laure (*se plaindre*) du bruit, elle (*dire*) qu'elle (*vouloir*) vivre dans la montagne à l'extérieur de Marseille. Les enfants (*dire*) qu'ils (*vouloir*) une villa en bord de mer. Et moi, je (*s'apercevoir*) de plus en plus que je (*ne pas avoir*) envie de quitter le centre-ville.

Description d'une villa

L'entrée (*conduire*) à la fois vers le séjour et la salle à manger. La salle à manger, très conviviale, (*s'ouvrir*) largement sur le séjour. Un office la (*faire*) communiquer avec la cuisine. Les deux chambres situées à l'étage (*comprendre*) chacune une vaste penderie. Elles (*bénéficier*) également d'une salle d'eau et de WC indépendants.

C *Version.* The following sentences describe the reasons why many people are moving out of towns and cities. Translate them into English and, whenever there is a difference in the use of articles between French and English, indicate which rule from the grammar section applies.

e.g. Les conditions de vie ...
→ Living conditions ... (page 2, section 3)

1. Les conditions de vie dans les grandes villes sont de plus en plus difficiles à cause de l'accroissement de la pollution, du bruit et de la circulation.
2. C'est pourquoi les gens tendent à choisir de vivre dans des zones rurales.
3. Ils recherchent un cadre de vie plus proche de la nature.
4. Avec l'amélioration des transports et de la communication électronique, les zones rurales offrent, en fait, une meilleure qualité de vie.
5. Grâce au télétravail, la possibilité de vivre loin des centres urbains n'est plus réservée aux seuls retraités.
6. La France n'est pas le seul pays où la vie à la campagne exerce un grand attrait. On observe la même tendance au Royaume-Uni.

L'alimentation

A In the following recipe, make the adjectives in brackets agree with the nouns they refer to.

Salade (*composé*)

Eléments de base* pour une (*seul*) personne :

2 œufs

1 (*petit*) laitue

1 (*gros*) tomate (*ferme*)

1 tranche (*épais*) de jambon

100 g. de gruyère

1 (*bon*) cuillerée de mayonnaise

herbes (*aromatique*)

sel et poivre

Faites cuire deux œufs (*dur*). Mettez-les ensuite dans une cuvette d'eau (*froid*) pour les faire refroidir : ils seront ainsi plus (*facile*) à écaler[1]. Prenez quatre (*beau*) feuilles de laitue, placez-les au fond d'un saladier après les avoir lavées. Coupez la tomate et les œufs en rondelles (*fin*). Coupez le jambon et le gruyère en (*petit*) dés[2]. Ajoutez la mayonnaise, salez et poivrez avant de mélanger le tout. Placez le mélange dans le saladier et garnissez-le d'herbes (*haché*).

* Pour varier un peu, remplacez le jambon par des lardons (*frit*), le gruyère par du fromage (*bleu*), la mayonnaise par un yaourt (*bulgare*) ou de la crème (*frais*) ; ajoutez également, selon la saison, des carottes (*râpé*), une betterave (*rouge*), une poignée de radis, etc.

B Write the verbs in brackets in the future tense.

Pour retrouver la forme

– Au lieu de grignoter[3] toute la journée, vous (*faire*) des repas réguliers.

– Il vous (*falloir*) manger moins de gras.

– Vous (*éviter*) de manger trop de sucre.

– Plus de[4] coca-cola ! Vous (*boire*) de l'eau minérale à la place.

– Et plus de petits gâteaux ! Vous (*s'habituer*) à manger des fruits frais.

– Au lieu de prendre la voiture ou l'autobus pour faire un kilomètre, vous (*aller*) à pied.

– Et quand vous (*se sentir*) en meilleure forme, vous (*pouvoir*) manger un hamburger de temps en temps.

---

[1] *écaler* : to shell eggs
[2] *couper en dés* : to cut into dice-shaped pieces, to dice
[3] *grignoter* : to nibble
[4] *plus de . . .* : no more . . .

Making adjectives agree

See pages 80–83, sections 1–14 for more about ADJECTIVES

1   An ADJECTIVE describes a noun. For example, the ADJECTIVE *blue* describes the noun *car* in the sentence:

> I bought a **blue** car

French ADJECTIVES agree with the noun they describe. In the following French sentence, **bleue** is a FEMININE SINGULAR ADJECTIVE, agreeing with **une voiture** which is a FEMININE SINGULAR NOUN:

> J'ai acheté une voiture **bleue**   *I bought a blue car*

2   To make a regular adjective FEMININE, add **-e**. To form the PLURAL, add an **-s** to the singular form:

	SINGULAR	PLURAL
MASCULINE	un problème important	des problèmes importants
FEMININE	une question importante	des questions importantes

Note: one adjective describing two or more nouns of different gender will always be MASCULINE PLURAL:

> Les explications (*fem.*) et les exemples (*masc.*) sont **importants**
> *Explanations and examples are important*

3   There are groups of adjectives which are different. Look out for the word endings and note the changes in the feminine and plural forms:

WORD ENDING	MASCULINE SINGULAR	MASCULINE PLURAL	FEMININE SINGULAR	FEMININE PLURAL	
-al	national	nation**aux**	nationale	nationales	*national*
-e	sale	sales	sale	sales	*dirty*
-eil	pareil	pareils	par**eille**	par**eilles**	*similar*
-el	naturel	naturels	naturel**le**	naturel**les**	*natural*
-er	premier	premiers	premi**ère**	premi**ères**	*first*
-et	discret	discrets	discr**ète**	discr**ètes**	*discreet*
-eur	trompeur	trompeurs	tromp**euse**	tromp**euses**	*deceiptful*
-f	actif	actifs	acti**ve**	acti**ves**	*active*
-ien	italien	italiens	itali**enne**	itali**ennes**	*Italian*
-s	gris	gris	gri**se**	gri**ses**	*grey*
-x	heureux	heureux	heur**euse**	heur**euses**	*happy*

Exceptions: meilleur, meilleure (*better / best*), inférieur, inférieure (*lower / inferior*), supérieur, supérieure (*higher / superior*)

Irregular adjectives

See sections 7–8 below for adjectives **tout** and **ce**

4   The following adjectives have irregular feminine forms. For the plural forms, add **-s** to the singular forms:

MASCULINE	FEMININE		MASCULINE	FEMININE	
bas	**basse**	*low*	franc	**franche**	*frank*
blanc	**blanche**	*white*	gentil	**gentille**	*nice*
bon	**bonne**	*good*	gras	**grasse**	*greasy*
bref	**brève**	*brief*	gros	**grosse**	*big*
doux	**douce**	*soft / gentle*	las	**lasse**	*weary*
épais	**épaisse**	*thick*	long	**longue**	*long*
faux	**fausse**	*fake / false*	public	**publique**	*public*
favori	**favorite**	*favourite*	sec	**sèche**	*dry*
frais	**fraîche**	*fresh*			

5   The adjectives below have irregular plural and feminine forms:

MASCULINE		FEMININE		
SINGULAR	PLURAL	SINGULAR	PLURAL	
beau / **bel**	**beaux**	**belle**	**belles**	*beautiful*
fou / **fol**	**fous**	**folle**	**folles**	*mad*
nouveau / **nouvel**	**nouveaux**	**nouvelle**	**nouvelles**	*new*
vieux / **vieil**	**vieux**	**vieille**	**vieilles**	*old*

Note: the masculine forms ending in **-l** (**bel, fol**, etc.) are used before nouns beginning with a vowel or unaspirated **h**:

un **nouveau** bar / un **nouvel** hôtel   mon **vieux** copain / mon **vieil** ami

Position of adjectives

6   Most adjectives go *after* the noun:

> une journée fatigante   *a tiring day*
> un problème national   *a national problem*

But the following commonly used adjectives go *before* the noun:

autre	excellent	jeune	nouveau	tout
beau	fou	joli	petit	vaste
bon	gentil	long	plusieurs	vieux
ce	grand	mauvais	premier	vilain
chaque	gros	meilleur	quelque	
court	haut	nombreux	tel	

une **longue** journée, *a long day*   un **mauvais** jour, *a bad day*

Note that there is only one form of **plusieurs**.

See page 80, sections 2–4 for more about position of adjectives

GRAMMAR 2

Adjectives tout and ce

See page 94, section 12 for **tout ce qui, que,** etc.
See page 121, section 5 for **tous ceux qui, que,** etc.

7   The adjective **tout** means *all, every, whole*:

	SINGULAR	PLURAL
MASCULINE	tout	**tous**
FEMININE	**toute**	**toutes**

Examples of how **tout** is used:

tout le monde	*everybody*
toute la journée	*all day long / the whole day*
tous les jours	*every day*
tous les deux jours	*every other day*
toutes les femmes	*all the women*

8   The adjective **ce** means *this / that* and *these / those*:

	SINGULAR	PLURAL
MASCULINE	ce / **cet**	**ces**
FEMININE	**cette**	**ces**

The form **cet** is used before a masculine noun or adjective beginning with a vowel or an unaspirated **h**:

	ce grand homme	*this / that great man*
BUT	**cet** homme célèbre	*this / that famous man*

Examples of how **ce** is used:

ce professeur	*this teacher / that teacher*
cet athlète	*this athlete / that athlete*
cette nuit	*tonight / this night / that night*
ces camions (*masc.*)	*these lorries / those lorries*
ces motos (*fem.*)	*these motorbikes / those motorbikes*

When it is necessary to distinguish between *this / these* and *that / those*, **-ci** and **-là** can be added to nouns used with **ce, cet, cette, ces**:

Ils ne seront pas chez eux à cette heure-**ci**
*They won't be at home at **this** time*
A ce moment-**là**, la police est intervenue
*At **that** point, the police intervened*

Expressing the future

9   The French future tense is used in much the same way as the English future:

   Il **recevra** ma lettre demain   *He **will receive** my letter tomorrow*
   Nous le **finirons** avant mardi   *We **shall finish** it by Tuesday*

10   The FUTURE TENSE is formed by adding **-ai, -as, -a, -ons, -ez, -ont** to the infinitive of the verb.
   Drop the final **-e** of **-re** verbs before adding the FUTURE ENDINGS:

-er verb:	parler	**-ir** verb:	finir	**-re** verb:	vendre
je	parler**ai**	je	finir**ai**	je	vendr**ai**
tu	parler**as**	tu	finir**as**	tu	vendr**as**
il / elle	parler**a**	il / elle	finir**a**	il / elle	vendr**a**
nous	parler**ons**	nous	finir**ons**	nous	vendr**ons**
vous	parler**ez**	vous	finir**ez**	vous	vendr**ez**
ils / elles	parler**ont**	ils / elles	finir**ont**	ils / elles	vendr**ont**

   See page 63, sections 16–19 for **-er** verbs with spelling changes in the future tense

11   Some verbs are irregular in the future. However, the FUTURE ENDINGS are the same for all verbs. For example, here is the future tense of **aller**:

j'	**irai**	nous	**irons**
tu	**iras**	vous	**irez**
il / elle	**ira**	ils / elles	**iront**

   Other verbs which are irregular in the future tense:

acquérir:	j'**acquerr**ai, etc.	pleuvoir:	il **pleuvr**a
s'asseoir:	je m'**assiér**ai	pouvoir:	je **pourr**ai
avoir:	j'**aur**ai	recevoir:	je **recevr**ai
courir:	je **courr**ai	savoir:	je **saur**ai
devoir:	je **devr**ai	tenir:	je **tiendr**ai
envoyer:	j'**enverr**ai	valoir:	je **vaudr**ai
être:	je **ser**ai	venir:	je **viendr**ai
faire:	je **fer**ai	voir:	je **verr**ai
falloir:	il **faudr**a	vouloir:	je **voudr**ai
mourir:	je **mourr**ai		

12   The IMMEDIATE FUTURE is formed with the PRESENT TENSE of **aller** and the INFINITIVE. It is used like the immediate future in English:

   On **va fêter** ton arrivée   *We **are going to** celebrate your arrival*
   Je **vais** leur **téléphoner** ce soir   *I'm **going to** call them this evening*

A Make the adjectives in brackets agree with the nouns they refer to.

Les (*nouveau*) habitudes (*alimentaire*) des Français

L'image (*traditionnel*) des Français ne correspond plus à la réalité (*quotidien*). Les différences avec les autres pays s'estompent, même si certaines traditions (*national*) et (*régional*) se maintiennent.

La consommation de pain est en baisse (*régulier*). Si le « steak-frites » reste encore le plat (*préféré*) des Français, ils consomment davantage de viande (*blanc*) et de poisson. Les plats (*préparé*) et les produits (*surgelé*) tendent à se substituer aux légumes (*frais*). Les fruits tendent à être remplacés par d'autres types de dessert : produits (*laitier*) ou crèmes (*glacé*). La consommation (*moyen*) de vin (*ordinaire*) a beaucoup diminué ; par contre, on achète plus de vins (*fin*). Parmi les boissons non (*alcoolisé*) la préférence va aux eaux (*minéral*) et aux boissons (*gazeux*).

B Write the verbs in brackets in the future tense.

Si les tendances actuelles se poursuivent ...

– Les repas (*être*) de plus en plus rapides.
– Les Français (*manger*) moins à chaque repas.
– Ils (*se limiter*) à un plat principal au lieu d'un repas complet.
– On (*voir*) le nombre de repas pris à l'extérieur augmenter.
– Les gens (*prendre*) de moins en moins le temps de cuisiner.
– Cependant la séparation entre repas quotidien et repas de fête (*se maintenir*).

Préparation d'un grand repas de fête

LOLA Il (*falloir*) faire toutes les courses à l'avance.
GABRIEL Tu crois que tu (*avoir*) le temps ?
LOLA Oui, ne t'inquiète pas. Je (*aller*) les faire vendredi soir.
GABRIEL Mais nous (*ne pas pouvoir*) tout préparer le jour même !
LOLA Mais si, il (*suffire*) de demander à Jacques de nous aider.
GABRIEL Bonne idée ! Vous (*faire*) cuire le plat principal. Et nous, on (*s'occuper*) du reste.

C *Thème.* Give the French for the following.

1. This excellent wine will be the ideal accompaniment for your dinner parties.
2. All our frozen meals and ice-creams are without artificial colouring.
3. This new dessert with fresh cream is completely natural.
4. This delicious pasta is imported from Italy.
5. Thanks to these moderately priced products, good food[1] is within everybody's reach.
6. The whole family will enjoy[2] these chocolates not only on Christmas Day but on the days that follow.

---

[1] good food : *les plaisirs de la table*
[2] translate as 'these chocolates will please the whole family'

La vie familiale

A Élise and her parents are being interviewed about their relationship. Insert **le**, **la**, **l'**, **les**, **lui** or **leur** as required.

Des relations familiales sans problèmes

• *Vous avez l'air de bien vous entendre. Vous passez beaucoup de temps ensemble ?*

ÉLISE   Pas pendant la semaine. Mon père et ma mère travaillent et je suis très occupée moi aussi. Je n'ai pas bien le temps de ＿＿ voir et de ＿＿ parler.

SON PÈRE   C'est vrai. On essaie de ＿＿ consacrer[1] le plus de temps possible et de ＿＿ encourager dans son travail, mais ce n'est pas toujours facile en semaine.

ÉLISE   Et puis, j'ai beaucoup de devoirs cette année. Alors, j'essaie de ＿＿ faire le soir pour avoir le week-end libre.

• *Comment se passe le week-end ?*

SA MÈRE   Le vendredi soir est sacré. On ＿＿ passe toujours avec Élise. On ＿＿ sort : on ＿＿ emmène au restaurant, ou on ＿＿ offre une soirée au cinéma ou au théâtre. Elle a beaucoup d'amis. On ＿＿ invite parfois à se joindre à nous.

ÉLISE   Le samedi, en général je sors toute seule. Tout ce que mes parents me demandent, c'est de ＿＿ dire où je vais et de ＿＿ téléphoner si j'ai du retard. Comme je ne veux pas qu'ils s'inquiètent, je ＿＿ fais sans problèmes.

B Christian is writing to his girlfriend to tell her about his holidays with his family. Write the verbs in brackets in the perfect tense (passé composé).

Ma chère Corinne,

Je (*ne pas avoir*) le temps de t'écrire plus tôt, excuse-moi. Quelles vacances ! C'est bien la dernière fois que je passe l'été en famille.

Mes parents (*se disputer*) en arrivant et ma mère (*bouder*) pendant deux jours. Si bien que le premier soir nous (*aller*) au restaurant sans elle et que le lendemain, elle (*ne pas vouloir*) venir à la piscine avec nous. Tout ça parce que mon père (*oublier*) d'apporter la table de camping. Mais c'est ma faute aussi, je (*intervenir*) pour dire que c'était ridicule de se fâcher pour si peu. Et évidemment, ça (*ne pas arranger*) la situation.

Ça va mieux depuis, mais je commence à perdre patience. Mardi, par exemple, mon cousin nous (*faire*) attendre pour partir au cinéma et nous (*manquer*) le début du film. Il (*ne pas y avoir*) un jour où nous (*être*) d'accord pour décider où passer l'après-midi. Finalement, hier, je (*partir*) me promener tout seul à pied, mais je (*s'ennuyer*).

L'an prochain, je pars en vacances avec toi ! En attendant je t'embrasse, Christian

---

[1] *consacrer du temps à quelqu'un* : to devote time to someone.

Subjects, direct objects and indirect objects

1 In a simple sentence, the SUBJECT of the verb (the person doing the action) usually comes at the beginning of the sentence.
The DIRECT OBJECT follows the verb directly, and the INDIRECT OBJECT has a preposition, usually **à**, before it:

SUBJECT	VERB	DIRECT OBJECT	INDIRECT OBJECT
Luc	a envoyé	une carte postale	**au** prof

Direct object pronouns: me, te, le, la, etc.

See also pages 112–113, sections 1–4

2 A DIRECT OBJECT can be replaced by a DIRECT OBJECT PRONOUN:

SUBJECT	VERB	DIRECT OBJECT	
Tu	achètes	**ce livre** ?	→ Tu **l'**achètes ?
J'	ai invité	**des amis**	→ Je **les** ai invités

Note: past participles agree with direct object pronouns – see section 15.

3 The examples below show all the DIRECT OBJECT PRONOUNS (**me, te, le**, etc.) and how they are used with the present and perfect tenses:

Il **me** voit	*He sees **me***	Il **m'**a vu(e)	*He saw **me***
Il **te** voit	*He sees **you***	Il **t'**a vu(e)	*He saw **you***
Il **le** voit	*He sees **him / it***	Il **l'**a vu	*He saw **him / it***
Il **la** voit	*He sees **her / it***	Il **l'**a vu(e)	*He saw **her / it***
Il **nous** voit	*He sees **us***	Il **nous** a vu(e)s	*He saw **us***
Il **vous** voit	*He sees **you***	Il **vous** a vu(e)s	*He saw **you***
Il **les** voit	*He sees **them***	Il **les** a vu(e)s	*He saw **them***

4 Some verbs take a DIRECT OBJECT (no preposition) in French, while their English equivalents take an indirect object (with prepositions *for, to*, etc.):

attendre le bus	*to wait **for** the bus*	écouter la radio	*to listen **to** the radio*
chasser ...	*to chase **away** ...*	payer ...	*to pay **for** ...*
chercher ...	*to look **for** ...*	regarder ...	*to look **at** ...*
demander ...	*to ask **for** ...*	soigner ...	*to look **after** ...*

Indirect object pronouns: me, te, lui, etc.

See also pages 112–113, sections 1–4

5 An INDIRECT OBJECT can be replaced by an INDIRECT OBJECT PRONOUN:

SUBJECT	VERB	DIRECT OBJECT	INDIRECT OBJECT	
Tu	offres	ce livre	**à Serge** ?	→ Tu **lui** offres ce livre ?

6   **me, te, lui, nous, vous, leur** are the INDIRECT OBJECT PRONOUNS which replace nouns referring to people. Examples with present and perfect tenses:

Il **me** parle	*He speaks to **me***	Il **m'**a parlé	*He spoke to **me***
Il **te** parle	*He speaks to **you***	Il **t'**a parlé	*He spoke to **you***
Il **lui** parle	*He speaks to **him / her***	Il **lui** a parlé	*He spoke to **him / her***
Il **nous** parle	*He speaks to **us***	Il **nous** a parlé	*He spoke to **us***
Il **vous** parle	*He speaks to **you***	Il **vous** a parlé	*He spoke to **you***
Il **leur** parle	*He speaks to **them***	Il **leur** a parlé	*He spoke to **them***

Note: the past participle does not agree with the indirect object pronoun.

7   With some verbs, the person referred to is the INDIRECT OBJECT, while the equivalent verb in English uses a DIRECT OBJECT to refer to the person:

   Il a envoyé une carte **à sa mère**   *He sent **his mother** a card*
   Il faudrait faire confiance **à vos amis**   *You should trust **your friends***

More examples of common verbs taking an indirect object:

demander quelque chose **à** quelqu'un	*to ask someone (for) something*
dire quelque chose **à** quelqu'un	*to tell someone something*
donner quelque chose **à** quelqu'un	*to give someone something*
faire confiance **à** quelqu'un	*to trust someone*
obéir **à** quelqu'un	*to obey someone*
offrir quelque chose **à** quelqu'un	*to give / offer someone something*
plaire **à** quelqu'un	*to be liked by / to please someone*
raconter quelque chose **à** quelqu'un	*to tell someone something*
ressembler **à** quelqu'un	*to resemble / look like someone*
téléphoner **à** quelqu'un	*to telephone / call someone*

See pages 171–178 for a list of common verbs and their constructions

The verb **plaire** is used as follows:

Notre voisin plaît à tout le monde	*Everybody likes our neighbour*
MEANS LITERALLY:	*Our neighbour pleases everybody*

Indirect object pronouns: y and en

See also pages 114–115, section 9

8   The INDIRECT OBJECT PRONOUN **y** replaces **à, au, à la, à l', aux** before a noun referring to a PLACE or THING:

à, à l', au, à la, aux → **y**	On va **à Marseille** → *We're going to **Marseilles***	On y va *We're going there*
	Je pense **à l'avenir** → *I am thinking about the future*	J'y pense *I am thinking about it*

9 The INDIRECT OBJECT PRONOUN **en** replaces **de, du, de la, de l', des** before a noun referring to a PLACE or THING:

de, de l', du, de la, des → en	Il n'a pas parlé **de ses projets** ? → *Didn't he talk about his plans ?*	Il n'**en** a pas parlé ? *Didn't he talk about them?*
	Nous avons **de l'argent** → *We have some money*	Nous **en** avons *We have some*
	Elle rentre **de la banque** → *She's back from the bank*	Elle **en** rentre *She's back from there*

10 **en** refers to both people and things with expressions of quantity:

Il donne **beaucoup de réceptions** → *He gives many parties*	Il **en** donne **beaucoup** *He gives many (of them)*
Il voulait inviter **douze personnes** → *He wanted to invite twelve people*	Il voulait **en** inviter **douze** *He wanted to invite twelve (of them)*

Perfect tense (le passé composé)

11 The PERFECT TENSE, or PASSÉ COMPOSÉ, is used to describe completed actions in the past. It is the equivalent of two tenses in English:

Elle **a garé** sa voiture   *She **has parked** her car / She **parked** her car*
Ils **sont arrivés**   *They **have arrived** / They **arrived***

12 The PERFECT TENSE consists of:

PRESENT TENSE of **avoir** or **être** + PAST PARTICIPLE of the verb

The PAST PARTICIPLES of verbs are formed in the following way:

verbs ending in **-er** e.g. **parler**,	remove **er** and add **é** :	parl**é**
verbs ending in **-ir** e.g. **finir**,	remove **ir** and add **i** :	fin**i**
verbs ending in **-re** e.g. **vendre**,	remove **re** and add **u** :	vend**u**

The following past participles are irregular:

s'asseoir:	**assis**	être:	**été**	recevoir:	**reçu**
acquérir:	**acquis**	s'enfouir:	**enfoui**	résoudre:	**résolu**
avoir:	**eu**	faire:	**fait**	rire:	**ri**
boire:	**bu**	falloir:	**fallu**	savoir:	**su**
conduire:	**conduit**	lire:	**lu**	suffire:	**suffi**
connaître:	**connu**	mettre:	**mis**	suivre:	**suivi**
courir:	**couru**	mourir:	**mort**	tenir:	**tenu**
craindre:	**craint**	naître:	**né**	valoir:	**valu**
croire:	**cru**	ouvrir:	**ouvert**	venir:	**venu**
croître:	**crû**	plaire:	**plu**	vivre:	**vécu**
devoir:	**dû**	pleuvoir:	**plu**	voir:	**vu**
dire:	**dit**	pouvoir:	**pu**	vouloir:	**voulu**
écrire:	**écrit**	prendre:	**pris**		

13 Most verbs take **avoir**, for example **parler**:

j'	**ai parlé**	nous	**avons parlé**
tu	**as parlé**	vous	**avez parlé**
il / elle	**a parlé**	ils / elles	**ont parlé**

14 All reflexive verbs take **être**, for example **s'amuser, se détendre, se fâcher, se reposer,** etc.

The following verbs also take **être**. Many are 'opposites' in meaning:

		AND THEIR COMPOUND FORMS
arriver	partir	
entrer	sortir	
descendre	monter	e. g. devenir, rentrer,
naître	mourir	redescendre, repartir,
aller	venir	revenir, redescendre, etc.
tomber	rester	
retourner	passer	

See page 75, section 11 for verbs which take both **avoir** and **être**.

The perfect tense of two **être** verbs, **s'amuser** and **venir**:

je me **suis amusé**(e)	je **suis venu**(e)
tu t'**es amusé**(e)	tu **es venu**(e)
il / elle s'**est amusé**(e)	il / elle **est venu**(e)
nous nous **sommes amusé**(e)s	nous **sommes venu**(e)s
vous vous **êtes amusé**(e)(s)	vous **êtes venu**(e)(s)
ils / elles se **sont amusé**(e)s	ils / elles **sont venu**(e)s

Past participle agreement

15 With verbs taking **avoir**, the past participle agrees with the DIRECT OBJECT if it comes before the verb (e.g. **les** and **la lettre** below). This is called the PRECEDING DIRECT OBJECT.

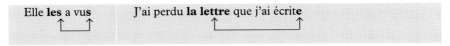

Elle **les** a vus   J'ai perdu **la lettre** que j'ai écrite

16 With verbs taking **être**, the past participle agrees with the SUBJECT:

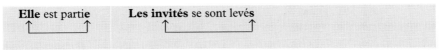

Elle est partie   **Les invités** se sont levés

Note that when **on** means *we* the past participle is plural:

On est partis à six heures   *We left at six o'clock*

See pages 74–75, sections 9–13 for more about PAST PARTICIPLE AGREEMENTS

A Replace the words underlined by a direct or indirect object pronoun.

La famille protectrice

– Dans ce type de famille, les parents adorent leur enfant mais ne traitent pas cet enfant comme un adulte.

– Ils ne se disputent jamais en famille car ils veulent donner à l'enfant une bonne image du couple.

– Bien qu'ils s'intéressent à la politique, ils discutent peu de politique devant lui; quant aux sujets délicats comme la sexualité, ils évitent ces sujets.

– A l'adolescence, l'enfant n'est pas toujours sûr d'obtenir l'autorisation de sortir lorsqu'il demande cette autorisation.

– Ses parents demandent à leur enfant d'être studieux car c'est à l'école que l'on construit son avenir et ils pensent à son avenir dès son plus jeune âge.

La famille ouverte

– Ici, les enfants sont considérés comme des êtres raisonnables et les parents poussent les enfants à devenir autonome.

– Ils font confiance aux enfants et laissent aux enfants une grande liberté.

– La sexualité n'est pas un sujet tabou : ils parlent librement de la sexualité.

– Les parents veulent préparer leur enfant à la vie en société et privilégient les qualités qui facilitent la vie en société.

– Ils sont convaincus que les activités culturelles et sportives lui seront bénéfiques, encouragent leur enfant à pratiquer deux ou trois activités.

B Write the verbs in brackets in the perfect tense. Make sure that the past participles agree, where necessary, with the subject or the object of the verb.

Témoignage

Je (grandir) à Paris avec mon frère et mes parents. À la naissance de mon frère, les relations familiales (se détériorer). Les conflits entre ma mère et mon père (se multiplier). Quand ils (divorcer), nous (connaître) des années difficiles. En effet, le divorce (se dérouler) dans de mauvaises conditions. Ma mère (se remarier) tout de suite et elle (partir) à l'étranger. Alors nous (aller) vivre chez mes grand-parents paternels. Malheureusement ma grand-mère (tomber) malade. Quand elle (mourir), c'est donc mon père qui nous (élever). Nous (faire) la connaissance de sa seconde femme et elle nous (plaire) tout de suite. Nous (prendre) l'habitude de nous confier à elle. À partir de ce moment-là, nous (vivre) dans un environnement familial très harmonieux.

C *Thème.*

1. Generally, children don't hesitate to tell their parents about their problems.
2. They ask them their opinion when they need advice.
3. When they've reached adulthood, their parents often keep helping them.
4. If they have lost their job, for example, their parents pay for their rent.

A In the following statements about young people, insert **le**, **la**, **les** or **un**, **une** as required. Where **l'** or **les** is used, say whether the word is masculine or feminine.

e.g. _____ amitié joue _____ rôle clé.
→ L'amitié [*fem.*] joue un rôle clé.

1. _____ tolérance est _____ des caractéristiques des jeunes.
2. _____ découverte de _____ amour est _____ période difficile pour eux.
3. _____ réalisme de la jeunesse est _____ facteur positif.
4. _____ consommation est _____ phénomène important dans _____ vie des jeunes.
5. Ils exercent _____ influence sur _____ décisions d'achat de leurs parents.

B Put the nouns in italics into the plural and alter the rest of the sentence accordingly.

1. *Ce jeu* électronique a connu beaucoup de succès.
2. *Ce festival* international de musique attirera les touristes.
3. Vous avez oublié *un détail* essentiel.
4. *Le travail* de la commission sera rendu public au cours *du mois* prochain.
5. *Le journal* a publié *un article* explosif.
6. Le gouvernement a respecté *le vœu* de la majorité.

C Replace the words in italics by a direct or indirect object pronoun and make the past participle agree whenever necessary.

Histoire de remariage –   1   Les difficultés d'Éva

Quand Éva a épousé Marc, un père divorcé, elle ne se doutait pas qu'elle allait avoir des difficultés à la fois avec ses enfants et ses parents. Au début, les enfants ne faisaient pas confiance *à Éva* et refusaient d'obéir *à Éva*. En outre, ses beaux-parents, qui gardaient un bon souvenir de la première femme de Marc, ont mal accueilli *Éva* : Éva ne plaisait pas *à ses beaux-parents* parce qu'elle ne ressemblait pas *à cette femme*. En fait, leur attitude aggravait la situation avec les enfants : Éva n'avait aucun soutien alors qu'elle avait bien besoin *de soutien*.

D Practise direct and indirect object pronouns further by replacing the words in italics by the appropriate pronoun.

Histoire de remariage –   2   Tout est bien qui finit bien

Une amie d' Éva a conseillé *à Éva* d'être patiente : « L'attitude de tes beaux-parents est tout à fait normale, ne t'inquiète pas *de leur attitude*. L'important, c'est avant tout de conquérir la confiance et l'affection des enfants de Marc ». Elle avait raison : lorsqu'Éva est parvenue à faire *cela*, ses beaux-parents ont adopté *Éva*. Elle a maintenant d'excellentes relations avec eux : si elle a besoin de conseils, elle va voir *ses beaux-parents* ou téléphone *à ses beaux-parents*.

E Write the following verbs in the present tense.

1. investir   ils _____
2. s'améliorer   il _____
3. soumettre   nous _____
4. surprendre   nous _____
5. s'apercevoir   on _____
6. connaître   elles _____
7. perdre   je _____

8. circuler   je _____
9. atteindre   elles _____
10. traduire   vous _____
11. ouvrir   je _____
12. voir   vous _____
13. pouvoir   tu _____
14. savoir   on _____

F Write the following verbs in the future tense.

1. comprendre   elles _____
2. décevoir   nous _____
3. venir   tu _____
4. se poursuivre   il _____
5. continuer   je _____
6. voir   vous _____
7. se rétablir   tu _____

8. maintenir   vous _____
9. pouvoir   elle _____
10. acquérir   ils _____
11. être   tu _____
12. savoir   on _____
13. envoyer   je _____
14. falloir   il _____

G Write the following verbs in the perfect tense.

1. recevoir   il _____
2. tenir   je _____
3. souffrir   tu _____
4. se plaindre   nous _____
5. reconstruire   ils _____
6. naître   elle _____
7. vouloir   tu _____

8. résoudre   ils _____
9. s'attendrir   je _____
10. admettre   on _____
11. entreprendre   tu _____
12. créer   nous _____
13. s'engager   vous _____
14. se conduire   elle _____

H The following text is about the pledges and achievements made by French Railways. Write the verbs in brackets in the appropriate tense (perfect, present, future).

Les engagements pris et tenus. L'an dernier, nous (*s'engager*) à offrir de meilleurs services et nous (*tenir*) nos engagements. Des milliers de clients (*recevoir*) à domicile leur billet commandé et payé par téléphone. Nous (*créer*) de nouvelles liaisons entre la France et l'Italie. Et enfin, nous (*entreprendre*) un programme de rénovation des gares.

La situation actuelle. Dans les trains « verts », les passagers (*pouvoir*) bénéficier aujourd'hui d'une réduction de 15 % sur le prix de base. Par ailleurs, la qualité des services accueil (*s'améliorer*) sans cesse. Ainsi, dans la banlieue parisienne, les guichets (*ouvrir*) à 5h 30 les lundis .

L'avenir. Dans les années à venir, le nombre de trains (*continuer*) à augmenter sur les grandes lignes. L'amélioration des services accueil (*se poursuivre*). Durant l'été, nos clients (*pouvoir*) bénéficier de billets à moitié prix à destination des plages. Nous (*maintenir*) notre politique d'indemnisation en cas de retard.

Les jeunes

A Here are some of the rules you should follow to keep your friends. The French equivalents of the words in brackets are **mon**, **ton**, **son**, etc. or **le mien**, **le tien**, **le sien**, etc. Fill the gaps without forgetting the agreements.

Les règles de l'amitié

1. Montrez-vous toujours aimable envers _____ copains et _____ copines. [*your, your*]
2. Si l'un d'entre _____ ou l'une d'entre _____ se moque de vous gentiment, surtout ne boudez pas. [*them* masc., *them* fem.]
3. Si au cours d'une soirée mouvementée, quelqu'un abîme _____ affaires, ne saccagez pas _____ pour vous venger. [*your, his/hers*]
4. N'essayez jamais de sortir avec le flirt de _____ meilleur(e) ami(e). [*your*]
5. N'oubliez pas qu'il faut toujours partager _____ affaires et ne pas tout garder pour _____ . [*one's, oneself*]
6. Ne refusez jamais d'accompagner les autres dans une sortie même si _____ choix ne vous plaît pas. [*their*]
7. Chacun a _____ opinion, ne critiquez pas continuellement les idées des autres. _____ ne sont pas infaillibles ! Acceptez donc _____ . [*his/her/one's, yours, theirs*]
8. Apprenez la discrétion : vos copains ne vous confieront pas _____ problèmes s'il savent que vous répétez _____ histoires. [*their, their*]
9. Sachez combiner l'amour et l'amitié : ne laissez pas tomber _____ copains et ne demandez à personne d'abandonner _____ . [*your, his/hers*]

B Write the verbs in brackets in the imperfect tense.

Témoignage – Premier amour

Tout a commencé l'année dernière lorsque j'ai fait la connaissance de Thomas, un garçon de ma classe. Il (*être*) super sympa, mais je (*ne pas penser*) du tout sortir avec lui. Un jour, alors que je (*être*) à la patinoire, je l'ai vu par hasard et il m'a souri. Une semaine plus tard, un de mes copains m'a dit qu'il (*vouloir*) sortir avec moi. Comme on (*ne pas se connaître*) très bien, j'ai répondu qu'il me (*falloir*) réfléchir. Ensuite, les grandes vacances sont arrivées et je l'ai un peu oublié.

À la rentrée, comme nous (*se trouver*) à nouveau dans la même classe, je lui ai demandé s'il (*avoir*) encore envie de sortir avec moi. Mais il n'a pas voulu me parler. Ma réaction a été intense : je (*se sentir*) profondément triste et je (*ne pas comprendre*) pourquoi il (*agir*) comme ça. C'est à ce moment-là que j'ai compris qu'il me (*plaire*) vraiment. Trop tard !

Possessive adjectives and pronouns

1 POSSESSIVE ADJECTIVES (**mon, ma, mes**, etc.) agree with the noun to which they refer:

> Elle m'a prêté **son** dossier   *She lent me her file*

2 Here are the forms of the POSSESSIVE ADJECTIVE in French:

	SINGULAR		PLURAL
	MASCULINE	FEMININE	MASCULINE AND FEMININE
my	**mon** salaire	**ma** nationalité	**mes** excuses
your	**ton** salaire	**ta** nationalité	**tes** projets
his / her / one's	**son** salaire	**sa** nationalité	**ses** loisirs
	MASCULINE AND FEMININE		
our	**notre** salaire		**nos** excuses
your	**votre** intelligence		**vos** projets
their	**leur** habitude		**leurs** loisirs

mon, ton, son replace **ma, ta, sa** before a vowel or an unaspirated **h**:

> **mon** amie (*fem.*)   **ton** habitude (*fem.*)   **son** autre fille (*fem.*)

Use a definite article and not a possessive adjective with parts of the body:

> Il m'a serré **la** main   *He shook **my** hand*

3 The POSSESSIVE PRONOUNS (*mine, yours, his*, etc.) agree with the noun they refer to and are always used with the definite articles **le, la, les**. They are used for emphasis and comparison:

> Ces affaires ? Ce sont **les nôtres**
> *Those things? They're **ours***
> Mon plan est plus précis que **le sien**
> *My map is more accurate than **his** / **hers***

4 Here are the forms of the POSSESSIVE PRONOUNS in French:

	SINGULAR		PLURAL	
	MASCULINE	FEMININE	MASCULINE	FEMININE
mine	**le mien**	**la mienne**	**les miens**	**les miennes**
yours	**le tien**	**la tienne**	**les tiens**	**les tiennes**
his / hers / one's	**le sien**	**la sienne**	**les siens**	**les siennes**
ours	**le nôtre**	**la nôtre**	**les nôtres**	
yours	**le vôtre**	**la vôtre**	**les vôtres**	
theirs	**le leur**	**la leur**	**les leurs**	

5 The possessive adjectives **son, sa, ses** and pronouns **le sien, la sienne**, etc. are the forms which are used with **on**. Example:

> **On** doit déclarer **ses** revenus   *One has to declare one's income*
> *You are obliged to declare your income*

Emphatic pronouns moi, toi, lui, etc.

6   EMPHATIC PRONOUNS refer to people and are used separately from the verb. For example, they are used after all PREPOSITIONS (**sans**, **à cause de**, etc.):

Elle l'a fait à cause de **lui**	*She did it because of **him***
Je suis fier de **moi**	*I am proud of **myself***
Rentrons **chez nous**	*Let's go home*

They are also used in comparisons, for emphasis and after **et**:

Il a écrit plus qu'**elle**	*- He has written more than **her***
Eux je les connais	*I know **them***
Et **moi**, je fais le travail	*As for **me**, I do the work*
Mon frère et **moi**, on est sortis	*My brother and **I** went out*

7   Here are the EMPHATIC PRONOUNS:

moi	*me*	**nous**	*us*
toi	*you*	**vous**	*you*
lui	*him*	**eux**	*them (masc.)*
elle	*her*	**elles**	*them (fem.)*
soi	*one*		

Note that **soi** is the emphatic pronoun which goes with the impersonal **on**:

On a du temps pour **soi**	*One has time for **oneself***

8   To emphasise possession, use the preposition **à** + EMPHATIC PRONOUN:

C'est l'avis du patron ? Non, c'est notre avis **à nous**
*Is it the boss's opinion ? No, it's **our** opinion*

Because **son avis** means both *his opinion* and *her opinion*, you sometimes need to use the emphatic pronoun to avoid confusion:

son avis à lui	*his opinion*	son avis à elle	*her opinion*

Myself, yourself, himself, etc.

9   The EMPHATIC PRONOUNS are used in combination with **-même** to produce the following forms:

moi-même	*myself*	**nous-mêmes**	*ourselves*
toi-même	*yourself*	**vous-même(s)**	*yourself, yourselves*
lui-même	*himself*	**eux-mêmes**	*themselves (masc.)*
elle-même	*herself*	**elles-mêmes**	*themselves (fem.)*
soi-même	*oneself*		

Elle rédige ses discours **elle-même**   *She writes her speeches herself*

Imperfect tense: forms and uses

10 The IMPERFECT TENSE is formed from the **nous** form of the present tense. Remove the **-ons** ending and replace it with the IMPERFECT TENSE endings:

je	parl**ais**	je	fin**issais**	je	vend**ais**
tu	parl**ais**	tu	fin**issais**	tu	vend**ais**
il / elle	parl**ait**	il / elle	fin**issait**	il / elle	vend**ait**
nous	parl**ions**	nous	fin**issions**	nous	vend**ions**
vous	parl**iez**	vous	fin**issiez**	vous	vend**iez**
ils / elles	parl**aient**	ils / elles	fin**issaient**	ils / elles	vend**aient**

The only exception to this rule is the verb **être**: **j'étais, tu étais**, etc.

See page 62, sections 14–15 for **-er** verbs with spelling changes in imperfect tense

11 The IMPERFECT TENSE has a number of different uses. While the perfect tense is used to describe completed actions, the imperfect tense is used for:

1. DESCRIPTION of appearance, age, state of mind and state of affairs:

    Les bâtiments **étaient** délabrés   *The buildings were dilapidated*
    Il **avait** 30 ans et il **était** marié   *He was 30 and (he was) married*

2. INTERRUPTED ACTION, where in English *was / were . . . ing* is often used:

    Le président **parlait** quand la bombe a explosé
    *The President **was** speaking when the bomb exploded*

3. HABITUAL ACTION, where in English ***used to*** or ***would*** is often used:

    Le ministre **consultait** son équipe le matin
    *The minister consulted his team in the morning / **used to** consult his team in the morning / **would** consult his team in the morning*

Note that when you mention that the action took place on a number of distinct occasions, rather than regularly, you must use the PERFECT TENSE:

Il m'**a consulté** à plusieurs reprises   *He consulted me several times*

Expressions of time: depuis, pendant and venir de

12 **depuis** (*since, for*) can be used to express a CONTINUING ACTION. The tenses are different in French and English.

1. If the action <u>is</u> still going on, the PRESENT TENSE is used in French:

    Elle **travaille** ici **depuis** juin
    She has been working here since June
    CONTINUING ACTION: SHE IS STILL WORKING HERE

2. If the action <u>was</u> still going on at the time, the IMPERFECT TENSE is used:

> Il **assistait** aux cours **depuis** mai
> *He had been attending lessons since May*
> CONTINUING ACTION: HE WAS STILL ATTENDING LESSONS
> J'**étais** à Paris **depuis** un mois   *I had been in Paris for a month*
> CONTINUING ACTION: I WAS STILL IN PARIS

This box summarises the differences in tense between the languages:

FRENCH			ENGLISH	
present tense	+ **depuis**	→	perfect	+ *for* or *since*
imperfect tense	+ **depuis**	→	pluperfect	+ *for* or *since*

Note that **ça fait ... que** (in conversation) and **il y a ... que** can also be used instead of **depuis**. The tenses used are the same as with **depuis**:

> Il y a un an que je la **connais**
> *I have known her for a year*
> Ça fait longtemps que tu y **travailles** ?
> *Have you been working there long?*

13 If the sentence is negative because the action did <u>not</u> take place, then the tenses used are similar to those used in English:

> On ne l'**a** pas **vu** depuis Pâques   *We haven't seen him since Easter*
> Je n'**avais** rien **fait** depuis un an   *I hadn't done anything for a year*

14 To express a COMPLETED ACTION in the past, use **pendant** (*for, during*) with the PERFECT TENSE:

> Elle a **travaillé** ici **pendant** six mois   *She worked here for six months*
> COMPLETED ACTION: SHE IS NO LONGER WORKING THERE

Note: **pendant** is omitted if the expression of time follows the verb directly:

> Elle a travaillé six mois ici   *She worked here for six months*
> J'ai habité un mois chez des amis   *I lived with friends for a month*

15 The expression **venir de** + INFINITIVE means *to have just* and is only used with the PRESENT and IMPERFECT tenses:

PRESENT	Elle **vient de** partir	*She has just left*
	Qu'est ce qu'il **vient de** dire ?	*What did he just say?*
IMPERFECT	Nous **venions de** déménager	*We had just moved house*
	Vous **veniez d'**appeler	*You had just phoned*

This box summarises the differences in tense between French and English:

FRENCH		ENGLISH	
present tense of **venir de**	→	perfect:	*have / has just ...*
imperfect tense of **venir de**	→	pluperfect:	*had just ...*

A Here are some descriptions of young people's attitudes to relationships. Change the subject of the underlined verb and alter the rest of the sentence accordingly, making sure that any necessary changes are made.

e.g. <u>Je respecte</u> les amis de mes amis et ils respectent les miens. *Elle* . . .
→ Elle respecte les amis de ses amis et ils respectent les siens.

1. En amour comme en amitié, <u>nous tenons</u> à notre indépendance. Nous <u>respectons</u> la liberté de l'autre et <u>exigeons</u> qu'il respecte la nôtre.
Je . . .

2. <u>Elle a</u> une bonne opinion d'elle-même, <u>elle est</u> sûre d'elle et <u>elle aime</u> séduire. Ses partenaires ont souvent une attitude comparable à la sienne.
Ils . . .

3. <u>Vous êtes</u> souvent frustré parce que votre timidité et votre anxiété vous empêchent de faire le premier pas. C'est plus fort que vous [1]!
Elle . . .

4. <u>Ils n'aiment pas</u> l'aventure. L'important pour eux, c'est que leurs parents acceptent la personne de leur choix et que les siens les accueillent bien.
Tu . . .

B Here is a description of the way fashion developed in the 1960s and 1970s. Put the verbs in brackets in the imperfect tense.

Dans les années 60, les jeunes (*devenir*) hippies par réaction contre leurs parents. L'anticonformisme qui (*prévaloir*) à l'époque (*se traduire*) notamment par les cheveux longs, les couleurs vives et l'absence de cravate. À partir de 1975, la traditionnelle réaction contre les parents (*tendre*) à disparaître. Pour les punks, par exemple, il (*s'agir*) surtout de se démarquer de leurs frères et sœurs ou des aînés de leur lycée qui (*être*) babas [2]. Au cours des décennies suivantes, l'accélération des mouvements de mode (*aller*) devenir telle que les générations de jeunes ne (*devoir*) plus durer qu'une ou deux années.

C Thème. Four people describe what were they like when they were seventeen.

SYLVIE   At seventeen, I was anti-establishment and the police arrested me twice. My appearance was very important to me. I used to wear short skirts underneath a very long coat. My friends had long hair and never took their jeans off.

JÉRÔME   On my seventeenth birthday, my parents gave me a scooter as a present. They were very proud of me because I had just passed my exams. Since our stay in England, the summer before, my friends and I only wore English clothes.

LAURA   My best friend and I sang in a punk group. Our hair was pink. My parents found it quite funny but hers were furious.

ÉTIENNE   When I reached the age of seventeen, I decided that I wanted to travel. I worked in a petrol station in the evening for a whole winter and the following year I went to Africa. I was in Rwanda when the civil war broke out.

---

[1] *c'est plus fort que vous !* : You can't help it!

[2] *un baba* : another word for 'hippy'

Les déplacements

A The following statements about car travel are only true in the negative. Put the verbs and phrases in italics into the negative as instructed.

e.g. Les hommes *conduisent mieux* que les femmes.　[not]
→ Les hommes ne conduisent pas mieux que les femmes.

1. *Tout le monde prétend* que les déplacements à pied ont augmenté.　[nobody]
2. En fait, *tout encourage* les gens à laisser leur voiture au garage.　[nothing]
3. L'utilisation de la voiture *a diminué* au cours des dernières années.　[not]
4. Pourtant, les achats de grosses cylindrées[1] *sont* aussi nombreux.　[no longer]
5. Aujourd'hui, la vitesse *est* aussi importante que la sécurité.　[not]
6. Au fond, le mouvement écologiste *a changé quelque chose.*　[nothing]
7. Les modes de transports collectifs *remplaceront* la voiture.　[never]

B Patrice, who has just won a competition organised by a travel insurance company, is being interviewed. Fill in the gaps before the infinitives with **à** or **de** if necessary.

e.g. J'ai réussi _____ partir mais j'ai dû _____ rentrer peu après.
→ J'ai réussi à partir mais j'ai dû rentrer peu après.

- *Patrice, vous venez _____ gagner le concours Assurtout. Comment comptez-vous _____ dépenser la somme d'argent qui vous est offerte ?*
- J'ai l'intention _____ passer trois mois _____ voyager en Europe. J'ai essayé _____ le faire, il y a quelques années, mais je n'ai réussi qu' _____ voir l'Italie.
- *Ah bon ? Vous voulez bien _____ nous raconter ce qui vous est arrivé ?*
- J'avais décidé _____ aller jusqu'en Roumanie à bicyclette. Et tout a bien commencé puisque je suis parvenu _____ faire les premiers 300 km en quatre jours.
- *Ah oui ! C'est remarquable ! Et ensuite ?*
- Arrivé en Italie, je me suis arrêté au bord de la route pour me reposer avant de me mettre _____ chercher une auberge de jeunesse pour la nuit. C'était l'été. Il commençait _____ faire très chaud. Bref ! Je me suis endormi ! À mon réveil, je me suis aperçu que mon vélo avait disparu. J'avais oublié _____ l'attacher à un arbre !
- *Et vous étiez assuré pour le vol ?*
- Non, malheureusement pas. Et je n'ai pas pu _____ retrouver mon vélo ! La police italienne a accepté _____ me conduire jusqu'à Turin et je suis rentré par le train. Depuis, je rêve _____ repartir. Cette aventure m'a appris _____ être plus prudent et mieux organisé. Cette fois-ci, j'espère bien _____ ne pas rentrer cinq jours après mon départ.

[1] *une grosse cylindrée* : a car with a big engine

Negative sentences

See pages 72–73, sections 1–7 for more about NEGATIVE SENTENCES

1   NEGATIVE SENTENCES are formed with **ne** and a NEGATIVE WORD:

ne … aucun(e)	*no, not one, not any*
ne … guère	*scarcely, hardly, not much*
ne … jamais	*never, not ever*
ne … ni … ni	*neither … nor, not … or*
ne … nulle part	*nowhere, not anywhere*
ne … nullement	*not at all*
ne … pas	*no, not any*
ne … personne	*no one / nobody, not anyone, not anybody*
ne … plus	*no more, not any more, no longer, not any longer*
ne … que	*only*
ne … rien	*nothing, not anything*

These examples illustrate the use of the above negative words:

Il **n'a aucune** idée originale	*He doesn't have any original ideas*
Il **ne** réfléchit **guère**	*He doesn't think much*
Il **n'a guère** d'ambition	*He has hardly any ambition*
Il **ne** sort **jamais**	*He never goes out*
Il **n'a jamais** d'initiative	*He doesn't ever show any initiative*
Il **n'a ni** diplôme **ni** expérience	*He has neither qualifications nor experience*
Il **ne** va **nulle part**	*He is not going anywhere*
Il **ne** comprend **pas**	*He doesn't understand*
Il **n'a pas** de patience	*He has no patience*
Il **ne** voit **personne**	*He sees nobody*
Il **ne** me voit **plus**	*He no longer sees me*
Il **ne** reçoit **plus** de lettres	*He doesn't receive letters any more*
Il **ne** travaille **que** quand il veut	*He only works when he wants to*
Il **ne** comprend **rien**	*He doesn't understand anything*
Je **ne** crois **nullement** en lui !	*I don't believe in him at all!*

Note: **ne** always comes before OBJECT PRONOUNS **me, te, le, lui**, etc.:

Nous **ne les** invitons plus	*We don't invite them any more*
Je **ne vous** ai jamais vu si fâché	*I have never seen you so angry*

2   **de** (or **d'**) replaces **du, de la, des** after a NEGATIVE:

POSITIVE SENTENCE with **du, de la, des**	NEGATIVE SENTENCE with **de**
Il a **de la** patience	Il n'a **pas de** patience
Il a **de l'**initiative	Il n'a **jamais d'**initiative
Il reçoit **des** lettres	Il ne reçoit **plus de** lettres

This does not apply to **ne ... que** which is not negative in meaning. For example, in the following sentence *they do buy clothes*, but *only in the sales*:

Ils n'achètent que **des** vêtements en solde
They only buy clothes in the sales

Position of negative words pas, rien, etc.

3   A negative sentence can begin with a negative word. **ne** must not be omitted:

Aucun de mes rêves **ne** s'est réalisé	*None of my dreams has come true*
Ni l'un **ni** l'autre **ne** gagnera	*Neither of them will win*
Pas un **ne** réussira	*Not one will succeed*
Personne ne m'a contacté	*Nobody has contacted me*
Rien ne me surprend	*Nothing surprises me*

4   Some negatives go before PAST PARTICIPLES and INFINITIVES. Others go after:

BEFORE PAST PARTICIPLE OR INFINITIVE	AFTER PAST PARTICIPLE OR INFINITIVE
guère	aucun(e)
jamais	ni ... ni
pas	nulle part
plus	nullement
rien	personne
	que

Examples of negatives with past participles:

Je n'ai **pas** vu cette exposition	*I haven't seen that exhibition*
Je n'ai **jamais** vu ce feuilleton	*I have never seen that serial*
Je n'ai **plus** vu mon patron	*I didn't see my boss any more*
Je n'ai vu **personne**	*I didn't see anyone*
Je n'ai vu **que** le début	*I only saw the beginning*
Je n'ai vu **ni** lui **ni** elle	*I saw neither him nor her*
Je n'ai vu **aucun** film	*I did not see one film*

Examples of negatives with infinitives:

Elle préfère ne **pas** voir cela	*She prefers not to see that*
Elle préfère ne **jamais** voir ce film	*She prefers never to see that film*
Elle préfère ne **plus** me voir	*She prefers not to see me any more*
Elle préfère ne voir **personne**	*She prefers not to see anyone*
Elle préfère ne voir **que** le début	*She prefers only to see the beginning*
Elle préfère ne voir **ni** lui **ni** elle	*She prefers to see neither him nor her*
Elle préfère ne voir **aucun** film	*She prefers not to see any films*

Infinitive after prepositions (avant de, pour, etc.)

See section 6 below for use of infinitive after prepositions à and **de**

5 Use the infinitive after prepositions (e.g. **pour**, **sans**, **avant de**, etc.):

Je disais cela **pour** les impressionner	*I was saying that to impress them*
Réfléchis **avant de** prendre une décision	*Think before making a decision*
Dépêche-toi **au lieu de** discuter	*Hurry up instead of talking*
Elle est **en train de** se reposer	*She is having a rest*
Nous étions **sur le point de** signer	*We were about to sign*

Exceptions: **en** takes the PRESENT PARTICIPLE – see page 000, section 10;
après takes the PAST INFINITIVE – see page 31 section 9.

Verbs taking à, de or no preposition before the infinitive

See page 94–95, sections 13–14 for more about TWO-VERB CONSTRUCTIONS
See pages 171 for a list of the most common verbs and how they are used before an infinitive

6 Where two verbs are used together, the second one will be in the INFINITIVE.
It is important to know what construction the first verb takes.

1. Certain verbs take the PREPOSITION **à** before an infinitive, for example:

commencer à ...	*to begin, to start to ...*	persister à ...	*to persist in ...*
se mettre à ...	*to begin, to start to ...*	réussir à ...	*to succeed in ...*
hésiter à ...	*to hesitate to ...*	etc.	

Vous **avez réussi à** le trouver ?	*Did you succeed in finding him?*
J'**hésite à** vous déranger	*I hesitate to disturb you*
Ils se **sont mis à** sortir ensemble	*They started to go out together*

2. Certain verbs take the PREPOSITION **de** before an infinitive, for example:

s'arrêter de ...	*to stop ...*	remercier de ...	*to thank for ...*
décider de ...	*to decide to ...*	regretter de ...	*to regret ...*
essayer de ...	*to try to ...*	etc.	

Arrêtez de fumer tout de suite	*Stop smoking immediately*
Elle **a décidé de** quitter son emploi	*She decided to leave her job*

3. Certain verbs take no preposition before an infinitive, for example:

aimer ...	*to like (to) ...*	pouvoir ...	*to be able to, can, may ...*
devoir ...	*to have to, must ...*	préférer ...	*to prefer ...*
espérer ...	*to hope to ...*	sembler ...	*to seem to ...*
penser ...	*to think of / about ...*	etc.	

Nous **espérons** partir avant minuit	*We hope to leave by midnight*
Elle **pense** déménager bientôt	*She is thinking of moving soon*

Forms and uses of the past infinitive

See page 4, section 10 for explanation of INFINITIVE

7   The PAST INFINITIVE is formed by **avoir** or **être** + PAST PARTICIPLE:

	PRESENT INFINITIVE	PAST INFINITIVE
verbs taking **avoir**	**manger**	**avoir mangé**
	to eat	*having eaten / eating*
	écrire	**avoir écrit**
	to write	*having written / writing*
verbs taking **être**	**partir**	**être parti(e)(s)**
	to leave	*having left / leaving*
	s'habiller	**s'être habillé(e)(s)**
	to get dressed	*having got dressed / getting dressed*

Note: past participle agreement rules are the same as for the perfect tense.

See page 17, sections 15–16 for PAST PARTICIPLE AGREEMENT
See page 17, sections 13–14 for verbs taking **avoir** and **être**

8   The PAST INFINITIVE refers to the past:

Elle est sortie sans **avoir mangé**	*She went out without eating*
	She went out without having eaten
Merci de **m'avoir écrit**	*Thanks for writing to me*
Ils ont regretté d'**être partis** si tôt	*They regretted leaving so early*
	They regretted having left so early
Après **s'être habillée**, elle est sortie	*After getting dressed, she went out*

Use of après and the past infinitive

9   Always use the PAST INFINITIVE form of the verb after **après**. The equivalent
in English is usually the *-ing* form of the verb:

Après **m'être endormi**, je n'ai rien entendu
After falling asleep, I didn't hear anything
Après **avoir quitté** la ville, elle a franchi la frontière
After leaving the town, she crossed the border
Après **vous être aperçus** du danger, vous avez appelé la police ?
After becoming aware of the danger, did you call the police?

A Here is some advice for people flying to a distant country. Fill in the gaps with the prepositions **à** or **de** if necessary.

C'est le moment du grand départ ! Depuis longtemps vous rêvez ____ partir à la recherche du soleil et de la détente. Vous avez choisi ____ passer quinze jours au Brésil où vous espérez ____ trouver un ciel toujours bleu et une plage de sable blanc. Si c'est la première fois que vous faites un aussi long voyage, suivez les conseils suivants :

– essayez ____ faire votre réservation sur un vol direct ;
– arrivez à l'aéroport à l'avance si vous voulez ____ choisir votre place ;
– armez-vous de patience : vous aurez ____ faire la queue avant ____ passer par le contrôle de sécurité ;
– pendant le vol, évitez ____ prendre une boisson alcoolisée surtout si vous souffrez du mal des transports ;
– pensez ____ mettre des vêtements d'été dans votre bagage de cabine, afin de pouvoir ____ vous changer avant l'arrivée. A moins, bien sûr, que vous ne préfériez ____ le faire à votre arrivée à l'hôtel.

B Join the following pairs of sentences by using **après**.
e.g. On a fini les examens. On est parties en France.
→ Après avoir fini les examens, on est parties en France.

1. On est arrivées à la gare du Nord à Paris. On a pris le métro pour aller à la gare de Lyon.
2. Je me suis renseignée sur les horaires. J'ai réservé des places pour le TGV.
3. On a composté nos billets. On est montées dans le train.
4. Ma compagne s'est installée dans le train. Elle s'est aperçue qu'elle avait oublié d'apporter de la lecture.

C *Thème.* Cars and lorries were banned from the centre of Pau yesterday (during the « Journée sans véhicules fumants »). How did the people manage? Here are some of the answers.

LUC	Instead of taking my car, I cycled to work. It didn't take long!
LÉA & GUY	We've never liked using public transport. Therefore we didn't go anywhere yesterday.
ALEX	After leaving my car outside the town, I hired an electric scooter. It was great! Now, I'm thinking of buying a scooter!
PAULA	As I didn't have any shopping to do, I decided not to go into the centre of town.
YOUSSEF	No one warned me that it was a no-car day. I went to work without knowing about it. I was about to cross the main bridge when the police stopped me.
ESTHER	At first we[1] tried to walk everywhere. But we took an electric taxi in the end. The children loved that. I've never seen them so excited. We didn't regret going into town.

[1] use *on*

Les loisirs

A Read the following extracts from tourist brochures and insert **qui, que, qu'**, **dont** or **où** as required.

Safari du Pin
- Un domaine _____ vous pourrez, en toute sécurité, observer des centaines d'animaux dans leur habitat naturel.
- La vedette du moment est un orang-outan _____ mesure 1,90 m et pèse 130 kilos.

Show aquatique laser
- Un spectacle exceptionnel _____ allie jeux d'eau, laser et feux d'artifices.
- Une soirée _____ vous n'êtes pas près d'oublier.

Excursions en autocar
- Visite des Gorges du Verdon _____ l'on peut admirer d'étonnants paysages.
- Une journée _____ toute la famille gardera un excellent souvenir.

B Here are some commentaries about the Tour de France. Fill the gaps with the present participle of the verbs in brackets.

1. Il a réalisé un véritable exploit en _____ cette étape[1]. *(remporter)*

2. Il s'est effondré en _____ la ligne d'arrivée. *(franchir)*

3. En _____ l'Italien, le Belge a réussi à prendre le maillot jaune[2]. *(battre)*

4. Tout en _____ fait une bonne course, le Niçois est arrivé troisième. *(avoir)*

5. _____ donné la pluie, on s'attend à des performances médiocres. *(être)*

C *Version.* Some people have been asked to say what they find relaxing.

SYLVIA   C'est en ayant plusieurs activités très différentes que je parviens à me défouler.

ÉRIC   Je combats le stress en pratiquant à la fois des sports d'équipe et des sports individuels.

KARIMA   Tout en m'intéressant au sport, je préfère les jeux sur ordinateur.

BEN & ÉLA   Le soir, pour se changer les idées, on écoute les informations à la radio en prenant un verre.

RACHID   Moi, pour me détendre en rentrant du travail, j'écoute de la musique.

CLAUDE   Étant donné que j'ai peu de temps libre, la télévision est ma distraction principale.

---

[1] *une étape* : a leg (of a race)
[2] *remporter le maillot jaune* : to become leader of the Tour de France race

Relative pronouns

See page 147, section 5 for use of **l'on** after **que** and **où**
See pages 92–93, sections 1–6 for RELATIVE PRONOUNS AFTER PREPOSITIONS
See page 94, sections 7–12 for relative pronouns **ce qui, ce que, ce dont, ce à quoi**

1   **qui**, **que**, **dont** and **où** are RELATIVE PRONOUNS:

Le médecin **qui** soigne Luc est absent	*The doctor who treats Luc is absent*
La cliente **que** tu détestes est partie	*The client who you hate has left*
Le papier **dont** on a besoin est là	*The paper (that) we need is there*
Le cinéma **où** vous allez est loin ?	*Is the cinema you are going to far?*

RELATIVE PRONOUNS link two sentences and refer to the noun they follow:

Le médecin soigne Luc + **Le médecin** est absent →	**Le médecin qui** soigne Luc est absent
La cliente est partie + Tu détestes **la cliente** →	**La cliente que** tu détestes est partie
Le papier est là + On a besoin **du papier** →	**Le papier dont** on a besoin est là
Le cinéma est loin ? + Vous allez **au cinéma** →	**Le cinéma où** vous allez est loin ?

qui and que

See pages 49–50, sections 7–10 for **qui** and **que** as question words

2   **qui** and **que / qu'** both mean *who, that* and *which*. They can be used for both people and things. How do you know whether to use **qui** or **que**? An easy way is to remember to use **qui** when the next word is a verb:

Le médecin **qui soigne** Luc est absent	*The doctor who treats Luc is absent*
Le colis **qui est arrivé** vient d'Aix	*The parcel that has arrived is from Aix*

The grammatical explanation is that **qui** is the SUBJECT of the next verb and **que** is the OBJECT of the next verb. See pages 34–40, sections 3–4.

3   **qui** replaces the SUBJECT of the next verb. The SUBJECT is the person or thing coming <u>before</u> the verb, for example **le médecin**:

SUBJECT	VERB	DIRECT OBJECT
le médecin	soigne	Luc

therefore **qui** is used to refer back to **le médecin**:

le médecin <u>qui</u> soigne Luc ...

More examples:

> L'employé **qui** a répondu ne savait rien
> *The employee who replied did not know anything*

l'employé is the SUBJECT of the verb **a répondu**: **l'employé** a répondu

> J'ai regardé le film **qui** est passé hier à la télévision
> *I watched the film that was on television yesterday*

le film is the SUBJECT of the verb **est passé**: **le film** est passé

4   **que** replaces the DIRECT OBJECT of the next verb. The DIRECT OBJECT is the person or thing coming <u>after</u> the verb, for example **la cliente** in the following:

SUBJECT	VERB	DIRECT OBJECT
tu	détestes	**la cliente**

therefore **que** is used to refer back to **la cliente**:

> **la cliente <u>que</u>** tu détestes ...

Unlike its English equivalents *who, whom, which, that*, **que** is never omitted in French.
More examples:

> Les gens **qu'**on a vus étaient mécontents
> *The people we saw were dissatisfied*

les gens is the DIRECT OBJECT of the verb **a vus**: on a vu **les gens**

> La décision **que** tu as prise m'étonne
> *The decision (that) you took surprises me*

la décision is the DIRECT OBJECT of the verb **as prise**: tu as pris **la décision**

que shortens to **qu'** before vowels and unaspirated **h**.

5   A past participle following **que** agrees with the word that **que** refers to:

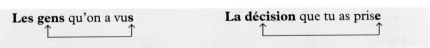

Les gens qu'on a vus   **La décision** que tu as prise

This is because the past participle agrees with the direct object when it comes before the verb – see page 17, section 15.

dont and où

6   **dont** is used for both *people* and *things*. It always replaces a phrase beginning with **de**:

SUBJECT	VERB	PHRASE WITH DE
tu	parlais	**de la comédienne**
on	a	besoin **du papier**
elle	est	responsable **du service**

> **La comédienne dont** tu parlais est morte
> *The actress (whom) you were talking about is dead*
> **Le papier dont** on a besoin est là
> *The paper we need is there*
> **Le service dont** elle est responsable est au premier étage
> *The department she is responsible for is on the first floor*

7   **dont** can express POSSESSION:

> Rémi, **dont** j'utilise la voiture, est à l'étranger
> *Rémi, whose car I am using, is abroad*

dont replaces **de Rémi**: la voiture **de Rémi**

> La ville **dont** le nom m'échappe n'est pas loin de Lille
> *The town whose name escapes me is not far from Lille*

dont replaces **de la ville**: le nom **de la ville**

Note that the word order is different in French, and that the definite article (**le, la, l', les**) is needed before the noun:

> Rémi, dont j'utilise **la voiture**, ...   *Rémi, whose car I am using, ...*
> La ville dont **le nom** m'échappe ...   *The town whose name escapes me ...*

8   **où** can refer to both PLACE and TIME:

> L'endroit **où** je suis allé est magnifique
> *The place I went to is wonderful*
> Mais le jour **où** je suis arrivé, il pleuvait
> *But on the day (when) I arrived it was raining*

Note the use of **où** in the expressions **au cas où** and **dans la mesure où**:

> **au cas où** il serait absent   *in case he is absent*
> **dans la mesure où** c'est possible   *inasmuch as it is possible*

See page 45, section 13.3 for use of conditional after **au cas où**

Forms and uses of the present participle

9   The PRESENT PARTICIPLE of verbs is formed by taking the **nous** form of the present tense, removing the **-ons** ending and replacing it by **-ant**.

parler:	nous **parl**ons	→	**parlant**
finir:	nous **finiss**ons	→	**finissant**
vendre:	nous **vend**ons	→	**vendant**
prendre:	nous **pren**ons	→	**prenant**

Some verbs are irregular:

avoir → ayant	**être → étant**	**savoir → sachant**

10 The preposition **en** (*on, when, by, while*) + PRESENT PARTICIPLE is used to describe an action closely followed by another, or overlapping with another:

En me **voyant**, il était fou de joie	***When he saw*** *me, he was overjoyed*
	On seeing *me, he was overjoyed*
Tu réussiras **en travaillant**	*You will succeed **by working***
Elle consultait la carte **en conduisant**	*She read the map **while driving***

In each sentence the subject of both the verb and the present participle is the same. If the subject changes, do <u>not</u> use the present participle:

Quand je l'ai vu, il était fou de joie
When I saw him, he was overjoyed
Elle consultait la carte **pendant que sa fille conduisait**
She read the map while her daughter drove

11 **tout en** + PRESENT PARTICIPLE is used for emphasis:

1. When two actions take place at the same time:

Tout en répondant au téléphone, il décachetait le courrier
While answering the telephone he opened the mail

2. When making a concession:

Tout en comprenant vos motifs, je ne peux pas les approuver
While understanding your motives I cannot approve of them
Although I understand your motives I cannot approve of them

12 The PRESENT PARTICIPLE is rarely used on its own in French. Note how the following phrases with *-ing* in English are translated by **qui** + VERB:

les personnes **qui voyagent**	*people travelling*
les enfants **qui ont besoin d'assistance**	*children needing help*

A Insert **qui, que, qu', dont** or **où** into the following sentences.

Les villages de vacances

Les villages de vacances, pourquoi ?
- Les parents _____ nous avons interrogés disent préférer partir en vacances avec leurs enfants.
- Les adolescents _____ nous avons rencontrés pensent différemment : ils préfèrent la compagnie des jeunes de leur âge.
- Ce sont ces attitudes contradictoires _____ expliquent le succès des villages de vacances.

Flexibilité et respect de l'individu
- Le village est un endroit _____ chacun peut jouir d'une certaine indépendance.
- Les activités _____ on propose aux vacanciers, jeunes et moins jeunes, sont variées.
- Les familles _____ veulent se séparer pendant la journée peuvent le faire.
- Le repas du soir est le moment _____ on peut raconter ses exploits de la journée.

Une formule réussie
- Les parents peuvent jouir de la tranquillité _____ ils rêvent toute l'année, sans être séparés de leurs enfants.
- Les enfants ont l'indépendance _____ ils souhaitent.
- C'est donc une formule _____ satisfait tout le monde.

B Give the French equivalent of the expressions in brackets, remembering to make any necessary agreements.

e.g. Où as-tu mis les vidéos ... ?   [that I forgot yesterday]
→ Où as-tu mis les vidéos que j'ai oubliées hier ?

1. Quel est le titre des deux films ... ?   [that they talked about]
2. Je vous recommande la pièce ... à Pau.   [that I have seen]
3. Vous avez reçu les deux livres ... ?   [that she sent you]
4. Tu peux nous prêter les CD ... ?   [that we need]
5. Elle devrait essayer la raquette ....   [that Lise used yesterday]
6. Ils n'ont pas pu regarder l'émission ....   [that you mentioned]
7. On a visité le village de vacances ....   [that she was responsible for]

C *Thème.*
1. I discovered the theatre by going to the Avignon Festival.
2. Although I take part in team sports, I prefer individual sports.
3. I love activities which combine music and movement.
4. With my personal stereo, I can listen to music all the time – on my way to work or while I do my shopping, for example.
5. When I get home in the evening, I visit some Internet sites to take my mind off things.

A Complete the sentences below using the instructions in brackets.
1. J'ai apporté mes affaires, mais pas [yours *sing*.].
2. J'ai téléphoné à mes parents, lui n'a même pas écrit [to his].
3. Il a posté son paquet, mais pas [theirs].
4. Ils ont pris ses billets, mais pas [theirs].
5. On a discuté de ses problèmes, mais je n'ai pas voulu parler [about mine].

B Write these negative sentences correctly using the imperfect tense of the verb.
1. Elles (*ne pas être*) au courant.
2. Je (*ne jamais conduire*) la nuit.
3. Vous (*ne guère se plaindre*) de votre travail.
4. Nous (*ne rien promettre*).
5. On (*ne décevoir personne*) à ce moment-là.
6. Nous (*ne plus comprendre*) les motifs de sa conduite.
7. Tu (*ne pas avoir*) le courage de lui annoncer ton départ ?
8. On (*se souvenir*) de rien.
9. Je (*voir*) aucune difficulté insurmontable.
10. Il (*s'appeler*) ni Renaud ni Roland ?
11. Elle (*souffrir*) nullement de la chaleur.
12. On (*pouvoir*) le joindre nulle part.

C Insert **qui**, **que**, **qu'**, **dont** or **où**:

Les centres de vacances

Les centres de vacances, _____ on appelait autrefois les « colonies de vacances », accueillent des centaines de milliers de jeunes. On distingue au moins trois catégories de centres :
- les centres maternels, _____ s'occupent des petits de quatre à six ans ;
- les centres pour mineurs, _____ accueillent les mineurs de six à quatorze ans ;
- et les camps d'adolescents, _____ s'adressent aux plus de quatorze ans.

Les activités _____ bénéficient les jeunes sont multiples : du sport à la vidéo, en passant par les séjours linguistiques et les stages informatiques. Dans les camps d'adolescents ce sont les activités physiques et sportives _____ dominent : camps de voile _____ les jeunes peuvent s'initier à la navigation à voile, camps d'équitation _____ ils apprennent à monter à cheval, etc.

Les jeunes _____ s'occupent les animateurs viennent en général de familles modestes vivant en milieu urbain. Ce sont, en majorité, des enfants _____ la mère travaille. Tous ceux _____ nous avons interrogés se sont déclarés enchantés de la formule.

D If the following sentences were true, nobody reading this advertisement would buy travel insurance from Assurtout. Rewrite each statement in the negative as suggested.

1. Tout le monde est à l'abri¹ d'un accident.   [Nobody ...]
2. Tout nous empêchera de vous porter assistance.   [Nothing ...]
3. Tous les efforts seront épargnés pour faciliter votre retour.   [No ...]
4. Un assuré s'est déclaré mécontent des prestations² d'Assurtout.
   [Not one ...]

E *Thème.*
1. After checking in their luggage, they helped me carry mine.
2. The plane was about to take off when one of the engines exploded. There were no casualties.
3. She has decided not to go away this year in order to save some money.
4. After obtaining information from a travel agent, they booked a flight on Air Littoral.
5. When I met her she was thinking of giving up her studies to look for a job.
6. While admitting that they were wrong, they refused to change their plans.
7. When we finally arrived at the airport, the coach that was supposed to take us to the hotel had just left.
8. In the rush hour, we used to avoid taking the train that stopped at every station.
9. The Spanish man whose flat we rented last winter would come every other week to check that everything was all right.
10. He has been learning to drive since Easter, but he has not yet taken his test.

F CAREFUL: the following passage contains some grammatical errors. Read and reread it carefully until you have corrected all fifteen mistakes. Check agreements (past participles, adjectives), verb endings, verb constructions (before infinitives), relative pronouns and negatives.

Extraits du Guide Suntours

La veille du départ. Il est possible que les horaires que nous vous avons donné au moment de votre réservation subissent des modifications par la suite. La veille de notre départ, prenez la précaution de vérifiez ces horaires auprès de vos agent de voyages.

Bagages. Essayez, si possible, voyager léger. Pour cela réfléchissez à votre style de vacances et ne vous encombrez pas de choses que vous aurez pas besoin. Évitez emporter des bijoux de valeur.

Au retour. Nous avons effectué des enquêtes que nous permettent de connaître l'évolution des besoins en matière de tourisme ainsi que les problèmes que surgissent au cours des séjours organisé. Cependant, aucun information n'est aussi précis que celle que vous pouvez nous faire parvenir personnellement, aussi nous vous recommandez de bien vouloir remplir, dès votre retour, les questionnaires que vous auront été remis. Nous vous remercions votre aimable coopération.

---

¹ *à l'abri de* : safe from
² *les prestations* : services

Le corps et la santé

A Jogging is a popular sport. Replace each expression in italics by an adverb with the same meaning and insert it in the right place so that each sentence makes sense.

e.g. *En ce moment*   Notre club est en plein essor.
→ Notre club est actuellement en plein essor.

Ils courent, ils courent ...

1. *d'une manière constante*
   Le nombre de « joggers » augmente.
2. *d'une manière physique*
   La plupart d'entre eux disent qu'ils ont besoin de se dépenser pour éviter le stress.
3. *d'habitude, d'une manière fréquente*
   Ils font partie d'un groupe ou d'un club, et s'entraînent.
4. *en général, d'une façon régulière*
   Âgés de 35 à 45 ans, ils se soumettent à un contrôle médical.
5. *d'une façon absolue, tout à fait*
   Ils cherchent à retrouver ou à garder leur jeunesse et sont convaincus que courir est la meilleure façon d'y parvenir.

B Write the verbs in brackets in the conditional tense.

De bonnes résolutions

Après avoir regardé à la télévision une émission intitulée « Bien vivre », je me suis dit que je (*se sentir*) mieux dans ma peau si je menais une vie plus équilibrée.

Comme j'étais en congé j'ai décidé que dès le lendemain je (*arrêter*) de fumer. Je (*sauter*) du lit à sept heures et demie et avant de déjeuner je (*faire*) un peu d'exercice physique. Le reste de la matinée (*être*) consacré à de menus travaux dans l'appartement et, au lieu d'aller acheter des plats tout prêts, je (*prendre*) la peine de préparer des légumes frais et une grillade pour midi. Je (*avoir*) le temps en début d'après-midi de lire un peu et je (*aller*) ensuite à la piscine. Après un repas léger, je (*rejoindre*) les copains mais plutôt que de traîner toute la soirée d'un endroit à l'autre je (*proposer*) toute une série d'activités culturelles. J'étais sûr que ce nouveau rythme de vie me (*convenir*) tout à fait et que je (*pouvoir*) ainsi mieux profiter de mes vacances.

Malheureusement, le lendemain je n'ai pas entendu mon réveil sonner. Quand je me suis réveillé il était déjà trop tard pour mettre mes résolutions en pratique.

Adverbs

1   ADVERBS can describe VERBS, ADJECTIVES and other ADVERBS:

Nous soutenons **activement** vos efforts	**activement** describes
*We **actively** support your efforts*	the VERB **soutenons**
Leurs articles sont **généralement** bons	**généralement** describes
*Their articles are **usually** good*	the ADJECTIVE **bons**
Notre idée a été **assez** bien reçue	**assez** describes
*Our idea was **quite** well received*	the ADVERB **bien**

How to form regular adverbs

2   Most ADVERBS are formed by adding **-ment** to the feminine adjective.
ADVERBS have only one form and do not agree with nouns or other words:

MASCULINE ADJECTIVE	FEMININE ADJECTIVE	ADVERB	
général	générale	**généralement**	*usually, generally*
entier	entière	**entièrement**	*entirely*
actif	active	**activement**	*actively*

Some adjectives do not have adverbial forms, for example **important**,
intéressant and **charmant**. See page 44, section 9.

3   If the masculine form of an adjective ends in a vowel (**a, e, i, o, u**), the
adverb is formed by adding **-ment** to the masculine form:

ADJECTIVE	ADVERB	
absolu	**absolument**	*absolutely, completely*
forcé	**forcément**	*necessarily, inevitably*
infini	**infiniment**	*extremely, infinitely*
résolu	**résolument**	*resolutely, determinedly*
vrai	**vraiment**	*really, truly*

Exception: **gaiement** (*gaily, cheerfully*) follows the rule in section 2 above.

4   With adjectives ending **-ant** / **-ent**, replace these endings by
-amment / **-emment**:

ADJECTIVE	ADVERB	
constant	**constamment**	*constantly, perseveringly*
courant	**couramment**	*fluently, usually, generally*
évident	**évidemment**	*obviously, evidently*
récent	**récemment**	*recently*
violent	**violemment**	*violently*

Exception: **lentement** (*slowly*) follows the rule in section 2 above.

Irregular adverbs

5 The following adverbs are irregular:

ADJECTIVE	ADVERB	
aveugle	**aveuglément**	*blindly*
commun	**communément**	*commonly, generally*
énorme	**énormément**	*enormously, tremendously*
précis	**précisément**	*precisely*
profond	**profondément**	*profoundly, deeply*
gentil	**gentiment**	*nicely, pleasantly*
bref	**brièvement**	*briefly*
bon	**bien**	*well*
meilleur	**mieux**	*better, best*
mauvais	**mal**	*badly*
rapide	**vite**	*fast, quickly*

Vite and bien

6 **vite** (*fast*) is an adverb and cannot be used as an adjective. The adjective **rapide** is generally used to translate *fast* when it describes a noun:

Ils roulent trop **vite** — *They drive too **fast***

BUT — Leur voiture est **rapide** — *Their car is **fast***

7 **bien** (*well*) also means *good* in English:

Ce serait **bien** s'il venait — *It would be good if he came*

Position of adverbs

8 Adverbs describing verbs usually go immediately <u>after</u> the verb in French:

Nous acceptons **entièrement** ses conseils
*We **entirely** accept his advice*
Il ne refuse pas **catégoriquement** de signer
*He does not **flatly** refuse to sign*

Where there is a PAST PARTICIPLE, adverbs usually go <u>before</u> it:

Elle a **complètement** oublié de m'appeler
She completely forgot to call me
J'ai **toujours** eu du mal à me réveiller
I've always had trouble waking up

Certain adverbs do go <u>after </u>the past participle:

1. All adverbs of place:
Cela s'est passé **ici** — *It happened here*
Je t'ai cherché **partout** — *I looked for you everywhere*

2. Certain adverbs of time e.g., **hier, aujourd'hui, demain, tôt, tard**:
Il l'a publié **hier** — *He published it yesterday*
Le film est passé **tard** — *The film was on late*

Adverbial phrases

9   Some adjectives, such as **charmant**, **important** and those listed below, do not have an adverbial form.

However, they can be used in ADVERBIAL PHRASES. These describe the way in which someone does something and are often translated by an adverb in English:

surprenant	Il a réagi **d'une manière surprenante**
	He reacted surprisingly / in a surprising way
enthousiaste	Elle a accepté ma proposition **avec enthousiasme**
	She accepted my suggestion enthusiastically
intéressant	Tu as traité le thème **d'une façon intéressante**
	You tackled the topic interestingly / in an interesting way
irrité	Elle a répondu **d'un ton irrité**
	She replied angrily

Note: use **de, d'** in front of **une manière**, **une façon** and **un ton**.

Adjectives used as adverbs

10   Some ADJECTIVES are used with certain verbs as adverbs:

aller **(tout) droit**	*to go straight on*	parler **fort**	*to speak loudly*
coûter **cher**	*to be expensive*	travailler **dur**	*to work hard*
parler **bas**	*to speak quietly*	voir **clair**	*to see clearly*

Cette moto coûte trop **cher**   *This motorbike is too expensive*
Parlez plus **fort**   *Speak up*

Note: these adjectives, when used as adverbs, do not agree with the noun.

The conditional and conditional perfect

11   To form the CONDITIONAL, add the CONDITIONAL ENDINGS to the infinitive of the verb. As with the future, drop the final **-e** of the infinitive of **-re** verbs:

-er verbs:	**parler**	**-ir** verbs:	**finir**	**-re** verbs:	**vendre**
je	parler**ais**	je	finir**ais**	je	vendr**ais**
tu	parler**ais**	tu	finir**ais**	tu	vendr**ais**
il / elle	parler**ait**	il / elle	finir**ait**	il / elle	vendr**ait**
nous	parler**ions**	nous	finir**ions**	nous	vendr**ions**
vous	parler**iez**	vous	finir**iez**	vous	vendr**iez**
ils / elles	parler**aient**	ils / elles	finir**aient**	ils / elles	vendr**aient**

12 Verbs which are irregular in the future are also irregular in the conditional. Some examples:

INFINITIVE	FUTURE	CONDITIONAL
aller	j'irai, etc.	**j'irais**, etc.
avoir	j'aurai, etc.	**j'aurais**, etc.
devoir	je devrai, etc.	**je devrais**, etc.
venir	je viendrai, etc.	**je viendrais**, etc.

See page 11, section 11 for verbs with irregular future forms

13 The conditional is used to express:

1. The FUTURE IN THE PAST:

   Elle pensait que nous **viendrions**   *She thought that we would come*

2. An action which is subject to a CONDITION:

   Ils **voyageraient** s'ils étaient riches   *They would travel if they were rich*

3. A NEED or PREFERENCE:

   Je **voudrais** présenter ma candidature   *I would like to apply*
   Nous **aimerions** la voir plus souvent   *We would like to see her more often*

   It is also used after **au cas où**:

   Appelle-moi **au cas où** je serais libre   *Call me in case I'm free*

See page 149, section 11 for use of conditional to imply what may or may not be true

14 The CONDITIONAL PERFECT consists of the CONDITIONAL of **avoir** or **être** + PAST PARTICIPLE:

parler	venir	se laver
j'**aurais** parlé	je **serais** venu(e)	je me **serais** lavé(e)
tu **aurais** parlé	tu **serais** venu(e)	tu te **serais** lavé(e)
il / elle **aurait** parlé	il / elle **serait** venu(e)	il / elle se **serait** lavé(e)
nous **aurions** parlé	nous **serions** venu(e)s	nous nous **serions** lavé(e)s
vous **auriez** parlé	vous **seriez** venu(e)(s)	vous vous **seriez** lavé(e)(s)
ils / elles **auraient** parlé	ils **seraient** venu(e)s	ils / elles se **seraient** lavé(e)s

15 The CONDITIONAL PERFECT is usually equivalent to *would have . . .* in English:

   Nous **aurions démissionné**   *We would have resigned*
   Elle **serait partie**   *She would have left*

See page 69, section 12 for use of the conditional and conditional perfect in sentences with **si**

A Replace the adjectives in italics by adverbs or adverbial phrases and then insert them into the sentences so that they describe the words underlined.

e.g. *récent*   Les médecines alternatives *ont connu* un grand essor.
→ Les médecines alternatives ont connu récemment un grand essor.

Les médecines alternatives

1. *fréquent, enthousiaste*
   Les Français qui <u>ont utilisé</u> les médecines dites « douces » en <u>parlent</u>.
2. *commun, relatif*
   Parmi celles-ci, on compte la phytothérapie, pratique fort ancienne, <u>appelée</u> « médecine par les plantes » et l'acuponcture <u>bien</u> acceptée de nos jours.
3. *général, particulier*
   Les gens <u>se tournent</u> vers les médecines alternatives lorsque la médecine traditionnelle s'est avérée <u>inefficace</u>.
4. *forcé, sérieux*
   Il y <u>aura</u> des sceptiques, mais le nombre des médecins généralistes qui <u>croient</u> aux bienfaits de ces médecines différentes est en augmentation croissante.
5. *sûr, net*
   Ces moyens thérapeutiques <u>auront</u> un rôle <u>plus</u> important à jouer à l'avenir.

B Write the verbs in brackets in the conditional tense.

1. Il (*falloir*) se préoccuper plus de son corps et de sa santé.
2. Vous (*être*) moins essoufflé si vous fumiez moins.
3. Le médecin a déclaré qu'elle ne lui (*prescrire*) plus de somnifères.
4. L'alcool ne (*faire*) de mal à personne, si les gens buvaient modérément.
5. Les gens (*souffrir*) moins du dos s'ils se tenaient correctement.

C Write the verbs in brackets in the conditional perfect tense.

1. Nous (*vouloir*) organiser une randonnée pédestre dans les Alpes.
2. Il (*prendre*) plus d'exercice physique s'il en avait eu le temps.
3. Tu (*devoir*) venir à pied au lieu de prendre la voiture.
4. Je (*préférer*) me faire soigner par un homéopathe.
5. On (*s'inscrire*) à un cours de yoga si on avait su.

D *Thème.*

1. If he went on a diet and ate in a sensible way he would lose weight quickly.
2. I would have thought that he would have gone to a homeopath, but when I told him so he replied angrily that he would never do such a thing.
3. At one time, everybody believed that antibiotics and vaccines would control disease for ever, but it is obviously not the case.
4. The arrival of AIDS has deeply shocked the public and dramatically changed our sexual habits. The opposite would have been surprising.

L'enseignement

A In a letter to a newspaper a pupil tries to explain what a good teacher is. Write the questions relating to the answers provided, using the question words and phrases suggested in the list below.

Qu'est-ce qu'un bon prof ?

Je peux aisément répondre à cette question parce que j'ai la chance d'avoir un excellent professeur d'histoire.

Un bon prof, c'est d'abord quelqu'un qui aime son métier. Notre professeur est heureuse d'enseigner parce que nous sommes heureux d'apprendre (enfin, c'est l'impression que j'ai !) et nous sommes heureux d'apprendre parce qu'elle aime enseigner. Pour les élèves comme pour elle, c'est donc un véritable plaisir d'être en cours. Elle est généreuse, disponible et sait donner à chacun d'entre nous le sentiment d'être important. C'est en nous prenant au sérieux qu'elle nous incite à produire un travail personnel. L'histoire me passionne maintenant. Plus que tout autre professeur jusqu'à présent, elle m'a donné envie d'apprendre.

Omar Latelli (17 ans)

1. Parce qu'il a la chance d'avoir un excellent professeur d'histoire.
2. C'est d'abord quelqu'un qui aime son métier.
3. Oui, elle est heureuse d'enseigner.
4. Pour les élèves comme pour elle.
5. En les prenant au sérieux.
6. L'histoire.
7. C'est elle qui lui en a donné envie.
8. Dix-sept ans.

   Comment ... ?   Quel ... ?   Est-ce que ... ?   Qu'est-ce que ... ?
   Qu'est-ce qui ... ?   Pour qui ... ?   Pourquoi ... ?   Qui est-ce qui ... ?

B Student life can be disappointing. Write the verbs in brackets in the pluperfect tense.

Déçus par la vie d'étudiant

JULIEN   La fac, ce n'est pas ce que je *(imaginer)*. Avant de venir je *(se dire)* que la fac serait pour moi l'occasion de découvrir des tas de choses. Je *(ne pas se rendre compte)* de ce que serait la vie sur un campus complètement coupé de tout, à plusieurs kilomètres du centre. Personne ne me *(prévenir)*.

RACHID   Même quand on s'intéresse à ses études, comme c'est notre cas, on ne peut pas faire que ça. On a besoin d'autre chose.
Personnellement, si je *(savoir)*, j'aurais essayé d'aller ailleurs.

CHLOÉ   Moi, je *(ne pas se faire)* d'illusions, alors c'est différent. Mais c'est vrai qu'on est isolé.

Asking questions with est-ce que ... ?

1 The most common way to ask a QUESTION in conversation is to use a questioning tone of voice:

> Vous aimez la musique ?   Il est parti à quelle heure ?

Another simple way of forming a question is to use **est-ce que ... ?**:

Est-ce que vous aimez la musique ?	*Do you like music?*
Quand **est-ce qu'**il est sorti ?	*When did he go out?*
Avec qui **est-ce que** vous avez fait cela ?	*Who did you do that with?*
A quelle heure **est-ce qu'**il est parti ?	*What time did he leave?*

Inversion of subject and verb: formal questions

See page 149, section 12 for the use of inversion after speech

2 To ask a question in formal language, use INVERSION. This means turning around (inverting) the subject and the verb:

> Cette guerre **peut-elle** continuer ? *Can this war go on?*
> A qui **s'adressera-t-on** ? *To whom will they turn?*

3 With a subject pronoun (e.g. **je, tu, il**) and a verb tense consisting of one word (e.g. **faudrait**), turn them round and join them with a hyphen (-):

Il faudrait →	**Faudrait-il** accepter ?	*Should they agree?*
Ils changeront →	**Changeront-ils** d'avis ?	*Will they change their mind?*

Use **-t-** to separate two vowels:

Il fera →	**Fera-t-il** des concessions ?	*Will he make concessions?*
On a →	**A-t-on** le droit d'en parler ?	*Can one talk about it?*

4 When the subject is a noun, it is repeated in the subject pronoun **il, elle, ils** or **elles**:

Le ministre fera-t-**il** des concessions ?	*Will the Minister make concessions?*
La grève va-t-**elle** continuer ?	*Will the strike go on?*

5 With tenses taking **avoir** or **être**, such as the perfect tense, invert **avoir** or **être** and not the past participle:

N'**ont-ils** pas assez souffert ?	*Have they not suffered enough?*
Le client **s'est-il** déclaré satisfait ?	*Did the client say he was pleased?*

6 Object pronouns (**me, le, lui,** etc.) stay before the verb, or **avoir** or **être**:

> Ne **nous** a-t-il pas dit la vérité ? *Has he not told us the truth?*

Asking *who ...?* and *what ...?*

7   Look at the beginning of each of these expressions:

qui est-ce qui ... ?	mean *who . . .?* and begin with **qui**
qui est-ce que ... ?	
qu'est-ce qui ... ?	mean *what . . .?* and begin with **qu'**
qu'est-ce que ... ?	

8   When *who ...?* and *what ...?* are SUBJECT of the verb, the expression ends with **qui**:

qui est-ce **qui** ... ? *(who ...?)*	qu'est ce **qui** ... ? *(what ...?)*

Qui est-ce **qui** fait ce bruit ?	***Who** is making that noise?*
Charlotte fait ce bruit	***Charlotte** is making that noise*

Charlotte is the SUBJECT of the verb **fait**

Qu'est-ce **qui** fait ce bruit ?	***What** is making that noise?*
Le moteur fait ce bruit	***The engine** is making that noise*

Le moteur is the SUBJECT of the verb **fait**

9   When *who ...?* and *what ...?* are the DIRECT OBJECTS of the verb, the expression ends with **que**, or **qu'** before a vowel or unaspirated **h**:

qui est-ce **que** ... ? *(who ...?)*	qu'est-ce **que** ... ? *(what ...?)*

Qui est-ce **qu'**il regarde ?	***Who** is he looking at?*
Il regarde **le chanteur**	*He is looking at **the singer***

le chanteur is the DIRECT OBJECT of the verb **regarde**

Qu'est-ce **qu'**il regarde ?	***What** is he looking at?*
Il regarde **le compteur**	*He is looking at the **speedometer***

le compteur is the DIRECT OBJECT of the verb **regarde**

10   **qui ... ?** and **que ... ?** are also used to mean *who ...?* and *what ..?* in formal language. Sometimes inversion of verb and subject is required:

LESS FORMAL, NO INVERSION	MORE FORMAL	
qui est-ce qui ... ?	**qui ... ?** no inversion	*who ...?*
qui est-ce que ... ?	**qui ... ?** with inversion	
qu'est-ce qui ... ?	(no shorter version)	*what ...?*
qu'est-ce que ... ?	**que ... ?** with inversion	

Some examples:

Qui a fait cette erreur ?	*Who made this mistake?*
(Qui est-ce qui a fait cette erreur ?)	
Qui avez-vous vu ?	*Who/whom did you see?*
(Qui est-ce que vous avez vu ?)	
Que font les joueurs ?	*What are the players doing?*
(Qu'est-ce que les joueurs font ?)	

Note: when **que** is followed by inversion of subject and verb, the subject is <u>not</u> repeated in the personal pronoun, unlike the examples in section 4 above.

Other question words (comment ... ?, pourquoi ... ?, etc.)

See page 48, section 1 about avoiding inversion by using **est-ce que ... ?**

11 In formal language, the other question words also require inversion:

comment ... ? *how ...?*	**Comment** le ministre a-t-il pu faire une telle déclaration ? *How could the Minister have made such a statement?*
pourquoi ... ? *why ...?*	**Pourquoi** a-t-il fait cette déclaration aujourd'hui ? *Why did he make it today?*
où ... ? *where ...?*	**Où** l'a-t-il faite ? *Where did he make it?*
quand ... ? *when ...?*	**Quand** l'a-t-il faite ? *When did he make it?*
combien (de) ... ? *how much/many ...?*	**Combien de** fois l'a-t-il répétée ? *How many times did he repeat it?*

Asking questions with prepositions (pour qui, etc.)

See page 48, section 1 about avoiding inversion by using **est-ce que ... ?**

12 When asking *who ...?* and *what ...?* questions with a preposition (**à**, **avec**, **de**, **pour**, etc.), use **qui ... ?** and **quoi ... ?**
In French, prepositions cannot be left 'hanging' as in English sentences like:

*What is he afraid **of**?   Who are you thinking **about**?*

1. Use **qui ... ?** when referring to PEOPLE (*who ...?*):

De **qui** a-t-il peur ?	*Who is he afraid of? (Of whom is he afraid?)*
A **qui** pensez-vous ?	*Who are you thinking about?*

2. Use **quoi ... ?** when referring to THINGS (*what ...?*):

De **quoi** as-tu peur ?	*What are you afraid of? (Of what are you afraid?)*
A **quoi** pensez-vous ?	*What are you thinking about?*

Question adjective quel ... ? and pronoun lequel ... ?

See page 48, section 1 about avoiding inversion by using **est-ce que ... ?**

13 **quel ... ?** *(which ...?, what ...?)* is the question adjective. It is always used with a noun, which it agrees with:

	SINGULAR	PLURAL
MASCULINE	quel	quels
FEMININE	quelle	quelles

Quels conseils vous a-t-elle donnés ?   *What advice did she give you?*
De **quels vêtements** a-t-elle besoin ?   *Which clothes does she need?*

14 **lequel ... ?** *(which ...?, which one ...?)* is the question pronoun. It is used alone and agrees with the noun it refers to:

	SINGULAR	PLURAL
MASCULINE	lequel	lesquels
FEMININE	laquelle	lesquelles

Tu veux des dossiers ? **Lesquels ?**   *Do you want some files? Which ones?*

The pluperfect tense

15 The PLUPERFECT TENSE consists of the IMPERFECT TENSE of **avoir** or **être** with the PAST PARTICIPLE:

parler	venir	se laver
j'**avais** parlé	j'**étais** venu(e)	je m'**étais** lavé(e)
tu **avais** parlé	tu **étais** venu(e)	tu t'**étais** lavé(e)
il/elle **avait** parlé	il / elle **était** venu(e)	il / elle s'**était** lavé(e)
nous **avions** parlé	nous **étions** venu(e)s	nous nous **étions** lavé(e)s
vous **aviez** parlé	vous **étiez** venu(e)(s)	vous vous **étiez** lavé(e)(s)
ils/elles **avaient** parlé	ils / elles **étaient** venu(e)s	ils / elles s'**étaient** lavé(e)s

See page 17, sections 15–16 for PAST PARTICIPLE AGREEMENT rules

16 The PLUPERFECT TENSE has its equivalent in English:

Elle **avait terminé** son mémoire avant de partir pour la France
*She **had finished** her report before leaving for France*
Je **m'étais reposé** avant le dîner, mais j'avais toujours sommeil
*I **had rested** before dinner, but I was still sleepy*

See page 54, section 3 for pluperfect in indirect questions
See page 69, section 12 for pluperfect with **si**

A Why do people send their children to private schools in France? Rewrite the questions in italics in a formal style using inversions.

Pourquoi met-on ses enfants dans le privé ?

- *Les enfants sont plus suivis dans leurs études ?* – Oui, dans certains cas.
- *Les classes sont moins chargées ?* – Non, pas toujours.
- *On obtient un meilleur pourcentage de réussite ?* – Pas vraiment.
- *Il y a un effort d'innovation pédagogique ?* – Cela dépend des écoles.
- *Le niveau universitaire des maîtres est plus élevé ?* – Certainement pas.
- *C'est pour des raisons religieuses ?* – Pas nécessairement.
- *C'est lié à la position sociale des parents ?* – Oui, mais il faudrait nuancer.

B The following text is about preparing for the « baccalauréat » at evening classes. The parts of the sentences in italics could be the answers to a series of eight questions. Write out the eight questions.

Les terminales du soir : une expérience positive

Les terminales du soir offrent une seconde chance *à ceux qui ont quitté le lycée et décidé par la suite de reprendre leurs études*. Elles s'adressent à ces élèves dont personne ne veut *parce qu'ils sont trop âgés ou trop faibles scolairement*. Avant de s'inscrire à des cours du soir, bon nombre d'entre eux ont essayé de travailler *seuls par correspondance* mais sans succès. Il leur manquait *l'ambiance de travail d'une classe*. En effet, la solidarité des élèves joue un rôle *considérable* : elle aide ces derniers à tenir le coup *dans les moments difficiles*.

C Your teacher returns your essays, explaining why you did not get good marks. Select the appropriate verbs from the list and write them in the pluperfect.

Vous auriez tous eu une bonne note ...

1. si vous _____ pour bien présenter votre copie.
2. si tout le monde _____ à fond le sujet.
3. si vos arguments _____ si mal construits.
4. si vos idées me _____ par leur originalité.
5. si vous _____ le temps de relire votre dissertation avant de la rendre.

enthousiasmer   ne pas être   s'appliquer   analyser   prendre

D *Thème.* You are inquiring about a new course.

1. Who is this course intended for[1]?
2. What qualifications do they ask for?
3. What do they teach to the first-year students?
4. What are the lectures about[2]?
5. What are the important subjects in the second year?

---

[1] use *s'adresser à*
[2] use *porter sur*

La sécurité

A You were a witness when a fire broke out and as a result were questioned by the police. Later on, your parents ask you about the interview. Rewrite the following questions as indicated and remember to change the tense of the second verb where necessary.

e.g. « Où étiez-vous exactement ? » *On m'a interrogé pour savoir …*
→ On m'a interrogé pour savoir où j'étais exactement.

Compte-rendu d'un témoignage

1. « Comment est-ce arrivé ? » *J'ai décrit …*
2. « Où s'est déclaré le sinistre[1] ? » *On m'a demandé …*
3. « Qu'est-ce qui a provoqué l'explosion ? » *Je n'ai pas su dire …*
4. « Quelle heure était-il ? » *J'ai indiqué …*
5. « Y avait-il d'autres témoins ? » *Il m'a fallu dire …*
6. « Qui a prévenu les sapeurs-pompiers ? » *Ensuite, on a voulu savoir …*
7. « A quelle heure sont-ils arrivés sur les lieux ? » *On m'a fait préciser …*
8. « Qu'avez-vous fait en les attendant ? » *Enfin, j'ai dû raconter …*

B Write the verbs in brackets in the imperative.

Sur la route, il est très important de bien voir et d'être vu

Si vous utilisez une voiture :
– *(nettoyer)* votre pare-brise régulièrement ;
– *(changer)* vos balais d'essuie-glaces quand ils sont usés ;
– *(s'assurer)* du parfait fonctionnement de vos éclairages.
Si vous utilisez un deux-roues :
– *(porter)* des vêtements clairs ;
– *(s'équiper)* d'éléments fluorescents pour rouler de nuit.

Recommandations amicales

Avant de quitter l'appartement, sois gentil(le) :
– *(faire)* attention à bien fermer les robinets ;
– *(sortir)* les ordures ;
– *(vérifier)* que les volets et les fenêtres sont fermés ;
– *(débrancher)* les appareils électriques ;
– *(éteindre)* toutes les lumières.
Et puis au moment de partir, *(ne pas oublier)* de fermer la porte d'entrée à clé.
Merci !

---

[1] *un sinistre* : a blaze

Indirect questions

See pages 48–51, sections 1–16 for direct questions

1   Here are some examples of DIRECT and INDIRECT QUESTIONS:

DIRECT QUESTION	INDIRECT QUESTION
Est-ce que tu l'as vue ?	Je voudrais savoir si **tu l'as vue**
Did you see her?	*I'd like to know **whether you saw her***
Qui habite ici ?	Il m'a demandé **qui habitait ici**
Who lives here?	*He asked me **who lived here***
Qu'est-ce qu'elle fera ?	Je vais leur demander **ce qu'elle fera**
What will she do?	*I'm going to ask them **what she will do***
Pour qui l'as-tu fait ?	Elle m'a demandé **pour qui je l'avais fait**
Who did you do it for?	*She asked me **who I had done it for***
Quel jour partira-t-il?	On demanda **quel jour il partirait**
On which day will he leave?	*They asked **on what day he would leave***

Note: inversion is <u>not</u> used in indirect questions.

2   The QUESTION WORD (**qui, quand,** etc.) becomes a RELATIVE PRONOUN in the indirect question. **qui, quand, pourquoi, combien, comment, où, quel,** and **lequel** do not change.
With the following question words, a change is needed:

1. qui est-ce qui and **qui est-ce que** become **qui**:

Qui est-ce que tu as vu ?	→	Il veut savoir **qui** j'ai vu
Who did you see?		*He wants to know who I saw*

2. qu'est-ce qui becomes **ce qui**:

Qu'est-**ce qui** te rend triste ?	→	Dis-moi **ce qui** te rend triste
What is making you sad?		*Tell me what is making you sad*

3. que and **qu'est-ce** become **ce que**:

Qu'est-**ce que** tu feras ?	→	Je vais lui demander **ce qu**'il fera
What will you do?		*I'm going to ask him what he will do*

3   When a question which was asked <u>in the past</u> is reported, the verb tense of the indirect question may be different from that of the direct question:

PRESENT TENSE →	IMPERFECT TENSE
Qui habite ici ?	Elle m'a demandé **qui habitait ici**
PERFECT TENSE →	PLUPERFECT TENSE
Pour qui l'as-tu fait ?	Elle m'a demandé **pour qui je l'avais fait**
FUTURE TENSE →	CONDITIONAL TENSE
Quel jour partira-t-il?	On demanda **quel jour il partirait**

Reported speech

4   INDIRECT QUESTIONS are used in REPORTED SPEECH, that is, a record of a conversation in the past. Compare this conversation between a minister and a journalist with the report in which the journalist records the conversation:

CONVERSATION:

LE JOURNALISTE	Est-ce que vous **avez pris** une décision ?
LA MINISTRE	Non, j'**attends** un rapport. Mais vous **pouvez** être sûrs que la position du gouvernement **sera connue** bientôt.

REPORTED SPEECH:

J'ai demandé à la ministre si elle **avait pris** une décision. Elle a répondu que non, qu'elle **attendait** un rapport. Mais elle a ajouté que nous **pouvions** être sûrs que la position du gouvernement **serait connue** bientôt.

The imperative

5   The IMPERATIVE is used to tell someone to do something, or to suggest that we do something.

Ecoute ! *Listen!*   **Partons** ! *Let's go!*   **Mangez** ! *Eat!*

To form the imperative, use the **tu**, **nous** and **vous** form of the present tense. With **-er** verbs, remove the final **-s** from the **tu** form:

	parler	**finir**	**vendre**
tu form	parle	finis	vends
nous form	parl**ons**	fin**issons**	vend**ons**
vous form	parl**ez**	fin**issez**	vend**ez**

6   Irregular verbs follow the rule in section 5 above, with these exceptions:

aller	va, allons, allez	**être**	sois, soyons, soyez
	(vas-y, *go ahead*)	**savoir**	sache, sachons, sachez
avoir	aie, ayons, ayez	**vouloir**	veuillez (only form used)

7   When you tell someone to do something, object pronouns and reflexive pronouns are placed <u>after</u> the verb and linked to it by hyphens:

assieds-**toi** ! *sit down!*   allons-**y** ! *let's go!*   parlez-**moi** ! *talk to me!*

Note: **me** and **te** change to **moi** and **toi** when they are used <u>after</u> the verb.

8   When you tell someone <u>not</u> to do something, object pronouns and reflexive pronouns are placed <u>before</u> the verb in the normal way:

ne t'assieds pas !   n'**y** allons pas !   ne **me** parlez pas !

A Read the following interview and complete the report below.

Interview accordée par M. le ministre de l'Intérieur à la suite du Congrès du CNPP.

1. • *Monsieur le ministre, que pensez-vous de l'œuvre accomplie par le CNPP [1] ?*
2. – J'éprouve un très grand intérêt à l'égard des multiples activités du CNPP et de ses initiatives en faveur de la sécurité.
3. • *Notre environnement est-il plus dangereux qu'avant ?*
4. – Oui, il y a, sans aucun doute, une évolution préoccupante. Les efforts des responsables de la sécurité permettront tout de même, je l'espère, de restreindre l'étendue des périls.
5. • *Qu'est-ce qui favorisera, selon vous, la réduction du nombre d'accidents dans les années à venir ?*
6. – Il faut avant tout mettre en place un réseau très dense d'information afin de rendre les Français plus responsables de leur sécurité.
7. • *Quelle impression générale ce congrès vous a-t-il laissée ?*
8. – Dans le domaine de l'information et de la prévention, l'action du CNPP semble exemplaire.

Compte-rendu de l'interview

1. J'ai tout d'abord demandé au ministre …
2. Il m'a répondu …
3. Je lui ai ensuite demandé …
4. Il m'a affirmé … , mais en ajoutant qu'il espérait …
5. J'ai voulu savoir …
6. Il a déclaré …
7. Je lui ai enfin demandé …
8. Il a dit pour conclure …

B Replace the words in italics by a pronoun, and insert it in the right place.

Skieurs oubliez tout sauf votre sécurité

1. Votre sécurité dépendra en grande partie de vos capacités physiques. Ne surestimez pas *vos capacités physiques*, surtout en fin de journée.
2. En montagne, le temps change vite. Les services météo sont là pour vous aider. Avant de partir, consultez *les services météo*.
3. Un équipement adapté et contrôlé, c'est aussi votre sécurité. Vérifiez *votre équipement*.
4. On peut contracter une assurance pour la responsabilité civile et les frais de secours. Pensez *à contracter une assurance* dès votre arrivée.
5. Il est risqué de s'aventurer hors des pistes. Si vous êtes inexpérimenté, ne vous écartez pas *des pistes*.
6. Pour pratiquer le ski en haute montagne, il est prudent de se faire accompagner par un guide. Même si vous êtes expérimenté, engagez un *guide*.

[1] le CNPP : *Centre National de Prévention et de Protection* (in charge of safety)

A Read the following story. The parts of the sentences in italics could be the answers to a series of questions. Write these questions.

e.g. *La direction de la SNCF* a regretté *l'accident d'hier soir* …
→ Qui est-ce qui a regretté l'accident d'hier soir ?
or Qui a regretté l'accident d'hier soir ?

Mort d'un voyageur

La direction de la SNCF a regretté *l'accident d'hier soir* qui a fait une victime, un père de famille d'*une quarantaine d'années*. D'après les témoins, tout a commencé *vers 17h 30* : M. Perrier ne possédait pas de *titre de transport* et il a réagi *de manière violente* lorsque deux contrôleurs l'ont taxé *d'une amende. Un autre voyageur* est intervenu *pour essayer de le calmer* mais sans résultat. Au cours de l'altercation qui a suivi, M. Perrier est tombé *du dernier* wagon en gare de Versin. Il a été transporté à l'hôpital *Pasteur* mais a succombé *à ses blessures* pendant le trajet.

B The following sentences present the same information as the text above but in a different way. Replace the adjective in italics by an adverb and insert into the sentence so that it makes sense.

1. *vif* La direction de la SNCF a regretté l'accident d'hier soir qui a fait une victime, un père de famille d'une quarantaine d'années.
2. *violent* M. Perrier ne possédait pas de titre de transport et il a réagi lorsque deux contrôleurs l'ont taxé d'une amende.
3. *gentil* D'après les témoins, un autre voyageur est intervenu pour essayer de le calmer mais n'y est pas parvenu.
4. *accidentel* Au cours de l'altercation qui a suivi, M. Perrier est tombé du dernier wagon en gare de Versin.
5. *immédiat* Il a été transporté à l'hôpital Pasteur mais a succombé à ses blessures pendant le trajet.

C Write the verbs in the required tenses.

		PLUPERFECT	CONDITIONAL	CONDITIONAL PERFECT
1.	suffire	il …	cela …	il …
2.	se présenter	les lycéens …	je …	elles …
3.	vivre	nous …	les malades …	on …
4.	ouvrir	on …	le magasin …	vous …
5.	suivre	vous …	on …	tu …
6.	mourir	ils …	les gens …	elle …
7.	valoir	cela …	il …	tout …
8.	ne jamais voir	je …	nous …	nous …
9.	ne pas faire	le président …	tu …	je …
10.	ne rien résoudre	ces mesures …	cela …	vous …

D The results of an opinion poll on teaching are described below. Use the results to complete the sentences which follow.

L'opinion des Français à l'égard du corps enseignant

La formation des enseignants de l'enseignement public est suffisante : 42 %
Les enseignants s'intéressent plutôt aux élèves les plus doués : 50 %
Les enseignants projettent leurs idées politiques dans leurs cours : 40 %
A l'avenir, les enseignants devront manifester un plus grand esprit d'innovation : 37 %

Analyse de ce sondage quelques années plus tard

42 % des personnes interrogées ont déclaré ...
50 % considéraient ...
40 % estimaient ...
Seuls, 37 % des Français semblaient convaincus ...

E Write the verbs in brackets in the imperative.

Lorsque vous séjournez dans des pays tropicaux, pour éviter les ennuis de santé, il vous suffit de prendre quelques précautions :
– (*savoir*) vous reposer, surtout après un long voyage ;
– (*avoir*) soin de vous protéger du soleil et des insectes ;
– (*ne boire*) que des boissons embouteillées si possible ;
– (*se munir*) d'un désinfectant intestinal ;
– (*ne jamais se baigner*) en eau douce.

F Replace each expression in italics by a pronoun.

Ceci est un médicament

1. Un médicament n'est pas un produit comme les autres, ne laissez pas *ce produit* à portée de main des enfants.
2. Les médicaments sont des produits actifs, n'abusez jamais *des médicaments*.
3. Votre médecin sait quels sont les médicaments dont vous avez besoin, consultez *votre médecin*.
4. Suivez le traitement prescrit, n'interrompez pas *le traitement*, ne reprenez pas *le traitement* de votre seule initiative.
5. Votre pharmacien connaît les médicaments : demandez des conseils *à votre pharmacien* si nécessaire.

G *Thème*.

1. The firemen asked them whether there had been any other witnesses.
2. The journalist asked the Minister which policy she intended to pursue.
3. The owners wanted to know what had happened during their absence.
4. The manager recently asked me what I would like to do next year.
5. The police asked who we were with and who we were looking for.

L'environnement

A Insert **le, la, l', les** making all necessary changes, or leave blank.

e.g. Contrairement à _____ oiseaux, _____ serpents sont mal protégés.
→ Contrairement aux oiseaux, les serpents sont mal protégés.

Sauvez ces vilaines bêtes

_____ forêt recule, _____ marais s'assèchent, _____ pollution augmente et c'est ainsi que disparaissent serpents, araignées, chauve-souris, vers et crapauds. Ces vilaines bêtes meurent dans _____ indifférence générale. En effet, seuls _____ mammifères – excepté _____ chauve-souris – et _____ oiseaux sont populaires auprès de _____ public. C'est pourtant dans cet univers oublié que se trouve l'essentiel de _____ biodiversité animale et la très grande majorité de _____ espèces menacées de disparition.
Deux exemples :
– le ver de terre géant de _____ famille des *Scherotheca*, qui vit généralement dans le sud de _____ France et se déplace _____ nuit à six ou sept mètres de profondeur, devient rarissime ;
– le rhinolophone, chauve-souris originaire de _____ pays tropicaux, est aujourd'hui au bord de _____ extinction. Il ne vit pas caché _____ jour, ce qui le rend très vulnérable.

B Write the verbs in brackets in the present tense.

La forêt

1. De nombreuses menaces (*peser*) sur la forêt, dont le feu et la surexploitation.
2. En Europe, pour éviter les incendies on (*nettoyer*) les sous-bois.
3. Dans les pays en voie de développement où la déforestation (*s'accélérer*), on essaie d'introduire de nouvelles méthodes agricoles.
4. Comme le feu, la surexploitation (*mener*) à la désertification.
5. Pour y remédier, les spécialistes (*suggérer*) de planter des arbres à croissance rapide surtout en Afrique.

C *Thème.*

1. The international conference on global warming which was convened in Japan from 21 May to 1 June was not as disappointing as expected.
2. It was the second conference on the reduction of greenhouse gas emissions since last year.
3. Environmental protection is not always a priority in developing countries.
4. China, India and Brazil supported the measures advocated by Europe.
5. The United States, on the other hand, feared a slowing down of economic growth and an increase in unemployment.

When to use the definite article (le, la, les)

See page 2, sections 1–3
See page 66, sections 1–4 for when not to use ARTICLES

le, la, les in general statements and with places

1 Use a DEFINITE ARTICLE (**le, la, l', les**) before abstract nouns and nouns used in a general sense, where the article is usually omitted in English:

> **La** politique m'ennuie   *Politics bores me*
> **L'**essence est en hausse   *Petrol is going up*

2 Use a definite article when referring to regularly attended places where the article is omitted in English:

> J'ai quitté **le** lycée en juin   *I left school in June*
> Il est toujours **à l'**hôpital   *He is still in hospital*

le, la, les with names of languages, parts of the body, titles, ranks and professions

3 Use **le, l'** before names of languages, except after the verb **parler**:

> Il apprend **l'**espagnol   *He is learning Spanish*
> Elle parle russe   *She speaks Russian*

4 Use a definite article before parts of the body:

> Il nous a serré la main   *He shook our hands*

Note the use of the definite article in descriptive phrases such as:

> ... **les** armes **à la** main   *... with their weapons in their hands*

5 Use a definite article before titles, ranks and professions:

> **Le** prince Charles est en visite officielle
> *Prince Charles is on an official visit*
> **Le** général de Gaulle est mort en 1970
> *General de Gaulle died in 1970*

le, la, les with fractions, dates, days, times and seasons

6 Use a definite article before fractions **quart** and **tiers** when followed by **de** or **du, de la, de l', des**:

> **les trois-quarts de la** ville   *three quarters of the town*

See pages 66–67, section 6 for use of **la moitié**

7   Use **le** before dates:

     Nous sommes **le** 17 juillet aujourd'hui   *It is the 17th of July today*
     Paris, **le** 2 avril [used at top of letters]   *Paris, 2 April*

   Note: **le premier** (abbreviated to **le 1ᵉʳ**) is used for the first of the month:

     Ils sont arrivés **le premier** octobre   *They arrived on the first of October*

8   Use **le** before days of the week to describe regular actions:

     J'y vais **le** samedi, jamais **le** lundi   *I go on Saturdays, never on Mondays*

   But if the action is not regular, **le** is not used:

     J'y vais samedi et non lundi   *I'm going on Saturday, not on Monday*

9   Use a definite article to refer to times of the day (e.g. *at night, in the morning*) and to express *last* or *next week, month* or *year*:

     Elle est de service **l'**après-midi   *She is on duty in the afternoon*
     Il part en vacances **le** mois prochain   *He is going on holiday next month*
     Je **l'**ai vu **l'**année dernière   *I saw him last year*

10   Use **le, l'** before the names of seasons:

     L'hiver aggravera la situation   *Winter will make things worse*

   Sometimes the definite article is used to mean *in*:

     Je ne pars jamais **l'**hiver   *I never go away in winter*

   Note: to express *in the ...*, use **en été**, **en automne**, **en hiver** and **au printemps**.

le, la, les with continents, regions and countries

11   Use a definite article before the names of continents, regions and countries:

     L'Afrique du Sud attire les touristes
     South Africa attracts tourists
     La Normandie est au nord de **la** France
     Normandy is in the north of France

12   Before continents, countries and regions which are MASCULINE or PLURAL, use **à** + DEFINITE ARTICLE (**au** or **aux**) to mean *in* or *to*, and **de** + DEFINITE ARTICLE (**du** or **des**) to mean *from*:

     La réunion aura lieu **aux** États Unis
     The meeting will take place in the United States
     Le président est rentré **du** Japon
     The President has returned from Japan

     See page 66, section 5 for *in*, *to* and *from* feminine singular countries and masculine singular countries beginning with a vowel

-er verbs with spelling changes (espérer, etc.)

Some verbs ending in **-er** change slightly in certain tenses, reflecting the way the verb is pronounced. The following sections give the change in the present tense and identify the other tenses affected. See verb tables on pages 160–167 for all the forms of these verbs.

Some of these verbs also change in the present subjunctive and the past historic. See grammar index for references to the use and forms of the subjunctive and the past historic.

13 With verbs like **espérer**, **é** changes to **è**:

PRESENT TENSE	
j'espère	Change also occurs in:
tu espères	IMPERATIVE: **tu** form
il / elle espère	PRESENT SUBJUNCTIVE: all forms except **nous**
nous espérons	and **vous**
vous espérez	
ils / elles espèrent	

See page 169, Appendix 3 for a list of verbs like **espérer**

14 All verbs ending in **-cer** change in certain forms to ensure that the soft sound is preserved: **c** becomes **ç** before **a** and **o**.

PRESENT TENSE	
je commence	Change also occurs in:
tu commences	IMPERATIVE: **nous** form
il / elle commence	IMPERFECT TENSE: all forms except **nous** and **vous**
nous commençons	PRESENT PARTICIPLE
vous commencez	PAST HISTORIC: all forms except **ils**
ils / elles commencent	

See page 169, Appendix 3 for a list of verbs like **commencer**

15 All verbs ending in **-ger** change in certain forms to ensure that the soft sound is preserved: **g** becomes **ge** before **a** and **o**.

PRESENT TENSE	
je partage	Change also occurs in:
tu partages	IMPERATIVE: **nous** form
il / elle partage	IMPERFECT TENSE: all forms except **nous** and **vous**
nous partageons	PRESENT PARTICIPLE
vous partagez	PAST HISTORIC: all forms except **ils**
ils / elles partagent	

See page 169, Appendix 3 for a list of verbs like **partager**

16 With verbs like **acheter**, **e** changes to **è** in certain forms.

PRESENT TENSE	
j'achète	Change also occurs in:
tu achètes	IMPERATIVE: **tu** form
il / elle achète	PRESENT SUBJUNCTIVE: all forms except **nous**
nous achetons	and **vous**
vous achetez	FUTURE and CONDITIONAL: all forms
ils / elles achètent	

See page 169, Appendix 3 for a list of verbs like **acheter**

17 With verbs like **rejeter**, **t** becomes **tt** in certain forms.

PRESENT TENSE	
je rejette	Change also occurs in:
tu rejettes	IMPERATIVE: **tu** form
il / elle rejette	PRESENT SUBJUNCTIVE: all forms except **nous**
nous rejetons	and **vous**
vous rejetez	FUTURE and CONDITIONAL: all forms
ils / elles rejettent	

See page 169, Appendix 3 for a list of verbs like **rejeter**

18 With verbs like **appeler**, **l** becomes **ll** in certain forms.

PRESENT TENSE	
j'appelle	Change also occurs in:
tu appelles	IMPERATIVE: **tu** form
il / elle appelle	PRESENT SUBJUNCTIVE: all forms except **nous**
nous appelons	and **vous**
vous appelez	FUTURE and CONDITIONAL: all forms
ils / elles appellent	

See page 169, Appendix 3 for a list of verbs like **appeler**

19 With verbs ending in **-oyer** and **-uyer**, **y** changes to **i** in certain forms.

PRESENT TENSE	
j'emploie	Change also occurs in:
tu emploies	IMPERATIVE: **tu** form
il / elle emploie	PRESENT SUBJUNCTIVE: all forms except **nous**
nous employons	and **vous**
vous employez	FUTURE and CONDITIONAL: all forms
ils / elles emploient	

See page 169, Appendix 3 for a list of verbs like **employer**

A Insert **le, la, les** or **du, de la, des** if required, making all necessary changes.

La guerre de l'eau

Un risque majeur de pénurie menace aujourd'hui _____ humanité. _____ eau douce, indispensable à _____ santé, à _____ bien-être et à _____ développement économique est, en effet, devenue un bien rare. _____ consommation d'eau progresse à un rythme deux fois supérieur à celui de _____ croissance économique.

Lors d'un forum international, qui s'est tenu _____ 24 et 25 mars dernier à _____ Maroc, _____ spécialistes ont annoncé que la quantité d'eau disponible par habitant en Afrique ne représenterait bientôt plus que _____ quart de ce qu'elle était en 1950. D'ici à 2025, les régions touchées par _____ pénurie s'étendront à _____ deux tiers environ de la population mondiale. Seuls _____ Australie, _____ Brésil, l'Europe _____ Nord et _____ Ouest, _____ Russie et _____ Afrique équatoriale resteront autosuffisants. Les autres devront avoir recours à _____ importation d'eau, à moins qu'ils n'aillent, _____ armes à _____ main, s'approvisionner chez leur voisin.

B Write the verbs in brackets in the present tense or the imperfect tense as required by the meaning of the sentence.

Des catastrophes naturelles plus nombreuses et plus destructrices

1. Les catastrophes naturelles (*se répéter*) plus souvent aujourd'hui.
2. Il y a quelques années encore, on (*considérer*) qu'il s'agissait-là de phénomènes exceptionnels.
3. A cette époque-là, on (*ne guère s'interroger*) sur le rôle joué par la concentration urbaine, la désertification rurale ou l'effet de serre.
4. Aujourd'hui les experts (*rejeter*) l'explication strictement « naturelle ».
5. Ils (*rappeler*) que les pays en développement sont souvent les plus touchés.
6. Ils (*révéler*) aussi qu'il existe désormais un nouveau type de réfugiés, les « réfugiés de l'environnement », qui fuient cyclones, sécheresses ou inondations.

C *Thème.* Use some of the vocabulary and constructions found in « La guerre de l'eau » above to produce the following sentences in French.

1. Fresh water, which is essential for life, has become rare.
2. Experts revealed the extent of the problem during the discussions held on 22 March last year in Brazil.
3. By 2025, North Africa, South Africa, the Middle-East, Asia, the United States, Mexico and parts of Europe will be affected by drought.
4. In certain countries, the amount of fresh water available per inhabitant will be a third of what it is today.
5. The possibility[1] of armed conflict raises deep concern.

---

[1] the possibility of ... : *les risques de ...*

La communication

A This text describes the growth of video which began in the 1980s. Fill the gaps with **du, de la, de l'**, **des** or simply **de, d'** as appropriate.

L'explosion de la vidéo

Des millions _____ foyers sont désormais équipés d'un magnétoscope. Si, pour la majorité _____ utilisateurs, le magnétoscope sert avant tout à enregistrer des émissions _____ télévision, la location _____ cassettes préenregistrées est un phénomène important.

Grâce aux vidéo clubs, les propriétaires _____ magnétoscopes ont un choix très diversifié _____ programmes : les longs métrages ne sont pas seuls à figurer dans les catalogues, on y trouve aussi bien des films _____ animation que des cours _____ tennis ou _____ langue, sans oublier, bien évidemment, les programmes _____ jeux. Mais loin de n'être qu'un instrument _____ reproduction, la vidéo est à la fois un outil _____ expression et un moyen _____ diffusion dans des secteurs comme la formation _____ personnel et l'enseignement à distance.

B Write the verbs in brackets in the appropriate tense.

Internet

1. Si vous (*souhaiter*) communiquer avec le monde entier, connectez-vous à Internet.
2. Si la tendance actuelle (*se poursuivre*), le Web jouera un rôle clé dans la vie de chacun.
3. Avant le Minitel[1] et Internet, si on (*vouloir*) la moindre information, il fallait se déplacer.
4. Si je (*ne pas contacter*) d'autres internautes[2], je n'aurais jamais trouvé ce renseignement.
5. Certains services (*ne plus être*) consultés s'ils n'étaient pas sur Internet.
6. D'autres (*ne jamais apparaître*), si Internet n'avait pas connu un tel succès.

C *Thème.*

1. She worked as a press photographer abroad and then as a project manager in the multimedia industry on her return from Germany.
2. She was recruited mainly because she was able to communicate with conviction and great clarity.
3. In France at the time, many young people without university qualifications or specialist training started working in multimedia.
4. Electronic publishing was only one aspect of this new employment sector.
5. The new technologies were beginning to play a key role in the communication policy of most large companies.
6. Within about ten years, they would completely transform the world of work.

[1] *le Minitel* : the French national computerised information system   [2] *un(e) internaute* : Internet user

When not to use an article

See pages 2–3, sections 1–4 for an introduction to ARTICLES
See pages 60–61, sections 1–12 for when to use the DEFINITE ARTICLE

1   Don't use **un** or **une** after **être**, **devenir** and **comme** when describing someone's occupation, religion or politics:

Gerard Depardieu **est acteur**	*Gerard Depardieu is an actor*
La reine **est protestante**	*The Queen is a Protestant*
Il est **devenu socialiste**	*He became a socialist*
Elle travaille **comme ingénieur**	*She is working as an engineer*

2   Don't use **un, une** or **des** after **ni ... ni** (*neither ... nor, either ... or*):

Il n'a **ni** chat **ni** chien   *He has neither a cat nor a dog*

But note that a definite article is used with nouns in a general sense:

Il n'aime ni les chats ni les chiens   *He likes neither cats nor dogs*

3   Don't use **un, une** or **des** after **sans** (*without*):

Elle voyage **sans** billet   *She is travelling without a ticket*

4   Don't use an article in adverbial expressions with **avec**. Adverbial expressions describe how someone does something and are often translated as an adverb (e.g. *intelligently*) in English:

Elle fait son travail **avec** intelligence   *She does her work intelligently*

Note that an article is used if there is an adjective (e.g. **remarquable**):

Elle fait son travail avec **une** intelligence remarquable
She does her work with remarkable intelligence

See page 44, section 9 for more about adverbial phrases

5   Don't use an article before feminine singular CONTINENTS, COUNTRIES and REGIONS after **en** (*in* or *to*) and **de** (*from*):

Mme Schmidt retourne **en** Afrique	*Mme Schmidt is going back to Africa*
M. Gonzalez vient **d'**Espagne	*M. Gonzalez is from Spain*

en and **de** are also used before masculine singular COUNTRIES:

On a tourné le film **en** Iran   *We made the film in Iran*

See page 61, section 12 for how to say *in, to* and *from* masculine singular and all plural countries

Using de with expressions of quantity

See pages 142–145, sections 1–24 for NUMBERS AND FIGURES

6   Use **de / d'** and not **du, de la, des** after most EXPRESSIONS OF QUANTITY. These include numbers and measurements like **un litre de**, etc.:

40 **litres** d'essence	*40 litres of petrol*
3 000 **tonnes de** charbon	*3,000 tonnes of coal*
un **million de** dollars	*a million dollars*
une **trentaine d'**années	*about thirty years*

and less precise quantities like **beaucoup de,** etc.:

beaucoup de jeunes	*many young people*
bon nombre de retraités	*many pensioners*
assez d'expérience	*enough experience*
peu de diplômes	*few qualifications*

But use **du, de la, de l', des** whenever *the* is used in English:

  Nombre **des** salariés sont mécontents   *Many of **the** staff are dissatisfied*

Remember that some expressions of quantity do <u>not</u> take **de**:

la plupart	**du, de la, des** (+ PLURAL VERB)	*most of*
la majeure partie	**du, de la, des** (+ SINGULAR VERB)	*most of*
la majorité	**du, de la, des** (+ SINGULAR VERB)	*the majority of*
la moitié	**du, de la, des** (+ SINGULAR VERB)	*half (of)*

la plupart des habitants	*most inhabitants*
la moitié du travail	*half the work*

Note: **la plupart d'entre eux** means *most of them*.

Using de and not du, de la, des after negatives

See pages 28–29, sections 1–4 and pages 72–73 sections 1–6 for NEGATIVE SENTENCES

7   Remember that **de / d'** is used after NEGATIVE WORDS like **pas**, **rien**, etc.:

POSITIVE SENTENCE	NEGATIVE SENTENCE
J'ai toujours **un** stylo sur moi	Je n'ai jamais **de** stylo sur moi
I always have a pen on me	*I never have a pen on me*
Ils ont **de l'**influence	Ils n'ont jamais **d'**influence
They have some influence	*They never have any influence*
Elle reçoit **des** lettres tous les jours	Elle ne reçoit plus **de** lettres
She receives letters every day	*She no longer receives any letters*

Use **un** and **une** and not **de** to mean *not one …* or *not a single …*:

  Il n'y a pas **un** instant à perdre   *There is not a minute to lose*

Using de in adjectival expressions and before adjectives

See pages 8–10, sections 1–8 for introduction to ADJECTIVES

8 Use **de** to link two nouns in ADJECTIVAL EXPRESSIONS. They are called adjectival expressions because the second noun (in bold type) acts like an adjective:

une campagne **de publicité**	a **publicity** campaign
la consommation **de pétrole**	**oil** consumption
les conditions **de travail**	**working** conditions
les vins **de France**	**French** wines

Note: there are some exceptions to this rule. When you are reading in French, note down for yourself expressions such as:

la politique de la France *French politics*
le marché de l'emploi *the labour market*

9 Use **de / d'** in formal language before plural adjectives coming before the noun:

Cet homme a **d'**excellentes idées *This man has excellent ideas*
De nombreuses directives paraîtront *Many important guidelines will appear*

Using de and not du, de la, des after certain verbs

10 Use **de** and not **du, de la, des** after some verbs. Two common examples are **changer de** (*to change one thing for another*) and **manquer de** (*to lack* or *to be short of something*):

L'entreprise a changé **de** nom *The company changed its name*
L'association manque **de** fonds *The association lacks funds*

si in sentences expressing a condition

See page 147, section 5 on use of **l'on** after **si**

11 **si**, meaning *if*, is used in sentences which express a CONDITION:

Elle serait contente **si** tu venais en France
She would be pleased if you came to France
Il serait venu **s'**il avait su
He would have come if he had known

Note: **si** is only shortened to **s'** in front of **il** and **ils**.

12 When **si** is used to express a CONDITION, the following tense rules apply:

CONDITION CLAUSE	RESULT CLAUSE
si + present	present, future or imperative
si + imperfect	conditional
si + pluperfect	conditional perfect

Examples:

si + present	present, future or imperative

Si le projet échoue, je pars   *If the project fails, I'm leaving*
Si le projet échoue, je partirai   *If the project fails, I'll leave*
Ne restez pas si le projet échoue   *Don't stay if the project fails*

si + imperfect	conditional

Si le projet échouait, je partirais   *If the project failed, I would leave*

si + pluperfect	conditional perfect

Si le projet avait échoué, je serais parti
If the project had failed, I would have left

Other meanings and uses of si

When **si** is not used in sentences expressing a condition, the tense rules in section 12 above do not apply.

13 **si** can mean *while* or *although*:

Si la situation est grave, elle n'est pas désespérée pour autant
Although the situation is serious, it is not necessarily hopeless

14 **si** can mean *whether* or *if* in an INDIRECT QUESTON:

Je me demande s'il viendra   *I wonder whether he will come*

See page 54, sections 1–3 for INDIRECT QUESTIONS

15 **si** can mean *when*:

Si je suis pressé, je prends le train   *When I am in a hurry, I take the train*

16 **si** can mean *supposing ...?*, *what if ...?*, *how about ...?*:

Et si les experts s'étaient trompés ?   *What if the experts had been wrong?*
Si on allait au cinéma ?   *How about going to the cinema?*

See page 73, section 4.2 for **si** meaning *yes* after negative questions and statements

A Fill the gaps with **du, de la, de l', des** or simply **de / d'** as appropriate.

Il faut que chaque culture ait son Internet

- *Pourquoi avez-vous créé une association pour les utilisateurs d'Internet en Afrique ?*
- Je l'ai créée dans le but de promouvoir la culture _____ Web dans les coins les plus reculés _____ Afrique. Le but est de faire d'Internet un outil _____ alphabétisation et _____ expression culturelle.
- *Comment résoudre les problèmes d'infrastructure téléphonique ?*
- Grâce aux réseaux _____ satellites mis en place actuellement par les pays riches, on peut se connecter en utilisant _____ petites antennes paraboliques.
- *Concrètement de quoi avez-vous besoin ?*
- Nous voulons créer _____ centres de formation. Pour cela, peu _____ moyens suffisent. On récupère _____ vieux ordinateurs et on les transforme en serveurs.
- *Quelle est votre ambition ultime ?*
- Les autoroutes _____ information devraient permettre l'édification d'une réelle solidarité planétaire. Si le tiers monde n'est pas présent sur Internet, ce sera la fin _____ diversité culturelle.

B Write the verbs in brackets in the required tense.

L'influence des médias

1. Si la concurrence entre les différents médias était moins effrénée, l'information (*être*) plus fidèle à la réalité.
2. Si les bonnes nouvelles (*se vendre*) aussi bien que les mauvaises, les médias ne seraient pas tentés de noircir la réalité.
3. Ainsi, l'an dernier, le public (*se sentir*) sécurisé si l'on avait vraiment parlé de la baisse de la criminalité.
4. Si l'utilité des médias est incontestable aujourd'hui, il (*paraître*) néanmoins essentiel de s'interroger sur leur effet sur la société.

C *Thème.*

1. As a general editor, Michel Blanc is very efficient. He runs the daily newspaper with amazing conviction and a great deal of courage. This is why the majority of the journalists treat him with so much respect. Recently, he published confidential documents without authorisation and a great many readers approved of his action.
2. Nowadays children spend less time watching television programmes than they did about fifteen years ago. In fact, most of them spend as much time in front of their television set as before but use it for other activities: video games, the Internet, etc. If this trend continues, the influence of television in children's lives will gradually diminish.
3. If, at the time when the first PCs arrived on the market, we had been told that they would soon be everywhere, we would not have believed it. In schools, although multimedia has not challenged the pedagogical role of teachers, it has changed teaching habits and methods.

L'action humanitaire

A *Version.* Translate this text describing the fate of refugees, with particular attention to negatives.

Le drame des réfugiés

La vague des réfugiés enfle de semaine en semaine : ils arrivent soit à pied en longues colonnes misérables soit entassés sur des charrettes à bœufs. Dès leur arrivée, ils sont pris en charge par les associations humanitaires. La vie reste cependant précaire pour ces déracinés qui n'ont plus rien ni nulle part où aller : la malnutrition ainsi que les épidémies sévissent. Une fois installés dans les camps, ils ne sont pas, non plus, à l'abri de la violence : la nuit, après le départ des représentants des organisations de solidarité internationale, les familles qui se terrent dans leur cahute ne sont plus protégées par personne.

Un tel dénuement ne paraît guère concevable pour ceux qui vivent dans l'abondance. La communauté internationale n'est ni spécialement généreuse ni consciente de ses responsabilités.

B Here is an extract from a letter which a Belgian nurse working for *Médecins sans frontières* has written to his family. Write the verbs in brackets in the perfect tense.

J'espère que vous (*passer*) un bon week-end. Le mien (*être*) assez mouvementé.

Samedi, à nouveau, la ville (*recevoir*) des obus. L'un d'eux (*tomber*) sur une maison proche de l'hôpital. Nous (*avoir*) le temps d'entendre un sifflement au-dessus de notre tête quand il (*passer*) au-dessus du toit. On (*se jeter*) au sol et il (*exploser*) à 100 mètres d'ici. On (*aller*) tout de suite voir s'il y avait des victimes et on (*sortir*) trois fillettes blessées des décombres. Deux d'entre elles (*mourir*) dans la nuit. Dimanche, les combats (*s'amplifier*). Les villages aux alentours de la ville (*souffrir*) et de nouveaux enfants blessés (*arriver*) à l'hôpital.

Malgré tout ça, je garde le moral et ne regrette pas d'être venu.

C Here is a letter written by a doctor to her boyfriend. Make the past participles in italics agree if necessary.

Cher toi,

En janvier, des journalistes de la Télé nationale sont *venu* faire un reportage. Tu m'as *vu* à la télévision ? Je suis très curieuse de connaître le résultat car les choses se sont *passé* très vite. Ils ont tout *enregistré* en une seule fois. Je n'ai pas eu la possibilité de recommencer quand je me suis *mis* à bafouiller. Il est évident que ces journalistes ne sont *venu* que pour récolter du sensationnel. Il n'y a que la salle des tuberculeux qui les a *intéressé*, parce qu'il y avait plein de gens en train de mourir ! Ils m'ont vraiment *dégoûté*.

J'espère que tu ne m'as pas *oublié*.

Je t'embrasse tendrement.

More about negative sentences

See pages 28–29, sections 1–4 for an introduction to NEGATIVE SENTENCES

1 More than one negative word can be used in a sentence:

Il ne la verra **plus jamais**	*He will never see her again*
Vous n'avez **plus rien** ?	*Don't you have anything left?*
Je ne vois **plus personne**	*I don't see anyone any more*
Il n'y a **plus que** vous	*You're the only one left*
Je n'ai **plus rien** à expliquer	*I have nothing more to explain*
Elle ne voit **jamais personne**	*She never sees anyone*
Ne parle **jamais ni** de politique **ni** de religion	*Never talk about politics or religion*
Il ne va **jamais nulle part**	*He never goes anywhere*
Il n'offre **jamais rien** à **personne**	*He never gives anyone anything*

The negative words are used in this order:

ne ...	plus .... jamais ...	ni . . . ni
		nulle part
		personne
		que
		rien
		guère

Note: **ne ... pas** can be used with **que** (*only*):

Il n'y avait **pas que** des enfants à bord   *There weren't only children on board*

and **plus** can be used with **guère**:

Je ne lui parle **plus guère**   *I hardly speak to him any more*

2 **ne ... que** means *only*. The **que** always goes before the noun it refers to, unlike *only* in English which can appear in other parts of the sentence:

Je ne l'ai vu **que trois fois**   *I saw him **only** three times*
*I **only** saw him three times*

See page 29, section 2 for use of **du, de la, des** after **ne ... que**

3 **ne ... que** cannot apply to the action of the verb. Use the construction **ne faire que** + INFINITIVE instead:

Il **ne fait que** parler   *All he does is talk*

4 **non** can mean *not*, and **oui** is not always translated as *yes*:

1. non, meaning *not* is used in formal language instead of **pas**:

C'est l'architecte et **non** l'entrepreneur qui est à blâmer
It is the architect and not the contractor who is to blame

non pas can be used for emphasis:

Je vous dis la vérité **non pas** pour vous effrayer mais pour vous prévenir
I am telling you the truth not to frighten you but to warn you

2. Use **si** to mean *yes* after a negative question or statement:

Vous n'avez pas d'emploi ? Mais **si**, j'ai été embauché hier
Don't you have a job? Yes, I was given a job yesterday
Il n'y a pas de Français ici. **Si**, j'en ai vu quelques–uns
There aren't any French people here. Yes there are, I have seen a few

3. ... **que non**, ... **que oui** and ... **que si** are used after verbs like **sembler**, **dire**, **croire**, etc.:

M. Leclerc était-il au courant ? Il semble **que non**
Was Mr Leclerc informed? It seems not
Mme Gonzalez sera-elle réélue ? La presse locale pense **que oui**
Will Mrs Gonzalez be re-elected? The local press thinks so

How to say *neither ... nor* and *either ... or*

5 **ni** ... **ni** translates both *neither ... nor* and *either ... or*:

La France **n'**a remporté **ni** la Coupe d'Europe **ni** la Coupe du monde
France won neither the European Cup nor the World Cup
France did not win (either) the European Cup or the World Cup

ni can be used after **pas**:

Il ne mange **pas** la viande, **ni** le poisson d'ailleurs
He doesn't eat meat, or fish for that matter

6 **non plus** can also mean *neither / either*. Like its opposite, **aussi** (*... as well, too, so* ...), it usually goes after the word it refers to:

Le comptable ne s'inquiète pas, moi **non plus**
The accountant is not worried, and neither am I
Il a été acquitté, son comptable **aussi**
He was acquitted and so was his accountant / and his accountant as well

7 **soit** ... **soit** ... can also be used to mean *either ... or* and is often used to present alternatives:

On peut le finir **soit** avant **soit** après la réunion
We can finish it either before or after the meeting

Summary of verb tenses using avoir and être

8   The table below summarises all the COMPOUND tenses, that is the verb tenses that contain **avoir** or **être** + PAST PARTICIPLE:

TENSE	EXAMPLES WITH **avoir**		EXAMPLES WITH **être**	
PERFECT	j'ai fini	*I have finished / I finished*	je suis parti(e)	*I have left / I left*
PLUPERFECT	j'avais fini	*I had finished*	j'étais parti(e)	*I had left*
FUTURE PERFECT	j'aurai fini	*I will have finished*	je serai parti(e)	*I will have left*
CONDITIONAL PERFECT	j'aurais fini	*I would have finished*	je serais parti(e)	*I would have left*
PAST INFINITIVE	avoir fini	*having finished / finishing*	être parti(e)(s)	*having left / leaving*

Note that the PERFECT SUBJUNCTIVE is also a compound tense. It is explained on page 106, sections 1–3.

See page 17, section 14 for which verbs take **être**
See page 126, sections 10–11 for forms and uses of the FUTURE PERFECT

Agreement of the past participle

See page 17, sections 15–16 for an introduction to PAST PARTICIPLES and agreement rules
See page 17, sections 13–14 for which verbs take **avoir** and **être**

9   With verbs taking **avoir**, the past participle only agrees with the PRECEDING DIRECT OBJECT. This could be a PRONOUN (e.g. **le**, **la**, **les**) or a NOUN (e.g. **les enfants**).

Look at the examples below. On the left, there is no agreement, because the direct object comes <u>after</u> the verb. On the right, the past participle does agree because the direct object comes <u>before</u> the verb.

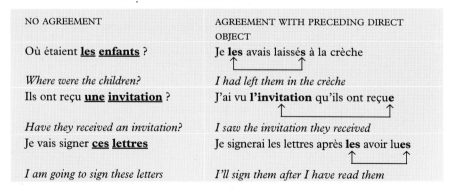

NO AGREEMENT	AGREEMENT WITH PRECEDING DIRECT OBJECT
Où étaient **les enfants** ?	Je **les** avais laissés à la crèche
Where were the children?	*I had left them in the crèche*
Ils ont reçu **une invitation** ?	J'ai vu **l'invitation** qu'ils ont reçu**e**
Have they received an invitation?	*I saw the invitation they received*
Je vais signer **ces lettres**	Je signerai les lettres après **les** avoir lu**es**
I am going to sign these letters	*I'll sign them after I have read them*

See page 14, section 1 for the difference between DIRECT and INDIRECT OBJECTS

10 With verbs taking **être** (**aller**, **venir**, etc.), which have no direct object, the past participle agrees with the subject of the verb:

Jeanne est descendue à la cuisine   *Jeanne came down to the kitchen*

Ils étaient partis de bonne heure   *They had left early*

11 Some verbs that usually take **être** are used with **avoir** and a direct object to mean something different. Here are the most common examples:

	with **être** (no direct object)	with **avoir** (with direct object)
descendre	*to go / come down*	*to take / bring (something) down*
monter	*to go / come up*	*to take / bring (something) up*
passer	*to pass / call by*	*to pass (something)*
sortir	*to go / come out*	*to take (something) out*

When used with **avoir**, the past participle of these verbs does not agree with the subject. It agrees with the PRECEDING DIRECT OBJECT when there is one:

Lucy a descendu les valises ?   *Has Lucy brought down the suitcases?*
Oui, elle **les** a descendu**es**   *Yes, she has brought them down*

Agreement of the past participle in reflexive constructions

12 Reflexive verbs take **être**. The past participle agrees with the SUBJECT:

elle s'est habill**ée**   *she got dressed*   **ils** se sont échappé**s**   *they escaped*

Note the agreements in sentences such as:

Elle s'est montrée généreuse   *She appeared generous*
Ils se sont déclaré**s** satisfaits   *They said they were satisfied*

13 Some reflexive constructions can take a DIRECT OBJECT after the verb. In the following sentence the reflexive pronoun **s'** tells us *who she bought the car for*:

Elle s'est acheté **une voiture**   *She bought (herself) a car*

If this direct object is before the verb, the past participle will agree with it:

La voiture qu'elle s'est achet**ée** ...   *The car that she bought ...*

A Give the French for the words in brackets, using the correct past tense.

L'aide internationale: un cadeau à double tranchant

Pour être efficace, l'aide doit obéir à des règles précises : secours correspondant aux besoins des populations, produits étiquetés dans la langue du pays receveur et triés au départ. Sinon, elle risque d'ajouter au chaos.

Lorsque la télévision [showed] des images de l'Arménie dévastée par un tremblement de terre, un immense mouvement de solidarité [was triggered off[1]]. Soixante-dix pays différents [sent] des centaines de tonnes de médicaments. Malheureusement quand ils [arrived], on [realised] que la plupart de ces médicaments [were] périmés. L'Arménie [had to] importer un coûteux incinérateur spécial pour les détruire sans polluer.

En Irak, certains réfugiés [mistook] des sachets de potages déshydratés pour des paquets de lessive parce qu'ils [were] incapables de déchiffrer le mode d'emploi écrit en anglais.

Même l'arrivée des secouristes, lorsqu'ils ne sont pas demandés par le pays victime d'une catastrophe, peut causer des difficultés. Après le tremblement de terre dont il [was] victime, l'Iran [could have] se passer des équipes de volontaires venus d'une dizaine de pays différents. En revanche, des experts [would have been] utiles pour l'assainissement[2].

B The following sentences present the same information as above but in a different way. Make the past participle in italics agree where necessary.

1. Les images que l'on a *montré* ont déclenché un vaste mouvement de solidarité.
2. Les médicaments que l'on a *envoyé* de l'étranger n'ont pas pu être utilisés.
3. Quand ils sont *arrivé*, on s'est *aperçu* que la plupart étaient périmés.
4. Après les avoir *reçu*, l'Arménie a dû détruire ces médicaments.
5. Le mode d'emploi des sachets de potage que les réfugiés ont *pris* pour des paquets de lessive était en anglais.
6. L'arrivée des secouristes que l'Iran n'avait pas *demandé* a causé des difficultés.
7. Par contre, les experts qui auraient *pu* être utiles sont *resté* chez eux.

C *Thème.*
1. These refugees no longer have anywhere to go.
2. They don't expect anything from anyone any more.
3. They only have food for a few days.
4. Soon they will have nothing left to eat.
5. They are not safe from disease either.
6. If nothing is done, thousands will have died before the end of the month.
7. And obviously, the war only makes things more difficult.
8. Until now this region has received neither food aid nor medical assistance from abroad.

---

[1] use *se déclencher*

[2] *une opération d'assainissement* : cleaning up operation

A Fill in the gaps with **le, la, l', les** or **de, du, de l', de la, des**.

L'électorat. Depuis une vingtaine d'années, les attitudes et les comportements
_____ électeurs ont considérablement évolué. L'image _____ partis et _____
politiques auprès _____ public s'est progressivement dégradée, et la France
est désormais un pays où le taux _____ abstention est élevé. En matière _____
politique, _____ électeurs se comportent en consommateurs : _____
programmes et _____ candidats sont considérés comme _____ produits que
l'on essaie et dont on change s'ils s'avèrent insatisfaisants.

Les partis traditionnels. Au fil des années, les discours et les programmes _____
droite et _____ gauche modérées se sont fortement rapprochés. _____
libéralisme et _____ préoccupations sociales ne sont plus l'apanage de telle ou
telle famille politique. En conséquence, un quart _____ électorat modéré est
susceptible de changer de bord, entre deux élections.

Les partis extrêmes. _____ extrême droite a bénéficié de la désaffection _____
Français pour _____ partis traditionnels. Elle a également profité de
l'inquiétude _____ Français devant _____ chômage, _____ inégalités sociales,
_____ immigration et la montée _____ intégrisme musulman.

B The police are making enquiries about a woman who has disappeared. Write
the verb in brackets in the appropriate tense (perfect, pluperfect, conditional
perfect). Don't forget to make the past participle agree where necessary.

Enquête

• *Nous savons que vous la* (licencier) *en juin. C'était pour quelle raison ?*
SON PATRON   Elle *(se mettre)* à s'absenter régulièrement sans motif.
• *Est-ce qu'elle* (dire) *qu'elle avait des problèmes récemment ?*
SON FRÈRE   Non, mais si elle *(avoir)* des problèmes, elle ne m'en aurait
          pas parlé.
• *Pourquoi est-ce que vous* (ne pas en parler) *ensemble ?*
SON FRÈRE   Parce qu'elle *(ne jamais se confier)* à moi.
• *Mais si elle* (être) *déprimée, vous l'auriez su !*
SES PARENTS   Oui, sans doute qu'on *(s'en apercevoir).*
• *Est-ce que vous la* (voir) *la semaine dernière ?*
SA VOISINE   Non. Mais la semaine précédente je la *(inviter)* à dîner en ville
          et elle avait refusé.
• *Pourriez-vous me dire si elle* (avoir) *des visites la veille de sa disparition ?*
LE GARDIEN   Si quelqu'un était venu dans la journée, je le *(remarquer).*
          Mais le soir, c'est différent !

C *Thème.* Having made additional enquiries, the detective summarises his
findings. Write his notes in French.

1. She never confided anything to anyone.
2. She never went anywhere any more.
3. Her neighbours never saw her with anyone before she disappeared[1].
4. She did not work much any more.
5. After Saturday, neither her parents nor her brother ever saw her again.

D A truckdriver and his partner explain why two major strikes have disrupted transport links with other countries. Put the verbs in brackets into the imperfect or the perfect tense.

La colère d'un gréviste et de sa compagne

DIDIER (32 ans, routier) Il y a deux ans, quand on (*se mettre*) à compter les heures de travail, on (*se rendre*) compte que notre salaire horaire (*être*) bien inférieur au Smic. Mais la première grève (*ne rien résoudre*) parce que les engagements (*ne pas être*) tenus. La plupart des entreprises (*continuer*) à faire comme elles (*faire*) avant et, par conséquent, la minorité d'entreprises qui (*vouloir*) appliquer la loi (*se trouver*) pénalisée.

JOSIANE (38 ans, la compagne de Didier) Didier aime son métier. Quand il (*décider*) de devenir routier, les conditions de travail et le salaire (*ne pas être*) mirobolantes mais on (*penser*) que ça (*aller*) s'améliorer. Pas du tout, c'est le contraire qui (*se passer*). Du fait de la concurrence, la situation (*se détériorer*). Pourtant ce n'est pas un job de tout repos ! Pendant des années, il (*faire*) l'Europe de l'Est. Quand il (*partir*) à l'étranger, je ne le (*voir*) presque jamais. L'an dernier, je (*finir*) par craquer et je (*insister*) pour qu'il travaille sur le réseau national.

E *Thème.*

1. Thousands of individuals and companies dump their waste anywhere. The French incinerate more than one third of their waste and recycle less than 10% of household rubbish. More often than not, they consider that it is primarily for the government and the industrialists to be concerned about protecting the environment and not for the simple consumer!

2. If France and the countries of the European Union had followed the example set by Switzerland and Austria instead of favouring road transport, the transport crisis would have become less serious. By neglecting to take into account the actual cost of road transport, France merely contributed to its development. The transfer of goods traffic from road to rail will prove long and difficult.

3. International organisations such as Friends of the Earth remind us constantly that protecting our natural environment is a responsibility that we all share[2]. It is by protecting the planet that we will guarantee our children's future. In one of their publications, environmentalists reveal that it takes 220 litres of water to produce ten litres of orange juice. If more people knew about it, would that lead them to change their consumer habits?

---

[1] translate as 'before her disappearance'

[2] a responsibility that we all share: *notre responsabilité à tous* or *notre affaire à tous*

L'Union européenne

A Some adjectives take **à, au, à l', à la, aux** while others take **de, du, de l',
de la, des**. Fill the gaps as necessary.

Comment voient-ils l'Europe ?

Les jeunes Français se déclarent plutôt favorables _____ Europe, même
s'ils ne sont pas toujours convaincus _____ rôle concret que peut jouer
l'Union européenne dans leur vie quotidienne. Ils semblent plutôt bien
informés _____ ce qui se passe dans les autres pays.

Même si l'Europe leur semble parfois assez éloignée _____ leurs
préoccupations, ils en attendent beaucoup. Ils sont surtout désireux _____
voir une Europe démocratique, en paix, et sans chômage. Une majorité
d'entre eux imaginent une Europe capable _____ jouer un rôle important
pour la défense de la paix dans le monde ainsi que celle des droits de
l'homme. Nombre d'entre eux se disent prêts _____ aller étudier ou travailler
dans un autre pays de l'Union. Conscients _____ difficultés existant sur le
marché du travail, les plus âgés pensent que l'Europe est susceptible _____
leur offrir demain des opportunités d'emploi.

B Rewrite the sentences beginning each one with the change of subject
suggested in italics.

e.g.   Cette analyse statistique n'est pas représentative.   *Ces chiffres ...*
→ Ces chiffres ne sont pas représentatifs.

1.   Le Parlement européen est devenu plus efficace.   *Les institutions ...*
2.   Le prochain sommet européen sera d'un intérêt capital.   *Il sera d'une
importance ...*
3.   Le rapprochement industriel s'est révélé fructueux.   *Notre collaboration ...*
4.   Où en sont les échanges commerciaux avec le Japon ?   *Où en sont les
négociations ... ?*
5.   La résolution définitive a été adoptée à l'unanimité.   *Le projet ...*
6.   Il faut revoir la politique régionale.   *Il faut réduire les déséquilibres ...*
7.   La prochaine décennie sera cruciale pour l'avenir de l'Europe.   *Les dix
prochaines années ...*

C *Thème.*
1.   The attitude of France has disappointed some of her European partners.
2.   During the various negotiations, Greece and Portugal adopted different
strategies.
3.   The British are no longer the only ones who disagree with the present policy.
4.   Only a complete review of the quotas will settle the crisis.
5.   The important thing is to reach a quick agreement.

More about the position of adjectives

See page 9, section 6 for an introduction to POSITION OF ADJECTIVES
See page 68, section 9 for use of **de** before plural ADJECTIVES

1   More than one ADJECTIVE can be used to describe a noun.

   1. Two adjectives that normally go before the noun keep their position:

      un **bon petit** restaurant   *a good little restaurant*

   2. When one adjective normally goes before and the other follows the noun, both keep their position:

      une **excellente** revue **internationale**   *an excellent international magazine*

   3. If both adjectives normally follow the noun, they are linked with **et** when they express two equal characteristics:

      une revue **sérieuse** et **respectée**   *a respected serious magazine*

   but not when both are necessary for meaning:

      une revue **mensuelle internationale**   *an international monthly magazine*

2   Some adjectives have one meaning when they are placed before the noun and a different meaning when they are placed afterwards:

l'**ancien** président	*the former President*
des bâtiments **anciens**	*old buildings*
certains amis	*certain (some) friends*
un fait **certain**	*a certain (undeniable) fact*
ces **chers** enfants	*these dear (beloved) children*
un article **cher**	*an expensive item*
son **dernier** film	*her / his latest (most recent) film*
la semaine **dernière**	*last (the one before this) week*
différentes versions	*various versions*
des versions **différentes**	*different versions*
la **même** attitude	*the same attitude*
l'image **même** de la santé	*the very picture of health*
mon **pauvre** ami	*my poor (to be pitied) friend*
une famille **pauvre**	*a poor (penniless) family*
leur **propre** appartement	*their own flat*
leur appartement **propre**	*their clean flat*

3   **prochain** (*next*) is similar to **dernier**. When it means *next* in the sense of *the one after this*, it comes after the noun, e.g. **la semaine prochaine, l'année prochaine**.

4   You will learn about the different possible positions of adjectives by reading and listening to authentic French.
Some adjectives can be used before or after the noun. When an adjective which normally follows the noun is used <u>before</u> the noun, this gives the adjective more importance:

      C'est une **remarquable** candidate   *She is an outstanding candidate*
      On a obtenu de **splendides** résultats   *We obtained some magnificent results*

seul and its meanings

5   **seul** has various meanings depending on its context and position:

1. Before a noun, **seul** means *only, single, sole*:

C'est ma **seule** amie	*She is my only friend*
Je suis leur **seul** héritier	*I am their sole heir*

2. After a noun, or referring back to a noun or pronoun, **seul** means *alone, on one's own, lonely*:

Un homme **seul** ne survivrait pas	*One man alone would not survive*
Elle se sentait **seule**	*She felt lonely*
Je l'ai fait tout(e) **seul(e)**	*I did it all on my own*

3. **seul** on its own, used as a noun, means *the only one*:

Vous êtes **le seul** à m'avoir aidé	*You are the only one who helped me*

4. **seul** can be used as an adjective on its own for emphasis, particularly at the beginning of a sentence:

Seuls les jeunes ont réagi	*Only young people reacted*

More about how adjectives are used in sentences

6   Adjectives can be used as NOUNS with **le, la, l', les**:

L'important est de prendre une décision
The important thing is to make a decision
Mais **l'essentiel**, c'est de prendre **la bonne**
But it is essential to make the right one

7   Adjectives can be linked to INFINITIVES by prepositions (page 179, Appendix 5).

1. The prepositions **à** and **de** link most adjectives to infinitives:

Il est **prêt à faire** des concessions	*He is ready to make concessions*
Nous sommes **ravis de** vous **revoir**	*We are delighted to see you again*

Note that **ce** and **il** can affect the preposition:

Il est difficile **d'**expliquer sa décision	*It is difficult to explain his decision*
Expliquer sa décision, **c'**est difficile **à** faire	

See pages 124–125, sections 1–5 for more about **ce** and **il**

2. When **assez** *(... enough)* or **trop** *(too...)* come before the adjective, use the preposition **pour** before the infinitive:

Il est **trop** faible **pour** sortir	*He is too weak to go out*
Il n'est pas **assez** fort **pour** sortir	*He not strong enough to go out*

8 Adjectives are linked to NOUNS by prepositions (see page 179, Appendix 5). Adjectives of FEELING (**triste, heureux**, etc.) generally take **de**:

> Elle est contente **de** son personnel   *She is pleased with her staff*

Note: when the adjective describes people's attitude towards other people, use the preposition **envers**:

> Il est dur **envers** ses employés   *He is tough with his employees*

9 Adjectives may be used with **rendre** which, in this context, means *to make*:

> Ce repas m'a **rendu malade**   *That meal made me ill*

Whenever possible, use a verb which conveys the same meaning:

> Cela vous **facilitera** la tâche   *It will make your task easy*

How to say *someone intelligent, nothing special,* etc.

10 The expressions **quelqu'un, quelque chose, personne** and **rien** are followed by **de** when used with an adjective:

> C'est **quelqu'un d'**intelligent   *She / he is someone intelligent*
> C'est **quelque chose d'**intéressant   *That's something interesting*
> Je n'ai vu **personne de** nouveau   *I didn't see anybody new*
> Je n'ai **rien** fait **de** spécial   *I did nothing special*

Note: **quelqu'un, quelque chose, personne** and **rien** are masculine singular and therefore the adjective is masculine singular.

Adjectives with particular spelling difficulties

See pages 8–9, sections 1–5 for ADJECTIVES and their feminine and plural forms

A number of abstract ADJECTIVES are often mis-spelt. The following sections list adjectives with particular spelling difficulties.

11 Adjectives ending in **-al**:

	SINGULAR	PLURAL
MASCULINE	**loyal**	**loyaux**
FEMININE	**loyale**	**loyales**

amical	global	original
commercial	international	postal
crucial	médical	primordial
familial	mondial	régional
fondamental	national	sentimental
général	normal	tropical, etc.

12 Adjectives ending in **-el**:

	SINGULAR	PLURAL
MASCULINE	**cruel**	**cruels**
FEMININE	**cruelle**	**cruelles**

conventionnel	annuel
exceptionnel	essentiel
fonctionnel	éventuel
interpersonnel	formel
personnel	individuel
professionnel	industriel
proportionnel	mensuel
sensationnel	naturel
traditionnel, etc.	potentiel, etc.

Note those double **n** spellings where there is a single **n** in English.

13 Adjectives ending in **-en**:

	SINGULAR	PLURAL
MASCULINE	**moyen**	**moyens**
FEMININE	**moyenne**	**moyennes**

aérien	égyptien	parisien
ancien	européen	quotidien
diluvien	méditerranéen	végétarien, etc.

14 Adjectives ending in **-f**:

	SINGULAR	PLURAL
MASCULINE	**vif**	**vifs**
FEMININE	**vive**	**vives**

actif	descriptif	progressif
chétif	inactif	réceptif
craintif	neuf	représentatif
définitif	primitif	veuf, etc.

A Using the list of common adjectives and their constructions on pages 179–180, Appendix 5 fill the gaps with **à** or **de**.

Les origines de l'Union européenne

L'idée d'une communauté européenne fut émise en 1950 par des hommes soucieux _____ assurer une paix durable. Seule une Europe unie leur semblait susceptible _____ empêcher une confrontation entre les deux blocs dominés par les États-Unis et l'URSS. Six pays (la Belgique, la France, le Luxembourg, l'Italie, les Pays-Bas et la République fédérale allemande) se déclarèrent disposés _____ participer aux négociations qui aboutirent en 1956 à la signature du traité de Rome instituant le Marché commun.

Au cours des décennies suivantes, de nombreuses étapes importantes furent franchies, surtout dans le domaine économique. Mais, dans la plupart des pays, l'opinion restait défavorable _____ une union politique forte. Sans politique étrangère et défense communes, l'Europe se trouva donc incapable _____ imposer ses propres solutions sur la scène internationale.

B Insert the adjective in the correct place and make it agree.

e g. *prochain, primordial*
Les ___ négociations ___ seront d'un ___ intérêt ___.
→ Les prochaines négociations seront d'un intérêt primordial.

1. *ancien, nouveau*
   La ___ présidente ___ du Parlement européen était favorable à de ___ mesures ___.
2. *commercial, certain*
   Le volume des ___ échanges ___ avec l'Afrique augmente depuis un ___ temps ___.
3. *pauvre, exceptionnel, dernier*
   Les ___ régions ___ ont bénéficié de ___ subventions ___ au cours des mois ___.
4. *progressif, vif*
   Le ___ élargissement ___ de l'Union européenne a fait l'objet de ___ discussions ___.
5. *positif, industriel*
   La Belgique a adopté une ___ attitude ___ en matière de ___ stratégie ___.
6. *unilatéral, gros*
   Les ___ décisions___ comportent toujours de ___ risques ___.

C *Thème.*
1. The European Commission did not propose anything new.
2. There is something very surprising in this lack of consensus.
3. Germany proved generous with her Southern European partners.
4. The Foreign Minister said that she was[1] pleased with the latest resolutions.
5. These measures are being implemented too badly to have an impact.
6. The serious current disagreements are not making the situation any better.

[1] to say that one is . . . : *se déclarer*

La société en question

A A journalist is interviewing a social worker after riots took place on a housing estate. Spot the subjunctive verbs in the passage below and underline the verb or the expression that they follow.

e.g. <u>Nous sommes déçus que</u> la situation se **soit** dégradée.

La banlieue s'enflamme

- *Pourquoi tant de violence ?*
- Quand plus de 20 % des jeunes d'une cité sont au chômage, il ne faut pas s'étonner qu'il y ait de la violence. En fait, tous les jours on s'attend à ce qu'il se produise un incident.
- *Mais la violence ne résout rien.*
- Non, mais c'est la seule manière pour ces jeunes de réclamer qu'on fasse quelque chose pour eux. Quand ils restent calmes, on les oublie.
- *Que veulent-ils ?*
- Ils veulent avant tout qu'on leur permette de jouer un rôle dans la société. Pour vivre, on a besoin de sentir que l'on sert à quelque chose.
- *La situation est-elle désespérée ?*
- Je ne pense pas du tout qu'elle soit désespérée. La banlieue est un lieu plein de vie et de dynamisme. J'aimerais tellement qu'on comprenne cela !

B Are you getting a feel for the subjunctive? Here are comments heard on the radio after the riots. Choose the appropriate form of the verb.

1. Je doute que le premier ministre (*prendra / prenne*) les mesures qui s'imposent.
2. Je ne suis pas sûre que les solutions proposées par le gouvernement (*sont / soient*) les meilleures.
3. N'attendons pas que la chose (*se reproduise / se reproduit*) pour créer des emplois pour les jeunes de la région !
4. J'insisterai auprès du gouvernement pour que les responsables (*sont / soient*) punis sévèrement.
5. Nous devons agir pour empêcher que toute une génération (*se sente / se sent*) exclue de la société.
6. Si l'on n'agit pas tout de suite, je crains que la haine ne (*devient / devienne*) un mode de vie pour tous ces jeunes.

C *Version.*

1. Mes frères sont au chômage. J'ai peur que ça soit la même chose pour moi !
2. On en a marre d'attendre que le gouvernement fasse quelque chose.
3. Mon père insiste pour que je poursuive mes études, mais ça sert à rien !
4. J'aurais aimé qu'on aille à la mairie pour discuter de nos problèmes, mais on n'a pas voulu nous recevoir. Pas étonnant qu'on ait mis le feu à la cité !

Introduction to the subjunctive

See page 102, section 7, pages 106–109, sections 2–9 and pages 148–149, sections 8–10 for uses of the SUBJUNCTIVE not covered in this chapter

See page 106, sections 1–3 for the PERFECT SUBJUNCTIVE

1   The SUBJUNCTIVE is a form of the verb in French which has no equivalent in English. Many expressions take the subjunctive. It is used, for example:

   1. after certain verbs, like **vouloir** when followed by **que**:

   Elle veut que tu **saches** la vérité   *She wants you to know the truth*

   2. after certain conjunctions, like **avant que**:
   Je lui téléphonerai avant qu'il **sorte**   *I'll call him before he goes out*

2   The subjunctive is used when there is a change of SUBJECT. If the subject is the same for both verbs, the infinitive is used:

NO CHANGE OF SUBJECT: INFINITIVE USED	CHANGE OF SUBJECT: SUBJUNCTIVE USED
Elle veut savoir la vérité	**Elle** veut que **tu** saches la vérité
She wants to know the truth	*She wants you to know the truth*
Je lui téléphonerai avant de sortir	**Je** lui téléphonerai avant qu'**il** sorte
I'll call him before I go out	*I'll call him before he goes out*

See page 14, section 1 for an explanation of subject of verb.

3   The main subjunctive tenses are the present, described in the next sections, and the perfect.

See page 106, sections 1–3 for the PERFECT SUBJUNCTIVE.

Forms of the present subjunctive

4   The PRESENT SUBJUNCTIVE is formed by taking the **ils** form of the present tense, removing **–ent** and adding the subjunctive endings **-e, -es, -e, -ions, -iez, -ent**:

parler: ils **parl**ent		finir: ils **finiss**ent		vendre: ils **vend**ent	
je	parl**e**	je	finiss**e**	je	vend**e**
tu	parl**es**	tu	finiss**es**	tu	vend**es**
il / elle	parl**e**	il / elle	finiss**e**	il / elle	vend**e**
nous	parl**ions**	nous	finiss**ions**	nous	vend**ions**
vous	parl**iez**	vous	finiss**iez**	vous	vend**iez**
ils / elles	parl**ent**	ils / elles	finiss**ent**	ils / elles	vend**ent**

5   The present subjunctive of the following verbs is irregular:

aller	aille, ailles, aille, allions, alliez, aillent
avoir	aie, aies, aie, ayons, ayez, aient
être	sois, sois, soit, soyons, soyez, soient
faire	fasse, fasses, fasse, fassions, fassiez, fassent
falloir	il faille
pouvoir	puisse, puisses, puisse, puissions, puissiez, puissent
savoir	sache, saches, sache, sachions, sachiez, sachent
vouloir	veuille, veuilles, veuille, voulions, vouliez, veuillent

6   The following verbs are irregular only in the **nous** and **vous** forms:

boire	boive, boives, boive, **buvions**, **buviez**, boivent
croire	croie, croies, croie, **croyions**, **croyiez**, croient
devoir	doive, doives, doive, **devions**, **deviez**, doivent
mourir	meure, meures, meure, **mourions**, **mouriez**, meurent
prendre	prenne, prennes, prenne, **prenions**, **preniez**, prennent
recevoir	reçoive, reçoives, reçoive, **recevions**, **receviez**, reçoivent
tenir	tienne, tiennes, tienne, **tenions**, **teniez**, tiennent
venir	vienne, viennes, vienne, **venions**, **veniez**, viennent
voir	voie, voies, voie, **voyions**, **voyiez**, voient

Note that some verbs with spelling changes to reflect pronunciation also change in some forms of the present subjunctive: verbs like **espérer**, **acheter**, **rejeter**, **appeler** and **employer** and **appuyer**.

See pages 62–63, sections 13–19 for more about these verbs

Use of the subjunctive after certain verbs and expressions

7   The subjunctive is used to express a WISH, PREFERENCE or EXPECTATION after certain verbs followed by **que**:

aimer que ...	to like ...
désirer que ...	to want / wish ...
souhaiter que ...	to hope / wish ...
vouloir que ...	to want ...
aimer mieux que ...	to prefer ...
préférer que ...	to prefer ...
s'attendre à ce que ...	to expect ...
attendre que ...	to wait for / wait until ...

On **préfère que** vous **déménagiez** tout de suite
We prefer you to move out immediately
Personne ne **s'attendait** pas **à ce que** le président **fasse un discours**
Nobody expected the President to give a speech

Note: one verb expressing a wish, **espérer que** ... (*to hope that ...*) does <u>not</u> take the subjunctive:

On **espère que** vous déménagerez tout de suite
We hope that you will move out immediately

8   The subjunctive is used to express an OPINION, FEELING or REACTION, for example:

avoir peur que ... ne	*to be afraid / frightened ...*
comprendre que ...	*to appreciate / understand ...*
craindre que ... ne	*to fear ...*
s'étonner que ...	*to be amazed ...*
s'opposer à ce que ...	*to be opposed / against ...*
regretter que ...	*to regret / be sorry ...*
être content que ...	*to be pleased ...*
être déçu que ...	*to be disappointed that ...*
être désolé que ...	*to be sorry ...*
être heureux que ...	*to be happy ...*
être surpris que ...	*to be surprised ...*

Elle **est surprise qu'il ait accepté**
She is surprised that he agreed
Je **comprends que** tu **sois** mécontent
I understand that you might be displeased
Il faut **s'opposer à ce qu'**il **soit** réélu
We must oppose him being reelected

Note that **avoir peur que** and **craindre que** take **ne** before the verb. This **ne** has no negative meaning, for example:

On **craint que** cet incident **ne déclenche** une crise mondiale
They fear that this incident might provoke a world crisis

9   The subjunctive is used to express PERMISSION or a COMMAND, for example:

consentir à ce que ...	*to consent / agree ...*
demander que ...	*to ask ...*
empêcher que ...	*to prevent / stop ...*
exiger que ...	*to demand ...*
insister pour que	*to insist ...*
réclamer que	*to demand ...*

Il **a consenti à ce que** son fils le **mette** dans une maison de retraite
He agreed to his son putting him in an old people's home
La société **insiste pour que** vous **passiez** une visite médicale
The company insists that you go for a medical examination

Use of the subjunctive to express possibility

10   The subjunctive is also used when something is considered a POSSIBILITY in the future:

Je suggère que vous **posiez** votre candidature
I suggest that you apply
Imaginons un instant que le président **démissionne**
Imagine for a moment that the President resigns

Verbs expressing degrees of certainty

11 When verbs and expressions which convey belief or conviction are used to express CERTAINTY, they do not take the subjunctive. Examples:

croire que ...	*to believe / think ...*
penser que ...	*to think ...*
être convaincu que ...	*to be convinced ...*
être sûr que ...	*to be sure ...*
être certain que ...	*to be certain ...*
il est certain que ...	*it is certain ...*
il est probable que ...	*it is probable ...*
il est sûr que ...	*it is sure ...*
il est vrai que ...	*it is true ...*

Je pense qu'ils sont au courant
I think they know what is going on
On est sûr que le gouvernement poursuivra son action
We are sure that the government will pursue its policy

However, when they are used to express uncertainty or doubt, expect to see the subjunctive used:

Je **ne peux pas croire** qu'ils **soient** au courant
I can't believe that they know what is going on
On **n'est pas sûr** que le gouvernement **poursuive** son action
We are not sure that the government will see its policy through
Il **est peu probable** qu'elle **sache** la vérité
It is unlikely that she knows the truth

In questions, the subjunctive may be used to suggest strong doubt:

Est-on sûr que le gouvernement **poursuive** son action ?
Can we be sure that the government will pursue its policy?

Note that **douter que** takes the subjunctive as it always expresses doubt:

Le comité **doute que** cette approche **soit** appropriée
The committee doubts whether this approach is suitable

A Various people are voicing their concerns about the future. Write the verbs in italics in the subjunctive.

Comment voient-ils l'avenir ?

PHILIPPE (travailleur social) Je suis inquiet. On dirait que les gens (*s'habituer*) à voir la misère autour d'eux. Je ne comprends pas qu'on (*faire*) preuve de tant d'indifférence.

ELVIRE (enseignante) Moi qui suis prof, c'est la violence à l'école qui m'inquiète le plus aujourd'hui. Je suis heureuse que le gouvernement (*avoir*) enfin décidé d'agir mais je crains qu'il ne (*être*) trop tard.

ROMAIN (ouvrier spécialisé) J'aimerais que mes enfants (*pouvoir*) être sûrs de trouver du travail, mais je ne crois pas que la situation de l'emploi (*s'améliorer*) du jour au lendemain.

LEILA (directrice commerciale) Nous vivons dans un monde qui bouge tout le temps, je ne pense pas qu'il (*falloir*) nécessairement s'inquiéter pour l'avenir. Au contraire, je m'attends à ce que les choses (*aller*) bien mieux d'ici quelques années.

B Rewrite the following statements about immigration using either the indicative or the subjunctive.

e.g. Un Français sur quatre est d'ascendance étrangère.
→ Il est exact qu'un Français sur quatre est d'ascendance étrangère.

Immigration

1. L'immigration a eu un effet très positif sur l'économie française jusqu'à la crise pétrolière de 1973. *Il est certain que …*
2. Les immigrés et leurs enfants sont les premières victimes du chômage. *Il est à craindre que …*
3. Les immigrés bénéficient plus du système de protection sociale que les Français. *Il n'est pas prouvé que …*
4. Il y a plus d'étrangers vivant en France aujourd'hui que dans les années 1930. *Il n'est pas vrai que …*
5. Le nombre d'étrangers vivant en France diminuera dans les quelques années à venir. *Il est probable que …*
6. Par la suite, on aura à nouveau besoin de main d'œuvre étrangère pour compenser la baisse du taux de natalité. *Les spécialistes sont convaincus que …*

C *Thème.*
1. We must do our utmost to prevent hatred from becoming a way of life.
2. People are tired of waiting for the Government to do something.
3. Young people would like the authorities to act rapidly to improve their living conditions on the estates.
4. They don't believe that there is a place for them in today's society.

L'entreprise

A Fill the gaps with either **qui** or **lequel**, **auquel**, etc. as appropriate.

Pour créer son entreprise

1. La priorité des priorités, c'est de connaître le marché à _____ on va s'attaquer.
2. C'est la raison pour _____ la réalisation d'une étude de marché est la première tâche à _____ il faut se consacrer.
3. Ensuite il s'agit de trouver les capitaux _____ vous permettront de créer votre entreprise.
4. Les institutions à _____ vous allez vous adresser voudront des chiffres, ne laissez rien au hasard.
5. Si aucun des organismes financiers auprès de _____ vous avez fait des démarches n'est intéressé par votre projet, sollicitez l'aide de votre famille.
6. Une fois les financements trouvés, choisissez soigneusement le personnel et les fournisseurs avec _____ vous travaillerez.

B Choose the appropriate word as required by the construction of the verbs.

Devenir commerçant

La Chambre de commerce et d'industrie (CCI) fournira (*au / du*) futur commerçant les renseignements qui (*le / lui*) permettront (*à / de*) prendre, en toute connaissance de cause, les décisions nécessaires à la réalisation de son projet. Elle (*le / lui*) suggérera, entre autres, (*à / de*) établir un plan de financement pour ses dépenses d'investissement et, suivant le type d'activité qu'il envisage, elle (*le / lui*) conseillera (*à / de*) contracter un emprunt auprès de tel ou tel établissement financier.

Le futur chef d'entreprise pourra aussi demander (*à / de*) la CCI (*à / de*) contacter certains organismes à sa place. Rien ne (*le / lui*) empêchera, par ailleurs, (*à / de*) chercher conseil auprès des organisations professionnelles.

C *Thème.*

Témoignage d'un jeune chef d'entreprise

1. My company has been in existence for three years and today I employ twenty people, which proves that the original idea was good.
2. I have paid back the money I had borrowed from my parents, which they are pleased about.
3. At present, the main problem for me is finding products which correspond to what I am looking for.
4. What worries me as well is the increasing lack of highly motivated staff.

Relative pronouns after prepositions

See pages 34–36, sections 1–8 for the uses of **qui**, **que**, **dont** and **où**

1   In English, the RELATIVE PRONOUN (*who / whom, which, that*) can be omitted, and the preposition (*with, from*, etc.) can be separated from the person or thing it refers to:

> *The pencil I was writing* **with** *has disappeared* instead of
> *The pencil* **with which** *I was writing has disappeared*

But in French you cannot omit the relative pronoun (**qui, lequel**, etc.) and the preposition (**avec, pour**, etc.) must come before the relative pronoun:

> Le crayon **avec lequel** j'écrivais a disparu

Prepositions + qui

See page 93, section 5 below for relative pronouns and **de**

2   Use **qui** to refer to PEOPLE after most PREPOSITIONS (**à, avec**, etc.) and prepositional phrases (**à propos de**, etc.). Some examples:

PREPOSITIONS		PREPOSITIONAL PHRASES	
sans qui	*without whom*	à propos de qui	*about whom*
avec qui	*with whom*	à côté de qui	*next to whom*
à qui	*to whom*	grâce à qui	*thanks to whom*
pour qui	*for whom*	loin de qui	*far from whom*

> la fille **avec qui** je sors   *the girl I am going out with*
> l'homme à côté **de qui** j'étais assis   *the man I was sitting next to*

Use **qui** where there is a PREPOSITION + NOUN + **de**:

> J'ai remercié les gens **sur les conseils de qui** j'ai continué mes études
> *I thanked the people on whose advice I continued my studies*

Prepositions + lequel, laquelle, etc.

See page 51, section 14 for forms of **lequel**

3   Use the forms **lequel, laquelle**, etc. to refer to THINGS after prepositions other than **à** and **de**:

> le dossier **sur lequel** ...   *the file on which ...*
> la voiture **dans laquelle** ...   *the car in which ...*
> les outils **avec lesquels** ...   *the tools with which ...*

Note that **la raison pour laquelle** can mean *why*:

la raison **pour laquelle** j'ai démissionné   *the reason why I resigned*

4   The forms of **lequel** combine with the preposition **à** as follows:

	SINGULAR	PLURAL
MASCULINE	**auquel**	**auxquels**
FEMININE	**à laquelle**	**auxquelles**

Use the forms **auquel**, etc. to replace **à** + NOUN and after prepositional phrases ending in **à** when referring to THINGS:

L'organisation **à laquelle** elle appartient est mondialement connue
The organisation she belongs to is known worldwide
Voici les témoignages **grâce auxquels** on a pu reconstruire la vérité
Here are the reports which enabled us to reconstruct the truth

5   The forms of **lequel** combine with the preposition **de** as follows:

	SINGULAR	PLURAL
MASCULINE	**duquel**	**desquels**
FEMININE	**de laquelle**	**desquelles**

Use the forms **duquel**, etc. after prepositional phrases ending in **de** when referring to THINGS:

l'usine **à côté de laquelle** ...   *the factory next to which ...*
les faits **à propos desquels** ...   *the facts about which ...*

But remember that **dont** (see page 36, sections 6–7) replaces **de** + NOUN:

les choses **dont** j'ai peur   *the things I am afraid of*

où meaning *at which, in which,* etc.

6   **où** is often used instead of **auquel**, etc. and **dans lequel,** etc. where the reference is to TIME or PLACE:

le siècle **où** se passent ces événements
the century in which these events take place
l'école **où** on m'a envoyé
the school to which they sent me

Note also the use of **où** after **cas**:

Il y a des cas **où** il n'est pas possible de trancher
There are cases in which it is impossible to make a clearcut decision

Relative pronouns ce qui, ce que, ce dont, ce à quoi

7 As we have seen so far, most relative pronouns refer to a particular noun. The relative pronouns in the following sections refer to an IDEA or a PHRASE, or to something as yet undefined:

Elle m'a dit **ce qu'**elle avait vu	*She told me what she had seen*
Il a tout nié, **ce qui** est normal	*He denied everything, which is normal*

8 **ce qui** refers to the SUBJECT of the verb that follows:

On ne sait pas **ce qui** se passe	*We don't know what is happening*
Elle ne sait rien, **ce qui** est curieux	*She knows nothing, which is odd*

9 **ce que / ce qu'** refers to the OBJECT of the verb that follows:

On ne sait pas **ce qu'**il fera	*We don't know what he will do*
Elle a refusé, **ce que** je comprends	*She refused, which I understand*

When the subject of the verb is long or consists of more than one word (e.g. **le premier ministre**), subject and verb are often inverted after **que**:

On ne sait pas ce que **fera le premier ministre**
We don't know what the Prime Minister will do

10 **ce dont** refers to an INDIRECT OBJECT introduced by **de**:

On ne sait pas **ce dont** ils ont besoin	*We don't know what they need*
Elle a refusé, **ce dont** je me doutais	*She refused, which did not surprise me*

11 **ce à quoi** refers to an INDIRECT OBJECT introduced by **à**:

On sait bien **ce à quoi** il pense	*We know what he is thinking about*
Il est parti, **ce à quoi** je m'attendais	*He has left, which is what I expected*

See page 54, section 2 for use of **ce qui, ce que** in INDIRECT QUESTIONS

12 **tout ce** + RELATIVE PRONOUN means *everything, all*, etc.:

Tout ce qui se trouve ici est à moi	*Everything here is mine*
C'est **tout ce que** nous savons	*That's all we know*
Dites-moi **tout ce dont** vous avez besoin	*Tell me everything you need*

Two-verb constructions

See page 30, section 6 for an introduction to TWO-VERB CONSTRUCTIONS
See pages 171–178 for list of common verbs and their constructions
See page 14, section 1 for DIRECT and INDIRECT OBJECTS

13 Most verbs meaning *to tell, advise, order, forbid*, etc. take **à** before the person being *told, advised*, etc. In other words they take an INDIRECT OBJECT. Their English equivalents take a DIRECT OBJECT.

These common verbs all take **à** before the person and **de** before the infinitive:

commander **à** quelqu'un **de** faire qch.	*to order someone to do sth.*
conseiller **à** quelqu'un **de** faire qch.	*to advise someone to do sth.*
déconseiller **à** quelqu'un **de** faire qch.	*to advise someone against doing sth.*
défendre **à** quelqu'un **de** faire qch.	*to forbid someone to do sth.*
demander **à** quelqu'un **de** faire qch.	*to ask someone to do sth.*
dire **à** quelqu'un **de** faire qch.	*to tell someone to do sth.*
interdire **à** quelqu'un **de** faire qch.	*to forbid someone to do sth.*
ordonner **à** quelqu'un **de** faire qch.	*to order someone to do sth.*
pardonner **à** quelqu'un **d'**avoir fait qch.	*to forgive someone for doing sth.*
permettre **à** quelqu'un **de** faire qch.	*to allow someone to do sth.*
promettre **à** quelqu'un **de** faire qch.	*to promise someone to do sth.*

Il a dit **aux ouvriers** de ne pas partir	*He told the workers not to leave*
J'ai promis **à la voisine** de l'appeler	*I promised the neighbour to call her*

Note that the verbs **prier** and **empêcher** are exceptions. They do not take **à** before the OBJECT:

prier **quelqu'un** de faire qch.	*to beg / request someone to do sth.*
empêcher **quelqu'un** de faire qch.	*to stop / prevent someone from doing sth.*

Priez **les visiteurs** d'attendre	*Ask the visitors to wait*
Il faut empêcher **les gens** de partir	*They must stop the people from leaving*

Verbs like voir, entendre, regarder, etc. + infinitive

14   The verbs **voir** (*to see*), **entendre** (*to hear*), **regarder** (*to watch*), **sentir** (*to feel*), **apercevoir** (*to notice*) do not take a preposition before the infinitive:

On nous **a vus quitter** le bâtiment	*We were seen leaving the building*
J'ai entendu la voiture **partir**	*I heard the car leave*

Note that **entendre dire** and **entendre parler** both mean *to hear* in the sense of *to find out*:

1. entendre dire is followed by **que** + verb phrase:

J'ai entendu dire **qu'il avait démissionné**
I heard (that) he had resigned

2. entendre parler is followed by **de** + noun:

J'ai entendu parler **de sa démission**
I heard about his resignation

Note: **entendre parler de** means *to hear about*.

A Complete the following sentences with the relevant relative pronoun, making all necessary changes.

Le nombre des faillites monte en flèche

1. On a enregistré quelque 50 000 faillites au cours des deux dernières années, _____ inquiète les pouvoirs publics.

2. Dans ces faillites, les victimes sont d'abord les salariés pour _____ il n'y a pas d'autre possibilité d'emploi.

3. Mais ce sont aussi les fournisseurs dont les factures restent impayées, _____ l'on oublie trop souvent.

4. Lorsqu'il s'agit d'une société importante, toute la région _____ elle est implantée se trouve sinistrée.

5. C'est _____ l'on a constaté lorsque la société Chabert a fermé ses portes.

6. Cette société, à _____ le gouvernement a refusé de porter secours, a dû licencier plus de 2 000 salariés.

7. Les circonstances à la suite de _____ Chabert a fait faillite étaient difficilement prévisibles.

8. Le chef d'entreprise, à _____ les salariés ont fait confiance jusqu'au bout, a tout fait pour essayer de sauver son entreprise.

9. _____ on peut être sûr c'est que pour lui le dépôt de bilan[1] n'a pas été une solution de facilité.

B In the following interview give the French for the phrases in brackets.

Fermeture d'usine

* *Avez-vous été prévenus à l'avance de la fermeture de l'usine ?*
– Non. Hier [we saw the director arrive] à son bureau, comme d'habitude.
* *Comment avez-vous donc appris cette fermeture ?*
– [We heard about it] pour la première fois à la télévision.
* *Comment les syndicats ont-ils réagi ?*
– [We heard them say] qu'ils s'attendaient à des licenciements depuis longtemps.

C *Thème.*

1. The turnover of Fauvet & Fils has doubled in less than a year, which is outstanding. If you ask Mr Fauvet why it has been so successful[2], he replies that it must be ascribed to his partners' quality of work. 'I have an extremely effective team, without whom the company would never be where it is today.'

2. On the occasion of a special dinner attended by many of the region's company heads, the Chambre de commerce promised to offer small companies a series of training sessions allowing them to become familiar with new management methods. It also intends to employ several advisers whose services the companies will be able to call on in times of difficulty.

---

[1] *le dépôt de bilan* : (voluntary) liquidation
[2] translate as 'the reasons for such success'

A Complete the following sentences by putting each adjective in the appropriate place and making it agree.

e.g. *tropical, phénoménal* La <u>médecine</u> a fait des <u>progrès</u>.
→ La médecine tropicale a fait des progrès phénoménaux.

1. *original, social* Il faut apporter des <u>solutions</u> aux <u>problèmes</u>.
2. *mensuel, moyen* Le <u>salaire</u> des <u>cadres</u> varie considérablement.
3. *industriel + européen* La <u>production</u> a atteint des chiffres record.
4. *international, paradoxal* L'amélioration des <u>relations</u> a eu certains <u>effets</u>.
5. *exceptionnel, postal* On annonce une <u>hausse</u> des <u>tarifs</u>.
6. *annuel, aérien* Les <u>bénéfices</u> des <u>compagnies</u> sont en baisse.
7. *proportionnel, dernier* On a introduit un nouveau type de <u>scrutin</u> aux <u>élections</u>.
8. *petit + individuel* Il ne faut pas tenir compte des <u>problèmes</u>.
9. *public, officiel, secret* L'<u>opinion</u> a été choquée à l'<u>annonce</u> de ces <u>négociations</u>.

B Rewrite the following sentences using the subjunctive.

e.g. On vous voit peu en France. *Je regrette que* ...
→ Je regrette qu'on vous voie peu en France.

Interviews de sportifs : ce qu'on leur demande parfois

1. Vous voulez bien nous parler de votre dernière saison ?
   Je voudrais que vous ...
2. Vous êtes moins décontractée que l'an dernier. Non ?
   Je crains que vous ...
3. On dit que vous avez l'intention de vous retirer de la compétition.
   Est-il vrai que vous ... ?
4. Un champion ressent parfois le besoin de faire une pause.
   Comprenez-vous qu'un champion ... ?
5. Vous avez déjà participé à des manifestations écologiques. Le referez-vous ?
   Faut-il s'attendre à ce que ...
6. Une championne comme vous a-t-elle un rôle social à jouer ?
   Pensez-vous qu'une championne comme vous ... ?

C Put the verbs in brackets in the correct tense of the indicative or in the present subjunctive.

Le sport et l'argent font bon ménage

1. Voilà plus de 30 ans que les athlètes consentent à ce qu'on (*se servir*) d'eux à des fins publicitaires.
2. Souvent les sportifs à la recherche de financement n'attendent pas qu'on (*venir*) les solliciter. Ils (*aller*) eux-mêmes tirer la sonnette des entreprises.
3. Aujourd'hui, on constate que le parrainage (*engendrer*) souvent le succès.
4. Il ne faudrait pas croire pour autant que les sponsors (*être*) des philanthropes.
5. Ce sont au contraire des hommes d'affaires qui espèrent que leur association au sport (*améliorer*) leur image de marque.

D A film director talks about the problems she encountered while making her last film. Rewrite the sentences with the appropriate relative pronoun.

Quelles sont les difficultés à _____ vous vous êtes heurtée pour réaliser ce film ?

• Le comédien à _____ on avait confié le rôle principal est tombé malade au dernier moment.

• La maison de production avec _____ on avait signé le premier contrat a fait faillite.

• Le cascadeur sur la présence de _____ je comptais ne s'est pas présenté le jour voulu.

• À cause du mauvais temps, on a dû reporter les scènes pour _____ il fallait du soleil.

• Enfin, malgré les difficultés _____ je vous parle, j'ai eu plaisir à faire ce film.

E Rewrite the following text by inserting **à, de** or **envers**.

Une banque pour les pauvres

La plupart des établissements bancaires considèrent que l'on ne peut pas faire confiance _____ pauvres en matière d'argent. C'est cette attitude _____ les plus démunis qui est en partie responsable _____ la misère actuelle. L'expérience de la Banque Grameen montre, en effet, qu'avec une aide financière minime, les pauvres sont capables _____ améliorer considérablement leurs conditions de vie.

La pauvreté découle souvent du fait que les travailleurs sont dans l'incapacité _____ bénéficier des fruits de leur travail. L'aide sociale distribuée par de nombreux pays industrialisés permet _____ plus démunis _____ survivre mais pas _____ éradiquer la misère. Si l'on veut supprimer la misère il faut donner _____ plus démunis les moyens de contrôler eux-mêmes leur destin. C'est ce que fait le micro-crédit. En accordant _____ chacun la possibilité _____ mettre ses compétences en application, il aide les pauvres _____ sortir des systèmes de dépendance.

F *Thème.*

Munoz was afraid of not being selected for the European Cup match because he wanted to play in front of his fans once more before retiring – which is understandable. Not only did he play, but the team manager, Luc Bertelli, insisted that he should do another season. Everyone thought that after all he had done for the club, he was too young to stop playing.

La publicité

A Rewrite the following sentences using the superlative form of the adjective in italics. Make sure that you put it in the right place and make it agree with the underlined noun.

e.g. *Histoire d'X*, le <u>livre</u> de l'année. *polémique*
→ *Histoire d'X*, le livre le plus polémique de l'année.

1. Natura, l'<u>eau minérale</u>. *riche en magnésium*
2. Nettol, les <u>produits d'entretien</u>. *économique*
3. Avec Excella, les <u>opérations</u> sont parfaitement maîtrisées. *complexe et long*
4. Le <u>modèle</u> a déjà fait preuve de ses qualités. *récent*
5. Les cafés Arabor sont torréfiés avec <u>soin</u> et <u>légèreté</u>. *grand … grand*
6. Le fond de teint Naouri, la <u>façon</u> de sublimer votre teint. *naturel*

B Complete these sentences using one of the following: **meilleur, le meilleur, mieux, le mieux, le pire** or **le moindre**. Make any necessary agreements.

1. Le four à micro-ondes Frank est celui qui se vend _____ cette année.
2. Notre assurance voyages ne vous empêchera pas d'avoir les _____ ennuis, mais elle en minimisera les conséquences.
3. Le moins cher n'est pas toujours le _____.
4. Un des avantages de ce lave-vaisselle, et non _____ , c'est sa rapidité.
5. Organisez-vous _____ avec un agenda Planning.
6. La Juva 4 a été choisie comme l'une des dix _____ voitures de l'année.

C *Version*. The director of a major advertising company explains the reasons for his success.

Publicité : les secrets de la réussite

Le bon publicitaire, c'est celui qui se croit le meilleur, qui dit qu'il est le meilleur mais qui, au fond, sait douter de lui. On ne peut pas se permettre de s'endormir, il faut toujours mieux faire. Avoir le goût du risque et se donner à fond dans son métier sans se prendre trop au sérieux, c'est ça le secret de la réussite.

La pub française a fait un bond vertigineux ces dernières années. C'est maintenant l'une des plus avancées du monde. Pourquoi ? Parce qu'elle a compris que moins on prend de risques moins on a de chances de réussir. Seule l'image excessive force l'attention du public. Il faut toujours aller plus loin, quitte parfois à déraper. En définitive, les « coups » époustouflants compensent les campagnes moins réussies. Mais pour réussir une grande campagne, il ne suffit pas d'être le meilleur, il faut le faire savoir. Le meilleur produit du publicitaire, c'est lui-même : il faut qu'il sache faire la publicité de la publicité.

Comparative adjectives

1   COMPARATIVE ADJECTIVES compare one thing or person to another:

Ce livre est **plus court**	*This book is shorter*
Cette revue est **moins intéressante**	*This magazine is less interesting*
Elle est **aussi célèbre** que vous	*She is as famous as you*

Comparative adjectives are formed with **plus**, **moins** and **aussi**. When one person or thing is being compared with another, **que** is used:

Il faut sensibiliser un **plus grand** nombre de gens
We must reach a larger number of people
Leur industrie est **moins performante que** la nôtre
Their industry is less competitive than ours
Les relations n'ont jamais été **aussi tendues qu'**à l'heure actuelle
Relations have never been as strained as today

Note the use of **de plus en plus** and **de moins en moins**:

Les attentats à la bombe se font **de plus en plus** fréquents
Bomb attacks are becoming more and more frequent
Les relations familiales sont **de moins en moins** stables
Family relations are less and less stable

2   If a comparative adjective is followed by **que** + a verb, **ne** is used before the verb. It has no negative meaning:

L'opinion des consommateurs est plus divisée qu'elle **ne** l'était
Consumer opinion is more divided than it was

See page 114, section 8 for use of **le** after comparatives

3   In French, some comparisons are more commonly expressed with **moins** + adjective than with **plus** + **adjective**, for example:

moins cher	*cheaper*		moins long	*shorter*
moins grand	*smaller*		moins rapide	*slower*

Superlative forms of adjectives

4   SUPERLATIVE ADJECTIVES refer to *the shortest*, *the most* or *the least interesting*, etc. person or thing. The definite articlec (**le**, **la**, **les**) is repeated if the adjective comes after the verb:

C'était le jour **le plus froid**	*It was the coldest day*
C'est l'hôtel **le moins cher**	*It is the cheapest hotel*

More examples:

> La faction **la plus militante** a appelé à la grève
> *The most militant faction called for a strike*
> C'est un des pays **les moins** peuplés
> *It is one of the least populated countries*

Note that **le, la, les** are used with an adjectival PHRASE

> la personne **la plus en colère**   *the angriest person*

5   **du, de la, des** (*from the, of the*) are used after a noun with a superlative adjective to mean *in the*:

> C'est un des pays **les moins** peuplés **du** monde
> *It is one of the least populated countries in the world*

Irregular comparative and superlative adjectives

6   The comparative and superlative forms of **bon** are irregular. **mauvais** and **petit** have two forms, one regular and one irregular:

ADJECTIVE	COMPARATIVE	SUPERLATIVE
bon *good*	**meilleur,** **meilleure**, etc. *better*	**le meilleur,** **la meilleure**, etc. *the best*
mauvais *bad*	**plus mauvais,** **plus mauvaise**, etc. *worse* **pire**, etc. *worse*	**le plus mauvais** **la plus mauvaise**, etc. *the worst* **le pire, la pire**, etc. *the worst*
petit *small / little*	**plus petit,** **plus petite**, etc. *smaller* **moindre**, etc. *lesser*	**le plus petit,** **la plus petite**, etc. *the smallest* **le moindre,** **la moindre**, etc. *the least*

Examples:

> La qualité de notre production est **meilleure** cette année
> *The quality of our produce is better this year*
> Le printemps a été **plus mauvais** que d'habitude
> *The spring weather was worse than usual*
> Il n'y a pas **le moindre** doute
> *There is not the least doubt*

Note that **plus mauvais** and **le plus mauvais** are the most common forms, but that **pire** and **le pire** are still used in set expressions:

> C'est **pire** que jamais   *It's worse than ever*
> On a évité **le pire**   *The worst was avoided*

The subjunctive after superlative adjectives

7   If a superlative adjective is followed by a verb, this verb will be in the subjunctive in formal French:

C'est la situation la plus inquiétante qui **puisse** être
It is the most alarming situation that there could be

See grammar index for references to forms and uses of the subjunctive

Comparative forms of adverbs

8   COMPARATIVE ADVERBS are also formed with **plus, moins** and **aussi**, followed by **que** when a comparison is being made:

Les otages ont été libérés **plus tôt**	*The hostages were freed earlier*
Cela arrive **moins fréquemment**	*It happens less frequently*
J'ai répondu **aussi vite que** j'ai pu	*I replied as quickly as I could*

Note the construction when **plus** and **moins** are first in the sentence:

Plus on vieillit, **moins** on est indépendant
The older you get, the less independent you are

9   After **plus** and **moins**, **ne** is used if a verb follows after **que**:

Cela arrive moins fréquemment qu'on **ne** le croit
It happens less frequently than one thinks

See page 114, section 8 for use of **le** after comparatives

Superlative forms of adverbs

10   SUPERLATIVE ADVERBS require the definite article **le**:

C'est ce qu'on utilise **le plus souvent**   *It is what we use most often*

Irregular comparative and superlative adverbs

11   Adverbs **bien, beaucoup** and **peu** have irregular forms:

ADVERB	COMPARATIVE	SUPERLATIVE
bien *well*	**mieux** *better*	**le mieux** (*the*) *best*
beaucoup *many, a lot*	**plus** *more*	**le plus** (*the*) *most*
peu *few*	**moins** *less*	**le moins** (*the*) *least*

Qu'est-ce qui vous inquiète **le plus** ?	*What worries you the most?*
C'est lui qui m'inquiète **le moins**	*He's the one who worries me least*

mieux and meilleur

12 Don't confuse the ADVERBS **mieux** (*better*) / **le mieux** (*the best*) and the
ADJECTIVES **meilleur** (*better*) / **le meilleur** (*the best*):

ADVERB	On mange **mieux** ici	*You eat **better** here*
	C'est ici qu'on mange **le mieux**	*This is where you eat **best***
ADJECTIVE	C'est un **meilleur** restaurant	*It's a **better** restaurant*
	C'est **le meilleur** restaurant	*It's the **best** restaurant*

Use of possible with comparatives and superlatives

13 **possible** is often used with comparative and superlative adjectives and
adverbs. Note the word order and the translations:

C'est la meilleure solution **possible**   *It's the best possible solution*
On les aide le plus **possible**   *We help them as much as possible*

More uses of the infinitive

14 INFINITIVES can be used as NOUNS:

Camper est une formule de vacances économique
Camping is a cheap way of going on holiday
Voyager, c'est **accepter** de vivre autrement
Travelling means accepting a different way of life

15 The INFINITIVE is used after **à** to express what is required or what is possible:

Il y a des décisions **à prendre**   *There are decisions to be made*
Mon appartement est **à vendre**   *My flat is for sale*
Il n'a rien **à** vous **reprocher**   *He has nothing to reproach you for*

16 The INFINITIVE is sometimes used instead of the imperative in formal French:

Envoyer CV et photo   *Send CV and photo*
Ne pas **affranchir**   *No stamp required*

17 **faire** + INFINITIVE is used to express the idea of *getting someone to do something
for you*:

Je le **ferai changer** d'avis   *I will make him change his mind*
Il faut **faire amender** cette loi   *We must have this law amended*

se faire + INFINITIVE is used to express the idea of *having something done to
yourself*:

Je **me suis fait teindre** les cheveux   *I had my hair dyed*
Ils **se sont fait** critiquer   *They were criticised*

A Fill the gaps using either **mieux** or **meilleur**, making any changes necessary.

1. Pour préparer votre voyage dans de _____ conditions, adressez-vous à notre agence-conseil.
2. La carte X : la _____ façon de gagner du temps et de l'argent.
3. Avec les produits solaires X, bronzez _____ en vous exposant moins.
4. Ce n'est pas le tout d'être bricoleur, encore faut-il posséder les _____ outils.
5. Pour _____ connaître les formules de financement possibles, adressez-vous à votre concessionnaire X.
6. De toutes les poudres à laver que j'ai essayées, c'est celle qui lave le _____
7. Nous vous offrons une qualité incomparable aux _____ prix.
8. Offrez-vous ce qui se fait de _____ en matière d'ameublement.

B Complete the following sentences with the correct tense of **faire** or **se faire**. Then translate them.

1. Le but d'une campagne publicitaire est de _____ vendre.
2. Elle y parvient en _____ mieux connaître les produits nouveaux.
3. Mais est-il bien nécessaire de _____ voir une femme nue pour vendre un parfum ?
4. Il est essentiel de créer une identité de marque si l'on veut _____ une réputation mondiale.
5. Les agences de publicité françaises ont mis longtemps à _____ accepter sur le marché américain.
6. Le Bureau de vérification de la publicité a parfois de la peine à _____ respecter la réglementation sur la publicité mensongère.

C *Thème.*

1. Sometimes restrictions can be more stimulating than a total lack of censorship: they force advertising professionals to be more creative. For instance, the measures designed to limit cigarette advertising have led them to create some of their finest advertising campaigns.
2. For a well known actor, a forty second commercial can be more profitable than any[1] feature film. Thirty years ago such an activity would have represented one of the worst humiliations for a star.
3. Losing weight has become an obsession with many women. Most people agree[2] that advertising is partly responsible for this phenomenon. But advertising agencies claim that they have nothing to feel guilty about.
4. It[3] is more and more desirable to inform the consumer as clearly as possible about the qualities of a product. But it is not the main aim of advertising.
5. If you have a car for sale or a flat to let, the simplest and the cheapest thing to do is to put an advertisement in the local paper. It is also the most efficient way that I know.

---

[1] any (meaning all of a group of things or people) : *n'importe quel + nom*

[2] use *s'accorder pour dire*

[3] see page 124, section 4

Le monde du travail

DIAGNOSTIC

A The impersonal expressions used in the following sentences about job interviews take the subjunctive when followed by **que**. Rewrite each sentence making any necessary changes.

e.g. Il est nécessaire d'être motivé. *Il est essentiel que vous ...*
  → Il est essentiel que vous soyez motivé.

L'entretien d'embauche

1. Il est naturel d'être anxieux avant un entretien. *Il est naturel que vous ...*
2. Mais il est important de rester calme. *Mais il est important que vous ...*
3. D'entrée, il faut faire preuve d'enthousiasme. *D'entrée, il faut que vous ...*
4. Il importe aussi de faire des réponses brèves et pertinentes. *Il importe aussi que vos réponses ...*
5. Et surtout n'oubliez pas qu'il est essentiel d'arriver à l'heure ! *Et surtout n'oubliez pas qu'il est essentiel que vous ...*

B Check the meaning of conjunctions **jusqu'à ce que**, **de manière à ce que**, **de peur que**, **pour que** and **sans que**, and select one for each gap.

Grève des contrôleurs aériens

Les aiguilleurs du ciel suspendront leur mouvement de grève pour le week-end _____ le retour des vacances de Pâques se fasse normalement. Ils ont néanmoins déposé un nouveau préavis de grève pour lundi matin. « Nous avons essayé de négocier tout l'hiver, _____ le gouvernement ait fait aucune concession. C'est pourquoi nous avons décidé de poursuivre notre mouvement de grève _____ nos revendications soient satisfaites » explique M. Bossi, responsable du syndicat national des contrôleurs aériens.

La plus importante de ces revendications concerne, rappelons-le, le calcul de la retraite. Les grévistes insistent également _____ la différence entre le travail « sur écran » et le travail « dans les bureaux » soit reconnue. Mais l'administration refuse toute concession _____ cela ne fasse boule de neige dans la fonction publique.

C In the following sentences about French trade unions, underline the verb in the subjunctive and the conjunction that takes the subjunctive.

e.g. Les syndicats s'essoufflent <u>sans qu</u>'il y <u>ait</u> des changements.

1. Bien que les centrales syndicales continuent à exercer d'importantes responsabilités, le syndicalisme français reste faible et divisé.
2. A moins qu'ils ne fassent de rapides progrès pour moderniser leur image, les syndicats risquent de perdre encore des adhérents.
3. Cela devrait pouvoir se faire à condition qu'ils tiennent compte des aspirations individuelles des salariés.

The perfect subjunctive

1 The PERFECT SUBJUNCTIVE consists of the present subjunctive of **avoir** or **être** + PAST PARTICIPLE

Example with **avoir**:

parler
j'**aie** parlé
tu **aies** parlé
il / elle **ait** parlé
nous **ayons** parlé
vous **ayez** parlé
ils / elles **aient** parlé

Examples with **être**:

arriver	s'asseoir
je **sois** arrivé(e)	je me **sois** assis(e)
tu **sois** arrivé(e)	tu te **sois** assis(e)
il / elle **soit** arrivé(e)	il / elle se **soit** assis(e)
nous **soyons** arrivé(e)s	nous nous **soyons** assis(e)s
vous **soyez** arrivé(e)(s)	vous vous **soyez** assis(e)(s)
ils / elles **soient** arrivé(e)s	ils / elles se **soient** assis(e)s

See page 16, section 12 for forms of PAST PARTICIPLE
See page 74–75, sections 9–13 for PAST PARTICIPLE agreement rules

Use of the present subjunctive and the perfect subjunctive

See pages 86–87, sections 4–6 for forms of PRESENT SUBJUNCTIVE

2 In modern French, the PRESENT SUBJUNCTIVE is used for actions taking place <u>after</u> the action of the first verb, whether or not these actions take place in the present or the past:

| Je suis content qu'elle **vienne** | *I'm pleased she is coming* |
| Je'étais content qu'elle **vienne** | *I was pleased she was due to come* |

3 The PERFECT SUBJUNCTIVE is used for actions taking place <u>before</u> the action of the first verb.

| Je regrette qu'elle **soit venue** | *I am sorry that she came* |
| J'ai regretté qu'elle **soit venue** | *I was sorry that she came* |

Conjunctions which take the subjunctive

4   The following CONJUNCTIONS take the subjunctive:

à condition que ...	*on condition that ...*
à moins que ... ne	*unless ...*
afin que ...	*so / in order that ...*
après que ...	*after ...*
avant que ... (ne)	*before ...*
bien que ...	*although ...*
de crainte que ... ne	*for fear that ...*
de façon à ce que ...	*so that ...*
de manière à ce que ...	*so that ...*
de peur que ... ne ...	*for fear that ...*
en attendant que ...	*until ...*
jusqu'à ce que ...	*until ...*
non que ...	*not that ...*
pour que ...	*so / in order that ...*
pourvu que ...	*provided that, if only ...*
quoique ...	*although ...*
sans que ...	*without ...*

Examples:

Son nom n'a pas été cité **quoiqu'**elle **ait été mise** en cause
Her name was not mentioned although she was implicated
On vous enverra un catalogue **pour que** vous **puissiez** choisir
We shall send you a catalogue so that you can make your choice
La réunion aura lieu **pourvu que** tout le monde **soit** là
The meeting will take place provided that everyone is there

Note: **après que** traditionally takes the indicative but is nowadays mainly used with the subjunctive.

5   **à moins que**, **de crainte que** and **de peur que** take **ne** before the verb:

A moins que le temps **ne** s'améliore, le match sera reporté
Unless the weather improves, the match will be postponed
On a évacué le quartier **de peur qu'**il **n'**y ait une seconde explosion
The area was evacuated for fear that a second explosion might occur

Note that you will also see **ne** used after **avant que**:

Il faudra plusieurs années **avant que** ce médicament **ne** soit au point
It will be several years before this drug is perfected

Conjunctions which take the indicative

6   The following CONJUNCTIONS take the indicative and not the subjunctive:

ainsi que	*just as*	pendant que	*while*
alors que	*at a time when,*	peut-être que	*perhaps*
	whereas	puisque	*since*
depuis que	*since*	selon que	*according to*
étant donné que	*given that*	tandis que	*while, whereas*
maintenant que	*now that*	vu que	*seeing that*
parce que	*because*		

Example:

> **Depuis que** la direction **a changé**, il n'y a pas eu d'amélioration
> *Since the management has changed, there has been no improvement*

See page 150, section 13 for **peut-être** + inversion

7   The following CONJUNCTIONS OF TIME also take the indicative:

(au fur et) à mesure que	*as*
après que	*after*
aussitôt que	*as soon as*
dès que	*as soon as*
lorsque	*when*
quand	*when*
tant que	*for as long as*

> **A mesure que** la médecine **progresse**, il y a de nouvelles maladies
> *As medicine progresses, new diseases appear*
> Ils ont envoyé des secours **aussitôt qu'**on les **a prévenus**
> *They sent help as soon as they were alerted*

See page 127, sections 12–14 for use of time conjunctions with future tenses

Conjunctions which can take either the indicative or the subjunctive

8   The following CONJUNCTIONS take the indicative or the subjunctive depending on the meaning of the sentence:

si bien que	
de sorte que	*so that, in such a way that*
de manière que	

They take the subjunctive when there is a sense of purpose:

> On a modifié cette loi **de sorte qu'**il n'y **ait** plus d'injustice
> *They have changed that law so that (in order that) it is no longer unfair*

and the indicative when the consequence is merely being mentioned as fact:

> On a modifié cette loi **de sorte qu'**il n'y a plus d'injustice
> *They have changed that law so that (in such a way that) it is no longer unfair*

Note that **de façon à ce que** and **de manière à ce que**, which convey a sense of intended purpose, always take the subjunctive.

Use of the subjunctive after impersonal constructions

9   The subjunctive is used after certain IMPERSONAL CONSTRUCTIONS expressing NECESSITY, COMMAND, OPINION such as:

Il est dommage que ...	*It is a shame / pity that ...*
Il est essentiel que ...	*It is essential that ...*
Il est étonnant que ...	*It is surprising / amazing that ...*
Il est important que ...	*It is important that ...*
Il est impossible que ...	*It is impossible that ...*
Il est juste que ...	*It is fair / right that ...*
Il est naturel que ...	*It is natural that ...*
Il est nécessaire que ...	*It is necessary that ...*
Il est possible que ...	*It is possible that ...*
Il est préférable que ...	*It is preferable that ...*
Il est temps que ...	*It is time that ...*
Il est utile que ...	*It is useful that ...*
Il convient que ...	*It is advisable / appropriate that ...*
Il faut que ...	*It is necessary that ...*
Il importe que ...	*It is important that ...*
Il se peut que ...	*It is possible that ...*
Il semble que ...	*It seems that ...*
Il suffit que ...	*It is enough that ...*
Il vaut mieux que ...	*It is better that ...*

Il est temps que vous **preniez** une décision définitive
It is time you made a final decision
Il se peut que notre chiffre d'affaires **augmente** cette année
Our turnover may increase this year

Note that **il semble que**, when used with indirect object pronouns (**me, te lui**, etc.) does not take the subjunctive:

Il me semble que notre chiffre d'affaires **augmentera** cette année
It seems to me that our turnover will increase this year

See page 89, section 11 for impersonal constructions expressing degrees of certainty

Use of infinitive after impersonal constructions

10 The infinitive is often used with the impersonal constructions listed in section 9 above, when the subject of the following verb is understood, or included as an indirect pronoun. Examples:

Il m'est impossible de démissioner	*It is impossible for me to resign*
Il lui importe de réussir	*It is important to her to be successful*
Il faudra attendre leur retour	*You must wait for them to return*

See page 131, section 4 for more about **falloir**

A Read the following sentences carefully and select one of the conjunctions according to whether the verb is in the indicative or the subjunctive.

L'informatique dans l'entreprise

1. *pourvu que / parce que* La production des entreprises est mieux adaptée aux besoins _____ les études de marché sont plus précises.
2. *avant que / pendant que* Les bureaux d'études peuvent simuler une ligne de production _____ elle ne soit réalisée.
3. *à condition que / au fur et à mesure que* _____ l'automatisation se développe dans les usines, l'intervention directe de l'homme dans les tâches d'exécution se réduit.
4. *sans que / tandis que* La robotique joue un rôle considérable _____ les entreprises soient pour autant peuplées de robots.
5. *de peur que / vu que* En effet, _____ les risques de pannes sont sensiblement accrus, l'automatisation rend le maintien d'une intervention humaine indispensable.
6. *en attendant que / alors que* Les effectifs d'ouvriers qualifiés continuent de diminuer _____ la création d'emplois de maintenance se poursuit.
7. *de sorte que / pour que* Dans les bureaux, l'informatisation est également la règle partout, _____ chaque employé se sert d'un terminal ou d'un micro-ordinateur.
8. *de sorte que / afin que* Dans ces conditions, l'entreprise doit développer la formation permanente _____ les salariés puissent constamment s'adapter aux nouvelles techniques.

B *Thème.*

In most companies, individual salaries are not officially disclosed, although certain firms have now made the decision to display these details.

'Here every employee is a shareholder. Therefore it is normal that he or she should have access to all the social and economic facts about the company', said[1] one managing director, 'and it is the best way of eliminating all sorts of rumours about salaries'. One management consultant points out that openness improves relations between management and employees.

Finding out what others are earning encourages some employees to put their name down for training courses or to show more initiative. For others, however, knowing that they have reached the top of their salary scale[2] is discouraging. 'When I find out that the foreman has had yet another increase, it makes me sick'[3], said[1] Mariama Ali, a[4] semi-skilled worker in a small electronics factory.

[1] use present tense
[2] *une fourchette de salaire*
[3] *ça me reste en travers de la gorge*
[4] omit the article

Les relations interpersonnelles

A Rewrite the following sentences replacing the underlined nouns with the relevant pronouns, e.g. **le / la / les, lui / leur, eux / elles, en / y**.

Écrire en collaboration

• *Vous avez co-signé un roman policier qui vient de paraître aux éditions de Midi. Qui a eu l'idée de ce livre ?*

AGNÈS   C'est moi qui ai eu l'idée <u>de ce roman,</u> mais je savais que Macha s'intéresserait <u>à cette idée</u> avant même que j'aie parlé <u>à Macha de cette idée.</u> On avait toujours dit qu'on ferait quelque chose ensemble un jour. J'ai donc tout de suite pensé <u>à Macha.</u>

• *Et vous avez accepté tout de suite, Macha ?*

MACHA   Dès qu'elle m'a soumis <u>son projet,</u> son projet m'a tentée. Mais j'ai tout de même demandé <u>à Agnès</u> de me donner une semaine pour réfléchir <u>au projet.</u> En fait, j'ai téléphoné <u>à Agnès</u> dès le lendemain pour dire <u>à Agnès</u> que j'acceptais.

• *Comment s'est organisé le travail à deux ? Vous rédigiez ensemble ?*

AGNÈS   Non. Une fois qu'on avait décidé du contenu de chaque chapitre, on rédigeait séparément. On se retrouvait donc avec deux versions, on comparait <u>les deux versions,</u> on discutait <u>des deux versions</u> et petit à petit on arrivait à une version unique.

• *Quand on travaille en équipe, n'y a-t-il pas des tensions ?*

MACHA   Pas vraiment. La collaboration exige que chacun accepte les critiques de l'autre et ne s'offusque pas <u>des critiques de l'autre.</u> On savait <u>qu'il fallait savoir accepter les critiques</u> avant de commencer. Il n'y a eu aucun problème de ce côté-là. Mais il nous est arrivé d'être incapables de choisir entre les versions successives : aucune <u>des versions</u> ne nous plaisait. C'est alors qu'on a demandé à Ali d'intervenir.

• *Vous vous êtes donc mis à travailler à trois ?*

AGNÈS   Oui. Ali était curieux de lire le roman. On a donc offert <u>à Ali</u> de devenir notre premier lecteur. Il a été formidable.

B Fill the gaps with **à, aux, de** or **des**.

Homosexuel et agriculteur

Si en ville l'homosexualité s'affiche, à la campagne elle se veut invisible. Dans une communauté rurale, seule la discrétion permet _____ l'homosexuel _____ mener une vie sans histoires. « Il serait impensable de parler _____ son homosexualité, mieux vaut la cacher _____ autres », nous dit Gérard. Il joue les célibataires endurcis et profite _____ fins de semaine pour retrouver quelques amis dans une des villes voisines.

À quand une plus grande ouverture ? « Cela dépendra _____ l'évolution des mœurs. »

Using two object pronouns together

See pages 14–16, sections 2–10 for an introduction to DIRECT and INDIRECT OBJECT PRONOUNS

1 More than one OBJECT PRONOUN can be used with a verb, in which case the order is as follows:

me				
te	le	lui		
se	la		y	en
nous	les	leur		
vous				

Examples:

Elle **me les** a rendus	*She gave them back to me*
Je compte **la leur** présenter	*I'm expecting to introduce her to them*
Ils **nous en** prêteront plusieurs	*They will lend us several (of them)*
Je ne **la lui** ai pas offerte	*I did not offer it to him*
Il **y en** a encore dix	*There are still ten of them*

2 In French, when a verb has two objects, one will be the DIRECT OBJECT and one will be the INDIRECT OBJECT:

SUBJECT	VERB	DIRECT OBJECT	INDIRECT OBJECT	
Nous	enverrons	une invitation	à nos clients →	Nous **la leur** enverrons
Luc	a montré	les échantillons	à la cliente →	Luc **les lui** a montrés

Note that, in English, unlike French, a verb <u>can</u> have two direct objects, that is two objects without prepositions:

Nous enverrons **une invitation à nos clients**
We shall send our clients an invitation
Luc a montré **les échantillons à la cliente**
Luc showed the client the samples

See page 15, section 7 for more about direct objects in French and English

Use of emphatic pronouns to refer to people after verbs

See page 23, sections 6–9 for EMPHATIC PRONOUNS
See pages 14–16, sections 5–10 for INDIRECT OBJECT PRONOUNS

3 We saw in Chapter 3 that the INDIRECT OBJECT PRONOUNS **me**, **te**, **lui**, etc. usually replace **à** + PEOPLE:

On a renvoyé le chèque **à Christine** →   On **lui** a renvoyé son chèque
They sent her back her cheque

However, with the following common verbs, **à** + EMPHATIC PRONOUN (**moi**, **toi**, etc.) are used to refer to PEOPLE:

s' adresser à ...	to address ..., to go / come to ...
comparer ... à ...	to compare ... with ...
faire appel à ...	to appeal to ...
faire attention à ...	to pay attention to ...
s' habituer à ...	to get used to ...
s' intéresser à ...	to be interested in ...
penser à ...	to think about ...
s'en remettre à ...	to leave it up to ...

Examples:

En cas d'urgence, adressez-vous **à moi et mon équipe**
→ En cas d'urgence, adressez-vous **à nous**
In an emergency, come to us
J'ai fini par m'habituer **à mon patron**
→ J'ai fini par m'habituer **à lui**
In the end I got used to him

But remember that, as with all other verbs, **y** is used to replace **à** + THINGS with the above verbs:

Adressez-vous **à la réception**	→ Adressez-vous-**y**
Go to the reception desk	→ *Go there*
J'ai fini par m'habituer **à ses manières**	→ J'ai fini par m'**y** habituer
In the end I got used to his ways	→ *In the end I got used to them*

4   With all verbs taking **de**, use **de** + EMPHATIC PRONOUN (**moi, toi**, etc.) to refer to PEOPLE:

Tout dépend **de Léon**	→ Tout dépend **de lui**
Everything depends on Léon	→ *Everything depends on him*
Vous avez profité **de notre société**	→ Vous avez profité **de nous**
You took advantage of our company	→ *You took advantage of us*

But remember that with all verbs taking **de**, the pronoun **en** replaces **de** + THINGS:

Tout dépend **de sa décision**	→ Tout **en** dépend
Everything depends on her decision	→ *Everything depends on it*
Vous avez profité **de la crise**	→ Vous **en** avez profité
You took advantage of the crisis	→ *You took advantage of it*

See page 15, section 8 for indirect object pronoun **y**
See page 16, sections 9–10 for indirect object pronoun **en**

Use of le with être and devenir, and to replace verb constructions

5 The pronoun **le** is used to reflect or to replace an adjective or a noun following the verbs **être** and **devenir** where *so*, or no pronoun at all, is used in English:

> Elle était **leader du parti** mais elle ne l'est plus
> *She was leader of the party but she isn't any more*
> Les résultats seront **positifs**, du moins nous l'espérons
> *The results will be positive, at least we hope so*
> Il n'était pas **ambitieux**, mais il l'est devenu
> *He was not ambitious, but has become so*

6 **le** replaces verb constructions where the verb takes a direct object:

Vous croyez **que c'est grave** ?	→ Oui, je **le** crois
Do you think it is serious?	→ *Yes, I think so*
Je sais **qu'il refusera**	→ Je **le** sais
I know that he will refuse	→ *I know / I know he will*

Note that an equivalent pronoun is not always required in English.

7 **le** is also used to reflect a verb construction within the same sentence:

> Comme l'a dit le président, **tout est possible**
> *As the President said, anything is possible*

8 **le** is used to reflect the first part of a comparative sentence containing **plus** or **moins**, when a verb follows the **que**:

> Cet article est **plus polémique** que je ne l'ai d'abord pensé
> *This article is more controversial than I first thought*

Note: **ne** is used after comparatives followed by a verb.

See page 100, section 2 and page 102 section 9 for **ne** after comparative adjectives and adverbs

Use of y and en to replace verb constructions

See page 23, sections 6–9 for forms and uses of EMPHATIC PRONOUNS
See pages 14–16, sections 5–10 for INDIRECT OBJECT PRONOUNS

9 Pronouns **y** and **en** can also replace **à** and **de** followed by a verb construction:

Il s'attendait **à échouer**	
He expected to fail	→ Il s'**y** attendait
Il s'attendait **à ce que l'on le fasse échouer**	*He expected it*
He expected them to fail him	

Elle se souvient **d'avoir appris cela à l'école**
She remembers learning that at school
Elle se souvient **de ce qu'on lui apprenait**
She remembers what they taught her

→ Elle s'**en** souvient
She remembers (it)

Note that a pronoun is not always required in English:

Comme on s'**y** attendait, la grève n'a pas réussi
As we expected, the strike was not successful

Verb constructions to remember

See also the list of common verbs and their constructions on pages 171–178

10 Verbs which express the idea of getting something from someone take **à** before a person. These include:

acheter qch. **à** qn	*to buy sth. from s.o.*
arracher qch. chose **à** qn	*to snatch / grab sth. from s.o.*
cacher qch. **à** qn	*to hide sth. from s.o.*
emprunter qch. **à** qn	*to borrow sth. from s.o.*
enlever qch. **à** qn	*to take sth. away from s.o.*
prendre qch. **à** qn	*to take sth. from s.o.*
voler qch. **à** qn	*to steal sth. from s.o.*

Examples:

Les médecins cachent souvent **aux malades** la gravité de leur cas
Doctors often hide from patients the seriousness of their condition
On **leur** a retiré leur permis de conduire
Their driving licences were taken away from them

Note: **acheter à** has two meanings:

Je **lui** ai acheté un billet d'avion   *I bought an airline ticket **from** her / him*
                                            *I bought an airline ticket **for** her / him*

11 Watch out for the prepositions that these verbs take:

dépendre **de**	*to depend on*
se diriger **vers**	*to make for*
s'excuser **de**	*to apologise for*
penser **à**	*to think of / about*
profiter **de**	*to profit by, to take advantage of*
remercier **de**	*to thank for*
rire **de**	*to laugh at*
vivre **de**	*to live on / off*

Ils se sont excusés **de** leur absence   *They apologised for their absence*
Les résultats dépendront **du** ministre   *The results will depend on the minister*

A Fill the gaps with **y**, **en** or **le**. If necessary, check the verb constructions in the list on pages 171–178, Appendix 4.

Une période d'adaptation

L'usine où René travaillait s'est vue obligée de licencier, il y a dix-huit mois : « Je m' ___ attendais, on ___ parlait depuis un certain temps. Mais tout de même, ça fait un choc ! » La préretraite était préférable au licenciement et, à son âge, René a pu ___ profiter. Juliette, sa femme, tire un bilan positif de leur situation : « La vie est faite d'étapes successives. La retraite ___ est une. »

Les premières difficultés ont été financières. Ils ___ ont beaucoup discuté ensemble. « Je ne ___ aurais jamais cru mais, en fait, cette période de crise n'a fait que resserrer les liens entre nous », explique René. Ensuite il a fallu trouver un autre mode de vie : « Avoir mon mari à la maison à temps complet a bouleversé mes habitudes, reprend Juliette. Au début, j'ai eu de la difficulté à m' ___ habituer. Quoi que je fasse, il fallait toujours qu'il s'___ mêle ! »

Se retrouver en tête à tête 24 heures sur 24 peut devenir un enfer et tourner à la catastrophe. René et Juliette semblent pourtant ___ avoir échappé.

B The sentences below take up some of the points René and Juliette have just made. Give the French for the phrases in brackets.

1. Bien que _____ , le licenciement a été un choc.   [René had expected it]
2. « _____ , cette période de crise a resserré les liens entre nous. »   [As I told you]
3. « Elle nous a beaucoup rapprochés, même si _____ .   [we did not notice[1] it immediately]
4. _____ _____ , les débuts ont été difficiles.   [As Juliette suspected]
5. Elle n'était pas patiente avec René, mais _____ .   [she became so]
6. En fait, se retrouver en tête à tête 24 heures sur 24 s'est avéré beaucoup _____ .   [more pleasant than they they had imagined]

C *Thème.*

1. Women, for whom sexual freedom was a recent gain, were all the more determined to use it and some women's magazines did not fail to encourage them to do so. The situation is noticeably different today. As recent surveys show, most of them realize that sexual freedom does not create happiness even if it contributes to it.
2. Homosexuality, considered for a long time to be an abnormality, even a disease, is finding wider acceptance[2]. As a result, homosexuals are less likely to conceal from others the nature of their relationships and the magazines which are intended for them are freely available.
3. Adolescence often starts earlier than parents imagine and the sexual experiences of the adolescents of today are more complex than they were 30 years ago. This[3] should enable them to reach in their adult life a balance that previous generations have not experienced.

---

[1] use *s'apercevoir de*   [2] to find wider acceptance : *obtenir droit de cité*   [3] see page 125, section 5

A Put the underlined adjective or adverb in the superlative form, making any necessary changes to the article before it.

L'entreprise et le client

Ce sont les Américains qui ont développé la notion de « service » dans les affaires. Le service consiste à procurer au client l'objet dont il a besoin, à un <u>bon</u> prix et dans une <u>bonne</u> qualité, tout en se mettant à sa disposition pour lui faciliter son achat. <u>Souvent</u>, c'est l'étude du marché qui permet de connaître les besoins du client. La technique <u>en faveur</u> pour l'étude du marché a été pendant très longtemps celle du sondage d'opinion.

Une fois que l'on connaît les caractéristiques et les qualités de l'objet que le client recherche <u>beaucoup</u> et que l'on sait dans quelles conditions cet objet se vend et s'achète <u>couramment</u>, il est possible de fabriquer un objet conforme au goût de la clientèle, de le lui offrir dans des conditions <u>favorables</u> et d'utiliser les arguments publicitaires qui retiennent <u>bien</u> l'attention et qui sont <u>efficaces</u>.

B Combine the two parts of each sentence by adding **plus ... plus**, **plus ... moins**, etc. depending on the sense of the sentence.

e.g. les parents regardent la télévision / les enfants la regardent
→ **Plus** les parents regardent la télévision, **plus** les enfants la regardent.

L'enfant et la télévision : quelques constatations
1. l'enfant est jeune / il est sensible au contenu réel des émissions.
2. les enfants grandissent / ils sont nombreux à dire que la télévision leur permet de s'ouvrir au monde extérieur.
3. leurs parents s'occupent d'eux / les enfants regardent la télévision.
4. leurs parents parlent avec eux de ce qu'ils ont vu / ils deviennent des spectateurs intelligents.

C Write the verbs in brackets in the present subjunctive, the infinitive or the correct tense of the indicative.

Embauche : les méthodes de recrutement des cadres

Vous venez de répondre à une annonce et vous avez envoyé, comme on vous le demandait, « curriculum vitae, lettre manuscrite et photo ». Il est certain que la première sélection (*se faire*) sur la base de votre CV, mais il se peut que la seconde (*être*) réalisée par un graphologue bien que les psychologues (*contester*) la validité des conclusions tirées de l'analyse de l'écriture. Quant à la photo, il est possible qu'elle (*être*) adressée à un morphopsychologue pour qu'il (*définir*) votre caractère à partir des traits de votre visage.

Les psychologues s'accordent pour dire qu'un entretien (*pouvoir*) largement suffire à choisir le meilleur candidat, pourvu qu'il (*être*) mené par une personne compétente connaissant bien l'entreprise. Dans ces conditions, pourquoi faire appel à des méthodes contestées ? Parce que pour le patron l'embauche (*être*) un risque. S'il s'adresse à des spécialistes de l'extérieur c'est de manière à leur (*faire*) endosser la responsabilité en cas d'erreur.

D Read each sentence carefully to ensure that you have understood it. Then put the verb in brackets into the perfect subjunctive.

Arts et spectacles : quelques commentaires

1. Cette représentation est bien la plus belle à laquelle je (*ne jamais assister*).
2. C'est le seul spectacle de la saison qui (*remporter*) un tel succès.
3. Il n'est pas surprenant que la prestation d'Auteuil lui (*valoir*) un prix.
4. Je ne crois pas que nous (*déjà voir*) ce groupe en si bonne forme.
5. Il est dommage que le public (*ne pas se montrer*) plus enthousiaste.
6. C'est un miracle que l'exposition (*ne pas être*) annulée.
7. Bien que je (*ne pas pouvoir*) assister à ce concert, j'en ai entendu le plus grand bien.

E In the following text certain verbs, nouns and adjectives take either **à** or **de**. Check the constructions and add **à** or **de**, making all necessary changes.

Les plaisirs du célibat

Nombreux sont les célibataires qui ont choisi _____ conjuguer leur vie au singulier. Ils tiennent _____ leur indépendance et refusent _____ la perdre.

Solène, 36 ans, est une de ces célibataires pour qui célibat n'est pas synonyme de solitude. Son désir d'indépendance résiste _____ le temps et _____ l'amour. Pourtant, Michel, son amant depuis deux ans, est très désireux _____ bâtir un couple avec elle : « Il essaie _____ me convaincre _____ habiter chez lui, explique-t-elle, mais je ne peux me résoudre _____ le faire ». Pour Solène, le célibat se résume _____ la possibilité _____ se retirer seule dans son appartement où elle n'est obligée _____ penser _____ personne d'autre, ni _____ s'habituer _____ les manies de quelqu'un d'autre.

L'indépendance est un luxe. Vivre seul coûte cher, et la possibilité _____ choisir ce mode de vie dépend en quelque sorte _____ le salaire dont on dispose. Autre difficulté : la maladie. On ne peut pas demander _____ son amant _____ venir jouer les gardes-malades pendant une semaine. Ressource inestimable pour les vrais célibataires : les amis. Dans les moments de crise, c'est _____ eux que l'on s'adresse. Il faut bien avoir quelqu'un _____ qui se confier.

F *Thème.*

1. It is better to set up a company without borrowing too much from the bank so as not to have high repayments to start with.
2. His family offered to lend him some money without his asking so that he would not have to go to a bank.
3. As she explained to us, the more shops she opens, the more her turnover grows without her profits falling.

Les relations internationales

A Replace the words in italics with the appropriate demonstrative pronoun (**celui-ci, celle-ci, ceux-ci** or **celles-ci**).

e.g. Le Chancellier allemand est arrivé ce matin à Paris en visite officielle.
  Cette visite officielle a pour but de renforcer le dialogue entre les deux pays.
→ Celle-ci à pour but de renforcer le dialogue entre les deux pays.

En bref ...

Proche-Orient
Israël et la Syrie viennent de reprendre leurs négociations. *Ces négociations* avaient été suspendues à la suite de l'attentat de Tel-Aviv.

Amérique du Sud
Le récent effondrement de la bourse de Buenos Aires en Argentine inquiète l'Uruguay. L'avenir de *l'Uruguay* dépend, en effet, de la santé économique de son puissant voisin.

Asie du Sud-Est
La crise qui bouleverse actuellement l'équilibre de toute la région est d'autant plus grave que *la région* n'y était nullement préparée.

Commerce international
Le contentieux entre les États-Unis et les pays européens s'aggrave bien que *les pays européens* aient accepté certains compromis.

B In the following passage, the verbs in italics are in the past historic. Identify the infinitive of each verb and then translate the whole text.

Le général de Gaulle : une certaine conception de la défense

Le général de Gaulle *se fit* connaître, dès les années 30, par ses écrits d'histoire politique et de stratégie militaire. Il *essaya* de faire prendre conscience à ses contemporains de la nécessité impérieuse de moderniser l'armée mais *se heurta*, pendant plus de quinze ans, à l'incompréhension des dirigeants militaires de l'époque. Quand il *fut* enfin nommé sous-secrétaire à la Défense nationale par Paul Reynaud, le 6 juin 1940, il était malheureusement trop tard pour mécaniser l'armée et résister à l'ennemi.

Nul doute que lorsqu'il *revint* au pouvoir en 1958, ce *fut* le souvenir du désastre de 1940 qui *détermina* le général de Gaulle à doter la défense des techniques les plus avancées. Le 2 novembre 1959, il *annonça* la mise sur pied d'une force nationale de dissuasion capable d'assurer l'indépendance nationale. Les gouvernements suivants ne *remirent* pas en cause la nécessité d'un armement stratégique nucléaire.

Demonstrative pronouns celui, celle, etc.

1 The demonstrative pronoun **celui** agrees with the noun it replaces:

	SINGULAR	PLURAL
MASCULINE	**celui** *this / that,* *the one*	**ceux** *these / those ones,* *the ones*
FEMININE	**celle** *this / that one,* *the one*	**celles** *these / those ones,* *the ones*

Quand **mon ordinateur** est en panne, j'emprunte **celui** de mon frère
When my computer isn't working, I borrow my brother's / that of my brother
Il préfère **les anciennes méthodes** à **celles** qu'on utilise aujourd'hui
He prefers the old methods to those (that) we use today

2 **celui**, etc. + RELATIVE PRONOUNS (**qui, que, dont**, etc.) mean *those which, the one who*, etc.:

On a demandé à **ceux qui** soutiennent notre action de signer une pétition
We have asked those who support our action to sign a petition
J'ai fait une réservation mais pas **celle que** je voulais
I have made a booking but not the one I wanted
Ce roman n'est pas **celui dont** je suis la plus fière
This novel is not the one I am most proud of

3 **celui**, etc. + **de** means *that / those of* or *the one(s) of*:

La séance de l'après-midi a été annulée et **celle du** soir également
The afternoon session was cancelled and so was the evening one
Si vous n'êtes pas au train de 18h, j'attendrai celui de 18h 45
If you are not on the six o'clock train, I shall wait for the 6.45 one

celui, etc. + **de** can indicate POSSESSION, which is often *'s* in English:

Ses arguments ressemblent à **ceux du** premier ministre
His arguments are similar to the Prime Minister's / those of the Prime Minister

4 **celui**, etc. + **-ci** and **-là** are used to distinguish between *this / these (-ci)* and *that / those (-là)*:

Prenez **celui-ci** ou **celui-là**
Take this one or that one

celui-ci also means *the latter* and **celui-là** means *the former*:

La tâche a été confiée à une commission d'enquête. **Celle-ci** fera connaître ses conclusions en décembre
The task has been put in the hands of a commission of enquiry. The latter will make its conclusions known in December

Note that **ce dernier** also means *the latter.*

tous ceux qui, toutes celles que, etc.

5   **tous ceux / toutes celles** + RELATIVE PRONOUN are used to express the idea of *all those that, everyone who,* etc.:

Je ne connaissais pas **toutes celles qui** étaient présentes
I didn't know all those who were there
Tous ceux que l'on a invités sont venus
Everyone we invited came
J'ai écrit à **tous ceux dont** je connaissais l'adresse
I wrote to everyone whose address I knew

Note that **tout ce** followed by a relative pronoun expresses the idea of *everything, all,* etc.:

Tout ce qui se trouvait dans l'appartement a été endommagé
Everything that was in the flat has been damaged

See page 94, section 12 for **tout ce qui, tout ce que**

Use of the past historic in contemporary French

6   The PAST HISTORIC or **passé simple,** is used instead of the PERFECT TENSE to describe completed actions in the past. It is never used in conversation.

1.   The past historic is often used in novels:

Lorsque le coup de feu **éclata**, il **eut** tout juste le temps de se retourner
When the shot rang out, he just had time to turn around

2.   You will see it in newspaper articles and in formal speeches:

Le ministre **félicita** la police et **fit** l'éloge de leur courage
The Minister congratulated the police and praised their courage
La création de l'OTAN **fut** un événement d'une importance capitale
The creation of NATO was an event of major importance

Note: the PRESENT TENSE is now used instead of the PAST HISTORIC or the PERFECT TENSE in many historical accounts.

See verb tables on pages 160–167 for the forms of the past historic

A Choose the right tense (past historic or imperfect) for the verbs in brackets.

Les projets de tunnels sous la Manche au XIXᵉ siècle

C'est à Albert Mathieu que l'on attribue généralement le projet le plus ancien d'un tunnel sous la Manche. (*Ce fut/C'était*) en 1802. La reprise des guerres napoléoniennes (*mit/mettait*) bientôt fin à son projet et (*jeta/jetait*) une ombre permanente sur les implications de l'entreprise. Albert Mathieu avait du moins ouvert la voie à des générations de visionnaires qui (*allèrent/allaient*) poursuivre son idée.

Les projets (*se succédèrent/se succédaient*) au cours du XIXᵉ siècle. Le plus près d'aboutir (*fut/était*) celui de Sir Edward Watkins, qui (*fit/faisait*) entreprendre le forage de puits et de galeries près de Douvres. L'on aurait pu croire que l'heure du tunnel avait sonné. A tort. Il (*fut/était*) encore trop tôt, semble-t-il. Le risque d'invasion, en cas de conflit armé avec la France, (*devint/devenait*) l'un des thèmes majeurs d'une violente campagne de presse contre la construction d'un tunnel au début des années 80. Alors qu'il avait déjà fait creuser une longue galerie d'environ deux kilomètres, Watkins (*dut/devait*) abandonner son projet sous la pression des militaires et des isolationnistes.

B The following statements comment on the text above. Fill the gaps with **celui de/du/de la**, etc. or **celui que/qui**, etc. as required.

1. Nombreux sont _____ l'idée d'un tunnel a fascinés.
2. Le projet le plus ancien d'un tunnel sous la Manche est _____ Mathieu.
3. Ni le projet de Mathieu, ni _____ Watkins ne purent être réalisés.
4. L'entreprise de Watkins est _____ fut le plus près d'aboutir.
5. Les objections des militaires ainsi que _____ isolationnistes firent échouer le projet de Watkins.

C *Thème.*

The United Nations Organisation was founded in 1945. Its mission is to maintain international peace and security and to promote co-operation between peoples. It is important not to confuse the various bodies.

- The General Assembly, which brings together all the member states of the United Nations, makes recommendations, although these are not mandatory.
- The Security Council is an executive body responsible for the maintenance of international security. For everything which falls within its remit, decisions are taken by majority vote. The ones that do not have the support of *all* the permanent Council members cannot be implemented.
- The Economic and Social Council, whose members are elected by the General Assembly, assists the latter in economic, social, cultural and humanitarian matters.
- The International Court arbitrates in disputes between member states of the United Nations. When the latter make an appeal to it, the decision made by the court is mandatory.

Sciences et techniques

A Emphasise the part of the sentence in italics by rewriting it using **c'est/ce sont … qui** or **c'est/ce sont … que.**

e.g. On doit les grandes avancées technologiques actuelles *aux militaires.*
→ C'est aux militaires qu'on doit les plus grandes avancées technologiques …

La technologie fille de la guerre

1. L'Amérique s'est intéressée aux recherches sur l'atome, *à la suite de l'humiliation de Pearl Harbour en 1943.*
2. De même, *la mise au point des bombes volantes V1 et V2 en Allemagne* a ouvert la voie à la conquête de l'espace.
3. Le premier calculateur électronique fut construit *pour calculer la trajectoire des premiers missiles balistiques intercontinentaux.*
4. Plus récemment, *les crédits militaires* ont permis à l'informatique, et plus généralement à l'électronique, de se développer à une allure stupéfiante.

B Rewrite the following sentences using the impersonal pronoun **il** to introduce the expressions in italics. Make all necessary changes.

e.g. Protéger les cultures *est essentiel* pour l'homme.
→ Il est essentiel pour l'homme de protéger les cultures.

Pesticides

1. De tout temps, se protéger contre tous les animaux nuisibles qui déciment les cultures et provoquent des famines *a été impératif* pour l'homme.
2. La prolifération des insectes ravageurs *est particulièrement difficile* à contrôler.
3. Recourir à des armes chimiques « lourdes » comme le DDT *s'est avéré dangereux* pour les insectes utiles et la santé de l'homme.
4. Contrecarrer le « boom démographique » de certains insectes, *c'est maintenant possible* grâce aux progrès réalisés en chimie organique et en biologie.
5. Les conséquences à long terme pour la santé humaine et l'environnement de la culture des plantes transgéniques *sont néanmoins malaisées à prévoir.*

C Write the verbs in brackets in the appropriate tense.

1. Lorsqu'on (*parler*) de technologie avancée, on pense surtout à l'informatique et aux biotechniques.
2. Tant que l'on (*ne pas connaître*) précisément les effets à long terme des produits transgéniques, il faudra faire preuve de prudence.
3. A mesure que l'on (*régler*) les problèmes, d'autres se présenteront.
4. Dès que les Américains et les Européens (*parvenir*) à un accord, la mise en place de systèmes multimédias par satellite s'accélèrera.

ce meaning *he, she, it, they*

1   **ce** can mean *he, she* and *they* as well as *it*. **ce** is used as a SUBJECT PRONOUN with **être**, **devoir être** and **pouvoir être**:

Ce sont des fonctionnaires	*They are civil servants*
C'est une grande vedette	*He is a great star*
Ç'a été un événement capital	*It was a decisive event*
Ce doit être la seule solution	*It must be the only solution*
Ce ne pouvait être qu'une erreur	*It could only be a mistake*

Note: before compound tenses the form **ç'** is used.

2   **ce** is generally used when **être** is followed by a NOUN or PRONOUN:

ce + être +	Monsieur Pernon, Martine, Serge, etc.; **un …, une …, des …** **le …, la …, les …** **mon …, ma …, mes …**, etc. **moi, toi, lui**, etc. **celui qui / que / dont**, etc.

C'est M. Pernon qui fut élu	*It was M. Pernon who was elected*
C'était un de nos candidats	*He was one of our candidates*
Ce devaient être des Français	*They must have been French*
C'était vous qui aviez raison	*You were the ones who were right*
C'est celle pour qui je voterai	*She is the one I will vote for*

il, ce and cela in formal French

3   In formal French, the IMPERSONAL SUBJECT PRONOUN **il** (and not **ce**) is used in EXPRESSIONS OF TIME:

Il était plus de minuit	*It was past midnight*
Il sera trop tard pour agir	*It will be too late to act*
Il est l'heure de partir	*It is time to go*

4   When **être** is followed by an ADJECTIVE, both **il** and **ce** are used to refer to a phrase or an idea rather than a specific noun.

  1. In formal French, **il** refers forward to something about to be mentioned:

  Il est surprenant que personne n'ait rien dit
  It's surprising that nobody said anything
  Il était essentiel de prendre une décision
  It was essential to make a decision
  Il est difficile de dire s'il a raison
  It is difficult to say whether he is right

  Note that the preposition **de** is used: **il est … de**.

2. **ce** is used to refer back to something just expressed:

> Personne n'a rien dit. **C'**est surprenant !
> *Nobody said anything. It is surprising!*
> Prendre une décision, **c'**était essentiel
> *Making a decision was essential*
> A-t-il raison ? **C'**est difficile à dire
> *Is he right? It is difficult to say*

Note that the preposition **à** is used: **c'est ... à**.

5   In formal French, **cela** (and not **ce** or **il**) is used to refer back to a phrase or an idea before verbs other than **être**:

> On augmentera le prix des cigarettes, mais **cela** ne **résoudra** rien
> *They will raise the price of cigarettes but it will not solve anything*
> Quel rôle a-t-il joué dans tout **cela** ?
> *What was his part in all that?*
> Les prisonniers se sont mutinés. **Cela s'était** déjà **produit** en mai dernier
> *The prisoners rioted. This had already happened last May*

In less formal French **cela** is abbreviated to **ça**:

> **Cela / Ça** ne la regarde pas   *This does not concern her*

Note that *this* tends to be translated by **cela**, not **ceci**, in modern French.

Using c'est ... qui and c'est ... que for emphasis

6   **c'est / ce sont ... qui** are used to emphasise the SUBJECT of the verb:

> **Les dirigeants** sont coupables   *The leaders are guilty*
> → **Ce sont** les dirigeants **qui** sont coupables

7   **c'est / ce sont ... que** are used to emphasise the DIRECT OBJECT of the verb:

> Ils veulent attirer **les jeunes**   *They want to attract young people*
> → **Ce sont les jeunes qu'**ils veulent attirer

8   **c'est ... que** is used to emphasise any other part of a sentence:

> L'Algérie obtint son indépendance **en 1962**
> *Algeria gained its independence in 1962*
> → **C'est** en 1962 **que** l'Algérie obtint son indépendance

> La situation a empiré **parce qu'on a trop attendu**
> *The situation worsened because they waited too long*
> → **C'est** parce qu'on a trop attendu **que** la situation a empiré

> Ces critiques s'adressaient **aux politiques**
> *Those criticisms were aimed at the politicians*
> → **C'est** aux politiques **que** s'adressaient ces critiques

Note the use of inversion in the last sentence.

9 As you can see from the examples on page 125 section 8, the present tense is generally used for emphasis (**c'est / ce sont … qui / que**).

Other tenses (imperfect, future, past historic) can be used provided that the same tense is used in both parts of the sentence:

> Ce **fut** en 1962 que l'Algérie **obtint** son indépendance
> **C'était** aux politiques que s'**adressaient** ces critiques

The future perfect tense

10 The FUTURE PERFECT TENSE is formed by using the FUTURE tense of **avoir** or **être** + PAST PARTICIPLE:

Example with **avoir**:

parler
j'**aurai** parlé
tu **auras** parlé
il / elle **aura** parlé
nous **aurons** parlé
vous **aurez** parlé
ils / elles **auront** parlé

Examples with **être**:

arriver	s'asseoir
je **serai** arrivé(e)	je me **serai** assis(e)
tu **seras** arrivé(e)	tu te **seras** assis(e)
il / elle **sera** arrivé(e)	il / elle se **sera** assis(e)
nous **serons** arrivé(e)s	nous nous **serons** assis(e)s
vous **serez** arrivé(e)(s)	vous vous **serez** assis(e)(s)
ils / elles **seront** arrivé(e)s	ils / elles se **seront** assis(e)s

See page 17, section 15–16 for PAST PARTICIPLE AGREEMENT RULES

11 The future perfect has its equivalent in English:

> Nous **aurons terminé** l'enquête avant lundi
> *We will have completed the investigation by Monday*
> J'**aurai** tout **fait** pour vous aider
> *I will have done everything to help you*

Tenses after conjunctions of time

12 Remember that the following conjunctions of time take the indicative:

aussitôt que	*as soon as*	lorsque	*when*
dès que	*as soon as*	quand	*when*
à mesure que	*as*	tant que	*for as long as*

See pages 107–108, sections 4–8 for more about conjunctions

13 With these conjunctions, the tenses used in French reflect time more closely than English. In the following examples, you will see that when future time is implied, a tense expressing the future is used in French:

Je règlerai **dès que je recevrai la facture**
I will pay as soon as I receive the invoice
Je règlerai **dès que j'aurai reçu la facture**
I will pay as soon as I have received the invoice
J'ai dit que je règlerais **dès que je recevrais la facture**
I said I would pay as soon as I received the invoice
J'ai dit que je règlerais **dès que j'aurais reçu la facture**
I said I would pay as soon as I had received the invoice

This table summarises the differences between French and English:

FRENCH	ENGLISH
FUTURE	PRESENT
dès que je recevrai …	*as soon as I receive …*
FUTURE PERFECT	PERFECT
dès que j'aurai reçu …	*as soon as I have received …*
CONDITIONAL	SIMPLE PAST
dès que je recevrais …	*as soon as I received …*
CONDITIONAL PERFECT	PLUPERFECT
dès que j'aurais reçu …	*as soon as I had received …*

14 The same tense rules apply to all the conjunctions of time listed in section 12 above:

Ils s'en souviendront **tant** qu'ils **vivront**
They will remember it for as long as they live
On sortira **dès que** la pluie **aura cessé**
We shall go out as soon as the rain has stopped
Ils ont déclaré qu'ils seraient prêts **lorsqu'**il le **faudrait**
They said they would be ready when the need arose
On pensait que l'ordre se rétablirait **quand** les esprits se **seraient calmés**
It was thought that order would return when tempers had cooled
Je t'avancerai de l'argent **à mesure que** tu en **auras** besoin
I shall give you money as you need it

A Complete the sentences with **il** (impersonal), **il(s)/elle(s)**, **ce** or **cela**.

Sciences et techniques : quelques définitions

1. *Les biotechnologies.* _____ est un mot qui désigne l'utilisation des propriétés de la matière vivante dans l'industrie. Les biotechnologies touchent des domaines extrêmement variés mais _____ est dans les secteurs de la santé, de l'agriculture et de l'alimentation que _____ sont les plus performantes.

2. *Les matières plastiques.* _____ symbolisent la civilisation du XXe siècle. _____ sont des polymères essentiellement produits à partir du pétrole. _____ remplacent les produits plus traditionnels (acier, bois, verre, etc.) et disposent d'un potentiel encore largement inexploité. _____ explique pourquoi certains chercheurs prétendent que l'histoire des matières plastiques n'en est qu'à ses débuts.

3. *Les matériaux composites.* La construction automobile et l'industrie aérospatiale font largement appel à de nouveaux matériaux : les composites. _____ sont, comme leur nom l'indique, des matériaux dans lesquels plusieurs constituants sont associés et qui possèdent un ensemble original de propriétés. _____ permettent, entre autres, de réaliser de grandes structures à la fois rigides, résistantes et légères. Ainsi, _____ est grâce à eux que les véhicules automobiles sont beaucoup plus performants aujourd'hui.

4. *Le laser*[1]. _____ est de plus en plus rare d'imprimer une lettre, d'écouter un disque ou même de passer un coup de téléphone sans recourir à la technologie du laser. Des supermarchés aux boîtes de nuit, des hôpitaux aux chantiers navals, _____ occupe une place essentielle dans la vie quotidienne et _____ ne fera que s'accentuer dans les années à venir.

B *Thème.*

It was Roland Dumas, then French Minister for Foreign Affairs, who launched the idea of a large European research programmme in the mid-1980s. He was convinced that once European governments had succeeded in encouraging an intensive exchange of information between companies and research institutes, the productivity and competitiveness of European industry would greatly improve. Some of his critics argued that, as a general rule, it is extremely difficult to ask competitors to share their secrets and that it is a mistake to believe that programmes of co-operation initiated by governments are more likely to succeed than spontaneous co-operation. As surprising as it may seem, given their position on the subject at the time, it was the British who supported the project most strongly.

---

[1] light amplification by simulated emission of radiation: *amplification de lumière par émission simulée de radiation*

Service information

A Using **jusqu' à**, **jusqu'à ce que**, **avant de**, **avant que** or **après** and the information given in brackets, complete each of the following sentences.

1. (*prendre le chemin des stations*)   Si vous suivez un traitement médical, consultez votre médecin _____ .

2. (*se lancer sur les pistes*)   Une mise en condition physique s'impose _____ , si vous êtes un sportif occasionnel.

3. (*se sentir en pleine possession de ses moyens*)   Respectez une progression dans la difficulté des exercices _____ .

4. (*passer une journée sur les pistes*)   _____ , donnez-vous le temps du repos.

5. (*le lendemain*)   Et enfin, en cas de mauvais temps, n'hésitez pas à remettre votre sortie _____ .

B *Version.*

Extrait de la loi « Informatique et Liberté »[1]

Article 1. « L'informatique doit être au service de chaque citoyen. Elle ne doit porter atteinte ni à l'identité humaine, ni aux droits de l'homme, ni à la vie privée, ni aux libertés individuelles ou publiques. »

Ce qu'il faut savoir sur l'existence des fichiers informatisés

– Il existe en France des centaines de milliers de fichiers. Chacun de nous est fiché plusieurs centaines de fois.

– C'est souvent utile : c'est grâce à eux que l'on peut, par exemple, greffer dans les plus brefs délais à un malade le rein d'un automobiliste tué dans un accident de la route.

– Mais c'est parfois inquiétant : des renseignements périmés, faux ou malveillants, peuvent vous porter préjudice ; des fichiers peuvent être utilisés abusivement par un tiers.

Ce qu'il faut savoir sur le droit d'accès et de rectification

– La Commission nationale de l'informatique et des libertés peut vous aider à savoir si vous figurez sur certains fichiers car tous les fichiers doivent lui être déclarés.

– Vous pouvez, si vous le voulez, consulter votre fiche. Pour cela, il faut vous adresser à l'organisme concerné.

– Vous pouvez faire modifier les informations vous concernant si elles sont inexactes. Signalez les erreurs. Le responsable du fichier devra procéder aux corrections nécessaires.

---

[1] *la loi « Informatique et Liberté »* : the data protection law

devoir, pouvoir, vouloir and falloir

1　Use **devoir** to express:

1. various ideas of OBLIGATION:

Elle **doit** signer le contrat	*She **has to / must** sign the contract*
	*She **is to / is due to** sign the contract*
	*She **is supposed to** sign the contract*
Vous **devriez** accepter son offre	*You **ought to / should** accept his offer*
J'aurais dû le dire	*I **ought to have / should have** said so*

2. PROBABILITY:

Il devait s'y attendre	*He **must have been** expecting it*
Elle **a dû** y réfléchir	*She **must have** thought about it*

2　Use **pouvoir** to express:

1. what someone is ABLE TO DO:

Il **pourra** bientôt se déplacer	*Soon he **will be able to** travel*
Vous **pouvez** bénéficier d'un prêt	*You **can** obtain a loan*
Cela **pourrait** se faire	*That **could** be arranged*

Note: **savoir**, <u>not</u> **pouvoir**, translates *can* when it means *to know how to*:

Savez-vous programmer?	*Can you program (a computer)?*

2. PERMISSION:

Vous **pouvez** fumer si vous voulez	*You **may** smoke if you wish*
Je ne **peux** pas quitter la région	*I **am** not **allowed to** leave the area*

3. POSSIBILITY:

Cela **peut** arriver à n'importe qui	*It **may / can** happen to anyone*
Ils **ont pu** faire une erreur	*They **may have** made a mistake*
Elle **pourrait le** regretter	*She **might** regret it*

4. REPROACH:

Vous **auriez pu** nous avertir	*You **might / could have** warned us*

3　Use **vouloir** to express:

1. WANTING, WISHING, LIKING:

On ne **voulait** pas de déchets	*We didn't **want** any waste*
Je ne **veux** pas que cela se sache	*I don't **wish** this **to** be known*
On **aurait voulu** éviter le conflit	*We **would have liked** to avoid conflict*

2. WILLINGNESS:

Ils **ont bien voulu** m'aider *They **were willing** to help me*
*They **were kind enough** to help me*

3. POLITE REQUESTS:

Veuillez accepter nos excuses *Please accept our apologies*

Note the use of **vouloir dire** and **en vouloir à quelqu'un**:

Que **veut dire** cette phrase ? *What does this sentence mean?*
Ne **lui** en **veuillez** pas *Do not hold it against him*

4 **falloir** is an impersonal verb, so **il** is always its subject. Use it:

1. with a NOUN, to express a NEED:

Il me **fallait** un soutien *I **needed** support*

See page 109, section 10 for use of indirect object pronouns with impersonal verbs

falloir ... pour is also used to express the TIME NEEDED to do something:

Il lui **a fallu** deux jours pour le finir *It **took** her two days to finish it*

2. with a verb, to express a NECESSARY COURSE OF ACTION:

Il faudra repartir à zéro *They **will have to** start again*
Il faut que la loi soit respectée *The law **must** be obeyed*

See page 109, section 9 for use of subjunctive after **il faut que**

Note: use **devoir**, not **falloir**, to express probability. See page 130, section 1.2.

5 Remember that the rules about use of tenses also apply to these verbs. For example, the distinction between the IMPERFECT and PERFECT tenses applies:

On **pouvait** recruter du personnel *We could (used to be able to) recruit staff*
On **a pu** recruter du personnel *We could (and did) recruit staff*

See page 24, section 11 for use of perfect and imperfect tenses

You can see from the translations of the examples on page 130–131, sections 1–4 that there is often a change of meaning according to the tense used:

| Je **devais** partir lundi | *I **was supposed** to leave on Monday*
*I **was to leave** on Monday*
*I **was due to leave** on Monday* |
| J'ai **dû** partir lundi | *I **had to leave** on Monday*
*I **must have left** on Monday* |

après, avant **and** pendant

6 **après** (*after*) is used as follows:

après	+ NOUN
après	+ PAST INFINITIVE where the subject is the same
après que	+ SUBJUNCTIVE where the subject is not the same

après + NOUN

Elle a démissioné **après les négociations**
She resigned after the negotiations

après + PAST INFINITIVE where the subject is the same

Elle a démissioné **après avoir entamé les négociations**
She resigned after starting the negotiations

après que + SUBJUNCTIVE where the subject is not the same

Elle a démissioné **après qu'ils aient entamé les négociations**
She resigned after they started the negotiations

Note that **après que** traditionally takes the indicative but is nowadays mainly used with the subjunctive.

7 **avant** (*before*) is used as follows:

avant	+	NOUN
avant de	+	PAST INFINITIVE where the subject is the same
avant que	+	SUBJUNCTIVE where the subject is not the same

avant + NOUN

Il fera une déclaration **avant la séance**
He will make a statement before the meeting

avant de + PAST INFINITIVE where the subject is the same

Il fera une déclaration **avant de participer à la séance**
He will make a statement before taking part in the meeting

avant que + SUBJUNCTIVE where the subject is not the same

Il fera une déclaration **avant que la séance commence**
He will make a statement before the meeting begins

8 **pendant** (*during / while*) is used as follows:

pendant	+	NOUN
pendant que	+	INDICATIVE whether the subject changes or not

pendant + NOUN

Vous avez changé d'attitude **pendant la grève**
You changed your attitude during the strike

pendant que + INDICATIVE whether the subject changes or not

Vous avez changé d'attitude **pendant que vous étiez en grève**
You changed your attitude while you were on strike
Vous avez changé d'attitude **pendant que les employés étaient** en grève
You changed your attitude while the employees were on strike

Using jusqu'à, avant and attendre to express *until*

9 **jusqu'à** (*until*) is used as follows:

jusqu'à	+	NOUN
jusqu'à ce que	+	SUBJUNCTIVE whether the subject changes or not

jusqu'à + NOUN

Nous persévérerons **jusqu'au printemps prochain**
We shall persevere until next spring

jusqu'à ce que + SUBJUNCTIVE whether the subject changes or not

Nous persévérerons **jusqu'à ce que nous obtenions des résultats**
We shall persevere until we get results
Nous persévérerons **jusqu'à ce que les résultats soient positifs**
We shall persevere until the results are positive

10 After a negative verb, use **avant / avant de / avant que** (see section 7):

Ne fais rien **avant de** me parler   *Don't do anything until you talk to me*

11 To express *to wait until*, use **attendre** as follows:

attendre	+	NOUN
attendre de	+	INFINITIVE where the subject is the same
attendre que	+	SUBJUNCTIVE where the subject is not the same

attendre + NOUN

J'attendrai **le printemps**   *I shall wait until spring*

attendre de + INFINITIVE where the subject is the same

J'attendrai **de le voir**   *I shall wait until I see him*

attendre que + SUBJUNCTIVE where the subject is not the same

J'attendrai **que tu sois** d'accord   *I shall wait until you agree*

A Write the verbs in brackets in the appropriate tense.

Au restaurant : vos droits

• *Dernièrement, j'ai trouvé une erreur dans ma note de restaurant. Si le propriétaire n'avait pas accepté de la rectifier, quelle attitude* (je – devoir) *adopter ?*
RÉPONSE Vous (*pouvoir*) lui payer ce que vous estimiez lui devoir. S'il avait refusé votre argent, (*falloir*) alors prévenir la Direction départementale de la concurrence et de la consommation.
• *Le nom du plat que j'avais commandé ne correspondait pas du tout à ce que l'on m'a servi.* (Falloir) *refuser de le payer ?*
RÉPONSE On (*devoir*) vous servir autre chose à la place. La prochaine fois, (*falloir*) insister et prendre les autres clients à témoin.

B Fill the gaps with the present or the infinitive of **devoir, pouvoir, falloir, vouloir, vouloir dire** and **savoir**.

Accession à la propriété

L'achat d'un logement compte parmi les gestes les plus importants de la vie. Si on _____ le réussir, _____ mettre toutes les chances de son côté.

Pour ne pas finir au contentieux[1], _____ être capable de faire un budget et de s'y tenir. Le coût de l'installation _____ être examiné avec soin. Un couple qui dispose de solides revenus _____ parfaitement s'en tirer moins bien qu'un ménage plus modeste qui, lui, _____ épargner. Non seulement il n'est pas drôle de finir au contentieux, mais les conséquences psychologiques _____ être désastreuses.

Aujourd'hui encore, on achète trop sur un coup de cœur. Si l'on ne _____ pas s'empoisonner la vie, la première question que _____ se poser, c'est « j'achète où ? » et non pas « j'achète quoi ? ». Y a-t-il des commerces, des transports en commun, des espaces verts ? On _____ ensuite se demander si ce dont on a envie correspond à ce dont on a besoin. Et enfin, méfiez-vous des modèles témoins « non-contractuels », ce qui _____ que la maison que vous achetez ne ressemble pas à celle qu'on vous montre.

C *Thème.*
What you need to know before planning a holiday abroad.
– *Passports.* Each member of a family should have his or her own passport. Children may be included on the passport of their parents, but cannot use it on their own.
– *Visas.* You may need a visa. Apply to the consulate of the country concerned well in advance. Do not wait until it is too late to apply.
– *Personal insurance policy.* It is advisable to take out a personal insurance policy. Should you have any claim to make, wait until you return.
– *Foreign currency.* If you take a suitable bank card with you, you will be able to make withdrawals at cash dispensers while abroad.

[1] *le contentieux* : litigation

A Here are some arguments against advertising. Fill the gaps using suitable pronouns: **il, elle, ce, cela, celui/celle**, etc. or **celui-ci/celle-ci**, etc.

La pub : information ou piège ?

On dit que la publicité informe. _____ est faux. Au sens propre, le mot publicité a le sens de faire connaître _____ qui est d'intérêt public. Mais en réalité à quoi sert la publicité sinon à vendre ? _____ n'éclaire pas le public ; _____ le manipule.

On prétend aussi que la publicité favorise la vie économique. _____ est faux. _____ est prouvé que l'augmentation du pouvoir d'achat aide davantage la consommation que toutes les publicités réunies. En vérité, _____ que la publicité favorise, _____ est la surconsommation de _____ qui ont déjà les moyens de consommer.

Enfin, faire croire que le bonheur est dans la consommation, _____ est répandre une illusion nocive. Bien des jeunes restent esclaves des modèles publicitaires parce que _____ les empêchent de découvrir leur idéal de vie authentique. Tout _____ est bien inquiétant.

B Put the verbs that are in the past historic and the imperfect into the present tense. Note the dramatic effect this has on this account of past events.

Hiroshima et Nagasaki, 6 et 9 août 1945

Le temps était clair et la journée s'annonçait belle. Il était huit heures et les habitants d'Hiroshima étaient au travail. La radio annonça l'approche de trois bombardiers américains puis, à 8h 15 exactement, une lumière aveuglante déchira l'horizon. La bombe venait d'éclater. Tout de suite après, des ondes de chaleur insupportables s'abattirent sur la ville qui se mit à brûler. Ensuite, une gigantesque montagne de nuages fit son apparition dans le ciel. Enfin, dix minutes plus tard une espèce de pluie noire tomba sur la ville.

Les habitants d'Hiroshima ignorèrent sur le moment qu'ils venaient d'être victimes de la première bombe atomique. Quelque 70 000 personnes périrent immédiatement et le nombre de victimes doubla au cours des mois suivants.

Trois jours après le bombardement d'Hiroshima, la ville de Nagasaki fut la cible du second bombardement nucléaire de l'histoire. Quelque 20 000 personnes moururent le jour même et 50 000 autres au cours de l'année 1945.

C The following statements comment on the text above. Rewrite them so as to emphasise the information in italics.

e.g. *La radio* a annoncé l'approche de trois B29 américains.
→ C'est la radio qui a annoncé l'approche de trois B29 américains.

1. *Des bombardiers américains* ont lâché la première bombe atomique.
2. La bombe a éclaté à *8h 15 exactement*.
3. *Une espèce de pluie noire* s'est abattue sur la ville dix minutes plus tard.
4. Les Américains ont ensuite pris *la ville de Nagasaki* pour cible.
5. La ville de Nagasaki a été bombardée *trois jours après Hiroshima*.

D Rewrite the following interview in formal French by replacing **ce** and **ça** with the appropriate pronoun where necessary.

Un acteur répond à nos questions

- *Pour quelles raisons avez-vous tourné le film qui sort cette semaine ?*
- J'ai accepté par estime pour le réalisateur. Et en raison, aussi, de la qualité des autres participants. C'est rare qu'un film réunisse les meilleurs comédiens d'un pays.
- *Vous avez souvent déclaré choisir vos films en fonction du réalisateur. J'ai l'impression que c'est une constante chez vous.*
- Ça m'a toujours paru essentiel. Ça correspond, chez moi, à une certaine idée du cinéma. C'est important de travailler avec des gens intègres qui ne font pas n'importe quoi sous prétexte de remplir les salles.
- *C'est pour des raisons semblables que vous êtes passé de l'autre côté de la caméra pour devenir vous-même réalisateur ?*
- C'était une progression naturelle. Et puis j'aime voir travailler les acteurs. Je trouve ça absolument fascinant.

E *Thème.*

1. Although it has hardly been spoken of recently, noise is on its way to becoming[1] the major scourge of our society. As is often the case, we have waited until the number of people with hearing impairments has considerably increased before assessing the extent of the problem. Noise pollution affects first and foremost town dwellers and those who live near an airport or a motorway, but it does concern us all. Our health will be at risk as long as the authorities do not take drastic measures.
2. The introduction of new varieties of cereals may have helped in the fight against hunger in the Third World, but one should not forget that it has also caused serious environmental change. The introduction of[2] genetically engineered plants might have similar consequences.
3. Many environmentalists fear that governments will continue to exploit fossil fuels until all the resources are exhausted, without investing enough in alternative energy sources. As long as this attitude prevails, there will be cause for[3] concern.

---

[1] to be on one's way to …ing : *être en passe de* + infinitive
[2] translate as 'that of' to avoid repetition
[3] use *de quoi* (see page 150, section 14)

La loi et le citoyen

A Replace each infinitive by the past participle and make an agreement if necessary.

Sécurité : les contrôles d'identité se multiplient

Les contrôles d'identité (*déclencher*) en octobre par le ministre de l'Intérieur ont entraîné une augmentation sensible de la présence policière dans la rue. Or, si la grande majorité des policiers fait correctement son travail, force est de constater que certains d'entre eux se livrent à des excès de zèle difficilement justifiables. De nombreuses bavures ont été (*signaler*) depuis quelques mois.

En voici deux illustrations. A Marseille, deux jeunes Maghrébins sont (*contrôler*) : ils montrent leurs papiers mais refusent de se laisser fouiller. Ils auraient, semble-t-il, eu droit à une correction en règle. Autre anecdote : cinq mineurs (*interpeller*) à Paris en fin de journée ont passé la nuit au poste de police sans que leurs parents soient (*alerter*).

Le ministre délégué à la sécurité affirme que tout ceci n'est qu'une campagne politique (*diriger*) contre le gouvernement. Les policiers, quant à eux, sont partagés. Certains considèrent qu'une poignée de bavures ont été (*monter*) en épingle et qu'il leur arrive souvent d'être eux-mêmes (*insulter*) ou (*agresser*). D'autres estiment que leurs collègues sont (*pousser*) à faire des interpellations et s'en inquiètent.

B *Version.*

Expulsion

Necmettin Erim, sa femme et ses trois enfants, qui ne disposaient pas de titre de séjour régulier, ont été expulsés de France, lundi dernier. Ils auraient été dénoncés[1] par leur propriétaire. Arrivé en 1997 en France, Necmettin Erim s'est vu refuser le statut de réfugié, pourtant accordé à son frère pour des motifs comparables.

Sa demande est[2] définitivement rejetée à l'automne dernier et le 13 avril, la préfecture signe son arrêt d'expulsion. Le jour même, Madame Erim et ses enfants sont arrêtés à leur domicile, en l'absence du chef de famille. A son retour, celui-ci se précipite chez son avocat qui refuse de le remettre aux policiers, venus entre-temps l'appréhender. Il faudra plus de trois heures de négociations pour que les autorités acceptent d'assouplir leur attitude. Si Monsieur Erim accepte de se livrer, il ne sera pas menotté et on lui laissera quelques heures pour liquider ses biens.

Dans ce cas comme dans bien d'autres, la loi a été appliquée dans toute sa fermeté mais les méthodes employées ont été, pour le moins, expéditives.

---

[1] voir page 149, section 11
[2] the present tense is commonly used for dramatic effect when relating past events

Passive constructions

See page 14, section 1 for explanation of SUBJECT, DIRECT OBJECT = and INDIRECT OBJECT

1 Any active sentence with a SUBJECT, VERB and DIRECT OBJECT can be changed into a PASSIVE sentence:

	SUBJECT	ACTIVE VERB	DIRECT OBJECT
ACTIVE SENTENCE	Greenpeace	ont alerté	la presse
	Greenpeace	*alerted the press*	

	SUBJECT	PASSIVE VERB	**par** + NOUN
PASSIVE SENTENCE	La presse	a été alertée	par Greenpeace
	The press	*were alerted*	*by Greenpeace*

Note that **la presse**, DIRECT OBJECT of the active sentence, becomes the SUBJECT of the passive sentence.
Passive constructions are common in formal French:

> La déclaration a été approuvée par le ministre
> *The statement was approved by the Minister*

2 An active sentence can only be turned into a passive sentence if the object is DIRECT. For example, the active sentence:

> Ils ont prié **cette personne** de partir
> *They asked this person to leave*

can be turned into a passive sentence because **prier** takes a DIRECT OBJECT:

> **Cette personne** a été priée de partir
> *This person was asked to leave*

The following sentence, however, <u>cannot</u> be turned into a passive sentence because **demander** takes an INDIRECT OBJECT:

> Ils ont demandé à cette personne de partir

3 Shortened versions of PASSIVE constructions are widely used. In the following examples, the person or thing doing the action is not mentioned:

> Les missiles **seront** bientôt **déployés**
> *The missiles will soon be deployed*
> Leur visite aurait dû **être annoncée**
> *Their visit should have been announced*

Note that the past participle is often all that remains of a passive construction:

> Une fois **publiée**, cette déclaration causera un scandale
> *Once (it has been) published, this statement will cause an outcry*

4   Passive verbs consist of **être** + PAST PARTICIPLE. Examples of tenses:

PRESENT INFINITIVE	la presse devrait **être alertée**
PAST INFINITIVE	après **avoir été alertée** ...
PRESENT	la presse **est alertée**
PERFECT	la presse **a été alertée**
IMPERFECT	la presse **était alertée**
PLUPERFECT	la presse **avait été alertée**
FUTURE	la presse **sera alertée**
CONDITIONAL	la presse **serait alertée**
PRESENT SUBJUNCTIVE	... que la presse **soit alertée**
PERFECT SUBJUNCTIVE	... que la presse **ait été alertée**

5   In common with other constructions using **être**, the PAST PARTICIPLE always agrees with the SUBJECT in a passive construction:

La déclaration a été approuvée par le ministre

6   When using the passive, remember the difference between the PERFECT TENSE (completed action) and the IMPERFECT TENSE (continuing or habitual action):

Les consignes de sécurité **ont été appliquées**
The safety regulations were enforced (and are now in place)
Les consignes de sécurité **étaient appliquées**
The safety regulations were enforced (were being enforced at that time)

See page 24, section 11 for the uses of the perfect and imperfect tenses

Other ways of expressing English passive constructions

See page 147, section 2 for **on** + verb to translate English passive constructions

7   Other constructions can be used instead of the passive.

1. **on** can be used when a passive is not possible, for example where the verb takes an indirect object and not a direct object (see section 6 above):

On a demandé à cette personne de partir   *They asked this person to leave*
On m'a montré les dégâts   *I was shown the damage*

2. **se voir** + INFINITIVE and **se faire** + INFINITIVE can be the equivalent of an English passive construction:

Il **s'est vu refuser**   *He was refused*
Elle **s'est fait renverser** par une voiture   *She was run over by a car*

3. Other reflexive constructions are often favoured instead of passives:

C'est un produit qui **se vend** partout
It is a product which is sold everywhere
La transaction **s'est faite** lundi
The transaction was carried out on Monday

A Put the verbs in brackets into the passive, selecting the appropriate tense from the following: perfect, imperfect, pluperfect.

Deux évadés retrouvés

Deux évadés de la prison des Baumettes (*retrouver*) dimanche matin dans un village de l'Hérault. Les deux hommes (*localiser*) grâce à un commerçant qui avait vu leur photo au journal télévisé de vingt heures, et a reconnu l'un d'entre eux. Ils (*interpeller*) alors qu'ils s'apprêtaient à reprendre la route. Ils (*ne pas armer*) et n'ont opposé aucune résistance.

La camionnette qui avait servi à leur évasion (*retrouver*) la veille près de Montélimar. Les deux détenus (*condamner*) pour attaques à main armée, en juin dernier.

B Rewrite the following sentences using a passive construction to replace the words in italics.

e.g. Le nombre de documents *qu'on exige* s'est multiplié.
→ Le nombre de documents qui sont exigés s'est multiplié.

Vos papiers !

1. Depuis quelques mois, *on a renforcé* les dispositifs de contrôle des conditions d'entrée et de séjour en France des non ressortissants européens.
2. Plusieurs exemples récents montrent *qu'on applique* ces dispositions avec la plus grande sévérité.
3. *On a refoulé* de nombreux ressortissants algériens au cours du mois dernier.
4. Ainsi *on a rapatrié* de façon expéditive une vieille dame algérienne, venue rendre visite à ses enfants.
5. Dans certaines capitales arabes, *on ressent* très mal ces dispositions.

C *Thème.*

Explosion at a chemical factory. One person was killed and a dozen slightly injured on Friday evening as a result of the explosion of a tank at a chemical factory. Three other tanks were also damaged. According to the police, the smoke cloud which was given off is not toxic. An inquiry into the causes of the accident has just been set up.

Terrorism. Following last week's bomb attack in Paris, some 1,000[1] soldiers have been called in to[2] patrol France's stations and airports; all left luggage facilities have been closed down and wastebins removed. In addition, the managers of large supermarkets have been urged to[3] work with the police to improve evacuation procedures.

[1] see pages 142–143, sections 1–9
[2] use *faire appel à quelqu'un pour* + infinitive
[3] use *conseiller vivement à quelqu'un de* + infinitive

Les données socio-économiques

A Rewrite the sentences, writing out the numbers in full.

e.g. Il y a 12 places de libre. → Il y a douze places de libre.

1. Nous avons eu quelque 2 800 visiteurs cette année.
2. Les ventes ont atteint un chiffre record : 7 590 000 francs.
3. Le bilan des accidents de la route a été de 380 morts en juillet.
4. Le nombre des victimes s'élève à 51.
5. Notre club compte 155 membres.
6. Ce jeu-concours a suscité près de 1 000 réponses.

B Give the French for the words in brackets.

1. 74 % des moins de 35 ans, [as opposed to] 61 % des plus de 35 ans, déclarent avoir accompli au moins une tâche domestique dans les dernières 24 heures.
2. Le nombre de réfugiés recensés par le Haut Commissariat des Nations unies pour les réfugiés atteint 4 563 600, [of which] 700 000 au Liban.
3. En raison de la grève des contrôleurs aériens, Air France a annulé six vols [out of] les 290 prévus aujourd'hui.
4. A la fin du mois dernier, cette entreprise comptait 3 000 salariés, [that is] 800 de moins que l'an dernier.
5. Le prix du cuivre a augmenté de [some] 20 % tandis que le plomb progressait de 17,5 %.

C *Version.*

1. Le taux de natalité a diminué en moyenne de 40 % depuis 1962, passant de 2,7 enfants par couple à 1,7.
2. Les plus de 65 ans représentaient moins de 5 % de la population vers 1850. Ils sont aujourd'hui près de 15 %. En 2020, ils devraient dépasser 20 %. Parmi eux, le nombre des plus de 85 ans serait supérieur à 2 millions.
3. Sur 800 000 personnes en âge de se marier, 600 000 se marient. 200 000 divorcent avant cinq ans, soit 33 %. 16,6 % des divorcés se remarient, dont 50 % avec un célibataire.
4. La cohabitation, ou union libre, poursuit sa progression. Les naissances hors mariage ont franchi le seuil de 30 % des naissances.
5. Selon les démographes, la population active (personnes titulaires d'un emploi ou en cherchant un) devrait augmenter de 1,5 millions de personnes d'ici à 2015, et atteindrait un total de 28 millions (contre 26,5 millions aujourd'hui).
6. Alors qu'avant la Seconde Guerre mondiale, deux Français sur dix vivaient en ville, ils sont aujourd'hui huit sur dix.

Use of commas and full stops in numbers

1 A comma is used in French where a decimal point is used in English:

6,5 milliards de dollars	*6.5 billion dollars*
un taux de 2,3 pour cent	*a rate of 2.3 per cent*
7,50 francs le litre	*7.50 francs per litre*

A full stop or a space is used in French to denote *thousands*:

3.000 francs / 3 000 francs	*3,000 francs*

How to spell numbers

2 Hyphens are inserted in compound numbers except before and after **et**, **cent** and **mille**:

quarante-trois jours	BUT	quarante et un jours
quatre-vingt-un membres	BUT	soixante et onze membres
trente-neuf victimes	BUT	cent trente-neuf victimes
soixante-quinze voix	BUT	mille soixante-quinze voix

3 **vingt** and **cent** take an **-s** when they are multiplied, unless they are followed by another number:

quatre-vingts ans	BUT	quatre-vingt-onze ans
cinq cents blessés	BUT	cinq cent trente blessés

4 **mille** (a thousand) never takes **-s**:

trente mille hommes

5 Do not use **un** before **cent** and **mille**:

mille réfugiés	*a / one thousand refugees*
cent voix	*a / one hundred votes*

6 The numbers **million** and **milliard** are NOUNS. Use **un / des** or a number before them, add **-s** when they are plural and use **de** before the next noun:

un million **de** réfugiés	*a / one million refugees*
deux milliards **de** francs	*two thousand million francs / two billion francs*

How to present approximate numbers

7 The following nouns are used to express approximate numbers. There is no direct equivalent for these words in English:

une dizaine	une cinquantaine
une vingtaine	une soixantaine
une trentaine	une centaine
une quarantaine	un millier

une dizaine d'années	*a decade or so*
une centaine de jours	*about a hundred days*
un millier de victimes	*around a thousand victims*
des milliers de gens	*thousands of people*
des centaines de milliers de victimes	*hundreds of thousands of victims*

Note the use of an article (**un, une, des**) before these expressions.

8 **près de, autour de** or **quelque** can also be used:

près de six millions de téléspectateurs	*about six million viewers*
autour de soixante-dix milliards d'euros	*around seventy billion euros*
quelque dix mille personnes	*about / some ten thousand people*

Note that **quelque**, when used to mean *about* or *some*, is always SINGULAR.

9 **environ** and **vers** are often used to express approximate distance or time:

à une distance d'**environ** 7 000 km	*at a distance of about 7,000 kms*
vers deux heures	*at about two o'clock*

Expressing *more* and *less*, *over* and *under*, *from* and *to*

10 When **plus** and **moins** INTRODUCE a figure they are followed by **de**:

Le prix de l'essence a connu une hausse de **plus de** 5 %
The price of petrol has increased by more than 5 %

11 When **plus** and **moins** FOLLOW a figure, they are introduced by **de**:

deux cents sièges **de moins**
two hundred fewer seats

12 After the verb **être**, use **supérieur à** and **inférieur à** rather than **de plus de** and **de moins de**:

Le nombre d'habitants est **supérieur à** 55 millions
The number of inhabitants is over 55 million
Le coût de l'affaire est nettement **inférieur** à quatre milliards de francs
The cost of the deal is well below four billion francs

13 To indicate a range, use **de ... à**:

Le gouvernement anticipe une hausse des prix **de** 2 **à** 3 %
The government anticipates a price rise of 2 to 3 %

See also page 144, sections 14–18 for other uses of **à** and **de**

How to present one figure

14 Use **être à** to indicate a level, and **être de** when you just give the figure:

    L'inflation **est à** 3 %   *Inflation is at 3 %*
    Le taux d'inflation **est de 3** %   *The rate of inflation is 3 %*

15 You can also use the verbs **s'élever à** (*to rise*) or **atteindre** (*to reach*):

    Le montant des effectifs **s'élève à** 2 000 salariés
    The total workforce is 2,000 employees
    Le déficit du commerce extérieur **atteint** plusieurs milliards de dollars
    The foreign trade deficit amounts to several billion dollars

Expressing upward and downward trends and changes

16 To show an UPWARD TREND, use **augmenter de** (*to increase ...*), **progresser de** (*to go up ...*) or **s'accroître de** (*to grow / increase ...*) to show by how much the number has increased:

    La population mondiale a **augmenté de** quelque 80 millions d'habitants
    The world population has increased by some 80 million people

17 To show a DOWNWARD TREND, use **diminuer de** (*to decrease ...*), **baisser de** (*to fall ...*), **chuter de** (*to fall ...*) or **être réduit de** (*to be reduced ...*) to show by how much the figure has decreased:

    Le nombre des demandeurs d'emploi **a diminué de** 0,4 %
    The number of unemployed people has dropped by 0.4 %

18 To show a CHANGE, use **de** (*from*) and **à** (*to*) with **passer, tomber** (*to drop*), **relever** (*to raise*), **ramener** (*to bring down*) or **abaisser** (*to lower*):

    De 7 % en 1985, l'inflation **a été ramenée** à 3,5 % en 1987
    Inflation was brought down from 7 per cent in 1985 to 3.5 % in 1987
    Les importations japonaises **sont passées** de 30 % à 30,6 % en deux ans
    Japanese imports rose from 30 % to 30.6 % within two years

Note that when **de ... à** is used with **augmenter, s'accroître, réduire, diminuer, baisser** or with the noun corresponding to each of these verbs, it indicates a range, not a change:

    Le nombre de bidonvilles augmente chaque année **de** 10 % à 12 %
    *The number of slums rises **by between** 10 % and 12 % every year*

See page 143, section 13 for use of **de** and **à** to indicate a range

Expressing contrast and proportion

19 To CONTRAST figures, use **contre**, and to show a PROPORTION, use **sur**:

Le taux est de 6 %, **contre** 6,5 %   *The rate is 6 % as opposed to 6.5 %*
On a licencié deux salariés **sur** cinq   *Two employees out of five were laid off*

More about verbs used to present figures

20 **s'accroître** (*to grow / increase*) and the noun **un accroissement** imply a
build-up. Use them to indicate an increase in population, production or
wealth, and to comment on socio-economic trends:

La production alimentaire **s'est accrue** de 29 % en dix ans
Food production increased by 29 % within a decade
L'**accroissement** de la violence est inquiétant
The increase in violent crime is worrying

While **accroître**, which takes a direct object, implies an ACTION,
s'accroître, which has no object, indicates a PROCESS:

On **a accru** les bénéfices   *We have increased the profits*
Les bénéfices **se sont accrus**   *The profits have increased*

Note that **accroître** and **un accroissement** are not used for prices and
wages.

21 **augmenter** (*to increase*) and the noun **une augmentation** are more widely
used than **accroître, s'accroître, un accroissement**, and can replace
them:

On **a augmenté** les bénéfices   *We have increased the profits*
Les bénéfices **ont augmenté**   *The profits have increased*

22 The use of **croître** (*to grow*) and the noun **une croissance**, and **décroître**
(*to decrease*) and the noun **une diminution** is limited. They indicate the rate
of growth:

L'économie **croît** au ralenti   *The economy is growing slowly*

23 **relever** (*to raise*) and the noun **un relèvement**, and **abaisser** (*to lower*) and
the noun **un abaissement** are used when an official body raises or lowers
something:

Le Smic **a été relevé** en mars   *The minimum wage was raised in March*

24 Three more useful verbs with figures: **représenter** and **constituer** (*to make
up*), and **comprendre** (*to consist of / include / comprise*):

Le blé **représente** 19 % de la production
Wheat makes up 19 % of production
Aujourd'hui il en **constitue** 19,5 %
Today it is 19.5 %
Le conseil **comprend** 11 membres
The council consists of 11 members

A After examining the tables, fill in the gaps with the appropriate words (**inférieur à, augmentation, représenter**, etc.).

Activité professionnelle des femmes dans la région d'Aix

Taux d'activité des femmes de 25 à 55 ans
- femmes sans enfants .... 74,7 %
- femmes avec 1 ou 2 enfants .... 69,8 %
- femmes avec 3 enfants ou plus .... 38,1 %

Part des femmes parmi	1988	1998	Évolution
– les ouvriers spécialisés (OS)	28 %	31 %	+ 3
– les ouvriers qualifiés	14 %	11 %	– 3

1. Parmi les femmes sans enfants le taux d'activité est _____ 74 %, mais parmi celles qui ont un ou deux enfants il est _____ 70 %.
2. Quand les femmes ont trois enfants ou plus, leur taux d'activité _____ 38,1 %.
3. Les femmes _____ 28 % des OS en 1988.
4. La part des femmes parmi les OS est en _____ : 31 % en 1998, _____ 28 % en 1988.
5. Quant à la part des femmes parmi les ouvriers qualifiés, elle _____ de 14 % à 11 % entre 1988 et 1998, soit une _____ de 3 %.

B Fill the gaps, using **être abaissé, baisser, passer, s'accroître** or **augmenter** in the appropriate tense.

1. L'âge de la retraite _____ de 65 à 60 ans dans certains pays.
2. Le nombre de touristes qui se rendent en Chine _____ considérablement.
3. Selon les estimations, la TVA devrait _____ de 1 à 2 %.
4. Le pourcentage de réussite _____ de 51 % à 67 % en moins de cinq ans.
5. Le taux d'échec _____ cette année : 5 % contre 7 % l'an dernier.

C *Thème.*

1. From 1975 to 1987, the birth rate in developed countries dropped on average by 28.6 %.
2. In the year 2020, people under 25 will make up[1] 27.5 % of the working population.
3. Today, between a thousand and fifteen hundred refugees arrive in Europe every month.
4. Out of a salaried population of 15.5 million, only some 10 % are members of a union.
5. They have just been awarded a 5 % rise.
6. The number of unemployed young people will reach some 900,000.
7. Economic growth was 3 to 4 % on average per year in the mid 1990s.
8. The inflation rate had been reduced from 4.2 % in 1996 to 3.5 % in 1997, but in 1998 it increased again to over 4 %.
9. Last year, France showed[2] a foreign trade deficit of 27.3 billion francs.

[1] use conditional tense and see page 149, section 11.
[2] use *enregistrer*

Use of on (and l'on)

1 **on** is an INDEFINITE subject pronoun used to refer to an unspecified person:

Maintenant **on** peut faire **ses** courses à domicile grâce à Internet
Now one can do one's shopping at home thanks to the Internet
Quand **on** est plusieurs, **on se** sent moins vulnérable
When there are several of you, you feel less vulnerable

2 Note that there is a slight difference in emphasis between **on** + VERB and a
passive construction. With **on** + active verb, the emphasis is on the <u>action</u>:

On l'a condamné à la réclusion à perpétuité
He was condamned to life imprisonment

With a passive construction, the emphasis is on <u>the outcome</u>:

Il a été condamné à la réclusion à perpétuité
His sentence was life imprisonment

3 As with the other indefinite pronouns (**chacun**, **personne**, **nul**), the
emphatic pronoun **soi** is used with **on** when it is used to mean *you, one* or
people:

On est bien chez **soi**   *It's good to be in your own home*

Note that **vous** is the object pronoun used:

Quand quelqu'un **vous** offre des conseils, **on** ne peut qu'écouter
When someone offers you advice, all you can do is listen

4 **on** is used frequently in informal French to mean *we*, in which case the object
pronoun used is **nous**:

Si **on** l'appelle, il viendra **nous** chercher   *If we call him, he will pick us up*

Note that past participles and adjectives agree according to the meaning:

On est tomb**és** sur lui par hasard   *We (masc.) ran into him by chance*
On était trop fatigu**ées** pour sortir   *We (fem.) were too tired to go out*

5 Use **l'on**, after **et, ou, où, que** and **si** in formal French:

La situation des handicapés s'aggravera **si l'on** ne répond pas à
leurs besoins
The plight of disabled people will get worse if we do not meet their needs

Note that **on** and <u>not</u> **l'on** is used before words beginning with the letter **l**:

Leur situation s'aggravera **si on les** traite comme des marginaux
Their plight will get worse if we marginalise them

Impersonal expressions il suffit de and il s'agit de

6   **il suffit de** (*it is enough ...*) is followed by a NOUN or an INFINITIVE:

> **Il suffit d'**une seule panne pour que toute la production soit arrêtée
> *One breakdown is enough to stop the whole production*
> Si vous avez besoin de quoi que ce soit, **il** vous **suffit de** me le faire savoir
> *If you need anything at all, just let me know*

7   **il s'agit de** (*it is a matter of ...*) is followed by a NOUN, a PRONOUN or an INFINITIVE:

> **De** quoi **s'agit il** ?   *What is it about?*
> **De** qui **s'agit il** ?   *Who is it about?*
> **Il s'agit de** lui   *It's about him*
> Je me souviens de **ce dont il s'agit**   *I remember what it's about*

Note that **il s'agit de** + INFINITIVE sometimes means the same as **il faut**:

> **Il** ne s'agit pas **de** s'affoler   *We / you / they must not panic*
> **Il s'agit** avant tout **de** le lui dire   *We must first of all tell her*

Subjunctive after indefinite expressions

8   Use the subjunctive in the following indefinite expressions:

qui que vous **soyez**	*whoever you are*
à qui que vous **parliez**	*whoever you talk to*
quoi que vous **fassiez**	*whatever you do*
où que vous **alliez**	*wherever you go*
d'où que vous **veniez**	*wherever you come from*

> Avez-vous besoin de **quoi que ce soit** ?
> *Do you need anything (at all)?*
> Il a refusé de parler à **qui que ce soit**   *He refused to talk to anybody*
> Je n'ai pas l'intention d'aller **où que ce soit**   *I don't intend to go anywhere*

Note the difference between **quoi que** (two words) and **quoique** (one word):

> Le parti la soutiendra **quoi qu'il** arrive
> *The party will support her whatever happens*
> Le parti la soutiendra **quoiqu'elle** ait perdu de sa popularité
> *The party will support her although she is less popular*

9   Use the subjunctive after **quel que**. **quel** agrees with the noun it refers to:

> Nous tiendrons compte de vos objections, **quelles qu'elles soient**
> *We will take your objections into account, whatever they are*

Note that **quel que** and **quoi que** both mean *whatever*:

FRENCH	ENGLISH
quel que soit + NOUN	*whatever* + NOUN
quoi que + VERB other than **être**	*whatever* + VERB

> **quelle que soit** votre décision   *whatever your decision may be*
> **quoi que** vous **décidiez**   *whatever you decide*

Subjunctive in relative clauses

10 The subjunctive is required in three kinds of RELATIVE CLAUSE.

1. After superlative adjectives and expressions like **le premier ...**, **le seul ...**, **le dernier ...**, **l'unique ...** :

   Vous êtes le seul qui **comprenne**
   You are the only one who understands
   C'est la première qu'on **ait reçue**
   It's the first one we have received

2. After a noun referring to someone or something rare or as yet non-existent:

   Je cherche **quelqu'un qui sache** faire preuve d'initiative
   I am looking for someone who can show some initiative

3. After a negative:

   Je n'ai **rien** trouvé qui me **plaise**
   I haven't found anything I like

Use of conditional to imply what may be true

11 The CONDITIONAL and CONDITIONAL PERFECT are often used to refer to something that is implied, and may or may not be true:

   Le président **serait** malade
   Some say that the President is ill

It is normal in formal French to introduce statistics and estimations with the CONDITIONAL, where in English a past or present tense is used:

   Le nombre de réfugiés dans ce pays **s'élèverait** à 15 000
   The number of refugees in that country is 15,000

Inversion of subject and verb after speech

See page 48, sections 2–6 for INVERSION of subject and verb in questions

12 When directly reporting someone's words, the SUBJECT and VERB following the quotation are inverted:

   « Nous attendons beaucoup de cette rencontre », **a déclaré le ministre**
   'We expect a great deal from this meeting', the Minister declared
   « Mais nous allons faire preuve de fermeté », **a-t-il précisé**
   'But we are going to stand firm', he specified

Note that unlike inversion in questions, the subject noun is not repeated in a pronoun:

QUESTION:	« **Le ministre a-t-il précisé** ses intentions ? »
QUOTATION:	« Nous allons faire preuve de fermeté », **a précisé le ministre**

peut-être **and** sans doute

13 **peut-être que** and **sans doute que** are both used at the beginning of a sentence:

> **Peut-être que** l'on parviendra à réduire le nombre des accidents de la route
> *Perhaps they will manage to reduce the number of road accidents*
> **Sans doute que** les campagnes de publicité auront un effet à long terme
> *Undoubtedly, information campaigns will have a long-term effect*

In more formal French, **peut-être** and **sans doute** are used without **que**, and the following SUBJECT and VERB are inverted:

> **Peut-être parviendra-t-on** à réduire le nombre des accidents de la route
> **Sans doute** les campagnes de publicité **auront-elles** un effet à long terme

avoir de quoi + infinitive

14 **avoir de quoi** + infinitive can indicate *enough* or a *sufficient quantity* of something:

> Les personnes âgées n'**ont** pas toujours **de quoi vivre**
> *Old people do not always have enough to live on*
> Vous **avez de quoi vous plaindre**
> *You have something to complain about*

Use of singular nouns

15 A singular noun is used to refer to something that two or more individuals have, if each of them has only one of whatever it is:

> Ils ont inscrit **leur nom** sur la liste
> *They entered their names on the list*
> **Le salaire** des jeunes est dérisoire
> *Young people's wages are ridiculous*

Note that this also applies to nouns referring to people, such as **une femme**, **un mari**, **une famille**, etc.:

> Nombre de femmes de commerçants travaillent avec **leur mari**
> *Many shopkeepers' wives work with their husbands*

A Using **on** or **l'on** as the subject, write the verbs in brackets in the appropriate tense. Fill the gaps with the appropriate pronoun and adjective.

e.g. (– *recommander*) de signaler _____ absences aux voisins.
→ **On recommande** de signaler **ses** absences aux voisins.

Voisins ? Connais pas !

Ce sont les femmes qui voisinent le plus, parce que le contact se fait avec les enfants. Et davantage encore dans les régions ensoleillées où (– *vivre*) beaucoup plus dehors. (– *voisiner*) bien aussi à la campagne et dans les petites villes.

En ville surtout, (– *rester*) chez _____ , en souvenir sans doute d'épouvantables histoires de voisinage comme (– *en voir*) autrefois. En partant du principe qu'à l'instar de la famille on subit bien plus _____ voisins que (– *les choisir*), (– *ne pas chercher*) à en faire des amis. Les cités-dortoirs ne sont guère plus propices au voisinage. Que dire de plus que « bonjour, bonsoir » à une personne que (– *croiser*) dans l'ascenseur aussi pressée que _____ de prendre son train ou de rentrer préparer le dîner ? Et dans les quartiers aisés, (– *ne pas fréquenter*) les gens auxquels (– *ne pas être*) présenté.

Alors (– *devoir*) se plaindre de cet excès de discrétion que (– *observer*) vis-à-vis de _____ voisins ? À trop vouloir éviter les problèmes de voisinage, (– *se priver*) de bien des facilités et des ressources de la solidarité.

B Replace the words or expressions in italics by **il suffit** or **il s'agit** in the appropriate tense and rewrite the sentences accordingly.

e.g. Acheter n'importe quel livre *ne suffit plus*.
→ Il ne suffit plus d'acheter n'importe quel livre.

Les livres pour enfants. Naguère, un unique livre de contes *suffisait* pour exciter l'imagination des enfants. Ce n'est plus le cas aujourd'hui : les enfants lisent de moins en moins et sont, de surcroît, des consommateurs exigeants. Pour les encourager à lire, *on doit* donc les motiver. Heureusement pour les parents que nous sommes, le marché du livre pour enfants s'est considérablement élargi et diversifié : bandes dessinées, aventure, mythologie, fantastique, il y en a pour tous les goûts. *Vous n'avez qu'à* choisir.

L'éducation civique des enfants. Il importe de plus en plus d'apprendre aux jeunes à devenir de bons citoyens. Connaître les règles de la vie collective *n'est pas une raison suffisante*, en effet, pour les appliquer. *Il faut* aussi comprendre et admettre leur utilité. Pour cela, il faut prendre conscience que la vie d'une collectivité s'appuie sur des règles qu'il convient de respecter sous peine d'en être exclu.

C Fill the gaps with either **quoi que** or **quel que soit**, **quelle que soit**, etc.

Les parents de divorcés

« Je sais bien que _____ il arrive, j'aurai du mal à m'habituer à la nouvelle compagne de mon fils », raconte Christian, un père effondré à l'idée de ne pas revoir sa belle-fille. On oublie trop souvent que, lorsqu'un couple se sépare, les parents qui ont établi des liens d'affection avec leur gendre ou leur belle-fille en souffrent. _____ les raisons de la rupture, ils éprouvent un sentiment de frustration, doublé d'un sentiment d'échec. Certains réussissent mieux que d'autres à faire face à la situation mais ils en ressentent tous douloureusement la blessure _____ leurs facultés d'adaptation.

D Write the verbs in brackets in the conditional and then translate into English.

Le travail des enfants. D'après certaines études, le nombre d'enfants au travail dans le monde (*pouvoir*) atteindre 200 millions. La grande majorité d'entre eux (*se trouver*) dans le tiers monde, même si le travail clandestin des enfants n'est pas inconnu en Europe. Ils (*être*) pour la plupart âgés de cinq à quatorze ans.

Populations à la dérive. Selon les estimations des associations caritatives, quelque 1,4 millions de personnes (*composer*) la population « en grande difficulté sociale » qui, en dépit de toutes les politiques sociales mises en œuvre, (*ne pas parvenir*) à se réinsérer dans la société française. Cette population (*recouvrir*), entre autres, 300 000 jeunes âgés de moins de 25 ans, 250 000 sans domicile fixe et 300 000 chômeurs de longue durée.

E A recruitment consultant talks about finding the right person for the job. Put the verb in brackets in the appropriate form.

En général, je cherche des gens qui (*savoir*) faire preuve d'enthousiasme et (*être*) vraiment qualifiés pour prendre des responsabilités. C'est souvent difficile à trouver. La dernière fois que nous (*passer*) une annonce, la première candidature que nous (*recevoir*) s'est avérée la bonne. Mais parfois il faut des mois pour trouver quelqu'un qui (*correspondre*) au profil recherché.

F *Thème.*
1. Whatever your children's age and interests, you must choose their books according to the quality of the texts and illustrations.
2. Nowadays it is not so difficult to find books that appeal to young people.
3. One wonders why many people never exchange more than a few words with their neighbours, particularly when their houses and gardens are next to one another.
4. The parents of divorced couples often find it extremely difficult to accept their children's new partners.
5. Of all those who have applied for the job, he is the only one who has the required qualifications.
6. The long-term unemployed complain that they do not have enough to live on.
7. Perhaps Western countries should stop importing goods from countries where children are forced to work.
8. One bomb attack was enough to jeopardise the peace process.
9. 'Whatever happens, we must pursue the talks', said the President.

A Rewrite the following sentences by putting the verb in the passive to emphasise what will be done by one of the television channels.

e.g. On conservera les émissions pour la jeunesse.
→ Les émissions pour la jeunesse seront conservées.

Télévision : la grille de la rentrée

1. On ne supprimera pas le film du dimanche soir.
2. On consacrera la soirée du mardi entièrement au cinéma.
3. On abordera les grands sujets d'actualité deux fois par mois, le jeudi soir, dans une émission à très gros moyens.
4. On maintiendra le grand show en direct du vendredi soir.
5. On investira près de 950 millions de francs dans la production de fictions françaises.

B Use a reflexive verb to replace the construction with **on**.

e.g. On mange souvent ce plat dans le Midi. *C'est un plat qui …*
→ C'est un plat qui se mange souvent dans le Midi.

Les plaisirs de la table : ce qui se fait

1. On voit souvent ce plat au menu des restaurants. *Ce plat …*
2. On sert généralement ce soufflé en hors-d'œuvre. *C'est un soufflé qui …*
3. On prépare ce dessert au dernier moment. *Ce dessert …*
4. Les gens apprécient beaucoup les fruits exotiques. *Les fruits exotiques …*
5. On boit ce vin très frais. *C'est un vin qui …*

C Select from the words in italics the single or plural noun according to the meaning of the sentence. Remember to make the verbs and adjectives in brackets agree.

1 La drogue progresse

Face au fléau de la drogue, les polices du monde entier semblent impuissantes. *Leur technique/Leurs techniques* (est/sont) de plus en plus (sophistiquée/sophistiquées) mais souvent (inadaptée/inadaptées) car les trafiquants, eux aussi, affinent *leur méthode/leurs méthodes. Leur virtuosité/Leurs virtuosités* et *leur audace/leurs audaces* sont sans limites. La liste des astuces est sans fin : on a trouvé de la drogue jusque dans *l'estomac/les estomacs* de cadavres rapatriés vers *leur pays d'origine/leurs pays d'origine.* Une autre technique répandue consiste à acheter une société de location de voitures. Les clients, en réalité des acheteurs de drogue, passent sans difficulté les frontières avec *leur cargaison/leurs cargaisons.* Qui aurait l'idée de vérifier et de démonter *la carrosserie/les carrosseries* et *le moteur/les moteurs* de toutes les voitures de location ?

2 Témoignage

Dans un livre intitulé « La Drogue : ses effets, ses dangers », Eric Fantin et Claude Deschamps expliquent, à partir de *leur propre expérience/leurs propres expériences*, les effets des différents types de stupéfiants et *le danger/les dangers* qu'ils font courir. Ils parlent *de la vie/des vies* que mènent les toxicomanes et montrent *quel rôle/quels rôles* (peut/peuvent) jouer *la famille/les familles* de ceux qui ont « plongé » dans la drogue et en sont devenus dépendants. Il leur semble essentiel que les parents soient informés des vrais problèmes, et capables de comprendre la logique *du comportement/des comportements* des drogués. Ils soulignent que bien souvent les parents commencent à s'intéresser à *leur enfant/leurs enfants* le jour où ils découvrent qu'*il se drogue/ils se droguent*. Or il semble que certains sujets soient plus prédisposés à la drogue que d'autres et que *leur fréquentation/leurs fréquentations* ne (joue/jouent) pas le rôle déterminant qu'on (lui/leur) attribue d'ordinaire. La prévention, c'est donc aussi *une affaire/des affaires* de famille.

D *Thème.*

1. Eighty-four people died last week as a result of[1] floods in the north-east of India. Over two million inhabitants of the State of Assam were affected. The floods, caused by heavy monsoon rains, destroyed hundreds of houses and devastated two hundred thousand hectares of crops.

2. In less than ten years, the majority of the inhabitants of this planet will live in towns. Barely two centuries ago, 90 % of them lived in the country. In 30 years time the urban population, which is growing at a rate of 2.5 % per year, could be as high as five billion people. One town-dweller out of ten will be living in a 'megacity' of more than ten million inhabitants.

3. It would be irresponsible to claim that certain individuals will become drug addicts whatever happens, whatever company they keep[2], and whatever the laws of the country in which they live may be. It is an illusion to believe that punishing young drug addicts will be enough to cure them of the desire to use illegal drugs.

4. In the fight against drug trafficking, banks have been obliged[3] to co-operate with the police to make money laundering more difficult. These days drug traffickers can be refused services which they used freely, without any questions asked[4], about ten years ago.

[1] to die as a result of : *être victime de*
[2] the company one keeps : *les fréquentations*
[3] use *se trouver* + infinitive
[4] use *on*

Using link words

The function of link words is to show the relation between various events and arguments. When you are reading newspaper and magazine articles in French, make a note of the way link words are used.

A Fill the gaps with one of the following link words, having checked their meaning: **mais, ainsi, par contre, en effet, car, d'autant plus que**.

Les peines de substitution

Depuis de nombreuses années déjà, les tribunaux s'efforcent de substituer à l'emprisonnement des peines de travail d'utilité publique. _____ deux jeunes délinquants de Grenoble viennent-ils d'être condamnés à 100 heures de travail pour une tentative de cambriolage.

Ces dispositions ont l'approbation de nombreux magistrats. La majorité d'entre eux considèrent, _____, que condamner un petit voleur à quelques semaines de prison n'a rien de rédempteur. Éviter aux petits délinquants le contact avec l'univers carcéral peut, _____, avoir quelque chose de salutaire, _____ les prisons françaises sont surpeuplées. _____ encore faut-il que les prévenus soient consentants _____ la loi précise que l'on peut refuser cette forme de condamnation et « préférer » être privé de sa liberté.

B Fill the gaps with one of the following link words, having checked their meaning: **d'abord, ensuite, de plus, en outre, en somme, tandis que, alors que**.

Les femmes et la dépression

Les statistiques révèlent que les femmes souffrent de dépression deux fois plus souvent que les hommes. Y seraient-elles génétiquement prédisposées ? Non, d'après certains spécialistes.

En examinant les données, ils ont _____ découvert une vérité d'évidence, à savoir qu'une femme soigne son mari souffrant à domicile _____ elle se voit hospitalisée si elle est elle-même atteinte. _____, les femmes font plus souvent appel au médecin et au psychologue que les hommes.

Ils ont _____ analysé le rôle de l'environnement professionnel ou familial. Les conclusions sont frappantes : les femmes seules ne sont pas plus atteintes par la dépression que les hommes. Les femmes mariées, elles, le sont, _____ les hommes mariés ont des dépressions moins fréquentes que les célibataires.

_____, les dépressions sont moins fréquentes chez les épouses qui travaillent que chez les femmes au foyer.

_____, dans ce domaine comme dans bien d'autres, on aurait tort de négliger les facteurs économiques et sociaux.

APPENDICES

Appendix

1

Acute and grave accents over the letter « e »

In the dictionary, various symbols are used to indicate the pronunciation of the letter **e**:
[e]: same sound as in **thé** and **les**.   [a]: same sound as in **canne** and **mal**.
[ɛ]: same sound as in **père** and **lait**.   [ã] or nasalised [a]: same sound as in **sans** and **temps**.
When the sound is [e] an acute accent – é – or no accent – e – is normally required.
When the sound is [ɛ] a grave accent – è – or no accent – e – is normally required.

You can usually tell whether or not an accent is required by looking at the letters following
the letter **e** and its position in the word.

No accent required

Unless indicated otherwise the sound is [ɛ]

Beginning or middle of word		*End of word*	
(...)ecc...	impe**cc**able [e]	...ec	un éche**c**, se**c**
...echn...	**techn**ique		
(...)ect(...)	éle**ct**rique, le resp**ect**		
(...)ecz...	l'**ecz**éma		
...ed	un pie**d** [e]		
(...)eff...	un **eff**et [e], **eff**acer [e]	...ef	un relie**f**, bre**f**
...egm...	un se**gm**ent		
...eill...	un surv**eill**ant	...eil	un rév**eil**
(...)ell...	une appe**ll**ation, nature**ll**e (*fem.*)	...el	nature**l** (*masc.*)
(...)elt...	sv**elt**e		
(...)emm...	**emm**ener [ã], une fe**mm**e [a]		
(...)enn...	un **enn**emi, un **enn**ui [ã]*		
...epp...	Die**pp**e	...ep	un ce**p**
...ept(...)	le sc**ept**icisme, un conc**ept**		
(...)erc(h)...	un c**erc**le, p**erc**evoir, p**erch**er	...er	envoy**er** [e], lég**er** [e]
(...)erg...	une én**erg**ie		
(...)erm...	une f**erm**eture		
(...)err...	une **err**eur, médit**err**anéen		
...erv...	én**erv**er		
(...)esb...	l'**esb**roufe		
(...)esc...	un **esc**roc, eff**erv**escent		
(...)esp...	un **esp**oir¹		
(...)esq...	**esq**uisser		
(...)ess...	**ess**ayer [e], la pr**ess**e, succ**ess**if		
(...)est(...)	il **est**, sur**est**imer		
...ett...	prom**ett**re, n**ett**e (*fem.*)	...et	un regr**et**, n**et**, discr**et**
(...)ex...	une **ex**périence, **ex**écuter		

¹ except *un téléspectateur* [telesp...] , *un télescope* [telesk...] and all words similarly formed

Accent required

Acute accent

Unless indicated otherwise, the sound is [e]

Beginning or middle of word

(...)éb...	**éb**ahir [eb]
(...)ébr...	**débr**ancher, célé**br**er
(...)éc...	**éc**arter, néc**c**essaire
(...)éch...	**éch**ouer, sé**ch**er, la sé**ch**eresse[1]
(...)écl...	**écl**ater
(...)écr...	**écr**aser, exé**cr**er
(...)éd...	un **éd**iteur, la tié**d**eur
(...)édr...	un **édr**edon
...éf...	un dé**f**aut, la mé**f**iance
(...)éfl...	ré**fl**échir
(...)éfr...	dé**fr**icher
(...)ég...	**ég**aler, ré**g**ional, pié**g**er
(...)égl...	l'**égl**ise, ré**gl**er
...égr...	**égr**ener
(...)égu...	un délé**gu**é
(...)éi...	ré**i**térer, un s**é**isme
(...)éj...	**éj**ecter, un s**é**jour
(...)él...	une **él**ection, la d**él**ation
(...)ém...	une **ém**ission, problé**m**atique
(...)én...	**én**oncer, un évé**n**ement[2]
(...)éo ...	**éo**lien
(...)ép ...	**ép**ais, se dé**p**êcher
(...)épl...	**épl**ucher, dé**pl**orer
(...)épr...	**épr**ouver
(...)équ...	le dés**équ**ilibre
(...)ér...	une **ér**uption, une pé**r**iode
(...)és...	hé**s**iter, dé**s**abusé
	...**ès**e
(...)ét...	**ét**ablir, le pé**t**role, synthé**t**ique
(...)étr...	dé**tr**uire, le kilomé**tr**age
(...)év...	**év**entuel, une dé**v**aluation

Grave accent

Unless indicated otherwise, the sound is [ɛ]

End of word

...**èb**e	un éph**èb**e
...**èb**re	fun**èb**re, célè**b**re
...**èc**e	une esp**èc**e
...**èch**e	une cr**èch**e, sè**ch**e(ment)[3]
...**ècl**e	le si**ècl**e
...**ècr**e	il exè**cr**e
...**èd**e	il poss**èd**e, tiè**d**e
...**èdr**e	Ph**èdr**e
...**èfl**e	un tr**èfl**e
...**èg**e	un collè**g**e, un piè**g**e
...**ègl**e	une r**ègl**e
...**ègr**e	allè**gr**e
...**ègu**e	un collè**gu**e
...**èl**e	le z**èl**e
...**èm**e	deuxi**èm**e, un probl**èm**e
...**èn**e	un phénom**èn**e
...**èp**e	un c**èp**e
...**èp**re	la l**èp**re
...**èqu**e	une biblioth**èqu**e
...**èr**e	une fili**èr**e, légè**r**e(té)[3]
...**ès**	d**ès**, tr**ès**, pr**ès**, un succ**ès**
	une hypoth**ès**e, une synth**ès**e
...**èt**e	un interpr**èt**e, discr**èt**e
...**èt**re	un kilom**èt**re
...**èv**e	une gr**èv**e, br**èv**e

[1] *sécheresse* is pronounced [seʃʀɛs]

[2] *événement* is pronounced [evɛnmã]

[3] when -*ment* or –*té* are added to a word the accent is unchanged

Appendix

2

Verb tables

Infinitive and Present Participle	Present Indicative		Perfect	Imperfect	Future and Conditional
avoir	ai	avons	ai eu	avais	aurai
	as	avez			
ayant	a	ont			aurais
être	suis	sommes	ai été	étais	serai
	es	êtes			
étant	est	sont			serais

Regular verbs

parler	parle	parlons	ai parlé	parlais	parlerai
	parles	parlez			
parlant	parle	parlent			parlerais
finir	finis	finissons	ai fini	finissais	finirai
	finis	finissez			
finissant	finit	finissent			finirais
vendre	vends	vendons	ai vendu	vendais	vendrai
	vends	vendez			
vendant	vend	vendent			vendrais

-er verbs with spelling changes

acheter	achète	achetons	ai acheté	achetais	achèterai
	achètes	achetez			
achetant	achète	achètent			achèterais
appeler	appelle	appelons	ai appelé	appelais	appellerai
	appelles	appelez			
appelant	appelle	appellent			appellerais
commencer	commence	commençons	ai commencé	commençais	commencerai
	commences	commencez			
commençant	commence	commencent			commencerais
employer	emploie	employons	ai employé	employais	emploierai
	emploies	employez			
employant	emploie	emploient			emploierais
espérer	espère	espérons	ai espéré	espérais	espérerai
	espères	espérez			
espérant	espère	espèrent			espérerais
partager	partage	partageons	ai partagé	partageais	partagerai
	partages	partagez			
partageant	partage	partagent			partagerais
projeter	projette	projetons	ai projeté	projetais	projetterai
	projettes	projetez			
projetant	projette	projettent			projetterais

Present Subjunctive		Past Historic		Imperative	Verbs similarly formed
aie	ayons	eus	eûmes	aie	
aies	ayez	eus	eûtes	ayons	
ait	aient	eut	eurent	ayez	
sois	soyons	fus	fûmes	sois	
sois	soyez	fus	fûtes	soyons	
soit	soient	fut	furent	soyez	
parle	parlions	parlai	parlâmes	parle	
parles	parliez	parlas	parlâtes	parlons	
parle	parlent	parla	parlèrent	parlez	
finisse	finissions	finis	finîmes	finis	
finisses	finissiez	finis	finîtes	finissons	
finisse	finissent	finit	finirent	finissez	
vende	vendions	vendis	vendîmes	vends	
vendes	vendiez	vendis	vendîtes	vendons	
vende	vendent	vendit	vendirent	vendez	
achète	achetions	achetai	achetâmes	achète	see page 169, Appendix 3
achètes	achetiez	achetas	achetâtes	achetons	
achète	achètent	acheta	achetèrent	achetez	
appelle	appelions	appelai	appelâmes	appelle	see page 169, Appendix 3
appelles	appeliez	appelas	appelâtes	appelons	
appelle	appellent	appela	appelèrent	appelez	
commence	commencions	commençai	commençâmes	commence	see page 169, Appendix 3
commences	commenciez	commenças	commençâtes	commençons	
commence	commencent	commença	commencèrent	commencez	
emploie	employions	employai	employâmes	emploie	see page 169, Appendix 3
emploies	employiez	employas	employâtes	employons	
emploie	emploient	employa	employèrent	employez	
espère	espérions	espérai	espérâmes	espère	see page 169, Appendix 3
espères	espériez	espéras	espérâtes	espérons	
espère	espèrent	espéra	espérèrent	espérez	
partage	partagions	partageai	partageâmes	partage	see page 169, Appendix 3
partages	partagiez	partageas	partageâtes	partageons	
partage	partagent	partagea	partagèrent	partagez	
projette	projetions	projetai	projetâmes	projette	see page 169, Appendix 3
projettes	projetiez	projetas	projetâtes	projetons	
projette	projettent	projeta	projetèrent	projetez	

Infinitive and Present Participle	Present Indicative		Perfect	Imperfect	Future and Conditional

Irregular verb groups

Infinitive and Present Participle	Present Indicative		Perfect	Imperfect	Future and Conditional
conduire	conduis	conduisons	ai conduit	conduisais	conduirai
	conduis	conduisez			
conduisant	conduit	conduisent			conduirais
craindre	crains	craignons	ai craint	craignais	craindrai
	crains	craignez			
craignant	craint	craignent			craindrais
ouvrir	ouvre	ouvrons	ai ouvert	ouvrais	ouvrirai
	ouvres	ouvrez			
ouvrant	ouvre	ouvrent			ouvrirais
partir	pars	partons	suis parti(e)	partais	partirai
	pars	partez			
partant	part	partent			partirais
recevoir	reçois	recevons	ai reçu	recevais	recevrai
	reçois	recevez			
recevant	reçoit	reçoivent			recevrais

Common irregular verbs

Infinitive and Present Participle	Present Indicative		Perfect	Imperfect	Future and Conditional
accroître	accrois	accroissons	ai accru	accroissais	accroîtrai
	accrois	accroissez			
accroissant	accroît	accroissent			accroîtrais
accueillir	accueille	accueillons	ai accueilli	accueillais	accueillerai
	accueilles	accueillez			
accueillant	accueille	accueillent			accueillerais
acquérir	acquiers	acquérons	ai acquis	acquérais	acquerrai
	acquiers	acquérez			
acquérant	acquiert	acquièrent			acquerrais
aller	vais	allons	suis allé(e)	allais	irai
	vas	allez			
allant	va	vont			irais
s'asseoir	m'assieds	nous asseyons	me suis assis	m'asseyais	m'assiérai
	t'assieds	vous asseyez			
s'asseyant	s'assied	s'asseyent			m'assiérais
battre	bats	battons	ai battu	battais	battrai
	bats	battez			
battant	bat	battent			battrais
boire	bois	buvons	ai bu	buvais	boirai
	bois	buvez			
buvant	boit	boivent			boirais
connaître	connais	connaissons	ai connu	connaissais	connaîtrai
	connais	connaissez			
connaissant	connaît	connaissent			connaîtrais
convaincre	convaincs	convainquons	ai convaincu	convainquais	convaincrai
	convaincs	convainquez			
convainquant	convainc	convainquent			convaincrais

Present Subjunctive		Past Historic		Imperative	Verbs similarly formed
conduise	conduisions	conduisis	conduisîmes	conduis	*see*
conduises	conduisiez	conduisis	conduisîtes	conduisons	page 5,
conduise	conduisent	conduisit	conduisirent	conduisez	Section 14
craigne	craignions	craignis	craignîmes	crains	*see*
craignes	craigniez	craignis	craignîtes	craignons	page 5,
craigne	craignent	craignit	craignirent	craignez	Section 14
ouvre	ouvrions	ouvris	ouvrîmes	ouvre	*see*
ouvres	ouvriez	ouvris	ouvrîtes	ouvrons	page 5,
ouvre	ouvrent	ouvrit	ouvrirent	ouvrez	Section 14
parte	partions	partis	partîmes	pars	*see*
partes	partiez	partis	partîtes	partons	page 5,
parte	partent	partit	partirent	partez	Section 14
reçoive	recevions	reçus	reçûmes	reçois	*see*
reçoives	receviez	reçus	reçûtes	recevons	page 5,
reçoive	reçoivent	reçut	reçurent	recevez	Section 14
accroisse	accroissions	accrus	accrûmes	accrois	croître[1]
accroisses	accroissiez	accrus	accrûtes	accroissons	décroître
accroisse	accroissent	accrut	accrurent	accroissez	
accueille	accueillions	accueillis	accueillîmes	accueille	cueillir
accueilles	accueilliez	accueillis	accueillîtes	accueillons	recueillir
accueille	accueillent	accueillit	accueillirent	accueillez	
acquière	acquérions	acquis	acquîmes	acquiers	conquérir
acquières	acquériez	acquis	acquîtes	acquérons	requérir
acquière	acquièrent	acquit	acquirent	acquérez	
aille	allions	allai	allâmes	va (*note:* vas-y)	
ailles	alliez	allas	allâtes	allons	
aille	aillent	alla	allèrent	allez	
m'asseye	nous asseyions	m'assis	nous assîmes	assieds-toi	asseoir
t'asseyes	vous asseyiez	t'assis	vous assîtes	asseyons-nous	
s'asseye	s'asseyent	s'assit	s'assirent	asseyez-vous	
batte	battions	battis	battîmes	bats	abattre
battes	battiez	battis	battîtes	battons	combattre
batte	battent	battit	battirent	battez	débattre, etc.
boive	buvions	bus	bûmes	bois	
boives	buviez	bus	bûtes	buvons	
boive	boivent	but	burent	buvez	
connaisse	connaissions	connus	connûmes	connais	(ap)paraître
connaisses	connaissiez	connus	connûtes	connaissons	disparaître
connaisse	connaissent	connut	connurent	connaissez	reconnaître, etc.
convainque	convainquions	convainquis	convainquîmes	convaincs	vaincre
convainques	convainquiez	convainquis	convainquîtes	convainquons	
convainque	convainquent	convainquit	convainquirent	convainquez	

[1] *croître* : past participle **crû**

Infinitive and Present Participle	Present Indicative		Perfect	Imperfect	Future and Conditional
courir	cours	courons	ai couru	courais	courrai
	cours	courez			
courant	court	courent			courrais
croire	crois	croyons	ai cru	croyais	croirai
	crois	croyez			
croyant	croit	croient			croirais
devoir	dois	devons	ai dû[2]	devais	devrai
	dois	devez			
devant	doit	doivent			devrais
dire	dis	disons	ai dit	disais	dirai
	dis	dites			
disant	dit	disent			dirais
écrire	écris	écrivons	ai écrit	écrivais	écrirai
	écris	écrivez			
écrivant	écrit	écrivent			écrirais
envoyer	envoie	envoyons	ai envoyé	envoyais	enverrai
	envoies	envoyez			
envoyant	envoie	envoient			enverrais
faire	fais	faisons	ai fait	faisais	ferai
	fais	faites			
faisant	fait	font			ferais
falloir	il faut		il a fallu	il fallait	il faudra
—					il faudrait
fuir	fuis	fuyons	ai fui	fuyais	fuirai
	fuis	fuyez			
fuyant	fuit	fuient			fuirais
lire	lis	lisons	ai lu	lisais	lirai
	lis	lisez			
lisant	lit	lisent			lirais
mettre	mets	mettons	ai mis	mettais	mettrai
	mets	mettez			
mettant	met	mettent			mettrais
mourir	meurs	mourons	suis mort(e)	mourais	mourrai
	meurs	mourez			
mourant	meurt	meurent			mourrais
naître	nais	naissons	suis né(e)	naissais	naîtrai
	nais	naissez			
naissant	naît	naissent			naîtrais
plaire	plais	plaisons	ai plu	plaisais	plairai
	plais	plaisez			
plaisant	plaît	plaisent			plairais
pleuvoir	il pleut		il a plu	il pleuvait	il pleuvra
pleuvant					il pleuvrait
pouvoir	peux[3]	pouvons	ai pu	pouvais	pourrai
	peux	pouvez			
pouvant	peut	peuvent			pourrais

[2] no circumflex accent when an agreement is made with the preceding direct object: **due, dus, dues**
[3] inverted form: **puis-je** . . . ?

Present Subjunctive		Past Historic		Imperative	Verbs similarly formed
coure	courions	courus	courûmes	cours	accourir
coures	couriez	courus	courûtes	courons	recourir
coure	courent	courut	coururent	courez	
croie	croyions	crus	crûmes	crois	
croies	croyiez	crus	crûtes	croyons	
croie	croient	crut	crurent	croyez	
doive	devions	dus	dûmes	dois	
doives	deviez	dus	dûtes	devons	
doive	doivent	dut	durent	devez	
dise	disions	dis	dîmes	dis	contredire[4]
dises	disiez	dis	dîtes	disons	interdire[4]
dise	disent	dit	dirent	dites	prédire[4]
écrive	écrivions	écrivis	écrivîmes	écris	décrire
écrives	écriviez	écrivis	écrivîtes	écrivons	inscrire
écrive	écrivent	écrivit	écrivirent	écrivez	prescrire, etc.
envoie	envoyions	envoyai	envoyâmes	envoie	renvoyer
envoies	envoyiez	envoyas	envoyâtes	envoyons	
envoie	envoient	envoya	envoyèrent	envoyez	
fasse	fassions	fis	fîmes	fais	défaire
fasses	fassiez	fis	fîtes	faisons	refaire
fasse	fassent	fit	firent	faites	satisfaire
il faille		il fallut		—	
fuie	fuyions	fuis	fuîmes	fuis	s'enfuir
fuies	fuyiez	fuis	fuîtes	fuyons	
fuie	fuient	fuit	fuirent	fuyez	
lise	lisions	lus	lûmes	lis	relire
lises	lisiez	lus	lûtes	lisons	élire
lise	lisent	lut	lurent	lisez	réélire
mette	mettions	mis	mîmes	mets	admettre
mettes	mettiez	mis	mîtes	mettons	commettre
mette	mettent	mit	mirent	mettez	permettre, etc.
meure	mourions	mourus	mourûmes	meurs	
meures	mouriez	mourus	mourûtes	mourons	
meure	meurent	mourut	moururent	mourez	
naisse	naissions	naquis	naquîmes	nais	renaître
naisses	naissiez	naquis	naquîtes	naissons	
naisse	naissent	naquit	naquirent	naissez	
plaise	plaisions	plus	plûmes	plais	déplaire
plaises	plaisiez	plus	plûtes	plaisons	
plaise	plaisent	plut	plurent	plaisez	
il pleuve		il plut		—	
puisse	puissions	pus	pûmes	—	
puisses	puissiez	pus	pûtes		
puisse	puissent	put	purent		

[4] present and imperative : (vous) **contredisez, interdisez, prédisez**

APPENDIX 2

Infinitive and Present Participle	Present Indicative		Perfect	Imperfect	Future and Conditional
prendre	prends	prenons	ai pris	prenais	prendrai
	prends	prenez			
prenant	prend	prennent			prendrais
résoudre	résous	résolvons	ai résolu	résolvais	résoudrai
	résous	résolvez			
résolvant	résout	résolvent			résoudrais
revêtir	revêts	revêtons	ai revêtu	revêtais	revêtirai
	revêts	revêtez			
revêtant	revêt	revêtent			revêtirais
rire	ris	rions	ai ri	riais	rirai
	ris	riez			
riant	rit	rient			rirais
rompre	romps	rompons	ai rompu	rompais	romprai
	romps	rompez			
rompant	rompt	rompent			romprais
savoir	sais	savons	ai su	savais	saurai
	sais	savez			
sachant	sait	savent			saurais
suffire	suffis	suffisons	ai suffi	suffisais	suffirai
	suffis	suffisez			
suffisant	suffit	suffisent			suffirais
suivre	suis	suivons	ai suivi	suivais	suivrai
	suis	suivez			
suivant	suit	suivent			suivrais
taire	tais	taisons	ai tu	taisais	tairai
	tais	taisez			
taisant	tait	taisent			tairais
tenir	tiens	tenons	ai tenu	tenais	tiendrai
	tiens	tenez			
tenant	tient	tiennent			tiendrais
valoir	vaux	valons	ai valu	valais	vaudrai
	vaux	valez			
valant	vaut	valent			vaudrais
venir	viens	venons	suis venu(e)	venais	viendrai
	viens	venez			
venant	vient	viennent			viendrais
vivre	vis	vivons	ai vécu	vivais	vivrai
	vis	vivez			
vivant	vit	vivent			vivrais
voir	vois	voyons	ai vu	voyais	verrai
	vois	voyez			
voyant	voit	voient			verrais
vouloir	veux	voulons	ai voulu	voulais	voudrai
	veux	voulez			
voulant	veut	veulent			voudrais

Present Subjunctive		Past Historic		Imperative	Verbs similarly formed
prenne	prenions	pris	prîmes	prends	entreprendre,
prennes	preniez	pris	prîtes	prenons	comprendre
prenne	prennent	prit	prirent	prenez	apprendre etc.
résolve	résolvions	résolus	résolûmes	résous	absoudre[5]
résolves	résolviez	résolus	résolûtes	résolvons	
résolve	résolvent	résolut	résolurent	résolvez	dissoudre[5]
revête	revêtions	revêtis	revêtîmes	revêts	vêtir
revêtes	revêtiez	revêtis	revêtîtes	revêtons	
revête	revêtent	revêtit	revêtirent	revêtez	
rie	riions	ris	rîmes	ris	sourire
ries	riiez	ris	rîtes	rions	
rie	rient	rit	rirent	riez	
rompe	rompions	rompis	rompîmes	romps	corrompre
rompes	rompiez	rompis	rompîtes	rompons	interrompre
rompe	rompent	rompit	rompirent	rompez	
sache	sachions	sus	sûmes	sache	
saches	sachiez	sus	sûtes	sachons	
sache	sachent	sut	surent	sachez	
suffise	suffisions	suffis	suffîmes	suffis	se suffire
suffises	suffisiez	suffis	suffîtes	suffisons	
suffise	suffisent	suffit	suffirent	suffisez	
suive	suivions	suivis	suivîmes	suis	poursuivre
suives	suiviez	suivis	suivîtes	suivons	
suive	suivent	suivit	suivirent	suivez	
taise	taisions	tus	tûmes	tais	se taire
taises	taisiez	tus	tûtes	taisons	
taise	taisent	tut	turent	taisez	
tienne	tenions	tins	tînmes	tiens	appartenir
tiennes	teniez	tins	tîntes	tenons	contenir
tienne	tiennent	tint	tinrent	tenez	maintenir, etc.
vaille	valions	valus	valûmes	vaux	prévaloir
vailles	valiez	valus	valûtes	valons	revaloir
vaille	vaillent	valut	valurent	valez	
vienne	venions	vins	vînmes	viens	devenir
viennes	veniez	vins	vîntes	venons	intervenir
vienne	viennent	vint	vinrent	venez	revenir, etc.[6]
vive	vivions	vécus	vécûmes	vis	survivre
vives	viviez	vécus	vécûtes	vivons	revivre
vive	vivent	vécut	vécurent	vivez	
voie	voyions	vis	vîmes	vois	entrevoir
voies	voyiez	vis	vîtes	voyons	prévoir[7]
voie	voient	vit	virent	voyez	revoir, etc.
veuille	voulions	voulus	voulûmes	veuille	
veuilles	vouliez	voulus	voulûtes	veuillons	
veuille	veuillent	voulut	voulurent	veuillez	

[5] past participle : *absous / absoute ; dissous / dissoute*
[6] **convenir**, **prévenir**, **subvenir** take the auxiliary verb **avoir**
[7] note that the future and conditional of **prévoir** are : **je prévoirai**, etc., and **je prévoirais**, etc.

-er verbs with spelling changes
(See Verb Tables page 160–161)

Verbs like *espérer*

accélérer, aliéner, céder, compléter, concéder, considérer, déléguer, délibérer, différer, exagérer, excéder, inquiéter, insérer, libérer, posséder, précéder, préférer, procéder, protéger (also like **partager**), refléter, réitérer, répéter, révéler, régénérer, sécher, suggérer

Verbs like *commencer*

acquiescer, amorcer, annoncer, avancer, balancer, décontenancer, dénoncer, devancer, distancer, s'efforcer, espacer, exercer, financer, (ren)forcer, (en)foncer, influencer, lancer, ménager, nuancer, (dé)placer, forcer, renoncer, tracer

Verbs like *partager*

abréger, affliger, allonger, aménager, arranger, bouger, changer, charger, corriger, diriger, engager, envisager, ériger, exiger, juger, mélanger, ménager, négliger, obliger, protéger (also like **espérer**), déranger, voyager

Verbs like *acheter*

achever, amener, congeler, crever, déceler, élever, (dé)geler, (re)lever, (em)mener, modeler, peser, promener, soulever, surgeler

Verbs like *rejeter*

cacheter, empaqueter, feuilleter, (re)jeter, projeter

Verbs like *appeler*

amonceler, chanceler, épeler, étinceler, ficeler, harceler, morceler, niveler, peler, rappeler, renouveler

Verbs like *employer*

apitoyer, appuyer, broyer, convoyer, côtoyer, coudoyer, ennuyer, (r)envoyer, essuyer, foudroyer, fourvoyer, nettoyer, noyer, octroyer, (dé)ployer, tutoyer, vouvoyer

Common verbs and their constructions

References are to the chapter number and the section number.

Abbreviations

qch.:	quelque chose
qn:	quelqu'un
sth.:	*something*
s.o:	*someone*

aboutir à qch.	*lead to, result in, end in sth.*
s'abstenir de qch.	*abstain from sth.*
s'abstenir de faire qch.	*abstain from doing sth.*
abuser de qch./qn	*use sth. excessively, misuse sth.; take advantage of sth./s.o.*
accepter de faire qch.	*agree to do sth.*
accorder qch. à qn	*give, grant, award sth. to s.o.*
accuser qn de qch.	*accuse s.o. of sth.*
accuser qn d'avoir fait qch.	*accuse s.o. of having done sth.*
acheter qch. à qn	*buy s.o. sth., buy sth. from s.o. (see 18.10)*
s'adonner à qch.	*devote oneself to, go in for sth.*
s'adresser à qn	*speak to, address s.o., come/go to s.o., come/go and ask s.o., be aimed at, intended for s.o. (see 18.3)*
s'agir: il s'agit de qch./qn	*see 24.7*
s'agir: il s'agit de faire qch.	*see 24.7*
aider qn à faire qch.	*help s.o. to do sth.*
aimer faire qch.	*like to do sth., enjoy doing sth.*
aller faire qch.	*go to do sth., go and do sth., be going to do sth. (see 2.12)*
amener qn à faire qch.	*induce, lead, bring s.o. to do sth.*
s'amuser à faire qch.	*enjoy oneself doing sth.*
apercevoir qn faire qch.	*notice, see s.o. doing sth.*
s'apercevoir de qch.	*become aware of, notice sth.*
apprendre à faire qch.	*learn to do sth.*
s'apprêter à faire qch.	*get ready, prepare to do sth.*
approuver qch./qn	*approve sth./s.o., agree with sth./s.o., approve of sth./s.o.*
s'appuyer sur qch./qn	*lean on, rely on the support of sth./s.o.*
arracher qch. à qn	*snatch, grab sth. from s.o. (see 18.10)*
s'arrêter de faire qch.	*stop doing sth.*
arriver à qch./qn	*happen to sth./s.o.*
arriver à faire qch.	*manage to, succeed in doing sth.*
assister à qch.	*attend, witness sth.*
s'assurer de qch.	*make sure of, check, ascertain sth.*
attendre qch./qn	*wait for sth./s.o.*
attendre de faire qch.	*wait until it is time to do sth.*
attendre que qn fasse qch.	*wait until s.o. does sth.*
s'attendre à qch.	*expect sth.*

s'attendre à faire qch.	*expect to do sth.*
s'attendre à ce que qn fasse qch.	*expect s.o. to do sth.*
s'attendrir sur qch./qn	*be moved by sth./s.o.; feel sorry, pity for s.o.*
attribuer qch. à qn	*grant, award s.o. sth., attribute sth. to s.o., credit s.o. with sth.*
s'avérer qch.	*prove to be, turn out to be sth.*
avoir à faire qch.	*have to do sth.*
avoir besoin de qch./qn	*need sth./s.o.*
avoir droit à qch.	*be entitled to, have a right to sth.*
avoir de la peine à faire qch.	*have trouble doing, difficulty in doing sth.*
avoir de quoi faire qch.	*see 24.14*
avoir du mal à faire qch.	*have trouble doing sth., find it difficult to do sth.*
avoir envie de qch.	*feel like, want sth.*
avoir envie de faire qch.	*feel like doing, want to do sth.*
avoir la chance de faire qch.	*be lucky enough, fortunate enough to do sth.*
avoir le courage de faire qch.	*be brave enough to, have the heart to do sth.*
avoir le droit de faire qch.	*be allowed to, have the right to do sth.*
avoir le temps de faire qch.	*have time to do sth.*
avoir les moyens de faire qch.	*be able to, can afford to do sth.*
avoir l'intention de faire qch.	*intend to do sth.*
avoir l'occasion de faire qch.	*have a chance to, the opportunity to do sth.*
avoir peur de qch./qn	*be afraid of, frightened of sth./s.o.*
avoir raison de faire qch.	*be right to do sth.*
avoir soin de faire qch.	*take care to do sth.*
avoir soin de qch./qn	*take care of sth./s.o.*
avoir tendance à faire qch.	*tend to, have a tendency to do sth.*
avoir tort de faire qch.	*be wrong to do sth.*
bénéficier de qch.	*get, have, enjoy sth., benefit from sth.*
cacher qch. à qn	*hide, conceal sth. from s.o. (see 18.10)*
cesser de faire qch.	*cease, stop doing sth.*
changer de qch.	*change, replace sth.*
changer qch.	*change, modify sth.*
charger qn de qch.	*entrust s.o. with sth., put sth. in the hands of s.o.*
charger qn de faire qch.	*entrust s.o. with doing sth.*
se charger de qch.	*undertake sth.*
se charger de faire qch.	*undertake to do sth.*
chasser qch./qn	*chase, chase away, hunt sth./s.o.*
chercher qch./qn	*look for sth./s.o.*
chercher à faire qch.	*try to, attempt to do sth.*
choisir de faire qch.	*choose to do sth.*
commander à qn de faire qch.	*order s.o. to do sth. (see 15.13)*
commencer à faire qch.	*begin to, start to do sth.*
commencer par faire qch.	*begin by, start by doing sth.*
comparer qch./qn à qch./qn	*compare sth./s.o. with sth./s.o. (see 18.3)*
compter faire qch.	*intend to, plan to, mean to do sth.*
concurrencer qch./qn	*compete with sth./s.o.*
se confier à qn	*confide in s.o.*

confier qch. à qn	entrust s.o. with sth., put sth. in the hands of s.o.
conseiller qn	give advice to, counsel s.o.
conseiller à qn de faire qch.	advise s.o. to do sth. (see 15.13)
consentir à qch.	consent to sth.
consentir à faire qch.	consent to do sth.
consentir à ce que qn fasse qch.	consent to s.o. doing sth.
consister à faire qch.	consist in doing sth.
se contenter de qch.	make do with sth.
se contenter de faire qch.	content oneself with doing sth.
continuer à faire qch.	continue to do sth.
contraindre qn à faire qch.	force, compel s.o. to do sth.
convaincre qn de faire qch.	persuade s.o. to do sth.
décider de qch.	decide on sth.
décider de faire qch.	decide to do sth.
décider qn à faire qch.	to persuade, induce s.o. to do sth.
se décider à faire qch.	make up one's mind to do sth.
déconseiller à qn de faire qch.	advise s.o. against doing sth. (see 15.13)
décourager qn de qch.	discourage s.o. from sth.
décourager qn de faire qch.	discourage s.o. from doing sth.
défendre qch. à qn	forbid s.o. sth.
défendre à qn de faire qch.	forbid s.o. to do sth. (see 15.13)
demander à qn de faire qch.	ask s.o. to do sth. (see 15.13)
demander qch. à qn	ask s.o. for sth.
dépendre de qch./qn	depend on sth./s.o.
déterminer qn à faire qch.	decide, determine s.o. to do sth.
devoir faire qch.	have to, must do sth. (see 21.1 and 5)
différer de qch./qn	differ from, be different from sth./s.o.
dire faire/avoir fait qch.	say that one does/has done sth.
dire à qn de faire qch.	tell s.o. to do sth. (see 15.13)
dire qch. à qn	tell s.o. sth., say sth. to s.o.
se diriger vers qch./qn	make for, make one's way towards sth./s.o.
discuter de qch.	argue about, discuss, debate sth.
disposer de qch.	have the use of sth., have sth. at one's disposal
dissuader qn de faire qch.	dissuade s.o. from doing sth., convince s.o. not to do sth.
donner qch. à qn	give s.o. sth.
donner à qn envie de faire qch.	make s.o. want to do sth., make s.o. feel like doing sth.
donner à qn la permission de faire qch.	give s.o. permission to do sth.
doter qch./qn de qch.	equip sth./s.o. with sth.
douter de qch./qn	doubt, question sth./s.o.
se douter de qch.	suspect sth.
échapper à qch./qn	escape from sth./s.o.
échouer à (un examen)	fail (an exam)
écouter qch./qn	listen to sth./s.o.
s'efforcer de faire qch.	do one's best to, strive to, make an effort to do sth.

s'emparer de qch.	get hold of, seize sth.
empêcher qn de faire qch.	prevent, stop s.o. from doing sth.
employer qn à faire qch.	employ s.o. to do sth.
emprunter qch. à qn	borrow sth. from s.o. (see 18.10)
s'encombrer de qch.	load, burden oneself with sth.
encourager qn à faire qch.	encourage s.o. to do sth.
s'engager à faire qch.	commit oneself to doing sth., undertake to do sth.
s'engager dans qch.	enter into, embark on sth.
enlever qch. à qn	take sth. away from s.o. (see 18.10)
s'entendre bien avec qn	get on well with s.o.
entendre dire qch.	hear sth. (see 15.14)
entendre parler de qch./qn	hear about sth./s.o. (see 15.14)
entendre qn faire qch.	hear s.o. doing sth.
entrer à qch.	go to (institution)
entrer dans qch.	enter sth.
espérer qch.	hope for sth.
espérer faire qch.	hope to do sth.
essayer de faire qch.	try to do sth.
être en droit de faire qch.	have a right to, the right to do sth., be entitled to do sth.
être en mesure de faire qch.	be in a position to do sth.
être en train de faire qch.	be (in the middle of) doing sth.
être sur le point de faire qch.	be about to do sth.
éviter qch.	avoid sth.
éviter à qn de faire qch.	save s.o. the trouble of doing sth.
éviter qch. à qn	spare s.o. sth.
éviter de faire qch.	avoid doing sth.
s'excuser de qch.	apologise for sth.
s'excuser d'avoir fait qch.	apologise for doing sth.
faire appel à qch./qn	appeal to, call on sth./s.o., call for sth./s.o. (see 18.3)
faire attention à qch./qn	pay attention to, be careful of sth./s.o. (see 18.3)
faire bien de faire qch.	do well to do sth.
faire confiance à qch./qn	trust sth./s.o.
faire du mal à qn	hurt, harm s.o.
faire faire qch.	see 16.17
se faire faire qch.	see 16.17
faire mieux de faire qch.	have better do sth., do better to do sth.
faire partie de qch.	belong to sth., be a member of sth.
faire pression sur qch./qn	put pressure on, influence sth./s.o.
faire preuve de qch.	show (evidence of) sth.
faire la preuve de qch.	prove sth.
falloir : il faut qch. à qn	see 21.4
falloir : il faut faire qch.	see 21.4
féliciter qn de qch.	congratulate s.o. for sth.
se féliciter de qch.	be pleased with sth., congratulate oneself on sth.
se féliciter d'avoir fait qch.	congratulate oneself on having done sth.

finir de faire qch.	*finish doing sth.*
finir par faire qch.	*do sth. in the end, eventually*
fournir qch. à qn	*provide, supply s.o. with sth.*
garder qch./qn	*look after sth./so.; keep sth.*
s'habituer à qch./qn	*become, get used to sth./s.o. (see 18.3)*
s'habituer à faire qch.	*become, get used to doing sth.*
hésiter à faire qch.	*hesitate to do sth.*
se heurter à qn	*come into conflict with s.o.*
heurter qch.	*collide with sth.*
heurter qn	*offend s.o.*
se heurter à qch.	*come up against, meet with sth.*
importer : il importe de faire qch.	*it is important to do sth.*
inciter qn à faire qch.	*urge, incite s.o. to do sth.*
influer sur qch./qn	*affect, influence sth./s.o.*
informer qn de qch.	*inform s.o about sth.*
s'inscrire à qch.	*enrol for, put one's name down for sth.*
insister pour faire qch.	*insist on doing sth.*
s'intégrer à qch.	*be, become integrated into sth.*
s'intéresser à qch./qn	*be interested in sth./s.o. (see 18.3)*
interdire à qn de faire qch.	*forbid s.o. to do sth. (see 15.13)*
inviter qn à qch.	*invite s.o. to sth.*
inviter qn à faire qch	*invite s.o. to do sth.*
jouer à qch.	*play (game)*
jouer de qch.	*play (musical instrument)*
jouir de qch.	*enjoy sth.*
se livrer à qch.	*engage in, be engaged in sth., practise sth., indulge sth.*
ne pas manquer de faire qch.	*be sure to do sth., do sth. without fail*
manquer de qch.	*be short of, lack sth.*
se méfier de qch./qn	*be careful about, mistrust sth./s.o.*
mêler qch. à qch.	*mix sth. with sth.*
se mêler de qch.	*meddle with, interfere with sth.*
menacer qn de qch.	*threaten s.o. with sth.*
menacer de faire qch.	*threaten to do sth.*
se mettre à qch.	*begin, start sth.*
se mettre à faire qch.	*begin, start doing sth.*
mettre (deux heures) à faire qch.	*take (two hours) to do sth.*
mettre fin à qch.	*put an end to sth.*
se munir de qch.	*equip, provide oneself with sth.*
négliger qch.	*overlook, neglect sth.*
négliger de faire qch.	*neglect, not bother to do sth.*
nuire à qch./qn	*harm sth./s.o.*
obéir à qn	*obey s.o.*
obliger qn à faire qch.	*compel, oblige s.o. to do sth.*
être obligé de faire qch.	*be compelled to, obliged to do sth.*

s'occuper de qch./qn	attend to, look after sth./s.o.; be in charge of, deal with sth.
s'occuper de faire qch.	see about, set about doing sth.
offrir qch. à qn	offer, give s.o. sth.
offrir de faire qch.	offer to do sth.
s'offusquer de qch.	be offended at, by sth.
s'opposer à qch./qn	conflict with, oppose sth./s.o.
s'opposer à ce que qn fasse qch.	oppose s.o. doing sth.
ordonner à qn de faire qch.	order s.o. to do sth. (see 15.13)
ôter qch. à qn	take sth. away from s.o. (see also verbs in 18.10)
oublier de faire qch.	forget to do sth.
s'ouvrir à qch.	become aware of, open one's mind to sth.
pardonner qch. à qn	forgive s.o. for sth.
pardonner à qn d'avoir fait qch.	forgive s.o. for doing sth. (see 15.13)
parler de qch./qn	talk about, speak about sth./s.o.
parler de faire qch.	talk about, speak about doing sth.
participer à qch.	take part in, participate in sth.
partir faire	leave, set off to do sth.
parvenir à faire qch.	succeed in doing sth., manage to do sth.
passer du temps à faire qch.	spend time doing sth.
payer qch.	pay for sth.
se pencher sur qch.	look into, turn one's attention to sth.
penser faire qch.	be thinking of doing sth., intend to do sth.
penser à qch./qn	think about, of sth./s.o. (see 18.3)
penser de qch./qn	think of, have an opinion of sth./s.o.
perdre du temps à faire qch.	waste time doing sth.
permettre (à qn) de faire qch.	allow, permit (s.o.) to do sth. (see 15.13)
permettre qch. à qn	allow s.o. sth.
persister à faire qch.	persist in doing sth.
se plaindre (à qn) de qch./qn	complain (to s.o.) about sth./s.o.
plaire à qn	be liked by s.o. (see 3.7)
porter atteinte à qch.	undermine sth.
porter sur qch.	be about, concern sth.
poser une question à qn	ask s.o. a question
pouvoir faire qch.	be able to, can, may do sth. (see 21.2 and 5)
préférer faire qch.	prefer to do sth.
prendre qch. à qn	take sth. from s.o. (see 18.10)
prendre qch./qn au sérieux	take sth./s.o. seriously
prendre qch./qn en charge	take charge of sth./s.o., take care of sth./s.o.
prendre conscience de qch.	become aware of, realise sth.
prendre part à qch.	take part in sth.
se préoccuper de qch./qn	be worried about, give one's attention to sth./s.o.
se présenter à qch.	sit, take (exam, etc.), apply for (job), stand at (election)
prêter assistance à qn	help s.o., go to s.o.'s aid
prévoir de faire qch.	plan on doing, plan to do sth.
prier qn de faire qch.	request, invite, beg s.o. to do sth.
procéder à qch.	set up, carry out, initiate sth.

profiter de qch./qn	*take advantage of sth./s.o., make the most of sth.*
promettre qch. à qn	*promise s.o. sth.*
promettre à qn de faire qch.	*promise s.o. that one will do sth. (see 15.13)*
promettre de faire qch.	*promise to do sth.*
proposer à qn de faire qch.	*offer to do sth., suggest that s.o. does sth.*
proposer de faire qch.	*offer to do sth., suggest doing sth.*
raconter qch. à qn	*tell s.o. sth.*
se rappeler qch.	*remember sth.*
rappeler qch. à qn	*remind s.o. of sth.*
recommander à qn de faire qch.	*recommend that s.o. does sth., advise s.o. to do sth.*
refléchir à qch.	*think about, consider sth.*
refuser qch. à qn	*refuse s.o. sth.*
refuser de faire qch.	*refuse to do sth.*
regarder qch./qn	*look at, watch sth./s.o.*
regarder qn faire qch.	*look at, watch s.o. doing sth.*
regretter d'avoir fait qch.	*regret doing sth.*
remercier qn de qch.	*thank s.o. for sth.*
remercier qn d'avoir fait qch.	*thank s.o. for doing sth.*
remettre qch. en cause	*question sth.*
s'en remettre à qn	*leave it up to s.o., leave the matter in s.o.'s hands*
se rendre compte de qch.	*be aware of, realise sth.*
renoncer à qch.	*give up, abandon sth.*
se renseigner sur qch./qn	*make enquiries about, find out about sth./s.o.*
répondre à qch./qn	*answer sth./s.o.*
se résigner à faire qch.	*resign oneself to doing sth.*
résister à qch.	*hold out against, resist sth.*
se résoudre à faire qch.	*resign oneself to doing sth., resolve to do sth., make up one's mind to do sth.*
ressembler à qn	*look like, resemble s.o.*
se résumer à qch.	*amount to, to come down to sth.*
retirer qch. à qn	*take away, remove sth. from s.o.*
réussir qch.	*make a success of sth.*
réussir à faire qch.	*succeed in doing sth.*
réussir à (un examen)	*pass (exam)*
rêver de qch./qn	*dream of sth./s.o.*
rêver de faire qch.	*dream of doing sth.*
rêver à qch.	*hope for sth.*
rire de qch./qn	*laugh at sth./s.o.*
risquer de faire qch.	*be likely to do sth., might well do sth., risk doing sth.*
savoir faire qch.	*know how to do sth., can do sth.*
sembler faire qch.	*seem to do sth.*
servir à qch.	*be used for sth.*
servir à faire qch.	*be used to do sth.*
se servir de qch.	*use sth., make use of sth.*
songer à qch.	*think about, consider sth.*

songer à faire qch.	*think about, consider doing sth.*
soigner qn/qch.	*look after s.o./sth., take care over sth.*
souhaiter qch.	*wish for, want sth.*
souhaiter faire qch.	*wish to, want to do sth.*
soumettre qn à qch., qch. à qn	*subject s.o. to sth., submit sth. to s.o.*
se soumettre à qch.	*submit to sth.*
se souvenir de qch./qn	*remember sth./s.o.*
se souvenir d'avoir fait qch.	*remember doing sth.*
suffire (à qn pour faire qch.)	*be enough (for s.o. to do sth.)*
suffire : il suffit de faire qch.	*it is enough, sufficient to do sth. (see 24.6)*
suggérer à qn de faire qch.	*suggest that s.o. does sth.*
teléphoner à qn	*telephone, call s.o.*
tenir à qch.	*value sth.*
tenir à faire qch.	*be anxious to, keen to do sth.*
tenir compte de qch.	*take sth. into account, into consideration*
tenter de faire qch.	*attempt to, try to do sth.*
tirer sur qch./qn	*fire at, shoot sth./s.o.*
tomber amoureux de qn	*fall in love with s.o.*
se tourner vers qch./qn	*turn to sth./s.o.*
user de qch.	*make use of use sth.*
valoir : il vaut mieux faire qch.	*it is better to do sth.*
venir faire qch.	*come and do sth., come to do sth.*
venir de faire qch.	*have just done sth. (see 4.15)*
viser qch./qn	*have sth. as one's aim; be intended for s.o.*
viser à qch.	*aim at sth.*
viser à faire qch.	*aim to do sth.*
vivre qch.	*live through, experience sth.*
vivre de qch.	*live on, off sth.*
voir qn faire qch.	*see s.o. doing sth.*
se voir faire qch.	*see 22.7*
voler qch. à qn	*steal sth. from s.o. (see 18.10)*
vouloir faire qch.	*want to, wish to do sth. (see 21.3)*
en vouloir à qn	*bear a grudge against, hold it against s.o.*

Common adjectives and their constructions

References are to the chapter number and the section number.

accompagné de qn	*accompanied by s.o.*
adapté à qch.	*suited to, suitable for sth.*
approprié à qch.	*appropriate for, suitable for sth.*
assuré de qch.	*confident of, sure of sth.*
capable de faire qch.	*capable of doing sth.*
censé faire qch.	*supposed to do sth.*
certain de qch.	*certain of, convinced of sth.*
certain de faire qch.	*certain to do sth.*
chargé de faire qch.	*responsible for doing sth.*
chargé de qch.	*in charge of sth., loaded with sth.*
conforme à qch.	*in keeping with, in accordance with sth.*
content de faire qch.	*pleased to, happy to do sth.*
content de qch./qn	*pleased with, happy with sth./s.o.*
contraint de faire qch.	*forced to, compelled to do sth.*
coupé de qch.	*cut off from sth.*
couvert de qch.	*covered with sth.*
curieux de faire qch.	*curious to, interested to, keen to do sth.*
décidé à faire qch.	*determined to do sth.*
défavorable à qch.	*against sth.*
désireux de faire qch.	*wanting to, anxious to do sth.*
destiné à qch./qn	*intended for sth./s.o.*
destiné à faire qch.	*intended to, meant to do sth.*
déterminé à faire qch.	*resolved to, determined to do sth.*
différent de qch./qn	*different from sth./s.o.*
difficile à faire	*difficult to do*
il est difficile de faire qch.	*it is difficult to do sth. (see 20.4)*
disposé à faire qch.	*inclined to do sth.*
dur à faire	*hard to do*
il est dur de faire qch.	*it is hard to do sth. (see 20.4)*
enchanté de qch./qn	*enchanted by, delighted with sth./s.o.*
enchanté de faire qch.	*delighted to, pleased to do sth.*
exclu de qch.	*excluded from sth.*
facile à faire	*easy to do*
il est facile de faire qch.	*it is easy to do sth. (see 20.4)*
favorable à qch.	*in favour of sth.*
fier de qch.	*proud of sth.*
heureux de faire qch.	*happy to do sth.*
impossible à faire	*impossible to do*
il est impossible de faire qch.	*it is impossible to do sth. (see 20.4)*

impressionné de faire qch.	*impressed at doing sth.*
impressionné par qch./qn	*impressed by s.o./sth.*
incapable de (faire) qch.	*incapable of (doing) sth.*
inconscient de qch.	*unaware of sth.*
inquiet de qch.	*worried about sth.*
inutile de faire qch.	*useless to do sth.*
lent à faire qch.	*slow to do sth.*
long à faire qch.	*a long time doing sth.*
mécontent de qch.	*dissatisfied with sth.*
nécessaire à qch.	*necessary for sth.*
obligé de faire qch.	*compelled to, obliged to do sth.*
prédisposé à qch.	*prone to sth.*
préférable à qch.	*preferable to sth.*
préjudiciable à qch./qn	*detrimental to, harmful to sth./s.o.*
pressé de faire qch.	*in a hurry to do sth.*
prêt à faire qch.	*ready to do sth.*
propre à qch.	*appropriate for, suitable for sth.*
propre à faire qch.	*suited to do sth.*
ravi de faire qch.	*delighted to do sth.*
responsable de qch./qn	*responsible for sth./s.o.*
ridicule de faire qch.	*ridiculous to do sth.*
satisfait de qch./qn	*satisfied with sth./s.o.*
sensible à qch.	*susceptible to sth.*
seul à faire qch.	*only one to do sth.*
soucieux de qch.	*concerned with sth., about sth.*
soucieux de faire qch.	*anxious to do sth.*
souhaitable de faire qch.	*desirable to do sth.*
stupéfait de faire qch.	*amazed to, astounded to do sth.*
sûr de qch./qn	*sure of sth./so., assured of sth.*
sûr de faire qch.	*sure of doing sth.*
susceptible de faire qch.	*liable to, likely to do sth., capable of doing sth.*
utopique de faire qch.	*utopian to, unrealistic to do sth.*

English–French vocabulary for translation exercises

Abbreviations

adj.	adjective
adv.	adverb
fem.	feminine
inf.	infinitive
masc.	masculine
pl.	plural
qn	quelqu'un
qch.	quelque chose
s.o.	someone
sth.	something

1970s **les années 1970, les années soixante-dix**

A

	able to	**capable de**
to be	able to	**pouvoir**
	abnormality	**une anomalie**
	about	**(à propos) de, sur, concernant**
to be	about	**porter sur**
	about [+ number]	**environ**
	about ten, fifteen, twenty, etc.	**une dizaine de, une quinzaine de, une vingtaine de, etc.**
to be	about to + *inf.*	**être sur le point de + *inf.***
	abroad	**à l'étranger**
to go	abroad	**partir à l'étranger**
	absence	**une absence**
to	accept	**accepter**
to have	access to sth.	**avoir accès à qch.**
	accident	**un accident**
	accompaniment	**un accompagnement**
	according to s.o.	**selon qn**
	according to sth.	**en fonction de qch.**
to	act	**agir**
	action	**une action**
	activity	**une activité**
	actor	**un acteur**
drug	addict	**un toxicomane**
in	addition	**en outre**
to	admit	**admettre**
	adolescence	**l'adolescence** *fem.*
	adolescent	**un(e) adolescent(e)**
to	adopt	**adopter**
	adult *adj.*	**adulte**
	adulthood	**l'âge adulte** *masc.*
well in	advance	**longtemps à l'avance**

	advertisement	une petite annonce
	advertising	la publicité
cigarette	advertising	la publicité pour les cigarettes
	advertising *adj.*	publicitaire
	advertising industry	la publicité
	advertising professional	un publicitaire
	advice	les conseils *masc. pl.*
	advisable	recommandé
	adviser	un conseiller
to	advocate	prôner
to	affect	toucher
	affected [by floods etc.]	sinistré
to be	afraid of	craindre
	Africa	l'Afrique *fem.*
	after	après
	after …ing	après + *past inf.*
	against	contre
	age	un âge
	agency	une agence
travel	agent	une agence de voyages
(one month)	ago	il y a (un mois)
to	agree that	s'accorder pour dire que
	agreement	un accord
	aid	l'aide *fem.*
	AIDS	le sida
	aim	un objectif
	airport	un aéroport
	all *adj.*	tout
to be	all right	aller bien
	all the more	d'autant plus
to	allow s.o. to do sth.	permettre à qn de faire qch.
	also	aussi, également
	alternative *adj.*	alternatif
	although	si, bien que
	although [while]	tout en + …ant
	always	toujours
	amazing *adj.*	remarquable
	amount	une quantité
	angrily	d'un ton irrité
	another	encore un(e), un(e) autre
	anti-establishment *adj.*	contestataire
	antibiotics	les antibiotiques *masc. pl.*
	any	n'importe quel
not	any	ne … pas, ne … aucun
	anyone, no one	ne … personne
	anything, nothing	ne … rien
	anywhere, nowhere	ne … nulle part (où)
	anywhere	n'importe où
to	appeal to s.o.	plaire à qn
to make an	appeal to [legal]	faire appel à
	appearance	le look

to apply for [document]	**faire une demande de**
to apply for [job]	**se présenter à**
to apply to [person, organisation]	**s'adresser à**
to approve of	**approuver**
to arbitrate in sth.	**juger qch.**
to argue that	**soutenir que, affirmer que**
to arm	**armer**
to arrest	**arrêter**
arrival	**une arrivée**
to arrive	**arriver**
artificial *adj.*	**artificiel**
as	**comme, en tant que**
as a result of	**à la suite de**
as … as	**aussi … que**
as … as it may seem	**aussi … que cela puisse paraître**
to be as high as	**atteindre**
as long as	**tant que**
as much … (as)	**autant de … (que)**
so as to	**pour**
as well	**aussi**
to ascribe to	**attribuer à**
to ask for	**demander**
to ask s.o. sth.	**demander qch. à qn**
aspect	**un aspect**
Assam	**Assam**
General Assembly [United Nations]	**l'Assemblée générale** *fem.*
to assess	**mesurer**
to assist	**assister**
assistance	**une assistance**
[bomb] attack	**un attentat**
to attend sth.	**assister à qch.**
attitude	**une attitude**
August	**août**
Austria	**l'Autriche** *fem.*
authorities	**les pouvoirs publics** *masc. pl.*
authorisation	**une autorisation**
available	**disponible**
freely available	**en vente libre**
on average	**en moyenne**
to avoid (…ing)	**éviter (de + *inf.*)**
to avoid sth.	**éviter qch.**
to award	**accorder**

B

badly	**mal**
balance	**un équilibre**
bank	**une banque**
bank card	**une carte bancaire**
barely	**à peine**
to be	**être**
to be about to	**être sur le point de**

to	be [statistics]	**représenter**
to	be ...ing	**être en train de + *inf*.**
	because	**parce que**
	because of	**à cause de**
to	become	**devenir**
to	become familiar with sth.	**s'initier à qch.**
	before	**avant**
the summer	before	**l'été précédent**
	before ...*ing*	**avant de + *inf*.**
to	begin (to + *inf*.)	**commencer (à + *inf*.)**
	Belgium	**la Belgique**
to	believe	**croire**
(the)	best *adj*.	**(le) meilleur**
to make	better	**améliorer**
it is	better	**il vaut mieux**
	between	**entre**
	billion	**un milliard**
	birth rate	**le taux de natalité, la natalité**
	birthday	**un anniversaire**
on my 17th	birthday	**le jour de mes dix-sept ans**
executive	body	**un organe exécutif**
	body [organisation]	**un organisme**
	bomb attack	**un attentat à la bombe**
	book	**un livre**
to	book [flight]	**faire une réservation**
to	borrow sth. from	**emprunter qch. à**
	Brazil	**le Brésil**
to	break out [war]	**éclater**
	bridge	**un pont**
to	bring together	**réunir**
	British *adj*.	**britannique**
the	British	**les Britanniques**
	brother	**un frère**
	but	**mais**
to	buy from	**acheter à**
to	buy s.o. sth.	**acheter qch. à qn**
	by	**par**
	by [+ year]	**d'ici à**
	by ...ing	**en ...ant**

C

to	call on s.o.	**faire appel à qn**
to	call s.o. in (to + *inf*.)	**faire appel à qn (pour + *inf*.)**
	campaign [advertising]	**une campagne**
	can *verb*	**pouvoir**
	car	**une voiture**
	card	**une carte**
to	carry	**porter**
to	carry out	**effectuer**
	case	**le cas**
in	case of	**en cas de**

	cash dispenser	**un distributeur de billets**
	casualty	**un(e) blessé(e)**
	cause	**une cause**
	cause for concern	**de quoi s'inquiéter**
to	cause	**causer**
	caused by	**dû à**
	censorship	**la censure**
	centre of town	**le centre-ville**
	century	**un siècle**
	cereal	**une céréale**
	certain *adj.*	**certain**
	certainly	**certainement**
to	challenge	**remettre en cause**
	Chamber of Commerce	**la Chambre de commerce**
	change	**une transformation**
to	change [replace]	**changer de**
to	change [transform]	**bouleverser, changer, modifier**
the	cheapest	**le moins cher**
to	check	**vérifier**
to	check in [luggage]	**faire enregistrer**
	chemical	**chimique**
	child	**un enfant**
	childhood	**l'enfance** *fem.*
	China	**la Chine**
	chocolate	**un bonbon au chocolat, un chocolat**
to	choose (to + *inf.*)	**choisir (de + *inf.*)**
	Christmas	**Noël**
	cigarette advertising	**la publicité pour les cigarettes**
	city	**une ville**
	civil *adj.*	**civil**
to	claim	**prétendre, affirmer**
	claim [insurance]	**une demande de remboursement**
	clarity	**la clarté**
	clearly	**clairement**
to	close down	**fermer**
	clothes	**les vêtements** *masc. pl.*
	cloud	**un nuage**
	club	**un club**
	coach	**un car**
	colouring	**un colorant**
to	combine	**allier**
	commerce	**le commerce**
	commercial	**un film publicitaire**
European	Commission	**la Commission européenne**
to	communicate	**communiquer**
	communication	**la communication**
	company	**une société, une entreprise**
	company head	**un chef d'entreprise**
the	company one keeps	**les fréquentations** *fem. pl.*
	competence	**une compétence**
	competitiveness	**la compétitivité**

	competitor	un concurrent
to	complain	se plaindre
	complete *adj.*	total
	completely	complètement, entièrement
	complex *adj.*	complexe
to	conceal from	cacher à
	concern	des inquiétudes *fem. pl.*
to	concern	concerner
to be	concerned about	se préoccuper de
	condition	une condition
	conference	une conférence
to	confide sth. in s.o.	confier qch. à qn
	confidential *adj.*	confidentiel
	conflict	un conflit
to	confuse	confondre
	consensus	un consensus
	consequence	une conséquence
to	consider (as)	considérer (comme)
	considerably	considérablement
	constantly	constamment
	consulate	un consulat
	consumer	le consommateur
	consumer habit	une habitude de consommation
	contagious *adj.*	contagieux
to	continue	se poursuivre
to	continue to + *inf.*	continuer à + *inf.*
on the	contrary	au contraire, en revanche
to	contribute (to sth.)	contribuer (à qch.)
to	control	contrôler
to be	convened	se réunir
	conviction	la conviction
to	convince	convaincre
	co-operation	la coopération
to	correspond to	correspondre à
	cost	le coût
at no	cost	gratuitement
	Council	le Conseil
	country	un pays
	countryside	la campagne
	couple	un couple
	courage	le courage
training	course	un stage de formation
	course [university]	des études *fem. pl.*
	Court [legal]	la Cour
	cream	une crème
to	create	créer
to	create happiness	faire le bonheur
	creative *adj.*	créatif
	crisis	la crise
	critic	un critique
	crop	une culture

to	cross	**traverser**
	cultural *adj.*	**culturel**
European	Cup	**la Coupe d'Europe**
to	cure	**guérir**
foreign	currency	**des devises** *fem. pl.*
	current *adj.*	**actuel**
to	cycle	**aller à bicyclette**
to	cycle to work	**aller travailler à bicyclette**

D

	daily newspaper	**un quotidien**
to	damage	**endommager**
	day	**un jour, une journée**
Christmas	day	**le jour de Noël**
no	car day	**une journée sans voitures**
a great	deal of	**beaucoup de**
	December	**décembre** *masc.*
to	decide (to + *inf.*)	**décider (de + *inf.*)**
	decision	**une décision**
to make the	decision to + *inf.*	**prendre la décision de + *inf.*,**
		décider de + *inf.*
	deep *adj.*	**profond**
	deeply	**profondément**
	deficit	**un déficit**
	delicious *adj.*	**délicieux**
to be	designed to	**viser à**
	designed to	**visant à**
	desirable *adj.*	**souhaitable**
	desire	**une envie**
	dessert	**un entremets**
	dessert with (fresh cream)	**un entremets à (la crème fraîche)**
to	destroy	**détruire**
	details *pl.*	**des informations** *fem. pl.*
	determined (to)	**décidé (à)**
to	devastate	**dévaster**
to	develop	**développer**
	developing	**en voie de développement**
	development	**le développement**
to	die	**mourir**
to	die as a result of	**être victime de**
to go on a	diet	**se mettre au régime**
	different *adj.* (from)	**différent (de)**
	difficult *adj.*	**difficile**
to find it	difficult to + *inf.*	**avoir du mal à + *inf.*,**
		avoir de la peine à + *inf.*
	difficulty	**une difficulté**
to	diminish	**diminuer**
	dinner	**un dîner**
special	dinner	**un grand dîner**
	dinner party	**un repas de fête**
to	disagree	**être en désaccord**

	disagreement	un désaccord
to	disappear	disparaître
	disappearance	une disparition
to	disappoint	décevoir
	disappointing *adj.*	décevant
to	disclose	divulguer
	discouraging *adj.*	décourageant
to	discover	découvrir
	discussion	une discussion
	disease	une maladie
to	display	afficher
	dispute	un différend
to	divorce	divorcer
	divorced couple	des divorcés *masc. pl.*
to	do	faire
	document	un document
to	double	doubler
a	dozen	une douzaine de
	dramatically	d'une manière dramatique, d'une façon dramatique
	drastic *adj.*	radical
to	drive	conduire
	driving licence	un permis de conduire
to	drop by [statistics]	diminuer de, baisser de
	drought	la sécheresse, la pénurie d'eau
	drug	une drogue
	drug addict	un toxicomane
	drug trafficker	un trafiquant de drogue
	drug trafficking	le trafic des stupéfiants, le trafic de la drogue
to	dump	jeter
	during	pendant, au cours de
town	dweller	un citadin

E

	each	chaque
	early	tôt
to	earn	gagner
Friends of the	Earth	Amis de la terre
	Easter	Pâques
	Eastern Europe	l'Europe *fem.* de l'Est
to	eat	manger
	Economic and Social Council	le Conseil économique et social
	economic *adj.*	économique
general	editor	un rédacteur en chef
	effective *adj.*	performant
	efficient *adj.*	efficace
not	either	non plus
to	elect	élire
	electric *adj.*	électrique
	electronic *adj.*	électronique

	electronics factory	une usine d'électronique
to	eliminate	éliminer
	emission	une émission
gas	emission	une émission de gaz
to	employ	employer
	employee	un(e) salarié(e), un(e) employé(e)
	employment sector	un secteur d'activité
to	enable s.o. to do sth.	permettre à qn de faire qch.
to	encourage	encourager
to	encourage s.o. to do sth.	encourager qn à faire qch.
	end	la fin
to ... in the	end	finir par ...
	energy	une énergie
	engine [aeroplane]	un réacteur
	England	l'Angleterre *fem.*
	English *adj.*	anglais
	enough	assez, suffisamment
to be	enough to	suffire à, suffire pour
to have	enough to + *inf.*	avoir de quoi + *inf.*
	environment	un environnement
	environmental *adj.*	de l'environnement
	environmentalist	un écologiste
	essential *adj.* for	indispensable à
	estate	une cité
	Europe	l'Europe *fem.*
	European	européen
Southern	European	d'Europe du Sud
	European Commission	la Commission européenne
	European Cup	la Coupe d'Europe
	European Union	l'Union européenne *fem.*
	evacuation	une évacuation
	even	même
	even if	même si
	even [indeed]	voire
	evening	un soir
for	ever	définitivement
	every *adj.*	chaque, tout
	every other week	tous les quinze jours
	every / per week, month, etc.	par semaine, mois, etc.
	everybody	tout le monde, tous
	everything	tout
	everywhere	partout
	exam	un examen
	example	un exemple
	example set by	l'exemple *masc.* de
for	example	par exemple
	excellent *adj.*	excellent
	exchange	un échange
to	exchange [words]	échanger
	excited *adj.*	excité
	executive *adj.*	exécutif

to	exhaust	**épuiser**
to be in	existence	**exister**
to	expect	**attendre**
to	expect sth.	**s'attendre à qch.**
	expected *adj*	**prévu**
	experience	**une expérience**
to	experience	**connaître**
	expert	**un(e) spécialiste**
to	explain sth. to s.o.	**expliquer qch. à qn**
to	explode	**exploser**
to	exploit	**exploiter**
	explosion	**une explosion**
	extent	**l'ampleur** *fem.*
	extremely	**extrêmement**
	eye	**un œil (***pl.* **des yeux)**

F

	fact	**une information**
in	fact	**en fait**
	factory	**une usine**
not to	fail to + *inf.*	**ne pas manquer de +** *inf.*
to	fall	**diminuer, être en baisse**
to	fall within sth.	**relever de qch.**
to become	familiar with sth.	**s'initier à qch.**
	family	**une famille**
	fans *pl.*	**le public**
	far from	**loin de**
to	favour	**privilégier**
to	fear	**craindre**
	feature film	**un long métrage**
to	feel + *adj.*	**se sentir +** *adj.*
to	feel guilty about sth.	**se reprocher qch.**
	festival	**un festival**
a	few	**quelques**
about	fifteen	**une quinzaine de**
	fight	**une lutte**
to	fight	**lutter**
	film	**un film**
	finally	**finalement**
to	find	**trouver**
to	find it difficult to + *inf.*	**avoir du mal à +** *inf.***, avoir de la peine à +** *inf.*
to	find out sth.	**apprendre qch.**
	fine *adj.*	**beau**
	fireman	**un pompier**
	firm	**une société, une entreprise**
	first *adj.*	**premier**
	first-year student	**un(e) étudiant(e) de première année**
at	first	**au début**
	first and foremost	**en tout premier lieu**
	flat	**un appartement**

flood	une inondation
to follow	suivre
following *adj.*	suivant
following sth.	à la suite de qch.
food	la nourriture
food aid	l'aide alimentaire *fem.*
for	pendant, depuis,
to force s.o. to	obliger qn à, forcer qn à
foreign *adj.*	étranger
Foreign Affairs	les Affaires étrangères *fem. pl.*
Foreign Minister	le / la ministre des Affaires étrangères
foreign trade	le commerce extérieur
foreman	le contremaître
to forget	oublier
fortnight	quinze jours
fossil fuel	un combustible fossile
to found	créer
franc	un franc
France	la France
free of charge	gratuitement
freedom	la liberté
freely	librement
freely available	en vente libre
French *adj.*	français
the French	les Français
fresh *adj.*	frais
fresh water	l'eau *fem.* douce
Friday	un vendredi
friend	un copain, une copine ; un ami, une amie
Friends of the Earth	Amis de la terre
coming from	de, en provenance de
in front of	devant
frozen meal	un plat surgelé
fuel	un combustible
funny *adj.*	amusant
furious *adj.*	furieux
future	l'avenir *masc.*

G

gain [victory]	une conquête
game	un jeu
garden	un jardin
greenhouse gas	les gaz *masc.* à effet de serre
General Assembly	l'Assemblée générale *fem.*
as a general rule	en règle générale
generally	en général, généralement
generation	une génération
generous *adj.* with s.o.	généreux envers qn
genetically engineered plant	une plante transgénique

	Germany	l'Allemagne *fem.*
to	get home	rentrer
to	give as a present	offrir
to	give s.o. sth.	donner qch. à qn
to	give up	abandonner
	given	étant donné
to be	given off	se dégager
	global warming	le réchauffement climatique
to	go	aller, partir
to	go away	partir
to	go on a diet	se mettre au régime
to	go out	sortir
to	go to s.o.	s'adresser à qn, faire appel à qn
	good *adj.*	bon
	goods	des marchandises *fem. pl.*
	government	le gouvernement
	gradually	progressivement
	great *adj.*	grand
it is	great	c'est formidable, c'est super
a	great deal of	beaucoup de
a	great many	bon nombre de, beaucoup de
	greatly	considérablement
	Greece	la Grèce
	greenhouse gas	les gaz *masc.* à effet de serre
	group	un groupe
to	grow	croître, augmenter
	growth	la croissance
to	guarantee	assurer
	guaranteed *adj.*	garanti
to feel	guilty about sth.	se reprocher qch.

H

	habit	une habitude
	hair	les cheveux *masc. pl.*
	half	la moitié
on the other	hand	par contre
to	happen	arriver, se passer
	happiness	le bonheur
to create	happiness	faire le bonheur
	hard *adj.*	dur
	hardly	ne ... guère
	hatred	la haine
to	have just (done)	venir de (faire)
to	have sth.	avoir qch., disposer de qch.
to	have to	avoir à, devoir
company	head	un chef d'entreprise
	Head of State	un chef d'État
	health	la santé
to	hear	entendre
to	hear about sth.	entendre parler de qch.
to	hear s.o. + *inf.*	entendre qn + *inf.*

s.o. with	hearing impairment	**un mal entendant**
	heavily	**très**
	heavy *adj.* [rain]	**fort**
	hectare	**un hectare**
to be	held	**se tenir**
to	help s.o. to + *inf.*	**aider qn à + *inf.***
	here	**ici**
to	hesitate	**hésiter**
	high *adj.*	**élevé, lourd**
to be as	high as [statistics]	**atteindre**
	highly	**hautement**
to	hire	**louer**
	holiday	**des vacances** *fem. pl.*
to get	home	**rentrer**
	homeopath	**un(e) homéopathe**
	homosexual	**un(e) homosexuel(le)**
	homosexuality	**l'homosexualité** *fem.*
	hotel	**un hôtel**
rush	hour	**les heures** *fem. pl.* **de pointe**
	house	**une maison**
	household rubbish	**les ordures ménagères** *fem. pl.*
	however	**cependant**
	humanitarian *adj.*	**humanitaire**
	humiliation	**une humiliation**
	hundreds of	**des centaines de**
	hunger	**la faim**

I

	ice-cream	**une crème glacée**
	idea	**une idée**
	ideal *adj.*	**idéal**
	if	**si**
	illegal *adj.*	**illicite**
it is an	illusion to	**il est illusoire de**
	illustration	**une illustration**
to	imagine	**imaginer**
	immediately	**tout de suite, immédiatement**
	impact	**un impact**
to be	implemented	**entrer en vigueur**
	implemented *adj.*	**appliqué**
to	import	**importer**
	important *adj.*	**important**
it is	important to	**il importe de**
to	improve	**s'améliorer**
to	improve sth.	**améliorer qch.**
to	incinerate	**incinérer**
to be	included in sth.	**figurer sur qch.**
	increase	**une augmentation**
to	increase	**augmenter**
	increasing *adj.*	**croissant**
	India	**l'Inde** *fem.*

	individual	un particulier
	individual *adj.*	individuel
	industrialist	un industriel
	industry	une industrie
advertising	industry	la publicité
	inflation	une inflation
	influence	une influence
to	inform s.o. about sth.	informer qn de qch.
	information	des informations *fem. pl.*
to obtain	information from [person, organisation]	se renseigner auprès de
	inhabitant	un habitant
	initiated by	dû à l'initiative de
	initiative	une initiative
to	injure	blesser
to	inquire	demander
	inquiry into	une enquête sur
to	insist (that)	insister (pour que)
for	instance	par exemple
	instead of	au lieu de
	institute	un institut
	insurance (policy)	une assurance
to	intend to	avoir l'intention de
to be	intended for [course]	s'adresser à
to be	intended for [publication]	être destiné à
	intensive *adj.*	intensif
	interest	un intérêt
	interest [personal]	un centre d'intérêt
to be	interested in	s'intéresser à
	international *adj.*	international
	International Court	la Cour internationale de justice
	Internet	Internet *masc.*
	introduction	une introduction
to	invest	investir
	irresponsible *adj.*	irresponsable
	issue	une question
	Italy	l'Italie *fem.*

J

	Japan	le Japon
	jeans	un jean
to	jeopardise	compromettre
	job	un emploi
	journalist	un(e) journaliste
	juice	le jus

K

to	keep on ...ing	continuer à + *inf.*
	key	une clé
	key role	un rôle clé
to	kill	tuer

	kitchen	une cuisine
to	know about	savoir
to	know [facts]	savoir
to	know [people and places]	connaître
well	known *adj.*	célèbre

L

	lack	un manque, une absence
	large *adj.*	grand
	last *adj.*	dernier
	late	tard
	latest	dernier
the	latter	ce dernier, cette dernière, etc.
to	launch	lancer
money	laundering	le blanchiment de l'argent
	laws [of a country]	la législation
to	lead s.o. to + *inf.*	amener qn à + *inf.*
to	learn	apprendre
at	least	du moins
to	leave	partir
to	leave sth.	laisser qch.
	lecture	un cours
	left-luggage facility	une consigne
to	lend s.o. sth.	prêter qch. à qn
	less	moins
	less than	moins de
	less … than	moins … que
to	let	louer
	life	la vie
to	like sth.	aimer qch.
to	like to + *inf.*	aimer, vouloir + *inf.*
to be	likely to + *inf.*	avoir tendance à + *inf.*
to be	likely to succeed	avoir des chances de réussir
to	limit	limiter
to	listen to	écouter
	litre	un litre
to	live	vivre, habiter
to	live on sth.	vivre de qch.
	living conditions	les conditions *fem. pl.* de vie
	local *adj.*	local
	long *adj.*	long
	long-term unemployed	les chômeurs *masc. pl.* de longue durée
for a	long time	longtemps
as	long as	tant que
	long *adv.*	longtemps
to	look for	chercher
to	lose	perdre
to	lose weight	perdre du poids, perdre des kilos
	loss	une perte
to	love sth.	adorer qch.

	low *adj.*	**bas**
	luggage	**les bagages** *masc. pl.*

M

	made up *adj.* [face]	**maquillé**
	magazine	**un magazine**
	main *adj.*	**principal, primordial, majeur**
	mainly	**principalement**
to	maintain [peace]	**sauvegarder**
	maintenance	**le maintien**
	major *adj.*	**majeur**
	majority	**la majorité**
by	majority vote	**à la majorité**
to	make + *adj.*	**rendre +** *adj.*
to	make better	**améliorer**
to	make up [statistics]	**constituer, représenter**
	management	**la direction**
	management consultant	**un conseiller en management**
	management method [finance]	**une méthode de gestion**
	manager	**un directeur**
	managing director	**un pdg (président-directeur général)**
to be	mandatory	**être obligatoire**
	many	**beaucoup de, de nombreux, bon nombre de**
a great	many	**un grand nombre de**
	March	**mars**
	market	**un marché**
	match	**un match**
in (social)	matters	**dans le domaine (social)**
	may *verb*	**pouvoir**
	meal	**un repas**
frozen	meal	**un plat surgelé**
	measure	**une mesure**
	medical	**médical**
to	meet	**voir, rencontrer**
	megacity	**une mégacité**
	member	**un membre**
to be a	member of a union	**être syndiqué**
to	mention	**mentionner**
	merely + *verb*	**ne faire que +** *inf.*
	method	**une méthode**
	Mexico	**le Mexique**
in the	mid 1980s	**vers le milieu des années 1980, vers le milieu des années quatre-vingts, vers 1985**
	Middle East	**le Moyen-Orient**
	million	**un million**
to take one's	mind off things	**se distraire**
	Minister	**un(e) ministre**
	ministry	**un ministère**
	mission	**une mission**

	mistake	une erreur
to	mistake sth. for sth.	prendre qch. pour qch.
	moderately priced	à petit prix
	money	l'argent *masc.*
	money laundering	le blanchiment de l'argent
	monsoon rain	une pluie de mousson
	month	un mois
	more	plus
	more and more	de plus en plus
once	more	une fois de plus
all the	more	d'autant plus
	morning	un matin
	most	la plupart de
	most of them	la plupart d'entre eux (*fem.* d'entre elles)
to	motivate	motiver
	motorway	une autoroute
	movement	un mouvement
	multimedia (industry)	le multimédia
	music	la musique
	must *verb*	devoir, falloir (il faut), s'agir de (il s'agit)

N

to put one's	name down for sth.	s'inscrire à qch.
	natural *adj.*	naturel
	nature	la nature
	near	près de, à proximité de
to	need sth.	avoir besoin de qch.
to	need to + *inf.*	avoir besoin de + *inf.*
to	neglect	négliger
	negotiation	une négociation
	neighbour	un(e) voisine
	neither ... nor	ne ... ni ...
	never	ne ... jamais
	new *adj.*	nouveau
daily	newspaper	un quotidien
	next	prochain
	next to one another [adjoining]	attenant
	no longer	ne ... plus
	noise	un bruit
	noise pollution	la pollution sonore
	no one	ne ... personne, personne ... ne
	normal	normal
	North Africa	l'Afrique *fem.* du Nord
	north-east	le nord-est
	not	ne ... pas
	not only	non seulement
	not ... any	pas ... de, ne ... aucun
	not ... anywhere	ne ... nulle part

	nothing	ne ... rien, rien ... ne
	nothing left	ne ... plus rien
to	notice sth.	s'apercevoir de qch.
	noticeably	sensiblement
	November	novembre
	now	maintenant, de nos jours
until	now	jusqu'à présent
	nowadays	aujourd'hui, à l'époque actuelle, à l'heure actuelle, de nos jours
	number	un nombre

O

to be	obliged to	se trouver obligé de
	obsession	une obsession
to	obtain information from [person, organisation]	se renseigner auprès de
	obviously	évidemment, bien sûr
on the	occasion of	lors de
to	offer s.o. sth.	offrir qch. à qn
to	offer to + *inf.*	offrir de + *inf.*
	officially	officiellement
	often	souvent
more	often than not	le plus souvent
	on average	en moyenne
	on ...ing	en ...ant
	once	une fois que
	only	uniquement ; ne ... que
not	only	non seulement
	only *adj.* + *noun*	seul
the	only one(s)	le seul, les seuls
	only + *verb*	ne faire que + *inf.*
to	open	ouvrir
	openness	la transparence
	opinion	un avis
public	opinion	l'opinion publique *fem.*
	opinion poll	un sondage d'opinion
the	opposite	le contraire
	orange juice	un jus d'orange
in	order to	pour
	organisation	une organisation
	original *adj.*	original
	other *adj.*	autre
on the	other hand	par contre
	other than	autre que
	others	d'autres
the	others	les autres
	out of [statistics]	sur
	outside	à l'extérieur (de)
	outstanding *adj.*	remarquable
	over [more]	plus de
	own *adj.*	propre

on one's	own	**seul**
	owner	**un(e) propriétaire**
	P	
	paper	**un journal**
	parents	**les parents** *masc. pl.*
	part	**un rôle**
	part of	**une partie de**
	particularly	**surtout**
	partly	**en partie**
	partner [personal, business]	**un(e) partenaire**
	partner [work]	**un collaborateur** *(fem.* **collaboratrice)**
	party [political]	**un parti**
dinner	party	**un repas de fête**
to	pass an exam	**réussir un examen**
	passport	**un passeport**
	pasta	**les pâtes** *fem. pl.*
to	patrol	**patrouiller**
to	pay back	**rembourser**
to	pay for	**payer**
	PC [computer]	**un PC**
	peace	**la paix**
	pedagogical *adj.*	**pédagogique**
a	people	**un peuple**
	people	**les gens** *masc. pl.*, **les personnes** *fem. pl.*
young	people	**les jeunes** *masc. pl.*
	per inhabitant	**par habitant**
	perhaps	**peut-être que, peut-être**
	permanent *adj.*	**permanent**
	person	**une personne**
	personal *adj.*	**personnel**
	petrol	**l'essence** *fem.*
	petrol station	**une station-service**
	phenomenon	**un phénomène**
	photographer	**un(e) photographe**
	pink	**rose**
	place	**une place**
	plan	**un plan, un projet**
	plane [aeroplane]	**un avion**
	planet	**la planète**
to	play	**jouer**
	pleasant *adj.*	**agréable**
to	please	**faire plaisir à**
	pleased *adj.* (with)	**satisfait (de)**
to be	pleased about	**se féliciter de, être ravi de**
to	point out	**souligner**
	police	**la police**
insurance	policy	**une assurance**
	politician	**un politique**

	pollution	la pollution
	population	la population
	Portugal	le Portugal
	position	une position
	possibility of	les risques de *masc. pl.*
to	prefer	préférer
	present *adj.*	actuel
at	present	actuellement
to give as a	present	offrir
	press	la presse
to	prevail	prévaloir
to	prevent sth. from …ing	empêcher qch. de + *inf.*
	previous *adj.*	précédent
moderately	priced	à petit prix
	primarily	essentiellement, principalement
	priority	une priorité
	problem	un problème, une difficulté
	procedure	une procédure
	process	un processus
to	produce	produire
	product	un produit
	productivity	la productivité
advertising	professional	un publicitaire
	profit	un bénéfice
	profitable *adj.*	rémunérateur
	programme	un programme
	programme [TV]	une émission
	project	un projet
to	promise s.o. sth.	promettre qch. à qn
to	promote	promouvoir
to	propose	proposer
to	protect	protéger, sauvegarder
	protecting	la protection, la sauvegarde
	protection	la protection
	proud *adj.* of	fier de
to	prove difficult	s'avérer difficile
to	prove generous	se montrer généreux
to	prove sth.	prouver qch.
	public *adj.*	public
	public transport	les transports collectifs *masc. pl.*
	publication	une publication
to	publish	publier
	publishing	l'édition *fem.*
to	punish	punir
	punk *adj.*	punk
to	pursue	poursuivre
to	put	mettre
to	put one's name down for sth.	s'inscrire à qch.

Q

qualification	**un diplôme**
quality	**une qualité**
quick *adj.*	**rapide**
quickly	**rapidement**
quite	**plutôt, assez**
quota	**un quota**

R

rail	**le rail**
rain	**la pluie**
to raise	**soulever**
rapidly	**rapidement**
rare *adj.*	**rare**
rate	**le taux**
at the rate of	**au rythme de**
to reach	**atteindre, arriver à**
to reach [an agreement]	**parvenir à**
to reach [statistics]	**atteindre, s'élever à**
within reach of	**à la portée de**
reader	**un lecteur** (*fem.* **lectrice**)
real *adj.*	**réel**
to realise	**s'apercevoir, se rendre compte**
reason	**une raison**
to receive	**recevoir**
recent *adj.*	**récent**
recently	**récemment**
to make recommendations	**formuler des recommandations**
to recruit	**embaucher, recruter**
to recycle	**envoyer au recyclage**
to reduce [statistics]	**ramener**
reduction	**une réduction**
refugee	**un(e) réfugié(e)**
to refuse	**refuser**
to be refused sth.	**se voir refuser qch.**
region	**une région**
to regret ...ing	**regretter de +** *inf.*
relation	**une relation**
relationship	**une relation**
to remind s.o.	**rappeler à qn**
to remove	**supprimer**
rent	**un loyer**
to rent	**louer**
repayment	**un remboursement**
to reply	**répondre**
to represent	**représenter**
required *adj.*	**requis**
research	**la recherche**
resolution	**une résolution**
resource	**une ressource**
respect	**le respect**

	responsibility	**une responsabilité**
	responsible *adj.* for	**responsable de**
	restriction	**une contrainte**
as a	result	**il en résulte que**
as a	result of sth.	**à la suite de qch.**
to	retire	**se retirer**
	return	**le retour**
on one's	return	**à son retour**
to	return	**rentrer**
to	reveal	**révéler**
	review	**une révision**
to be all	right	**aller bien**
	rise	**une augmentation**
at	risk	**en danger**
	road	**la route**
	road transport	**le transport routier**
	role	**un rôle**
	rubbish	**les ordures** *fem. pl.*
	rumour	**une rumeur**
to	run [company, newspaper]	**diriger**
	rush hour	**les heures** *fem. pl.* **de pointe**

S

	safe from	**à l'abri de**
	salaried *adj.*	**salarié**
	salary	**un salaire**
	salary scale	**une fourchette de salaire**
	Saturday	**un samedi**
to	save [time, money]	**économiser**
to	say	**dire, déclarer**
to	say that one is + *adj.*	**se déclarer +** *adj.*
	school	**une école**
	scooter	**un scooter**
	scourge	**un fléau**
	season	**une saison**
	second	**une seconde**
	second *adj.*	**second, deuxième**
	secret	**un secret**
employment	sector	**un secteur d'activité**
	security	**la sécurité**
	Security Council	**le Conseil de sécurité**
to	see	**voir**
to	see again	**revoir**
to	see s.o. + *inf.*	**voir qn +** *inf.*
to	select	**sélectionner**
to	sell	**vendre**
	semi-skilled worker	**un ouvrier spécialisé** (*fem.* **ouvrière spécialisée**)
to	send	**envoyer**
to	send s.o. sth.	**envoyer qch. à qn**
	sensible *adj.*	**raisonnable**

	series	une série
	serious *adj.*	grave, profond
	service	un service
training	session	un cours
television	set	un téléviseur
to	set an example	donner l'exemple *masc.*
to	set up a company	créer une entreprise
to	set up an inquiry	ouvrir une enquête
to	settle a crisis	résoudre une crise
	several	plusieurs
	sexual *adj.*	sexuel
to	share	partager
	shareholder	un(e) actionnaire
to	shock	choquer
	shopping	les courses *fem. pl.*
	short *adj.*	court
to	show	indiquer
to	show [evidence of]	faire preuve de
to	show [images]	montrer
	similar *adj.*	semblable
	simple *adj.*	simple
	since	depuis
to	sing	chanter
	site	un site
	situation	une situation
	skirt	une jupe
	slightly	légèrement
	slowing down	un ralentissement
	small *adj.*	petit
	smoke	la fumée
	so	si, tellement
	so as to	pour
	so much	tant de
	so that	pour que
	social *adj.*	social
	society	la société
	soldier	un soldat
	some	du (de la, des), quelques, certains
	some of	quelques-uns de (*fem.* quelques-unes de), certains de (*fem.* certaines de)
	some [+ number]	quelque
	someone	quelqu'un
	someone + *adj.*	quelqu'un de + *adj.*
	something	quelque chose
	something + *adj.*	quelque chose de + *adj.*
	sometimes	parfois
	soon	bientôt
	sort	une sorte
	source	une source
	South Africa	l'Afrique *fem.* du Sud

	Southern Europe	l'Europe *fem.* du Sud
	Southern European	d'Europe du Sud
	Spanish man	un Espagnol
to	speak of s.o. / sth.	parler de qn / qch.
	special dinner	un grand dîner
to	specialise	se spécialiser
	specialist training	une formation spécialisée
to	spend	passer
to	spend time …ing	passer du temps à + *inf.*
	spontaneous *adj.*	spontané
	sport	un sport
team	sport	un sport d'équipe
	staff	le personnel
	star [cinema, music]	une vedette
to	start	commencer
to	start with	au début, pour commencer
to	start …ing	commencer à + *inf.*
	state	un État
petrol	station	une station-service
railway	station	une gare
	stay	un séjour
	stimulating *adj.*	stimulant
to	stop	s'arrêter
to	stop s.o. / sth.	arrêter qn / qch.
to	stop …ing	arrêter de + *inf.*
	strategy	une stratégie
	strongly	vigoureusement
	student	un(e) étudiante
	studies	les études *fem. pl.*
	subject [school, university]	une matière
on the	subject	à ce sujet, sur ce point
to	succeed	réussir
to	succeed in …ing	réussir à + *inf.*
	success	un succès
	such	de tels (*fem.* de telles)
	such a	un tel (*fem.* une telle)
	such a thing	une telle chose, une chose pareille
	such as	comme
	suitable *adj.*	approprié
	summer	un été
large	supermarket	une grande surface
to	support	soutenir
to have the	support of	bénéficier du soutien de
	supposed to + *inf.*	censé + *inf.*
	surprising *adj.*	surprenant, étonnant
	survey	une étude
to	suspect sth.	se douter de qch.
	Switzerland	la Suisse

T

to	take	prendre
to	take [exam, test]	passer

to	take an hour	**prendre une heure**
to	take into account	**prendre en compte**
to	take long [i.e. time]	**prendre longtemps**
to	take off [aeroplane]	**décoller**
to	take off [clothes]	**quitter**
to	take out an insurance policy	**prendre une assurance,**
		contracter une assurance
to	take part in [sport]	**pratiquer**
to	take s.o.	**emmener qn**
to	take sth. with oneself	**se munir de qch.**
it	takes sth. to + *inf.*	**il faut qch. pour + *inf.***
	talk	**une négociation**
to	talk to s.o. about sth.	**parler à qn de qch.**
	tank	**un réservoir**
	taxi	**un taxi**
to	teach s.o. sth.	**enseigner qch. à qn**
	teacher	**un(e) enseignant(e), un professeur**
	teaching methods	**les méthodes *fem.* d'enseignement**
	team	**une équipe**
	team manager	**le directeur de l'équipe**
	technology	**une technologie**
	television	**la télévision**
	television set	**un téléviseur**
to	tell s.o. about sth.	**parler à qn de qch.**
to	tell s.o. sth.	**dire qch. à qn, raconter qch. à qn**
about	ten	**une dizaine de**
	terrorism	**le terrorisme**
	test [driving]	**un permis (de conduire)**
	text	**un texte**
	thanks to	**grâce à**
	theatre	**le théâtre**
and	then	**puis**
	there is / are	**il y a**
	therefore	**donc**
	thing	**une chose**
to	think	**penser**
to	think about sth.	**penser à qch., réfléchir à qch.**
to	think of …ing [plan]	**penser faire**
to	think of …ing [remember]	**penser à + *inf.***
	third [fraction]	**un tiers**
	Third World	**le tiers monde**
	thousands of	**des milliers de**
	time	**le temps**
at one	time	**à un moment donné**
at the	time	**à l'époque**
for a long	time	**longtemps**
at the	time when …	**au moment où …**
in	times of	**en période de**
	tired *adj.* of	**fatigué de, las de**
	today	**aujourd'hui**
	today's	**actuel**

	too (much)	**trop**
	top [scale]	**le plafond**
	total *adj.*	**total**
	town	**une ville**
centre of	town	**le centre-ville**
	town dweller	**un citadin**
	toxic *adj.*	**toxique**
	trade union	**un syndicat**
to be a	trade union member	**être syndiqué**
	traditional *adj.*	**traditionnel**
	traffic [road]	**le trafic**
	trafficker	**un trafiquant**
	trafficking [drug]	**le trafic**
	train	**un train**
	training	**une formation**
	training course	**un stage de formation**
	training session	**un cours**
	transfer	**le transfert**
to	transform	**transformer**
	transport	**le transport**
public	transport	**les transports collectifs** *masc. pl.*
road	transport	**le transport routier**
to	travel	**voyager**
	travel agent	**une agence de voyages**
to	treat	**traiter**
	trend	**tendance**
to	trigger off	**déclencher**
to	try	**essayer**
to	try to + *inf.*	**essayer de + *inf.***
	turnover	**un chiffre d'affaires**
	twice	**deux fois**

U

	UN [United Nations]	**l'Onu**
people	under 25	**les moins de 25 ans**
	underneath	**sous**
	understandable *adj.*	**compréhensible**
	unemployed people	**les chômeurs** *masc. pl.*
	unemployment	**le chômage**
	United Nations	**les Nations unies** *fem. pl.*
	United Nations Organisation	**l'Organisation** *fem.* **des Nations unies** *fem. pl.*
	United States	**les États-Unis** *masc. pl.*
	university qualification	**un diplôme universitaire**
	until	**jusqu'à ce que**
	until now	**jusqu'à présent**
	urban *adj.*	**urbain**
to	urge s.o. to + *inf.*	**conseiller vivement à qn de + *inf.***
to	use sth.	**se servir de qch., utiliser qch.**
to do one's	utmost to ...	**faire tout ce qu'on peut pour ...,** **faire tout son possible pour ...**

V

	vaccine	un vaccin
	variety	une variété
	various *adj.*	différent
	very	très
	video *adj.*	vidéo [*does not agree*]
	video games	des jeux vidéo
	visa	un visa
to	visit	visiter

W

	wage	un salaire
to	wait	attendre
to	wait until	attendre que, attendre de
to	walk	aller à pied
	Walkman	un baladeur
to	want	vouloir
to	want to + *inf.*	vouloir + *inf.*
	war	la guerre
global	warming	le réchauffement climatique
to	warn s.o. about sth.	prévenir qn de qch.
	waste	les déchets *masc. pl.*
	wastebin	une poubelle
to	watch	regarder
	water	l'eau *fem.*
fresh	water	l'eau *fem.* douce
	way	une façon, une manière ; une formule
	way of life	un mode de vie
on one's	way to becoming	en passe de devenir
on my	way to work	en allant travailler
to	wear [clothes]	porter
	week	une semaine
	well	bien
	well known *adj.*	célèbre
as	well	aussi
	Western *adj.*	occidental
	when	quand, lorsque
	where	où
	whether	si
	while	(tout) en (+ …ant)
	while	pendant (que)
	whole	tout ; entier
	why	pourquoi, la raison pour laquelle
	wine	un vin
	winter	un hiver
	with	avec
to make a	withdrawal	retirer de l'argent
	within [years]	en, en l'espace de
	within reach of	à la portée de
	without (any)	sans (aucun)

	without ...ing	**sans + *inf*.**
	witness	**un témoin**
	woman	**une femme**
	women's magazine	**un magazine féminin**
to	wonder	**se demander**
	word	**un mot**
	work	**le travail**
to go to	work	**aller travailler**
to	work	**travailler**
to	work with	**coopérer avec**
	worker	**ouvrier (*fem.* ouvrière)**
	working population	**la population active, les actifs** *masc. pl.*
	world	**le monde**
Third	World	**le tiers monde**
to	worry s.o.	**inquiéter qn**
the	worst of	**le pire de**
to be	wrong	**avoir tort**

Y

	year	**une année, un an**
	yesterday	**hier**
not	yet	**ne ... pas encore**
	young *adj.*	**jeune**

GRAMMAR INDEX

References are to the chapter number, the section number and the page number. For example, the reference **2.5 (p.15)** refers the reader to chapter 2, section 5, page 15.

Index of grammatical terms

Grammar index

GRAMMAR INDEX

GRAMMAR INDEX

GRAMMAR INDEX

GRAMMAR INDEX

GRAMMAR INDEX

KEY TO EXERCISES

In the answers to the *Reinforcement, Revision* and *Practice* exercises, you will find references to the relevant grammar explanations. References are to the chapter number and the section number: for example, the reference 2.5 refers you to chapter 2, section 5.

Chapter 1 Diagnostic, p. 1

A Ils ont décidé de vivre en zone rurale

1. Après **des** études de droit, Bernard est retourné dans son village natal pour cultiver **des** fruits biologiques et fabriquer **des** confitures.
2. Daniel, qui fabriquait **de la** bière pendant ses loisirs, a décidé d'en faire son activité principale. Il s'est rendu **au** Canada et **aux** États-Unis pour étudier les nouvelles méthodes de fabrication avant de s'installer **à la** campagne.
3. **Au** début de l'année, Béatrice a ouvert une auberge dans un petit village situé à l'est d'Avignon. La restauration est l'activité principale **de l'**auberge mais Béatrice loue également **des** chambres. Elle a mis **des** plats traditionnels au menu et organise **des** cours de cuisine destinés **aux** vacanciers.
4. Irène vient **de la** banlieue parisienne. Elle a quitté la ville pour créer une entreprise dans un village **du** Nord. Grâce **au** télétravail, elle peut travailler à domicile.

B La vie en banlieue

• *Laurence, vous **êtes** mère célibataire et vous **assurez** un emploi. Dites-moi, vous **devez** avoir des journées bien chargées ?*
– Oui, plutôt ! Je **suis** debout à six heures et je **réveille** les enfants vers sept heures. Pendant qu'ils **font** leur toilette, je **fais** un peu de ménage. Je les **conduis** ensuite chez ma mère et je **vais** prendre mon train. Il me **faut** en général une heure pour arriver à l'agence de voyages où je **travaille**. Nous **ouvrons** à neuf heures et nous **finissons** vers six heures.
• *C'est toujours votre mère qui **s'occupe** de vos enfants en votre absence ?*
– Oui. Le matin, elle les **fait** déjeuner et elle les **accompagne** à l'école. A midi, ils **prennent** leur repas à la cantine. Le soir, ma mère **va** les chercher à la sortie de l'école et les **aide** à faire leurs devoirs. L'été ils **viennent** parfois m'attendre à la gare. Heureusement que ma mère **habite** tout près et que je **peux** compter sur elle !

Chapter 1 Reinforcement p. 6

A (See 1.6 and 1.7)

1. **Une** ville est **une** agglomération urbaine.
2. **Un** appartement est **un** logement.
3. **Un** immeuble est **un** bâtiment à plusieurs étages.
4. **Une** résidence est **un** ensemble d'immeubles luxueux.
5. **Un** HLM est **une** habitation à loyer modéré.
6. **Un** embouteillage est **un** encombrement de la circulation.

B (See 1.11–14)

Vous déménagez ?

- *Vous **comptez** toujours déménager ?*
- Oui, mais on **ne sait pas** où. On ne **parvient** pas à se mettre d'accord sur un endroit ! Laure **se plaint** du bruit, elle **dit** qu'elle **veut** vivre dans la montagne à l'extérieur de Marseille. Les enfants **disent** qu'ils **veulent** une villa en bord de mer. Et moi, je **m'aperçois** de plus en plus que je **n'ai pas** envie de quitter le centre-ville.

Description d'une villa

L'entrée **conduit** à la fois vers le séjour et la salle à manger. La salle à manger, très conviviale, **s'ouvre** largement sur le séjour. Un office la **fait** communiquer avec la cuisine. Les deux chambres situées à l'étage **comprennent** chacune une vaste penderie. Elles **bénéficient** également d'une salle d'eau et de WC indépendants.

C Version

1. Living conditions (1.3) in cities are more and more difficult because of the increase in pollution (1.3), noise (1.3) and traffic (1.3).
2. This is why people (1.3) tend to choose to live in rural areas (1.4).
3. They are looking for a living environment that is closer to nature (1.3).
4. With improved transport (1.4) and electronic communication (1.4), rural areas (1.3) do offer, in fact, a better quality of life.
5. Thanks to teleworking (1.3), the opportunity to live outside urban areas (1.3) is no longer only the privilege of retired people (1.3).
6. France (1.3) is no longer the only country where country life (1.3) is a great attraction. A similar trend is noticeable in the United Kingdom.

Chapter 2 Diagnostic, p. 7

A Salade composée

Eléments de base* pour une **seule** personne:

2 œufs	*100 g. de gruyère*
1 petite laitue	*1 bonne cuillerée de mayonnaise*
1 grosse tomate ferme	*herbes aromatiques*
1 tranche épaisse de jambon	*sel et poivre*

Faites cuire deux œufs **durs**. Mettez-les ensuite dans une cuvette d'eau **froide** pour les faire refroidir : ils seront ainsi plus **faciles** à écaler. Prenez quatre **belles** feuilles de laitue, placez-les au fond d'un saladier après les avoir lavées. Coupez la tomate et les œufs en rondelles **fines**. Coupez le jambon et le gruyère en **petits** dés. Ajoutez la mayonnaise, salez et poivrez avant de mélanger le tout. Placez le mélange dans le saladier et garnissez-le d'herbes **hachées**.
* Pour varier un peu, remplacez le jambon par des lardons **frits**, le gruyère par du fromage **bleu**, la mayonnaise par un yaourt **bulgare** ou de la crème **fraîche** ; ajoutez également, selon la saison, des carottes **râpées**, une betterave **rouge**, une poignée de radis, etc.

B Pour retrouver la forme

–   Au lieu de grignoter toute la journée, vous **ferez** des repas réguliers.
–   Il vous **faudra** manger moins de gras.
–   Vous **éviterez** de manger trop de sucre.
–   Plus de coca-cola! Vous **boirez** de l'eau minérale à la place.
–   Et plus de petits gâteaux ! Vous **vous habituerez** à manger des fruits frais.
–   Au lieu de prendre la voiture ou l'autobus pour faire un kilomètre, vous **irez** à pied.
–   Et quand vous **vous sentirez** en meilleure forme, vous **pourrez** manger un hamburger de temps en temps.

Chapter 2 Reinforcement, p. 12

A Les nouvelles (2.5) habitudes alimentaires (2.2) des Français

L'image **traditionnelle** (2.3) des Français ne correspond plus à la réalité **quotidienne** (2.3). Les différences avec les autres pays s'estompent, même si certaines traditions **nationales** (2.3) et **régionales** (2.3) se maintiennent.

La consommation de pain est en baisse **régulière** (2.3). Si le « steak-frites » reste encore le plat **préféré** (2.2) des Français, ils consomment davantage de viande **blanche** (2.4) et de poisson. Les plats **préparés** (2.2) et les produits **surgelés** (2.2) tendent à se substituer aux légumes **frais** (2.4). Les fruits tendent à être remplacés par d'autres types de dessert : produits **laitiers** (2.3) ou crèmes **glacées** (2.2). La consommation **moyenne** (2.3) de vin **ordinaire** (2.2) a beaucoup diminué ; par contre, on achète plus de vins **fins** (2.2). Parmi les boissons non **alcoolisées** (2.2) la préférence va aux eaux **minérales** (2.3) et aux boissons **gazeuses** (2.3).

B (See 2.9 and 2.10)
Si les tendances actuelles se poursuivent ...

–   Les repas **seront** de plus en plus rapides.
–   Les Français **mangeront** moins à chaque repas.
–   Ils **se limiteront** à un plat principal au lieu d'un repas complet.
–   On **verra** le nombre de repas pris à l'extérieur augmenter.
–   Les gens **prendront** de moins en moins le temps de cuisiner.
–   Cependant la séparation entre repas quotidien et repas de fête **se maintiendra**.

Préparation d'un grand repas de fête

LOLA   Il **faudra** faire toutes les courses à l'avance.
GABRIEL   Tu crois que tu **auras** le temps ?
LOLA   Oui, ne t'inquiète pas. *J'irai* les faire vendredi soir.
GABRIEL   Mais nous **ne pourrons pas** tout préparer le jour même !
LOLA   Mais si, il **suffira** de demander à Jacques de nous aider.
GABRIEL   Bonne idée ! Vous **ferez** cuire le plat principal. Et nous, on **s'occupera** du reste.

KEY TO EXERCISES

C *Thème*

1. Cet (2.8) excellent (2.6) vin sera (2.10) l'accompagnement idéal de vos repas de fête.
2. Tous (2.7) nos plats surgelés (2.2) et toutes (2.7) nos crèmes glacées (2.2) sont sans colorant artificiel (2.3).
3. Ce (2.8) nouvel (2.5) entremets à la crème fraîche (2.4) est entièrement naturel (2.3).
4. Ces (2.8) pâtes savoureuses (2.3) sont importées (2.2) d'Italie.
5. Grâce à ces (2.8) produits à petit (2.6) prix, les plaisirs de la table sont à la portée de tout (2.7) le monde [*or* à la portée de tous].
6. Ces (2.8) bonbons au chocolat [*or* Ces chocolats] feront (2.10) plaisir à toute (2.7) la famille, non seulement le jour de Noël mais les jours suivants (2.2).

Chapter 3 Diagnostic, p. 13

A Des relations familiales sans problèmes

• *Vous avez l'air de bien vous entendre. Vous passez beaucoup de temps ensemble ?*

ÉLISE   Pas pendant la semaine. Mon père et ma mère travaillent et je suis très occupée moi aussi. Je n'ai pas bien le temps de **les** voir et de **leur** parler.

SON PÈRE   C'est vrai. On essaie de **lui** consacrer le plus de temps possible et de **l'**encourager dans son travail, mais ce n'est pas toujours facile en semaine.

ÉLISE   Et puis, j'ai beaucoup de devoirs cette année. Alors, j'essaie de **les** faire le soir pour avoir le week-end libre.

• *Comment se passe le week-end ?*

SA MÈRE   Le vendredi soir est sacré. On **le** passe toujours avec Élise. On **la** sort : on **l'**emmène au restaurant, ou on **lui** offre une soirée au cinéma ou au théâtre. Elle a beaucoup d'amis. On **les** invite parfois à se joindre à nous.

ÉLISE   Le samedi, en général je sors toute seule. Tout ce que mes parents me demandent, c'est de **leur** dire où je vais et de **leur** téléphoner si j'ai du retard. Comme je ne veux pas qu'ils s'inquiètent, je **le** fais sans problèmes.

B

Ma chère Corinne,

Je **n'ai pas eu** le temps de t'écrire plus tôt, excuse-moi. Quelles vacances ! C'est bien la dernière fois que je passe l'été en famille.

Mes parents **se sont disputés** en arrivant et ma mère **a boudé** pendant deux jours. Si bien que le premier soir nous **sommes allés** au restaurant sans elle et que le lendemain, elle **n'a pas voulu** venir à la piscine avec nous. Tout ça parce que mon père **a oublié** d'apporter la table de camping. Mais c'est ma faute aussi, **je suis intervenu** pour dire que c'était ridicule de se fâcher pour si peu. Et évidemment, ça **n'a pas arrangé** la situation.

Ça va mieux depuis, mais je commence à perdre patience. Mardi, par exemple, mon cousin nous **a fait** attendre pour partir au cinéma et nous **avons manqué** le début du film. Il **n'y a pas eu** un jour où nous **avons été** d'accord pour décider où passer l'après-midi. Finalement, hier, je **suis parti** me promener tout seul à pied, mais je **me suis ennuyé**.

L'an prochain, je pars en vacances avec toi ! En attendant je t'embrasse, Christian

Chapter 3 Reinforcement, p. 18

A La famille protectrice

– Dans ce type de famille, les parents adorent leur enfant mais ne **le** (3.3) traitent pas comme un adulte.
– Ils ne se disputent jamais en famille car ils veulent **lui** (3.6-7) donner une bonne image du couple.
– Bien qu'ils s'intéressent à la politique, ils **en** (3.9) discutent peu devant lui ; quant aux sujets délicats comme la sexualité, ils **les** (3.3) évitent.
– A l'adolescence, l'enfant n'est pas toujours sûr d'obtenir l'autorisation de sortir lorsqu'il **la** (3.4) demande.
  - Ses parents **lui** (3.7) demandent d'être studieux car c'est à l'école que l'on construit son avenir et ils **y** (3.8) pensent dès son plus jeune âge.

La famille ouverte

– Ici, les enfants sont considérés comme des êtres raisonnables et les parents **les** (3.3) poussent à devenir autonomes.
– Ils **leur** (3.7) font confiance et **leur** (3.6) laissent une grande liberté.
– La sexualité n'est pas un sujet tabou : on **en** (3.9) parle librement.
– Les parents veulent préparer leur enfant à la vie en société et privilégient les qualités qui **la** (3.3) facilitent.
– Ils sont convaincus que les activités culturelles et sportives lui seront bénéfiques, et **l'** (3.3) encouragent à **en** (3.9) pratiquer deux ou trois.

B Témoignage (See 3.12–16)

J'**ai grandi** à Paris avec mon frère et mes parents. À la naissance de mon frère, les relations familiales **se sont détériorées.** Les conflits entre ma mère et mon père **se sont multipliés.** Quand ils **ont divorcé,** nous **avons connu** des années difficiles. En effet, le divorce **s'est déroulé** dans de mauvaises conditions. Ma mère **s'est remariée** tout de suite et elle **est partie** à l'étranger. Alors **nous sommes allés** vivre chez mes grand-parents paternels. Malheureusement ma grand-mère **est tombée** malade. Quand elle **est morte,** c'est donc mon père qui nous **a élevés.** Nous **avons fait** la connaissance de sa seconde femme et elle nous **a plu** tout de suite. Nous **avons pris** l'habitude de nous confier à elle. À partir de ce moment-là, nous **avons vécu** dans un environnement familial très harmonieux.

C Thème

1. En général [*or* Généralement] les enfants n'hésitent pas à raconter (3.7) leurs problèmes à (3.7) leurs parents.

or En règle générale, les enfants n'hésitent pas à parler de leurs problèmes à leurs parents.

2. Ils leur (3.6-7) demandent leur avis quand ils [*or* lorsqu'ils] ont besoin de conseils.
3. Lorsqu'ils ont atteint (3.12) l'âge adulte, leurs parents continuent souvent à les (3.3) aider.

    or Quand ils sont arrivés à l'âge adulte …
4. S'ils ont perdu (3.12) leur emploi, par exemple, leurs parents paient (3.4) leur loyer.

Revision 1–3, p. 19

A (See 1.6–7)

1. **La** tolérance est **une** des caractéristiques des jeunes.
2. **La** découverte de l'amour est **une** période difficile pour eux.
3. **Le** réalisme de la jeunesse est **un** facteur positif.
4. **La** consommation est **un** phénomène important dans **la** vie des jeunes.
5. Ils exercent **une** influence sur **les** décisions d'achat de leurs parents.

B (See 1.9)

1. **Ces jeux électroniques ont connu** beaucoup de succès.
2. **Ces festivals internationaux** de musique **attireront** les touristes.
3. Vous avez oublié **des détails essentiels**.
4. **Les travaux** de la commission **seront rendus publics** au cours **des mois prochains**.
5. **Les journaux ont publié des articles explosifs**.
6. Le gouvernement a respecté **les vœux** de la majorité.

C Histoire de remariage – 1 Les difficultés d'Éva

Quand Éva a épousé Marc, un père divorcé, elle ne se doutait pas qu'elle allait avoir des difficultés à la fois avec ses enfants et ses parents. Au début, les enfants ne **lui** (3.6–7) faisaient pas confiance et refusaient de **lui** (3.6–7) obéir. En outre, ses beaux-parents, qui gardaient un bon souvenir de la première femme de Marc, l' (3.3) ont mal accueillie (3.15) : Éva ne **leur** (3.6–7) plaisait pas parce qu'elle ne **lui** (3.6–7) ressemblait pas. En fait, leur attitude aggravait la situation avec les enfants : Éva n'avait aucun soutien alors qu'elle **en** (3.9) avait bien besoin.

D Histoire de remariage – 2 Tout est bien qui finit bien

Une amie d'Éva **lui** (3.6–7) a conseillé d'être patiente : « L'attitude de tes beaux-parents est tout à fait normale, ne t'**en** (3.9) inquiète pas. L'important, c'est avant tout de conquérir la confiance et l'affection des enfants de Marc ». Elle avait raison : lorsqu'Éva est parvenue à **le** (3.3) faire, ses beaux-parents **l'** (3.3) ont adoptée (3.15). Elle a maintenant d'excellentes relations avec eux : si elle a besoin de conseils, elle va **les** (3.3) voir ou **leur** (3.6–7) téléphone.

KEY TO REVISION

E (See 1.10–14)
Present tense
1. ils investissent
2. il s'améliore
3. nous soumettons
4. nous surprenons
5. on s'aperçoit
6. elles connaissent
7. je perds
8. je circule
9. elles atteignent
10. vous traduisez
11. j'ouvre
12. vous voyez
13. tu peux
14. on sait

F (See 2.9–10)
Future tense
1. elles comprendront
2. nous décevrons
3. tu viendras
4. il se poursuivra
5. je continuerai
6. vous verrez
7. tu te rétabliras
8. vous maintiendrez
9. elle pourra
10. ils acquerront
11. tu seras
12. on saura
13. j'enverrai
14. il faudra

G (See 3.12–16)
Perfect tense
1. il a reçu
2. j'ai tenu
3. tu as souffert
4. nous nous sommes plaints
5. ils ont reconstruit
6. elle est née
7. tu as voulu
8. ils ont résolu
9. je me suis attendri(e)
10. on a admis
11. tu as entrepris
12. nous avons créé
13. vous vous êtes engagé(e)s
14. elle s'est conduite

H (See 3.12–16)

Les engagements pris et tenus. L'an dernier, nous **nous sommes engagés** à offrir de meilleurs services et nous **avons tenu** nos engagements. Des milliers de clients **ont reçu** à domicile leur billet commandé et payé par téléphone. Nous **avons créé** de nouvelles liaisons entre la France et l'Italie. Et enfin, nous **avons entrepris** un programme de rénovation des gares.

(See 1.11–14)

La situation actuelle. Dans les trains « verts », les passagers **peuvent** bénéficier aujourd'hui d'une réduction de 15 % sur le prix de base. Par ailleurs, la qualité des services accueil **s'améliore** sans cesse. Ainsi, dans la banlieue parisienne, les guichets **ouvrent** à 5 h 30 les lundis.

(See 2.9–10)

L'avenir. Dans les années à venir, le nombre de trains **continuera** à augmenter sur les grandes lignes. L'amélioration des services accueil **se poursuivra**. Durant l'été, nos clients **pourront** bénéficier de billets à moitié prix à destination des plages. Nous **maintiendrons** notre politique d'indemnisation en cas de retard.

Chapter 4 Diagnostic, p. 21

A Les règles de l'amitié

1. Montrez-vous toujours aimable envers **vos** copains et **vos** copines.
2. Si l'un d'entre **eux** ou l'une d'entre **elles** se moque de vous gentiment, surtout ne boudez pas.
3. Si au cours d'une soirée mouvementée, quelqu'un abîme **vos** affaires, ne saccagez pas **les siennes** pour vous venger.
4. N'essayez jamais de sortir avec le flirt de **votre** meilleur(e) ami(e).
5. N'oubliez pas qu'il faut toujours partager **ses** affaires et ne pas tout garder pour **soi**.
6. Ne refusez jamais d'accompagner les autres dans une sortie même si **leur** choix ne vous plaît pas.
7. Chacun a **son** opinion, ne critiquez pas continuellement les idées des autres. **Les vôtres** ne sont pas infaillibles ! Acceptez donc **les leurs**.
8. Apprenez la discrétion : vos copains ne vous confieront pas **leurs** problèmes s'il savent que vous répétez **leurs** histoires.
9. Sachez combiner l'amour et l'amitié : ne laissez pas tomber **vos** copains et ne demandez à personne d'abandonner **les siens**.

B Témoignage – Premier amour

Tout a commencé l'année dernière lorsque j'ai fait la connaissance de Thomas, un garçon de ma classe. Il **était** super sympa, mais je **ne pensais pas** du tout sortir avec lui. Un jour, alors que **j'étais** à la patinoire, je l'ai vu par hasard et il m'a souri. Une semaine plus tard, un de mes copains m'a dit qu'il **voulait** sortir avec moi. Comme on **ne se connaissait pas** très bien, j'ai répondu qu'il me **fallait** réfléchir. Ensuite, les grandes vacances sont arrivées et je l'ai un peu oublié.

À la rentrée, comme nous **nous trouvions** à nouveau dans la même classe, je lui ai demandé s'il **avait** encore envie de sortir avec moi. Mais il n'a pas voulu me parler. Ma réaction a été intense : je **me sentais** profondément triste et je ne **comprenais** pas pourquoi il **agissait** comme ça. C'est à ce moment-là que j'ai compris qu'il me **plaisait** vraiment. Trop tard !

Chapter 4 Reinforcement, p. 26

A (See 4.2–9)

1. En amour comme en amitié, **je tiens à mon indépendance. Je respecte** la liberté de l'autre et **exige** qu'il respecte **la mienne**.
2. **Ils ont** une bonne opinion **d'eux-mêmes, ils sont sûrs d'eux** et **ils aiment** séduire. **Leurs** partenaires ont souvent une attitude comparable à la **leur**.
3. **Elle est** souvent **frustrée** parce que **sa** timidité et **son** anxiété l'**empêchent** de faire le premier pas. C'est plus fort **qu'elle** !
4. **Tu n'aimes** pas l'aventure. L'important **pour toi**, c'est que **tes** parents acceptent la personne de **ton** choix et que les siens **t'**accueillent bien.

B (See 4.10)

Dans les années 60, les jeunes **devenaient** hippies par réaction contre leurs parents. L'anticonformisme qui **prévalait** à l'époque **se traduisait** notamment par les cheveux longs, les couleurs vives et l'absence de cravate. À partir de 1975, la traditionnelle réaction contre les parents **tendait** à disparaître. Pour les punks, par exemple, il **s'agissait** surtout de se démarquer de leurs frères et sœurs ou des aînés de leur lycée qui **étaient** babas. Au cours des décennies suivantes, l'accélération des mouvements de mode **allait** devenir telle que les générations de jeunes ne **devaient** plus durer qu'une ou deux années.

C *Thème*

SYLVIE   À dix-sept ans, j'étais (4.10, 4.11.1) contestataire et la police m'a arrêtée (4.11.3 note) deux fois. Le look était (4.10, 4.11.1) très important pour moi (4.6–7). Je portais (4.10, 4.11.3) des jupes courtes sous un manteau très long. Mes (4.2) copains [*or* amis] (4.10, 4.11.1) les cheveux longs et ne quittaient (4.10, 4.11.3) jamais leur jean (*see* 24.15).

JÉRÔME   Le jour de mes (4.2) dix-sept ans, mes (4.2) parents m'ont offert un scooter. Ils étaient (4.10, 4.11.1) très fiers de moi (4.6–7) parce que je venais (4.15) de réussir mes (4.2) examens. Depuis notre (4.2) séjour en Angleterre, l'été précédent, mes (4.2) copains [*or* amis] et moi (4.6–7), nous portions (4.10, 4.12.2) uniquement des vêtements anglais [*or* … mes copains et moi, on ne portait que des vêtements anglais].

LAURA   Ma (4.2) meilleure amie [*or* copine] et moi (4.6–7), nous chantions (4.10, 4.11.3) [*or* on chantait] dans un groupe punk. On avait (4.10, 4.11.1) les cheveux roses. Mes (4.2) parents trouvaient (4.10, 4.11.1) ça assez [*or* plutôt] amusant [*or* drôle], mais les siens (4.4) étaient (4.10, 4.11.1) furieux.

ÉTIENNE   Quand je suis arrivé à l'âge de dix-sept ans, j'ai décidé que je voulais (4.10, 4.11.1) voyager. J'ai travaillé (4.14) le soir dans une station-service pendant tout un hiver et l'année suivante je suis parti en Afrique. J'étais (4.10, 4.11.2) au Rwanda lorsque la guerre civile a éclaté.

or Lorsque j'ai atteint l'âge de de dix-sept ans, j'ai décidé que je voulais (4.10, 4.11.1) voyager. J'ai travaillé (4.14) le soir dans une station-service pendant un hiver entier et l'année suivante je suis allé en Afrique. J'étais (4.10, 4.11.2) au Rwanda quand la guerre civile a éclaté.

Chapter 5 Diagnostic, p. 27

A

1. **Personne ne prétend** que les déplacements à pied ont augmenté.
2. En fait, **rien n'encourage** les gens à laisser leur voiture au garage.
3. L'utilisation de la voiture **n'a pas diminué** au cours des dernières années.
4. Pourtant, les achats de grosses cylindrées **ne sont plus** aussi nombreux.

5. Aujourd'hui, la vitesse **n'est pas** aussi importante que la sécurité.
6. Au fond, le mouvement écologiste **n'a rien changé**.
7. Les modes de transports collectifs **ne remplaceront jamais** la voiture.

B

• *Patrice, vous venez **de** gagner le concours Assurtout. Comment **comptez-vous** dépenser la somme d'argent qui vous est offerte ?*
– J'ai l'intention **de** passer trois mois à voyager en Europe. J'ai essayé **de** le faire, il y a quelques années, mais je n'ai réussi qu'**à** voir l'Italie.
• *Ah bon ? Vous **voulez** bien nous **raconter** ce qui vous est arrivé ?*
– J'avais décidé **d'**aller jusqu'en Roumanie à bicyclette. Et tout a bien commencé puisque je suis parvenu à faire les premiers 300 km en quatre jours.
• *Ah oui ! C'est remarquable ! Et ensuite ?*
– Arrivé en Italie, je me suis arrêté au bord de la route pour me reposer avant de me mettre **à** chercher une auberge de jeunesse pour la nuit. C'était l'été. Il commençait à faire très chaud. Bref ! Je me suis endormi ! À mon réveil, je me suis aperçu que mon vélo avait disparu. J'avais oublié **de** l'attacher à un arbre !
• *Et vous étiez assuré pour le vol ?*
– Non, malheureusement pas. Et je n'**ai** pas **pu retrouver** mon vélo ! La police italienne a accepté **de** me conduire jusqu'à Turin et je suis rentré par le train. Depuis, je rêve **de** repartir. Cette aventure m'a appris **à** être plus prudent et mieux organisé. Cette fois-ci, **j'espère** bien **ne pas rentrer** cinq jours après mon départ.

Chapter 5 Reinforcement, p. 32

A (See 5.6)

C'est le moment du grand départ ! Depuis longtemps vous rêvez **de** partir à la recherche du soleil et de la détente. Vous avez choisi **de** passer quinze jours au Brésil où vous **espérez trouver** un ciel toujours bleu et une plage de sable blanc. Si c'est la première fois que vous faites un aussi long voyage, suivez les conseils suivants :
– essayez **de** faire votre réservation sur un vol direct ;
– arrivez à l'aéroport à l'avance si vous **voulez choisir** votre place ;
– armez-vous **de** patience : vous aurez **à** faire la queue avant **de** passer par le contrôle de sécurité ;
– pendant le vol, évitez **de** prendre une boisson alcoolisée surtout si vous souffrez du mal des transports ;
– pensez **à** mettre des vêtements d'été dans votre bagage de cabine, afin de **pouvoir vous changer** avant l'arrivée. A moins, bien sûr, que vous ne **préfériez le faire** à votre arrivée à l'hôtel.

B (See 5.7 and 5.9)

1. Après être arrivées à la gare du Nord à Paris, on a pris le métro pour aller à la gare de Lyon.

2. Après m'être renseignée sur les horaires, j'ai réservé des places pour le TGV.
3. Après avoir composté nos billets, on est montées dans le train.
4. Après s'être installée dans le train, ma compagne s'est aperçue qu'elle avait oublié d'apporter de la lecture.

C *Thème*

LUC — Au lieu de prendre (5.5) ma voiture je suis allé travailler à bicyclette. Ça n'a pas pris longtemps (5.1, 5.4) !

LÉA & GUY — Nous n'avons jamais aimé utiliser (5.6.3) les transports collectifs. Nous ne sommes donc allés nulle part (5.1, 5.4) hier.

ALEX — Après avoir laissé (5.9) ma voiture à l'extérieur de la ville, j'ai loué un scooter électrique. C'était formidable ! [*or* C'était super !] Maintenant, je pense acheter (5.6.3) un scooter !

PAULA — Comme je n'avais pas de courses (5.1) à faire, j'ai décidé de ne pas aller (5.4) au centre-ville.
or Comme je n'avais aucune course (5.1) à faire …

YOUSSEF — Personne ne m'a prévenu (5.2, 5.4) que c'était une journée sans voitures. Je suis allé travailler sans le savoir (5.5). J'étais sur le point de traverser (5.5) le pont principal quand [*or* lorsque] la police m'a arrêté.

ESTHER — Au début, on a essayé d'aller (5.6.2) partout à pied. Mais on a fini par (5.5) prendre un taxi électrique. Les enfants ont adoré [ça]. Je ne les ai jamais vus (5.1, 5.4) si excités. On n'a pas regretté d'être allés (5.6.2, 5.7–8) en ville.

Chapter 6 Diagnostic, p. 33

A

Safari du Pin
– Un domaine **où** vous pourrez, en toute sécurité, observer des centaines d'animaux dans leur habitat naturel.
– La vedette du moment est un orang-outan **qui** mesure 1,90 m et pèse 130 kilos.

Show aquatique laser
– Un spectacle exceptionnel **qui** allie jeux d'eau, laser et feux d'artifices.
– Une soirée **que** vous n'êtes pas près d'oublier.

Excursions en autocar
– Visite des Gorges du Verdon **où** l'on peut admirer d'étonnants paysages.
– Une journée **dont** toute la famille gardera un excellent souvenir.

B

1. Il a réalisé un véritable exploit en **remportant** cette étape.
2. Il s'est effondré en **franchissant** la ligne d'arrivée.
3. En **battant** l'Italien, le Belge a réussi à prendre le maillot jaune.
4. Tout en **ayant** fait une bonne course, le Niçois est arrivé troisième.
5. **Étant** donné la pluie, on s'attend à des performances médiocres.

C *Version*

SYLVIA   I manage to relax by having several activities that are quite different.

ÉRIC   I cope with stress by taking part in team sports as well as individual sports.

KARIMA   Although I am interested in sport, I prefer computer games.

BEN & ÉLA   In the evening, in order to take our mind off things, we listen to the news on the radio while having a drink.

RACHID   As for me, I relax by listening to music when I get home.

CLAUDE   Given that I have little free time, television is my main source of entertainment.

Chapter 6 Reinforcement, p. 38

A Les villages de vacances

Les villages de vacances, pourquoi ?

- Les parents **que** (6.4) nous avons interrogés disent préférer partir en vacances avec leurs enfants.
- Les adolescents **que** (6.4) nous avons rencontrés pensent différemment : ils préfèrent la compagnie des jeunes de leur âge.
- Ce sont ces attitudes contradictoires **qui** (6.3) expliquent le succès des villages de vacances.

Flexibilité et respect de l'individu

- Le village est un endroit **où** (6.8) chacun peut jouir d'une certaine indépendance.
- Les activités **qu'**on (6.4) [*or* que l'on (24.5)] propose aux vacanciers, jeunes et moins jeunes, sont variées.
- Les familles **qui** (6.3) veulent se séparer pendant la journée peuvent le faire.
- Le repas du soir est le moment **où** (6.8) on [*or* où l'on (24.5)] peut raconter ses exploits de la journée.

Une formule réussie

- Les parents peuvent jouir de la tranquillité **dont** (6.6) ils rêvent toute l'année, sans être séparés de leurs enfants.
- Les enfants ont l'indépendance **qu'**ils (6.4) souhaitent.
- C'est donc une formule **qui** (6.3) satisfait tout le monde.

B

1. Quel est le titre des deux films dont ils ont parlé ? (6.6)
2. Je vous recommande la pièce que j'ai vue à Pau. (6.4–5)
3. Vous avez reçu les deux livres qu'elle vous a envoyés ? (6.4–5)
4. Tu peux nous prêter les CD dont nous avons besoin ? (6.6)
   or Tu peux nous prêter les CD dont on a besoin ? (6.6)
5. Elle devrait essayer la raquette que Lise a utilisée hier. (6.4–5)
   or Elle devrait essayer la raquette dont Lise s'est servie hier. (6.6, 6.5)
6. Ils n'ont pas pu regarder l'émission que vous avez mentionnée. (6.4–5)
7. On a visité le village de vacances dont elle était responsable. (6.6)
   or On a visité le village de vacances dont elle s'occupait. (6.6)

C *Thème*

1. C'est en allant (6.9–10) au festival d'Avignon que j'ai découvert le théâtre. *or* J'ai découvert le théâtre en allant (6.9–10) au festival d'Avignon.
2. Tout en pratiquant (6.11) les sports d'équipe, je préfère les sports individuels.
3. J'adore les activités alliant [*or* qui allient (6.12)] la musique et le mouvement.
4. Avec mon baladeur, je peux écouter de la musique tout le temps – en allant (6.10) travailler ou en faisant (6.10) mes courses, par exemple.
5. Le soir en rentrant (6.10), je visite quelques sites Internet pour me distraire.

Revision 4–6, p. 39

A (See 4.4)

1. J'ai apporté mes affaires, mais pas **les tiennes**.
2. J'ai téléphoné à mes parents, mais lui n'a même pas écrit **aux siens**.
3. Il a posté son paquet, mais pas **le leur**.
4. Ils ont pris ses billets, mais pas **les leurs**.
5. On a discuté de ses problèmes, mais je n'ai pas voulu parler **des miens**.

B (See 5.1)

1. Elles n'étaient pas au courant.
2. Je ne conduisais jamais la nuit.
3. Vous ne vous plaigniez guère de votre travail.
4. Nous ne promettions rien.
5. On ne décevait personne à ce moment-là.
6. Nous ne comprenions plus les motifs de sa conduite.
7. Tu n'avais pas le courage de lui annoncer ton départ ?
8. On ne se souvenait de rien.
9. Je ne voyais aucune difficulté insurmontable.
10. Il ne s'appelait ni Renaud ni Roland ?
11. Elle ne souffrait nullement de la chaleur.
12. On ne pouvait le joindre nulle part.

C (See 6.3–8)

Les centres de vacances

Les centres de vacances, **qu'**on appelait autrefois les « colonies de vacances », accueillent des centaines de milliers de jeunes. On distingue au moins trois catégories de centres :
- les centres maternels, **qui** s'occupent des petits de quatre à six ans ;
- les centres pour mineurs, **qui** accueillent les mineurs de six à quatorze ans ;
- et les camps d'adolescents, **qui** s'adressent aux plus de quatorze ans.

Les activités **dont** bénéficient les jeunes sont multiples : du sport à la vidéo, en passant par les séjours linguistiques et les stages informatiques. Dans les camps d'adolescents ce sont les activités physiques et sportives **qui** dominent : camps de voile **où** les jeunes peuvent s'initier à la navigation à voile, camps d'équitation **où** ils apprennent à monter à cheval, etc.

KEY TO REVISION

Les jeunes **dont** s'occupent les animateurs viennent en général de familles modestes vivant en milieu urbain. Ce sont, en majorité, des enfants **dont** la mère travaille. Tous ceux **que** nous avons interrogés se sont déclarés enchantés de la formule.

D (See 5.1–4)

1. Personne n'est à l'abri d'un accident
2. Rien ne nous empêchera de vous porter assistance.
3. Aucun effort ne sera épargné pour faciliter votre retour.
4. Pas un assuré ne s'est déclaré mécontent des prestations d'Assurtout.
   or Aucun assuré ne s'est déclaré mécontent des prestations d'Assurtout.

E *Thème*

1. Après avoir fait (5.7–9) enregistrer leurs (4.2) bagages, ils m'ont aidé(e) à (App. 4) porter les miens (4.4).
2. L'avion était sur le point de décoller (5.5) quand un [*or* l'un] des réacteurs a explosé. Il n'y a eu aucun (5.1–4) blessé.
   or … lorsqu'un des réacteurs a explosé. Il n'y a pas eu de (5.3) blessés.
3. Elle a décidé de (5.6.2) ne pas (5.4) partir cette année pour économiser (5.5) de l'argent.
4. Après s'être renseignés (5.7–9) auprès d'une agence de voyages, ils ont fait une réservation avec Air Littoral.
5. Lorsque je l'ai rencontrée, [*or* Quand je l'ai vue, …] elle pensait (5.6.3) abandonner ses études pour (5.5) chercher un emploi.
6. Tout en admettant (6.11) qu'ils avaient tort, ils ont refusé de (App. 4) changer de plans.
7. Lorsque nous sommes finalement arrivés à l'aéroport [*or* Quand on est finalement arrivés à l'aéroport], le car qui (6.3) était censé nous emmener à l'hôtel venait de (4.15) partir.
8. Aux heures de pointe, nous évitions de (4.11.3) prendre [*or* Aux heures de pointe, on évitait de (4.11.3) prendre] le train qui s'arrêtait à toutes les gares.
9. L'Espagnol dont nous avons loué l'appartement l'hiver dernier venait (4.11.3) tous les quinze jours vérifier que tout allait bien (4.11.1).
10. Il apprend (4.12) à conduire depuis Pâques, mais il n'a pas encore passé son permis.

F Extraits du Guide Suntours

La veille du départ. Il est possible que les horaires que nous vous avons donné**s** (6.5) au moment de votre réservation subissent des modifications par la suite. La veille de **votre** (4.2) départ, prenez la précaution de vérifier ces horaires auprès de **votre** (4.2) agent de voyages.

Bagages. Essayez, si possible, **de** (5.6.2) voyager léger. Pour cela réfléchissez à votre style de vacances et ne vous encombrez pas de choses **dont** (6.6) vous **n'**aurez pas besoin. Évitez **d'** (App. 4) emporter des bijoux de valeur.

Au retour. Nous avons effectué des enquêtes **qui** (6.3) nous permettent de connaître l'évolution des besoins en matière de tourisme ainsi que les problèmes **qui** (6.3) surgissent au cours des séjours organisé**s**. Cependant, aucune (5.1) information n'est aussi précise que celle que vous pouvez nous faire parvenir personnellement, aussi nous vous recommand**ons** de bien vouloir remplir, dès votre retour, les questionnaires **qui** (6.3) vous auront été remis. Nous vous remercions **de** (App. 4) votre aimable coopération.

Chapter 7 Diagnostic, p. 41

A Ils courent, ils courent ...

1. Le nombre de « joggers » augmente **constamment**.
2. La plupart d'entre eux disent qu'ils ont besoin de se dépenser **physiquement** pour éviter le stress.
3. Ils font **habituellement** [*or* **Habituellement** ils font] partie d'un groupe ou d'un club et s'entraînent **fréquemment**.
4. **Généralement** âgés de 35 à 45 ans, ils se soumettent **régulièremen**t à un contrôle médical.
5. Ils cherchent **absolument** à retrouver ou à garder leur jeunesse et sont **entièrement** [*or* **profondément**] convaincus que courir est la meilleure façon d'y parvenir.

B De bonnes résolutions

Après avoir regardé à la télévision une émission intitulée « Bien vivre », je me suis dit que je **me sentirais** mieux dans ma peau si je menais une vie plus équilibrée.

Comme j'étais en congé j'ai décidé que dès le lendemain. **J'arrêterais** de fumer. Je **sauterais** du lit à sept heures et demie et avant de déjeuner je **ferais** un peu d'exercice physique. Le reste de la matinée **serait** consacré à de menus travaux dans l'appartement et, au lieu d'aller acheter des plats tout prêts, je **prendrais** la peine de préparer des légumes frais et une grillade pour midi. **J'aurais** le temps en début d'après-midi de lire un peu et **j'irais** ensuite à la piscine. Après un repas léger, je **rejoindrais** les copains mais plutôt que de traîner toute la soirée d'un endroit à l'autre je **proposerais** toute une série d'activités culturelles. J'étais sûr que ce nouveau rythme de vie me **conviendrait** tout à fait et que je **pourrais** ainsi mieux profiter de mes vacances.

Malheureusement, le lendemain je n'ai pas entendu mon réveil sonner. Quand je me suis réveillé il était déjà trop tard pour mettre mes résolutions en pratique.

Chapter 7 Reinforcement, p. 46

A Les médecines alternatives

1. Les Français qui **ont utilisé fréquemment** (7.4) les médecines dites « douces » en **parlent avec enthousiasme** (7.9).
2. Parmi celles-ci, on compte la phytothérapie, pratique fort ancienne, **communément appelée** (7.3) « médecine par les plantes » et l'acuponcture **relativement bien** (7.2) acceptée de nos jours.
3. Les gens **se tournent généralement** (7.2) vers les médecines alternatives lorsque la médecine traditionnelle s'est avérée **particulièrement inefficace** (7.2).
4. **Il y aura forcément** (7.3) des sceptiques, mais le nombre des médecins généralistes qui **croient sérieusement** (7.2) aux bienfaits de ces médecines différentes est en augmentation croissante.
5. Ces moyens thérapeutiques **auront sûrement** (7.2) un rôle **nettement plus** (7.2) important à jouer à l'avenir.

KEY TO EXERCISES

B (See 7.11–12)

1. Il **faudrait** se préoccuper plus de son corps et de sa santé.
2. Vous **seriez** moins essoufflé si vous fumiez moins.
3. Le médecin a déclaré qu'elle ne lui **prescrirait** plus de somnifères.
4. L'alcool ne **ferait** de mal à personne, si les gens buvaient modérément.
5. Les gens **souffriraient** moins du dos s'ils se tenaient correctement.

C (See 7.14)

1. Nous **aurions voulu** organiser une randonnée pédestre dans les Alpes.
2. Il **aurait pris** plus d'exercice physique s'il en avait eu le temps.
3. Tu **aurais dû** venir à pied au lieu de prendre la voiture.
4. J'**aurais préféré** me faire soigner par un homéopathe.
5. On **se serait inscrits** (see 3.16 note) à un cours de yoga si on avait su.

D *Thème*

1. S'il se mettait au régime et mangeait d'une façon raisonnable (7.9) [*or* d'une manière raisonnable (7.9)], il perdrait rapidement du poids.
2. J'aurais pensé (7.14) qu'il serait allé (7.14) chez un homéopathe, mais lorsque je lui ai dit cela il a répondu d'un ton irrité (7.9) qu'il ne ferait jamais une telle chose.

   or J'aurais pensé (7.14) qu'il serait allé (7.14) voir un homéopathe, mais quand je le lui ai dit il a répondu d'un ton irrité (7.9) qu'il ne ferait jamais une chose pareille.
3. A un moment donné, tout le monde pensait que les antibiotiques et les vaccins contrôleraient (7.11) définitivement (7.2) les maladies contagieuses, mais ce n'est évidemment (7.4) pas le cas.
4. L'arrivée du sida a profondément (7.3) choqué l'opinion publique et a changé d'une manière dramatique (7.9) [*or* d'une façon dramatique (7.9)] nos habitudes sexuelles. Le contraire aurait été (7.14) surprenant [*or* étonnant].

Chapter 8 Diagnostic, p. 47

A Qu'est-ce qu'un bon prof ?

1. Pourquoi est-ce qu'il peut aisément répondre à cette question ?
   or Pourquoi peut-il aisément répondre à cette question ?
2. Un bon prof, qu'est-ce que c'est ?
   or Qu'est-ce qu'un bon prof ?
3. Est-ce que leur professeur est heureuse d'enseigner ?
   or Leur professeur est-elle heureuse d'enseigner ?
4. Pour qui est-ce que c'est un vrai plaisir d'être en cours ?
   or Pour qui est-ce un vrai plaisir d'être en cours ?
5. Comment est-ce qu'elle les incite à produire un travail personnel ?
   or Comment les incite-t-elle à produire un travail personnel ?
6. Qu'est-ce qui le passionne maintenant ?

7. Qui est-ce qui lui a donné envie d'apprendre ?
   or Qui lui a donné envie d'apprendre ?
8. Quel âge a Omar Latelli ?

B Déçus par la vie d'étudiant

JULIEN   La fac, ce n'est pas ce que j'**avais imaginé**. Avant de venir je **m'étais dit** que la fac serait pour moi l'occasion de découvrir des tas de choses. Je **ne m'étais pas rendu compte** de ce que serait la vie sur un campus complètement coupé de tout, à plusieurs kilomètres du centre. Personne **ne m'avait prévenu**.

RACHID   Même quand on s'intéresse à ses études, comme c'est notre cas, on ne peut pas faire que ça. On a besoin d'autre chose. Personnellement, si j'**avais su** j'aurais essayé d'aller ailleurs.

CHLOÉ   Moi, je **ne m'étais pas fait** d'illusions, alors c'est différent. Mais c'est vrai qu'on est isolé.

Chapter 8 Reinforcement, p. 52

A (See 8.3–4)
Pourquoi met-on ses enfants dans le privé ?

- Les enfants sont-ils plus suivis dans leurs études ?
- Les classes sont-elles moins chargées ?
- Obtient-on un meilleur pourcentage de réussite ?
- Y a-t-il un effort d'innovation pédagogique ?
- Le niveau universitaire des maîtres est-il plus élevé ?
- Est-ce pour des raisons religieuses ?
- Est-ce lié à la position sociale des parents ?

B Les terminales du soir : une expérience positive

1. A qui (8.12) les terminales du soir offrent-elles une seconde chance ?
   or A qui est-ce que (8.1, 8.12.1) les terminales du soir offrent une seconde chance ?
2. Pourquoi (8.11) personne ne veut-il (8.4) de ces élèves ?
   or Pourquoi est-ce que (8.1) personne ne veut de ces élèves ?
3. Comment (8.11) bon nombre d'entre eux ont-ils travaillé (8.4–5) avant (de s'inscrire à des cours du soir) ?
   or Comment est-ce que (8.11) bon nombre d'entre eux ont travaillé avant … ?
4. Que (8.10) leur manquait-il ?
   or Qu'est-ce qui (8.8) leur manquait ?
5. Quel (8.13) rôle la solidarité des élèves joue-t-elle (8.4) ?
   or Quel rôle est-ce (8.1, 8.13) que la solidarité des élèves joue ?
6. Quand (8.11) la solidarité aide-t-elle (8.4) les élèves à tenir le coup ?
   or Quand est-ce que (8.1, 8.11) la solidarité aide les élèves à tenir le coup ?

C See 8.15

Vous auriez tous eu une bonne note ...

1. si vous **vous étiez appliqués** pour bien présenter votre copie.
2. si tout le monde **avait analysé** à fond le sujet.
3. si vos arguments **n'avaient pas été** si mal construits.
4. si vos idées m'**avaient enthousiasmé(e)** par leur originalité.
5. si vous **aviez pris** le temps de relire votre dissertation avant de la rendre.

D *Thème*

1. A qui (8.12.1) s'adressent ces études ?
   or A qui (8.12.1) est-ce que (8.1) ces études s'adressent ?
2. Quels (8.13) diplômes demande-t-on ?
   or Quels (8.12.1) diplômes est-ce qu' (8.1) on demande ?
3. Qu'est-ce qu'on (8.9) enseigne aux étudiants de première année ?
   or Qu'enseigne-t-on (8.10) aux étudiants de première année ?
4. Sur quoi (8.12.2) portent les cours ?
5. Quelles (8.13) sont les matières importantes la seconde [*or* la deuxième] année ?
   or Quelles sont les matières (8.13) importantes en seconde [*or* deuxième] année ?

Chapter 9 Diagnostic, p. 53

A Compte-rendu d'un témoignage

1. J'ai décrit comment c'était arrivé.
2. On m'a demandé où s'était déclaré le sinistre.
3. Je n'ai pas su dire ce qui avait provoqué l'explosion.
4. J'ai indiqué quelle heure il était.
5. Il m'a fallu dire s'il y avait-il d'autres témoins.
6. Ensuite, on a voulu savoir qui avait prévenu les sapeurs-pompiers.
7. On m'a fait préciser à quelle heure ils étaient arrivés sur les lieux.
8. Enfin, j'ai dû raconter ce que j'avais fait en les attendant.

B

Sur la route, il est très important de bien voir et d'être vu

Si vous utilisez une voiture :
- **nettoyez** votre pare-brise régulièrement ;
- **changez** vos balais d'essuie-glaces quand ils sont usés ;
- **assurez-vous** du parfait fonctionnement de vos éclairages.

Si vous utilisez un deux-roues :
- **portez** des vêtements clairs ;
- **équipez-vous** d'éléments fluorescents pour rouler de nuit.

Recommandations amicales

Avant de quitter de l'appartement, sois gentil(le) :
- **fais** attention à bien fermer les robinets ;
- **sors** les ordures ;

- **vérifie** que les volets et les fenêtres sont fermés ;
- **débranche** les appareils électriques ;
- **éteins** toutes les lumières.

Et puis au moment de partir, **n'oublie pas** de fermer la porte d'entrée à clé. Merci !

Chapter 9 Reinforcement, p. 56

A Compte–rendu de l'interview accordée par M. le ministre de l'Intérieur

1. J'ai tout d'abord demandé au ministre ce qu' (9.2.3) il pensait (9.3) de l'œuvre accomplie par le CNPP.
2. Il m'a répondu qu'il éprouvait (9.3) un très grand intérêt à l'égard des multiples activités du CNPP et de ses initiatives en faveur de la sécurité.
3. Je lui ai ensuite demandé si (9.1) notre environnement était (9.3) plus dangereux qu'avant.
   or Je lui ai ensuite demandé s' (9.1) pensait (9.3) que notre environnement était (9.3) plus dangereux qu'avant.
4. Il m'a affirmé qu'il y avait (9.3), sans aucun doute, une évolution préoccupante, mais en ajoutant qu'il espérait que les efforts des responsables de la sécurité permettraient (9.3), tout de même, de restreindre l'étendue des périls.
5. J'ai voulu savoir ce qui (9.2.2) favoriserait (9.3), selon lui, la réduction du nombre d'accidents dans les années à venir.
6. Il a déclaré qu'il fallait (9.3) avant tout mettre en place un réseau très dense d'information afin de rendre les Français plus responsables de leur sécurité.
7. Je lui ai enfin demandé quelle impression générale ce congrès lui avait laissée (9.3).
8. Il a dit pour conclure que, dans le domaine de l'information et de la prévention, l'action du CNPP semblait (9.3) exemplaire.

B Skieurs oubliez tout sauf votre sécurité

1. Votre sécurité dépendra en grande partie de vos capacités physiques. Ne **les** (9.5, 9.8) surestimez pas, surtout en fin de journée.
2. En montagne, le temps change vite. Les services météo sont là pour vous aider. Avant de partir, consultez-**les** (9.5, 9.7).
3. Un équipement adapté et contrôlé, c'est aussi votre sécurité. Vérifiez-**le** (9.5, 9.7).
4. On peut contracter une assurance pour la responsabilité civile et les frais de secours. Pensez-**y** (9.5, 9.7) dès votre arrivée.
5. Il est risqué de s'aventurer hors des pistes. Si vous êtes inexpérimenté, ne vous **en** (9.5, 9.8) écartez pas.
6. Pour pratiquer le ski en haute montagne, il est prudent de se faire accompagner par un guide. Même si vous êtes expérimenté, engagez-**en** (9.5, 9.7) un.

KEY TO EXERCISES

Revision 7–9, p. 57

A Mort d'un voyageur

- Qu'est-ce que (8.9) la direction de la SNCF a regretté ?
- Quel (8.13) âge avait la victime ?
  or Quel (8.13) âge la victime avait-elle (8.4) ?
- Vers / À quelle (8.13) heure est-ce que (8.1) tout à commencé ?
  or Vers / À quelle heure tout a-t-il commencé (8.5) ?
- Qu'est-ce qu' (8.9) il ne possédait pas ?
  or Que (8.10) ne possédait-il pas (8.3) ?
- Comment est-ce qu'il (8.1) a réagi ?
  or Comment a-t-il réagi (8.5) ?
- De quoi (8.12.2) est-ce que (8.1) les deux contrôleurs l'ont taxé ?
  or De quoi (8.12.2) les deux contrôleurs l'ont-ils taxé (8.4–5) ?
- Qui est-ce qui (8.8) est intervenu ?
  or Qui (8.10) est intervenu ?
- Pourquoi est-ce qu' (8.1) un autre voyageur est intervenu ?
  or Pourquoi un autre voyageur est-il intervenu (8.4) ?
- De quel (8.13) wagon est-ce qu' (8.1) il est tombé ?
  or De quel (8.13) wagon est-il tombé (8.5) ?
- Dans quel (8.13) hôpital est-ce qu' (8.1) il a été transporté ?
  or Dans quel (8.13) hôpital a-t-il été transporté (8.5) ?
- À quoi (8.12.2) est-ce qu' (8.1) il a succombé ?
  or À quoi (8.12.2) a-t-il succombé (8.5) ?

B

1. La direction de la SNCF a **vivement** (7.2) regretté l'accident d'hier soir qui a fait une victime, un père de famille d'une quarantaine d'années.
2. M. Perrier ne possédait pas de titre de transport et il a **violemment** (7.4) réagi lorsque deux contrôleurs l'ont taxé d'une amende.
3. D'après les témoins, un autre voyageur est **gentiment** (7.3) intervenu pour essayer de le calmer mais n'y est pas parvenu.
4. Au cours de l'altercation qui a suivi, M. Perrier est **accidentellement** (7.2) tombé du dernier wagon en gare de Versin.
5. Il a été **immédiatement** (7.2) transporté à l'hôpital Pasteur mais a succombé à ses blessures pendant le trajet.

C Pluperfect (See 8.15)

1. suffire	il avait suffi
2. se présenter	les lycéens s'étaient présentés
3. vivre	nous avions vécu
4. ouvrir	on avait ouvert
5. suivre	vous aviez suivi
6. mourir	ils étaient morts
7. valoir mieux	cela avait mieux valu
8. ne jamais voir	je n'avais jamais vu
9. ne pas faire	le président n'avait pas fait
10. ne rien résoudre	ces mesures n'avaient rien résolu

C Conditional (See 7.11–12)

1.	suffire	cela suffirait
2.	se présenter	je me présenterais
3.	vivre	les malades vivraient
4.	ouvrir	le magasin ouvrirait
5.	suivre	on suivrait
6.	mourir	les gens mourraient
7.	valoir mieux	il vaudrait mieux
8.	ne jamais voir	nous ne verrions jamais
9.	ne pas faire	tu ne ferais pas
10.	ne rien résoudre	cela ne résoudrait rien

C Conditional perfect (See 7.14)

1.	suffire	il aurait suffi
2.	se présenter	elles se seraient présentées
3.	vivre	on aurait vécu
4.	ouvrir	vous auriez ouvert
5.	suivre	tu aurais suivi
6.	mourir	elle seraient mortes
7.	valoir mieux	tout aurait mieux valu
8.	ne jamais voir	nous n'aurions jamais vu
9.	ne pas faire	je n'aurais pas fait
10.	ne rien résoudre	vous n'auriez rien résolu

D See 9.3

Analyse de sondage quelques années plus tard

42 % des personnes interrogées ont déclaré que la formation des enseignants de l'enseignement public était suffisante.

50 % considéraient que les enseignants s'intéressaient plutôt aux élèves les plus doués.

40 % estimaient que les enseignants projetaient leurs idées politiques dans leurs cours.

Seuls, 37 % des Français semblaient convaincus qu'à l'avenir les enseignants devraient manifester un plus grand esprit d'innovation.

E (See 9.5–8)

Lorsque vous séjournez dans des pays tropicaux, pour éviter les ennuis de santé, il vous suffit de prendre quelques précautions :
- **sachez** vous reposer, surtout après un long voyage ;
- **ayez** soin de vous protéger du soleil et des insectes ;
- **ne buvez** que des boissons embouteillées si possible ;
- **munissez-vous** d'un désinfectant intestinal ;
- **ne vous baignez jamais** en eau douce.

F (See 3.2–10 and 9.7–8)

Ceci est un médicament

1. Un médicament n'est pas un produit comme les autres, ne **le** laissez pas à portée de main des enfants.
2. Les médicaments sont des produits actifs, n'**en** abusez jamais.
3. Votre médecin sait quels sont les médicaments dont vous avez besoin, consultez-**le**.
4. Suivez le traitement prescrit, **ne l'**interrompez pas, ne **le** reprenez pas de votre seule initiative.
5. Votre pharmacien connaît les médicaments : demandez-**lui** des conseils si nécessaire.

G *Thème*

1. Les pompiers leur ont demandé s' (9.1) il y avait eu (9.3) d'autres témoins.
2. Le journaliste a demandé au ministre quelle (8.13) politique elle avait (9.3) l'intention de poursuivre.
3. Les propriétaires voulaient savoir ce qui (9.2.2) était arrivé (9.3) pendant leur absence.
   or Les propriétaires ont voulu savoir ce qui (9.2.2) s'était passé (9.3) pendant leur absence.
4. Le directeur m'a récemment (7.4, 7.8) demandé ce que (9.2.3) j'aimerais (9.3) faire l'année prochaine.
   or Le directeur m'a récemment (7.4, 7.8) demandé ce que (9.2.3) je voudrais (9.3) faire l'an prochain.
5. La police a demandé [*or* nous a demandé] avec qui (8.12.1) nous étions (9.3) et qui (9.2.1) nous cherchions (9.3).

Chapter 10 Diagnostic, p. 59

A Sauvez ces vilaines bêtes

La forêt recule, **les** marais s'assèchent, **la** pollution augmente et c'est ainsi que disparaissent serpents, araignées, chauve-souris, vers et crapauds. Ces vilaines bêtes meurent dans **l'**indifférence générale. En effet, seuls **les** mammifères – excepté **la** chauve-souris – et **les** oiseaux sont populaires auprès **du** public. C'est pourtant dans cet univers oublié que se trouve l'essentiel **de la** biodiversité animale et la très grande majorité **des** espèces menacées de disparition.

Deux exemples :

– le ver de terre géant de **la** famille des *Scherotheca*, qui vit généralement dans le sud de **la** France et se déplace **la** nuit à six ou sept mètres de profondeur, devient rarissime ;

– le rhinolophone, chauve-souris originaire **des** pays tropicaux, est aujourd'hui au bord **de l'**extinction. Il ne vit pas caché **le** jour, ce qui le rend très vulnérable.

B La forêt

1. De nombreuses menaces **pèsent** sur la forêt, dont le feu et la surexploitation.
2. En Europe, pour éviter les incendies on **nettoie** les sous-bois.
3. Dans les pays en voie de développement, où la déforestation **s'accélère**, on essaie d'introduire de nouvelles méthodes agricoles.
4. Comme le feu, la surexploitation **mène** à la désertification.
5. Pour y remédier, les spécialistes **suggèrent** de planter des arbres à croissance rapide, surtout en Afrique.

C *Thème*

1. La conférence internationale sur le réchauffement climatique qui s'est réunie au Japon du 21 mai au 1er juin n'a pas été aussi décevante que prévu.
2. C'était la seconde [*or* la deuxième] conférence sur la réduction des émissions de gaz à effet de serre depuis l'an dernier.
3. La protection de l'environnement n'est pas toujours une priorité dans les pays en voie de développement.
4. La Chine, l'Inde et le Brésil ont soutenu les mesures prônées par l'Europe.
5. Les États-Unis, par contre, craignaient un ralentissement de la croissance économique et une augmentation du chômage.

Chapter 10 Reinforcement, p. 64

A La guerre de l'eau

Un risque majeur de pénurie menace aujourd'hui **l'**humanité (10.1). **L'**eau (10.1) douce, indispensable **à la** santé (10.1), **au** bien-être (10.1) et **au** développement économique (10.1) est, en effet, devenue un bien rare. **La** consommation (10.1) d'eau progresse à un rythme deux fois supérieur à celui **de la** croissance économique (10.1).

Lors d'un forum international, qui s'est tenu **les** 24 et 25 mars dernier (10.7) **au** Maroc (10.12), **les** spécialistes (10.1) ont annoncé que la quantité d'eau disponible par habitant en Afrique ne représenterait bientôt plus que **le** quart (10.6) de ce qu'elle était en 1950. D'ici à 2025, les régions touchées par **la** pénurie (10.1) s'étendront **aux** deux tiers (10.6) environ **de la** population mondiale (10.1). Seuls **l'**Australie (10.11), **le** Brésil (10.11), l'Europe **du** Nord et **de** l'Ouest (10.11), **la** Russie (10.11) et **l'**Afrique équatoriale (10.11) resteront autosuffisants. Les autres devront avoir recours à **l'**importation d'eau, à moins qu'ils n'aillent, **les** armes à **la** main (10.4), s'approvisionner chez leur voisin.

B Des catastrophes naturelles plus nombreuses et plus destructrices

1. Les catastrophes naturelles **se répètent** (10.13) plus souvent aujourd'hui.
2. Il y a quelques années encore, on **considérait** (10.13) qu'il s'agissait-là de phénomènes exceptionnels.
3. A cette époque-là, on ne **s'interrogeait** (10.15) guère sur le rôle joué par la concentration urbaine, la désertification rurale ou l'effet de serre.
4. Aujourd'hui, les experts **rejettent** (10.17) l'explication strictement « naturelle ».

5. Ils **rappellent** (10.18) que les pays en développement sont souvent les plus touchés.

6. Ils **révèlent** (10.13) aussi qu'il existe désormais un nouveau type de réfugiés, les « réfugiés de l'environnement », qui fuient cyclones, sécheresses ou inondations.

C *Thème*

1. L' (10.1) eau douce, indispensable à la (10.1) vie, est devenue rare.
   or L' (10.1) eau douce, qui est indispensable à la (10.1) vie, est devenue un bien rare.

2. Les (10.1) spécialistes ont révélé l'étendue du problème au cours des discussions qui se sont tenues le (10.7) 22 mars dernier au Brésil.

3. D'ici à 2025, l' (10.11) Afrique du Nord, l' (10.11) Afrique du Sud, le Moyen-Orient, l' (10.11) Asie, les (10.11) États-Unis, le (10.11) Mexique et une partie de l' (10.11) Europe seront touchés par la sécheresse (10.1) [*or* par la (10.1) pénurie d'eau].

4. Dans certains pays, la quantité d'eau douce disponible par habitant représentera le (10.6) tiers de ce qu'elle est aujourd'hui.

5. Les risques de conflit armé soulèvent (10.16) de profondes inquiétudes.

Chapter 11 Diagnostic, p. 65

A L'explosion de la vidéo

Des millions **de** foyers sont désormais équipés d'un magnétoscope. Si, pour la majorité **des** utilisateurs, le magnétoscope sert avant tout à enregistrer des émissions **de** télévision, la location **de** cassettes préenregistrées est un phénomène important.

Grâce aux vidéo clubs, les propriétaires **de** magnétoscopes ont un choix très diversifié **de** programmes : les longs métrages ne sont pas seuls à figurer dans les catalogues, on y trouve aussi bien des films **d'**animation que des cours **de** tennis ou **de** langue, sans oublier, bien évidemment, les programmes **de** jeux. Mais loin de n'être qu'un instrument **de** reproduction, la vidéo à la fois un outil **d'**expression et un moyen **de** diffusion dans des secteurs comme la formation **du** personnel et l'enseignement à distance.

B Internet

1. Si vous **souhaitez** communiquer avec le monde entier, connectez-vous à Internet.

2. Si la tendance actuelle **se poursuit**, le Web jouera un rôle clé dans la vie de chacun.

3. Avant le Minitel et Internet, si on **voulait** la moindre information, il fallait se déplacer.

4. Si je **n'avais pas** contacté d'autres internautes, je n'aurais jamais trouvé ce renseignement.

5. Certains services **ne seraient plus** consultés s'ils n'étaient pas sur Internet.

6. D'autres **ne seraient jamais apparus**, si Internet n'avait pas connu un tel succès.

C *Thème*

1. Elle a travaillé comme photographe de presse à l'étranger puis comme directeur de projet dans le multimédia à son retour d'Allemagne.
    or Elle a travaillé en tant que photographe de presse à l'étranger puis en tant que directeur de projet dans le multimédia à son retour d'Allemagne.
2. Elle a été embauchée [*or* recrutée] principalement parce qu'elle était capable de communiquer avec conviction et une grande clarté.
3. En France, à l'époque, de nombreux jeunes gens [*or* jeunes] sans diplôme universitaire ni formation spécialisée ont commencé à travailler dans le multimédia.
4. L'édition électronique n'était qu'un aspect de ce nouveau secteur d'activité.
5. Les nouvelles technologies commençaient à jouer un rôle clé dans la politique de communication de la plupart des grandes entreprises.
6. En une dizaine d'années, elles transformeraient complètement le monde du travail.
    or En l'espace d'une dizaine d'années, elles transformeraient entièrement le monde du travail.

Chapter 11 Reinforcement, p. 70

A Il faut que chaque culture ait son Internet

*   *Pourquoi avez-vous créé une association pour les utilisateurs d'Internet en Afrique ?*
–   Je l'ai créée dans le but de promouvoir la culture **du** Web dans les coins les plus reculés **d'** (11.5) Afrique. Le but est de faire d'Internet un outil **d'** (11.8) alphabétisation et **d'** (11.8) expression culturelle.
*   *Comment résoudre les problèmes **d'** (11.8) infrastructure téléphonique ?*
–   Grâce aux réseaux **de** (11.8) satellites mis en place actuellement par les pays riches, on peut se connecter en utilisant **de** (11.9) petites antennes paraboliques.
*   *Concrètement de quoi avez-vous besoin ?*
–   Nous voulons créer **des** centres de formation. Pour cela, peu **de** (11.6) moyens suffisent. On récupère **de** (11.9) vieux ordinateurs et on les transforme en serveurs.
*   *Quelle est votre ambition ultime ?*
–   Les autoroutes **de l'**information devraient permettre l'édification d'une réelle solidarité planétaire. Si le tiers monde n'est pas présent sur Internet, ce sera la fin **de la** diversité culturelle.

B L'influence des médias (See 11.12)

1. Si la concurrence entre les différents médias était moins effrénée, l'information **serait** plus fidèle à la réalité.
2. Si les bonnes nouvelles **se vendaient** aussi bien que les mauvaises, les médias ne seraient pas tentés de noircir la réalité.
3. Ainsi, l'an dernier, le public **se serait senti** sécurisé si l'on avait vraiment parlé de la baisse de la criminalité.
4. Si l'utilité des médias est incontestable aujourd'hui, il **paraît** néanmoins essentiel de s'interroger sur leur effet sur la société.

C *Thème*

1. En tant que (11.1) [*or* Comme (11.1)] rédacteur en chef, Michel Blanc est très efficace. Il dirige le quotidien avec une (11.4 note) conviction remarquable et beaucoup de (11.6) courage. C'est la raison pour laquelle [*or* C'est pourquoi] la majorité des (11.6) journalistes le traite avec tant de respect. Récemment, il a publié des documents confidentiels sans autorisation et un grand nombre de (11.6) lecteurs [*or* bon nombre de (11.6) lecteurs] ont approuvé son action.

2. A l'heure actuelle, les enfants passent moins de temps à regarder des émissions de télévision qu'il y a une quinzaine d' (11.6) années. En fait, la plupart d'entre eux (11.6 note) passent autant de temps devant leur téléviseur qu'avant mais ils l'utilisent pour d' (11.9) autres activités : jeux vidéo, Internet, etc. Si cette tendance se poursuit, l'influence de la télévision dans la vie des enfants diminuera progressivement.

3. Si, au moment où les premiers PC sont arrivés sur le marché, on nous avait dit qu'ils seraient bientôt partout, on ne l'aurait pas cru (11.12). À l'école, si (11.13) le multimédia n'a pas remis en cause le rôle pédagogique des enseignants [*or* des professeurs], il a bouleversé [*or* changé *or* modifié] les habitudes et les méthodes d'enseignement.

Chapter 12 Diagnostic, p. 71

A Le drame des réfugiés

The wave of refugees swells from week to week: they arrive either on foot in pitiful columns or crammed into ox-drawn carts. As soon as they arrive, the humanitarian agencies take care of them. Life, however, is precarious for these people who, having been displaced, have nothing left and nowhere to go. Malnutrition and disease are rife. Even when they have settled in the camps, they are still not safe from violence: at night, when representatives of the international organisations have left, the families hiding in their shacks no longer have anyone to protect them.

Such deprivation is hardly conceivable for those who live in plenty. The international community is neither particularly generous nor aware of its responsibilities.

B J'espère que vous **avez passé** un bon week-end. Le mien **a été** assez mouvementé.

Samedi, à nouveau, la ville **a reçu** des obus. L'un d'eux **est tombé** sur une maison proche de l'hôpital. Nous **avons eu** le temps d'entendre un sifflement au-dessus de notre tête quand il **est passé** au-dessus du toit. On **s'est jetés** au sol et il **a explosé** à 100 mètres d'ici. On **est allés** tout de suite voir s'il y avait des victimes et on **a sorti** trois fillettes blessées des décombres. Deux d'entre elles **sont mortes** dans la nuit. Dimanche, les combats **se sont amplifiés**. Les villages aux alentours de la ville **ont souffert** et de nouveaux enfants blessés **sont arrivés** à l'hôpital.

Malgré tout ça, je garde le moral et ne regrette pas d'être venu.

C Cher toi,

En janvier, des journalistes de la Télé nationale sont **venus** faire un reportage. Tu m'as **vue** à la télévision ? Je suis très curieuse de connaître le résultat car les choses se sont **passées** très vite. Ils ont tout **enregistré** en une seule fois. Je n'ai pas eu la possibilité de recommencer quand je me suis **mise** à bafouiller. Il est évident que ces journalistes ne sont **venus** que pour récolter du sensationnel. Il n'y a que la salle des tuberculeux qui les a **intéressés**, parce qu'il y avait plein de gens en train de mourir ! Ils m'on vraiment **dégoûtée**.

J'espère que tu ne m'as pas **oubliée**.

Je t'embrasse tendrement.

Chapter 12 Reinforcement, p. 76

A (See 12.8 and also 4.11) for use of perfect and imperfect tenses
L'aide internationale: un cadeau à double tranchant

Pour être efficace, l'aide doit obéir à des règles précises : secours correspondant aux besoins des populations, produits étiquetés dans la langue du pays receveur et triés au départ. Sinon, elle risque d'ajouter au chaos.

Lorsque la télévision **a montré** des images de l'Arménie dévastée par un tremblement de terre, un immense mouvement de solidarité **s'est déclenché**. Soixante-dix pays différents **ont envoyé** des centaines de tonnes de médicaments. Malheureusement quand ils **sont arrivés**, on **s'est aperçu** que la plupart de ces médicaments **étaient** périmés. L'Arménie **a dû** importer un coûteux incinérateur spécial pour les détruire sans polluer.

En Irak, certains réfugiés **ont pris** des sachets de potages déshydratés pour des paquets de lessive parce qu'ils **étaient** incapables de déchiffrer le mode d'emploi écrit en anglais.

Même l'arrivée des secouristes, lorsqu'ils ne sont pas demandés par le pays victime d'une catastrophe, peut causer des difficultés. Après le tremblement de terre dont il **a été** victime, l'Iran **aurait pu** se passer des équipes de volontaires venus d'une dizaine de pays différents. En revanche, des experts **auraient été** utiles pour l'assainissement.

B

1. Les images que l'on a **montrées** (12.9) ont déclenché un vaste mouvement de solidarité.
2. Les médicaments que l'on a **envoyés** (12.9) de l'étranger n'ont pas pu être utilisés.
3. Quand ils sont **arrivés** (12.10), on s'est **aperçu** (12.12) que la plupart étaient périmés.
4. Après les avoir **reçus** (12.9), l'Arménie a dû détruire ces médicaments.
5. Le mode d'emploi des sachets de potage que les réfugiés ont **pris** (12.9) pour des paquets de lessive était en anglais.
6. L'arrivée des secouristes que l'Iran n'avait pas **demandés** (12.9) a causé des difficultés.
7. Par contre, les experts qui auraient **pu** (12.9) être utiles sont **restés** (12.10) chez eux.

KEY TO EXERCISES

C *Thème*

1. Ces réfugiés n'ont plus nulle part (12.1) où aller.
2. Ils n'attendent plus rien (12.1) de personne.
3. Ils n'ont de la nourriture que (12.2) pour quelques jours.
4. Bientôt ils n'auront plus rien (12.1) à manger.
5. Ils ne sont pas à l'abri de la maladie non plus (12.6).
   or Ils ne sont pas à l'abri des épidémies non plus.
6. Si rien n' (5.2) est fait, des milliers seront morts avant la fin du mois.
7. Bien sûr [*or* Évidemment], la guerre ne fait que (12.3) rendre les choses plus difficiles.
8. Jusqu'à présent, cette région n'a reçu ni (12.5) aide alimentaire ni (12.5) assistance médicale de l'étranger.

Revision 10–12, p. 77

A (See 10.1–12 and 11.1–10)

L'électorat. Depuis une vingtaine d'années, les attitudes et les comportements **des** électeurs ont considérablement évolué. L'image **des** partis et **des** politiques auprès **du** public s'est progressivement dégradée, et la France est désormais un pays où le taux **d'**abstention est élevé. En matière **de** politique, **les** électeurs se comportent en consommateurs : **les** programmes et **les** candidats sont considérés comme **des** produits que l'on essaie et dont on change s'ils s'avèrent insatisfaisants.

Les partis traditionnels. Au fil des années, les discours et les programmes **de la** droite et **de la** gauche modérées se sont fortement rapprochés. **Le** libéralisme et **les** préoccupations sociales ne sont plus l'apanage de telle ou telle famille politique. En conséquence, un quart **de l'**électorat modéré est susceptible de changer de bord, entre deux élections.

Les partis extrêmes. **L'**extrême droite a bénéficié de la désaffection **des** Français pour **les** partis traditionnels. Elle a également profité de l'inquiétude **des** Français devant **le** chômage, **les** inégalités sociales, **l'**immigration et la montée **de** l'intégrisme musulman.

B Enquête

*Nous savons que **vous l'avez licenciée** (12.9) en juin. C'était pour quelle raison ?*
SON PATRON **Elle s'était mise** (12.12) à s'absenter régulièrement sans motif.

- *Est-ce qu'**elle vous a dit** qu'elle avait des problèmes récemment ?*
SON FRÈRE   Non, mais si **elle avait eu** des problèmes, elle ne m'en aurait pas parlé.

- *Pourquoi est-ce que **vous n'en auriez pas parlé** ensemble?*
SON FRÈRE   Parce-qu'**elle ne s'est jamais confiée** (12.12) à moi [*meaning that she never did*].
             or Parce qu'**elle ne se serait jamais confiée** (12.12) à moi [*meaning that she would never have done it*].

- *Mais si **elle avait été** déprimée, vous l'auriez su !*

SES PARENTS Oui, sans doute qu'**on s'en seraient aperçus** (12.12) !

• *Est-ce que **vous l'avez vue** (12.9) la semaine dernière ?*

SA VOISINE Non. Mais la semaine précédente **je l'avais invitée** (12.9) à dîner en ville et elle avait refusé.

• *Pourriez-vous me dire si **elle a eu** des visites la veille de sa disparition ?*

LE GARDIEN Si quelqu'un était venu dans la journée, **je l'aurais remarqué**. Mais le soir, c'est différent !

C *Thème*

1. Elle ne confiait jamais rien (12.1) à personne.
2. Elle n'allait plus jamais nulle part (12.1).
3. Ses voisins ne l'ont jamais vue (12.9) avec personne avant sa disparition.
4. Elle ne travaillait plus guère (12.1 note).
5. Après samedi, ni (12.5) ses parents ni (12.5) son frère ne l'ont jamais revue (12.9).

D (See 3.11–14, 4.10–11 and 12.9–13)

La colère d'un gréviste et de sa compagne

DIDIER (*32 ans, routier*) Il y a deux ans, quand on **s'est mis** à compter les heures de travail, on **s'est rendu** compte que notre salaire horaire **était** bien inférieur au Smic. Mais la première grève **n'a rien résolu** parce que les engagements **n'ont pas été** tenus. La plupart des entreprises **ont continué** à faire comme elles faisaient avant et, par conséquent, la minorité d'entreprises qui **a voulu** appliquer la loi **s'est trouvée** pénalisée.

JOSIANE (*38 ans, la compagne de Didier*) Didier aime son métier. Quand il **a décidé** de devenir routier, les conditions de travail et le salaire **n'étaient pas** mirobolantes mais on **pensait** que ça **allait** s'améliorer. Pas du tout, c'est le contraire qui **s'est passé**. Du fait de la concurrence, la situation **s'est détériorée**. Pourtant ce n'est pas un job de tout repos ! Pendant des années, il **a fait** l'Europe de l'Est. Quand il **partait** à l'étranger, je **ne le voyais** presque jamais. L'an dernier, j'**ai fini** par craquer et j'**ai insisté** pour qu'il travaille sur le réseau national.

E *Thème*

1. Des milliers de (11.6) particuliers et d'entreprises jettent (10.17) leurs déchets n'importe où. Les Français incinèrent (10.13) plus d'un tiers de leurs déchets et envoient moins de 10 % des ordures ménagères au recyclage. Le plus souvent, ils considèrent (10.13) que c'est essentiellement [*or* principalement] au gouvernement et aux industriels de se préoccuper de la protection de l'environnement et non au simple consommateur !

2. Si la (10.11) France et les pays de l'Union européenne avaient suivi l'exemple de la (10.11) Suisse et de l' (10.11) Autriche, au lieu de privilégier le (10.1) transport routier, la crise des transports serait devenue (12.10) moins grave. En négligeant (10.15) de prendre en compte le coût réel du (10.1) transport routier, la (10.11) France n'a fait que (12.3) contribuer à son développement. Le transfert du (10.1) trafic de marchandises de la route au rail s'avérera (10.13) long et difficile.

3. Les (10.1) organisations internationales comme Amis de la terre nous rappellent (10.18) constamment que la sauvegarde (10.1) [*or* la protection] de notre environnement naturel est notre responsabilité à tous [*or* est notre affaire à tous]. C'est en protégeant (10.15) la planète que nous assurerons l'avenir de nos enfants. Dans une de leurs publications, les (10.1) écologistes révèlent (10.13) qu'il faut 220 litres d' (11.6) eau pour produire dix litres de (11.6) jus d'orange. Si plus de gens le savaient, cela les amènerait-il (10.16) à modifier leurs habitudes de (11.8) consommation ?

Chapter 13 Diagnostic, p. 79

A Comment voient-ils l'Europe ?

Les jeunes Français se déclarent plutôt favorables **à** l'Europe, même s'ils ne sont pas toujours convaincus **du** rôle concret que peut jouer l'Union européenne dans leur vie quotidienne. Ils semblent plutôt bien informés **de** ce qui se passe dans les autres pays.

Même si l'Europe leur semble parfois assez éloignée **de** leurs préoccupations, ils en attendent beaucoup. Ils sont surtout désireux **de** voir une Europe démocratique, en paix, et sans chômage. Une majorité d'entre eux imaginent une Europe capable **de** jouer un rôle important pour la défense de la paix dans le monde ainsi que celle des droits de l'homme. Nombre d'entre eux se disent prêts **à** aller étudier ou travailler dans un autre pays de l'Union. Conscients **des** difficultés existant sur le marché du travail, les plus âgés pensent que l'Europe est susceptible **de** leur offrir demain des opportunités d'emploi.

B

1. Les institutions sont devenues plus efficaces.
2. Il sera d'une importance capitale.
3. Notre collaboration s'est révélée fructueuse.
4. Où en sont les négociations commerciales avec le Japon ?
5. Le projet définitif a été adopté à l'unanimité.
6. Il faut réduire les déséquilibres régionaux.
7. Les dix prochaines années seront cruciales pour l'avenir de l'Europe.

C *Thème*

1. L'attitude de la France a déçu certains de ses partenaires européens.
2. Au cours des différentes négociations, la Grèce et le Portugal ont adopté des stratégies différentes.
3. Les Britanniques ne sont plus les seuls à être en désaccord avec la politique actuelle.
4. Seule une révision totale des quotas résoudra la crise.
5. L'important est de parvenir à un accord rapide.

Chapter 13 Reinforcement, p. 84

A (See 13.7–8 and Appendix 5, p.179)
Les origines de l'Union européenne

L'idée d'une communauté européenne fut émise en 1950 par des hommes soucieux d'assurer une paix durable. Seule une Europe unie leur semblait susceptible d'empêcher une confrontation entre les deux blocs dominés par les États-Unis et l'URSS. Six pays (la Belgique, la France, le Luxembourg, l'Italie, les Pays-Bas et la République fédérale allemande) se déclarèrent disposés à participer aux négociations qui aboutirent en 1956 à la signature du traité de Rome instituant le Marché commun.

Au cours des décennies suivantes, de nombreuses étapes importantes furent franchies, surtout dans le domaine économique. Mais, dans la plupart des pays, l'opinion restait défavorable à une union politique forte. Sans politique étrangère et défense communes, l'Europe se trouva donc incapable d'imposer ses propres solutions sur la scène internationale.

B (See 2.2–6 and 13.11–14 for forms of adjectives)

1. **L' ancienne** (13.2) **présidente** du Parlement européen était favorable à **de nouvelles mesures**.
2. Le volume **des échanges commerciaux** avec l'Afrique augmente depuis **un certain** (13.2) **temps**.
3. **Les régions pauvre**s (13.2) ont bénéficié de subventions **exceptionnelles** (13.4) au cours **des derniers** (13.2) **mois**.
4. **L'élargissement progressif** de l'Union européenne a fait l'objet **de vives discussions**.
5. La Belgique a adopté **une attitude positive** en matière **de stratégie industrielle**.
6. **Les décisions unilatérales** comportent toujours **de gros risques**.

C *Thème*

1. La Commission européenne n'a rien proposé de nouveau (13.10).
2. Ce manque de consensus a quelque chose de très étonnant (13.10) [*or* surprenant].
   or Il y a quelque chose de très étonnant (13.10) à ce manque de consensus.
3. L'Allemagne s'est montrée généreuse (12.12) envers (13.8) ses partenaires d'Europe du Sud.
4. La ministre des Affaires étrangères s'est déclarée satisfaite (12.12) des dernières (13.2) résolutions.
5. Ces mesures sont trop mal appliquées pour (13.7.2) avoir un impact.
6. Les graves (13.4) désaccords actuels n'améliorent (13.9) pas la situation.

Chapter 14 Diagnostic, p. 85

A La banlieue s'enflamme

- *Pourquoi tant de violence ?*
- Quand plus de 20 % des jeunes d'une cité sont au chômage, il ne faut pas <u>s'étonner qu'</u>il **y ait** de la violence. En fait, tous les jours on <u>s'attend à ce</u> qu'il **se produise** un incident.
- *Mais la violence ne résout rien.*
- Non, mais c'est la seule manière pour ces jeunes de <u>réclamer qu'</u>on **fasse** quelque chose pour eux. Quand ils restent calmes, on les oublie.
- *Que veulent-ils ?*
- Ils <u>veulent</u> avant tout qu'on leur **permette** de jouer un rôle dans la société. Pour vivre, on a besoin de sentir que l'on sert à quelque chose.
- *La situation est-elle désespérée ?*
- <u>Je ne pense pas</u> du tout **qu'**elle **soit** désespérée. La banlieue est un lieu plein de vie et de dynamisme. <u>J'aimerais</u> tellement <u>qu'</u>on **comprenne** cela !

B

1. Je doute que le premier ministre **prenne** les mesures qui s'imposent.
2. Je ne suis pas sûre que les solutions proposées par le gouvernement **soient** les meilleures.
3. N'attendons pas que la chose **se reproduise** pour créer des emplois pour les jeunes de la région !
4. J'insisterai auprès du gouvernement pour que les responsables **soient** punis sévèrement.
5. Nous devons agir pour empêcher que toute une génération **se sente** exclue de la société.
6. Si l'on n'agit pas tout de suite, je crains que la haine ne **devienne** un mode de vie pour tous ces jeunes.

C Version

1. My brothers are unemployed. I am afraid that it will be the same for me!
2. We are sick of waiting for the government to do something.
3. My father insists on my staying on at school but it's pointless!
4. I would have liked us to go to the town hall to discuss our problems, but they refused to see us. So it's not surprising that we set fire to the estate!

Chapter 14 Reinforcement, p. 90

A Comment voient-ils l'avenir ? (See 14.4–6)

PHILIPPE (*travailleur social*) Je suis inquiet. On dirait que les gens **s'habituent** à voir la misère autour d'eux. Je ne comprends pas qu'on **fasse** preuve de tant d'indifférence.

ELVIRE (*enseignante*) Moi qui suis prof, c'est la violence à l'école qui m'inquiète le plus aujourd'hui. Je suis heureuse que le gouvernement **ait** enfin décidé d'agir mais je crains qu'il ne **soit** trop tard.

ROMAIN (*ouvrier spécialisé*) J'aimerais que mes enfants **puissent** être sûrs de trouver du travail, mais je ne crois pas que la situation de l'emploi **s'améliore** du jour au lendemain.

LEILA (*directrice commerciale*) Nous vivons dans un monde qui bouge tout le temps, je ne pense pas qu'il **faille** nécessairement s'inquiéter pour l'avenir. Au contraire, je m'attends à ce que les choses **aillent** bien mieux d'ici quelques années.

B Immigration

1. Il est certain que l'immigration **a eu** (14.11) un effet très positif sur l'économie française jusqu'à la crise pétrolière de 1973.
2. Il est à craindre que les immigrés et leurs enfants **soient** (14.8) les premières victimes du chômage.
3. Il n'est pas prouvé que les immigrés **bénéficient** [*indicative*] (14.11) plus du système de protection sociale que les Français.
4. Il n'est pas vrai qu'il y **ait** (14.11) plus d'étrangers vivant en France aujourd'hui que dans les années 1930.
5. Il est probable que le nombre d'étrangers vivant en France **diminuera** (14.11) dans les quelques années à venir.
6. Les spécialistes sont convaincus que par la suite on **aura** (14.11) à nouveau besoin de main d'œuvre étrangère pour compenser la baisse du taux de natalité.

C *Thème*

1. On doit faire tout ce qu'on peut pour empêcher que la haine devienne (14.9) un mode de vie.
   or Il faut faire tout notre possible pour empêcher que la haine devienne (14.9) un mode de vie.
   or On doit faire tout ce qu'on peut pour empêcher la haine de devenir (15.13 note) un mode de vie.
2. Les gens sont fatigués [*or* las] d'attendre que le gouvernement fasse (14.7) quelque chose.
3. Les jeunes voudraient que les pouvoirs publics agissent [*subjunctive*] (14.7) rapidement pour améliorer leurs conditions de vie dans les cités.
4. Ils ne croient pas qu'il y ait (14.11) une place pour eux dans la société actuelle.

Chapter 15 Diagnostic, p. 91

A Pour créer son entreprise

1. La priorité des priorités, c'est de connaître le marché **auquel** on va s'attaquer.
2. C'est la raison pour **laquelle** la réalisation d'une étude de marché est la première tâche **à laquelle** il faut se consacrer.
3. Ensuite il s'agit de trouver les capitaux **qui** vous permettront de créer votre entreprise.
4. Les institutions **auxquelles** vous allez vous adresser voudront des chiffres, ne laissez rien au hasard.

5. Si aucun des organismes financiers auprès **desquels** vous avez fait des démarches n'est intéressé par votre projet, sollicitez l'aide de votre famille.
6. Une fois les financements trouvés, choisissez soigneusement le personnel et les fournisseurs avec **qui** vous travaillerez.

B Devenir commerçant

La Chambre de commerce et d'industrie (CCI) fournira **au** futur commerçant les renseignements qui **lui** permettront **de** prendre, en toute connaissance de cause, les décisions nécessaires à la réalisation de son projet. Elle **lui** suggérera, entre autres, **d'**établir un plan de financement pour ses dépenses d'investissement et, suivant le type d'activité qu'il envisage, elle **lui** conseillera **de** contracter un emprunt auprès de tel ou tel établissement financier.

Le futur chef d'entreprise pourra aussi demander **à** la CCI **de** contacter certains organismes à sa place. Rien ne **l'**empêchera, par ailleurs, **de** chercher conseil auprès des organisations professionnelles.

C Thème
Témoignage d'un jeune chef d'entreprise

1. Mon entreprise existe depuis trois ans et j'emploie aujourd'hui vingt personnes, ce qui prouve que l'idée originale était bonne.
2. J'ai remboursé l'argent que j'avais emprunté à mes parents, ce dont ils se félicitent.
   or J'ai remboursé l'argent que j'avais emprunté à mes parents, ce dont ils sont ravis.
3. Actuellement, pour moi, la difficulté majeure [*or* le problème majeur] est de trouver des produits correspondant à ce que je cherche.
4. Ce qui m'inquiète aussi, c'est le manque croissant de personnel hautement motivé.

Chapter 15   Reinforcement, p. 96

A Le nombre des faillites monte en flèche

1. On a enregistré quelque 50 000 faillites au cours des deux dernières années, **ce qui** (15.8) inquiète les pouvoirs publics.
2. Dans ces faillites, les victimes sont d'abord les salariés pour **qui** (15.2) il n'y a pas d'autre possibilité d'emploi.
3. Mais ce sont aussi les fournisseurs dont les factures restent impayées, **ce que** (15.9) l'on oublie trop souvent.
4. Lorsqu'il s'agit d'une société importante, toute la région **où** (15.6) elle est implantée se trouve sinistrée.
5. C'est **ce que** (15.9) l'on a constaté lorsque la société Chabert a fermé ses portes.
6. Cette société, à **laquelle** (15.4) le gouvernement a refusé de porter secours, a dû licencier plus de 2 000 salariés.
7. Les circonstances à la suite **desquelles** (15.5) Chabert a fait faillite étaient difficilement prévisibles.

8. Le chef d'entreprise, à **qui** (15.2) les salariés ont fait confiance jusqu'au bout, a tout fait pour essayer de sauver son entreprise.
9. **Ce dont** (15.10) on peut être sûr c'est que pour lui le dépôt de bilan n'a pas été une solution de facilité.

B Fermeture d'usine (See 15.14)

• *Avez-vous été prévenus à l'avance de la fermeture de l'usine ?*
– Non. Hier on a vu le directeur arriver à son bureau, comme d'habitude.
• *Comment avez-vous donc appris cette fermeture ?*
– On en a entendu parler pour la première fois à la télévision.
• *Comment les syndicats ont-ils réagi ?*
– On les a entendu dire qu'ils s'attendaient à des licenciements depuis longtemps.

C *Thème*

1. L'entreprise Fauvet & Fils a vu son chiffre d'affaires doubler en moins d'un an, ce qui (15.8) est remarquable. Si l'on demande à (15.13) M. Fauvet d' (15.13) expliquer les raisons d'un tel succès, il répond qu'il faut l'attribuer à la qualité du travail de ses collaborateurs. « J'ai une équipe extrêmement performante sans laquelle (15.3) l'entreprise ne serait pas où elle est aujourd'hui. »
or Le chiffre d'affaires de l'entreprise Fauvet & Fils a doublé en moins d'un an, ce qui (15.8) est remarquable. […] « Je dispose d'une équipe extrêmement performante sans laquelle (15.3) l'entreprise ne serait pas où elle est aujourd'hui. »
2. Lors d'un grand dîner auquel (15.4) assistaient de nombreux chefs d'entreprises de la région, la chambre de commerce a promis d' (15.13) offrir aux (15.13) petites entreprises une série de cours leur (15.13) permettant de (15.13) s'initier aux nouvelles méthodes de gestion. Elle a également l'intention d'engager plusieurs conseillers aux services desquels (15.5) les entreprises pourront faire appel en période de difficulté.

Revision 13–15, p. 97

A (See 13.1–3 and 13.11–14)

1. Il faut apporter des solutions **originales** aux problèmes **sociaux**.
2. Le salaire **mensuel** des cadres **moyens** varie considérablement d'un pays à l'autre.
3. La production **industrielle européenne** a atteint des chiffres record.
4. L'amélioration des relations **internationales** a eu certains effets **paradoxaux**.
5. On annonce une hausse **exceptionnelle** des tarifs **postaux**.
6. Les bénéfices **annuels** des compagnies **aériennes** sont en baisse.
7. On a introduit un nouveau type de scrutin **proportionnel** aux **dernières** élections.
8. Il ne faut pas tenir compte des **petits** problèmes **individuels**.
9. L'opinion **publique** a été choquée à l'annonce **officielle** de ces négociations **secrètes**.

KEY TO REVISION

B Interviews de sportifs : ce qu'on leur demande parfois (See 14.4-6)

1. Je voudrais que vous nous parliez de votre dernière saison.
2. Je crains que vous ne soyez moins décontractée que l'an dernier.
3. Est-il vrai que vous ayez l'intention de vous retirer de la compétition ?
4. Comprenez-vous qu'un champion ressente parfois le besoin de faire une pause ?
5. Faut-il s'attendre à ce que vous participiez à nouveau à des manifestations écologiques ?
6. Pensez-vous qu'une championne comme vous ait un rôle social à jouer ?

C Le sport et l'argent font bon ménage

1. Voilà plus de 30 ans que les athlètes consentent à ce qu'on **se serve** (14.9) d'eux à des fins publicitaires.
2. Souvent les sportifs à la recherche de financement n'attendent pas qu'on **vienne** (14.7) les solliciter. Ils **vont** eux-mêmes tirer la sonnette des entreprises.
3. Aujourd'hui, on constate que le parrainage **engendre** [*indicative*] (14.11) souvent le succès.
4. Il ne faudrait pas croire pour autant que les sponsors **soient** (14.11) des philanthropes.
5. Ce sont au contraire des hommes d'affaires qui espèrent que leur association au sport **améliorera** (14.7 note) leur image de marque.

D (See 15.2-5)

- *Quelles sont les difficultés **auxquelles** vous vous êtes heurtée pour réaliser ce film ?*
- Le comédien à **qui** on avait confié le rôle principal est tombé malade au dernier moment.
- La maison de production avec **laquelle** on avait signé le premier contrat a fait faillite.
- Le cascadeur sur la présence de **qui** je comptais ne s'est pas présenté le jour voulu.
- À cause du mauvais temps, on a dû reporter les scènes pour **lesquelles** il fallait du soleil.
- Enfin, malgré les difficultés **dont** je vous parle, j'ai eu plaisir à faire ce film.

E Une banque pour les pauvres

La plupart des établissements bancaires considèrent que l'on ne peut pas faire confiance **aux** (3.7) pauvres en matière d'argent. C'est cette attitude **envers** (13.8 note) les plus démunis qui est en partie responsable **de** (App. 5) la misère actuelle. L'expérience de la Banque Grameen montre, en effet, qu'avec une aide financière minime, les pauvres sont capables **d'** (App. 5) améliorer considérablement leurs conditions de vie.

La pauvreté découle souvent du fait que les travailleurs sont dans l'incapacité **de** bénéficier des fruits de leur travail. L'aide sociale distribuée par de nombreux pays industrialisés permet **aux** (15.13) plus démunis **de** (15.13) survivre mais pas **d'** (15.13) éradiquer la misère. Si l'on veut supprimer la misère il faut donner **aux** (3.7) plus démunis les moyens de contrôler eux-mêmes leur destin. C'est ce que fait le micro-crédit. En accordant **à** (App. 4) chacun la possibilité **de** mettre ses compétences en application, il aide les pauvres **à** (App. 4) sortir des systèmes de dépendance.

F *Thème*

Munoz craignait de ne pas être (14.2) sélectionné pour le match de la Coupe d'Europe parce qu'il voulait jouer (14.2) une fois de plus devant son public avant de se retirer – ce qui (15.8) est compréhensible. Non seulement il a joué, mais le directeur de l'équipe, Luc Bertelli, a insisté pour qu'il fasse (14.9) encore une saison. Tout le monde à pensé qu'après tout ce qu'il (15.9, 15.12) avait fait pour le club, il était trop jeune pour (13.7.2) arrêter de jouer.

Chapter 16 Diagnostic, p. 99

A
1. Natura, l'eau minérale **la plus riche en magnésium**.
2. Nettol, les produits d'entretien **les plus économiques**.
3. Avec Excella, les opérations **les plus complexes et les plus longues** sont parfaitement maîtrisées.
4. Le modèle **le plus récent** a déjà fait preuve de ses qualités.
5. Les cafés Arabor sont torréfiés avec **le plus grand** soin et **la plus grande** légèreté.
6. Le fond de teint Naouri, la façon **la plus naturelle** de sublimer votre teint.

B
1. Le four à micro-ondes Frank est celui qui se vend **le mieux** cette année.
2. Notre assurance voyages ne vous empêchera pas d'avoir **les pires** ennuis, mais elle en minimisera les conséquences.
3. Le moins cher n'est pas toujours **le meilleur**.
4. Un des avantages de ce lave-vaisselle, et non **le moindre**, c'est sa rapidité.
5. Organisez-vous **mieux** avec un agenda Planning.
6. La Juva 4 a été choisie comme l'une des dix **meilleures** voitures de l'année.

C Publicité : les secrets de la réussite

The good advertising professional is the one who believes that he is the best, who says that he is the best but is prepared to question himself. You cannot afford to be complacent, you must always do better. The secret of success is to enjoy taking risks and to be totally dedicated to your job without taking yourself too seriously.

French advertising has made a tremendous leap in the past few years. It is now one of the most innovative in the world. Why? Because it has understood that the fewer risks you take the less chance you have of being successful. Only sensational images capture the attention of the public. You must always go one step further, even at the risk of slipping up. In the end, the big *coups* make up for the less successful campaigns. But to make a big campaign successful, it is not enough to be the best, you must let it be known. The best product of the publicist is himself or herself: he or she must know how to advertise advertising.

Chapter 16 Reinforcement, p. 104

A (See 16.12)

1. Pour préparer votre voyage dans de **meilleures** conditions, adressez-vous à notre agence-conseil.
2. La carte X : la **meilleure** façon de gagner du temps et de l'argent.
3. Avec les produits solaires X, bronzez **mieux** en vous exposant moins.
4. Ce n'est pas le tout d'être bricoleur, encore faut-il posséder les **meilleurs** outils.
5. Pour **mieux** connaître les formules de financement possibles, adressez-vous à votre concessionnaire X.
6. De toutes les poudres à laver que j'ai essayées, c'est celle qui lave **le mieux**.
7. Nous vous offrons une qualité incomparable aux **meilleurs** prix.
8. Offrez-vous ce qui se fait de **mieux** en matière d'ameublement.

B (See 16.17)

1. Le but d'une campagne publicitaire est de **faire** vendre.
2. Elle y parvient en **faisant** mieux connaître les produits nouveaux.
3. Mais est-il bien nécessaire de **faire** voir une femme nue pour vendre un parfum ?
4. Il est essentiel de créer une identité de marque si l'on veut **se faire** une réputation mondiale.
5. Les agences de publicité françaises ont mis longtemps à **se faire** accepter sur le marché américain.
6. Le Bureau de vérification de la publicité a parfois de la peine à **faire** respecter la réglementation sur la publicité mensongère.

Translation

1. The aim of an advertising campaign is to sell.
2. It manages to do so by making people more aware of new products.
3. But is it really necessary to show a naked woman in order to sell a perfume?
4. It is essential to create a brand identity if you want to build a worldwide reputation.
5. It was a long time before French advertising agencies broke into the American market.
6. The *Bureau de vérification de la publicité* (advertising standards authority) sometimes finds it difficult to ensure that advertisers comply with the regulations about misleading advertising.

C *Thème*

1. Parfois les contraintes peuvent être plus stimulantes qu' (16.1) une absence totale de censure : elles obligent les publicitaires à être plus créatifs (16.1). Par exemple, les mesures visant à limiter la publicité [*or* les mesures qui visaient à limiter la publicité] pour les cigarettes les ont amenés à créer quelques-unes de leurs plus belles campagnes (16.4).
2. Pour un acteur célèbre, un film publicitaire de quarante secondes peut être plus rémunérateur (16.1) que n'importe quel long métrage. Il y a trente ans

une telle activité aurait représenté la pire (16.6) des humiliations pour une vedette.

3. Perdre (16.14) du poids [*or* des kilos] est devenu une obsession pour beaucoup de femmes. La plupart des gens s'accordent pour dire que la publicité est en partie responsable de ce phénomène. Mais les agences publicitaires prétendent qu'elles n'ont rien à se reprocher.

4. Il est de plus en plus (16.1 note) souhaitable d'informer le consommateur aussi clairement (16.8) que possible (16.1) des qualités d'un produit. Mais ce n'est pas l'objectif principal de la publicité.
   or ... le plus clairement possible (6.13) des qualités d'un produit. Mais ce n'est pas l'objectif primordial de la publicité.

5. Si vous avez une voiture à vendre (16.15) ou un appartement à louer (16.15), le plus simple (13.6, 16.4) et le moins cher (13.6, 16.3–4) est de mettre une petite annonce dans le journal local. C'est aussi [*or* également] la formule la plus efficace (16.4) que je connaisse (16.7).

Chapter 17 Diagnostic, p. 105

A L'entretien d'embauche

1. Il est naturel que vous soyez anxieux avant un entretien.
2. Mais il est important que vous restiez calme.
3. D'entrée, il faut que vous fassiez preuve d'enthousiasme.
4. Il importe aussi que vos réponses soient brèves et pertinentes.
5. Et surtout n'oubliez pas qu'il est essentiel que vous arriviez à l'heure !

B Grève des contrôleurs aériens

Les aiguilleurs du ciel suspendront leur mouvement de grève pour le week-end **de manière à ce que** le retour des vacances de Pâques se fasse normalement. Ils ont néanmoins déposé un nouveau préavis de grève pour lundi matin. « Nous avons essayé de négocier tout l'hiver, **sans que** le gouvernement ait fait aucune concession. C'est pourquoi nous avons décidé de poursuivre notre mouvement de grève **jusqu'à ce que** nos revendications soient satisfaites » explique M. Bossi, responsable du syndicat national des contrôleurs aériens.

La plus importante de ces revendications concerne, rappelons-le, le calcul de la retraite. Les grévistes insistent également **pour que** la différence entre le travail « sur écran » et le travail « dans les bureaux » soit reconnue. Mais l'administration refuse toute concession **de peur que** cela ne fasse boule de neige dans la fonction publique.

C

1. Bien que les centrales syndicales continuent [*same form as indicative present*] à exercer d'importantes responsabilités, le syndicalisme français reste faible et divisé.
2. A moins qu'ils ne fassent de rapides progrès pour moderniser leur image, les syndicats risquent de perdre encore des adhérents.
3. Cela devrait pouvoir se faire à condition qu'ils tiennent compte des aspirations individuelles des salariés.

Chapter 17 Reinforcement, p. 110

A (See 17.6–8)
L'informatique dans l'entreprise

1. La production des entreprises est mieux adaptée aux besoins **parce que** les études de marché sont plus précises.
2. Les bureaux d'études peuvent simuler une ligne de production **avant qu**'elle ne soit réalisée.
3. **Au fur et à mesure que** l'automatisation se développe dans les usines, l'intervention directe de l'homme dans les tâches d'exécution se réduit.
4. La robotique joue un rôle considérable **sans que** les entreprises soient pour autant peuplées de robots.
5. En effet, **vu que** les risques de pannes sont sensiblement accrus, l'automatisation rend le maintien d'une intervention humaine indispensable.
6. Les effectifs d'ouvriers qualifiés continuent de diminuer **alors que** la création d'emplois de maintenance se poursuit.
7. Dans les bureaux, l'informatisation est également la règle partout, **de sorte que** chaque employé se sert d'un terminal ou d'un micro-ordinateur.
8. Dans ces conditions, l'entreprise doit développer la formation permanente **afin que** les salariés puissent constamment s'adapter aux nouvelles techniques.

B *Thème*

Dans la plupart des entreprises [*or* sociétés], les salaires individuels ne sont pas divulgués officiellement, bien que certaines sociétés [*or* entreprises] aient (17.4) maintenant décidé d'afficher ces informations.
or Dans la plupart des entreprises [*or* sociétés], les salaires individuels ne sont pas dévoilés officiellement, bien que certaines d'entre elles aient (17.4) maintenant pris la décision d'afficher ces informations.

« Ici chaque employé est actionnaire. Il est donc normal qu'il ou elle ait accès à toutes les informations économiques et sociales concernant [*or* sur] l'entreprise, déclare un pdg, et c'est la meilleure façon d'éliminer toutes sortes de rumeurs sur [*or* concernant] les salaires ». Un conseiller en management souligne que la transparence améliore les relations entre la direction et les employés.

Apprendre ce que gagnent les autres encourage certains employés à s'inscrire à des stages de formation ou à faire preuve d'initiative. Pour d'autres, cependant, savoir qu'ils ont atteint le plafond de leur fourchette de salaire est décourageant. « Quand j'apprends que le contremaître a encore eu une augmentation, ça me reste en travers de la gorge », dit Mariana, ouvrière spécialisée dans une petite usine d'électronique.

Chapter 18 Diagnostic, p. 111

A Écrire en collaboration

- *Vous avez co-signé un roman policier qui vient de paraître aux éditions de Midi. Qui a eu l'idée de ce livre ?*

AGNÈS   C'est moi qui **en** ai eu l'idée, mais je savais que Macha s'**y** intéresserait avant même que je **lui en** aie parlé. On avait toujours dit qu'on ferait quelque chose ensemble un jour. J'ai donc tout de suite pensé à **elle**.

- *Et vous avez accepté tout de suite, Macha ?*

MACHA   Dès qu'elle me **l'**a soumis, son projet m'a tentée. Mais je **lui** ai tout de même demandé de me donner une semaine pour **y** réfléchir. En fait, je **lui** ai téléphoné dès le lendemain pour **lui** dire que j'acceptais.

- *Comment s'est organisé le travail à deux ? Vous rédigiez ensemble ?*

AGNÈS   Non. Une fois qu'on avait décidé du contenu de chaque chapitre, on rédigeait séparément. On se retrouvait donc avec deux versions, on **les** comparait, on **en** discutait et petit à petit on arrivait à une version unique.

- *Quand on travaille en équipe, n'y a-t-il pas des tensions ?*

MACHA   Pas vraiment. La collaboration exige que chacun accepte les critiques de l'autre et ne s'**en** offusque pas. On **le** savait avant de commencer. Il n'y a eu aucun problème de ce côté-là. Mais il nous est arrivé d'être incapables de choisir entre les versions successives : aucune d'**elles** ne nous plaisait. C'est alors qu'on a demandé à Ali d'intervenir.

- *Vous vous êtes donc mis à travailler à trois ?*

AGNÈS   Oui. Ali était curieux de lire le roman. On **lui** a donc offert de devenir notre premier lecteur. Il a été formidable.

B Homosexuel et agriculteur

Si en ville l'homosexualité s'affiche, à la campagne elle se veut invisible. Dans une communauté rurale, seule la discrétion permet **à** l'homosexuel **de** mener une vie sans histoires. « Il serait impensable de parler **de** son homosexualité, mieux vaut la cacher **aux** autres », nous dit Gérard. Il joue les célibataires endurcis et profite **des** fins de semaine pour retrouver quelques amis dans une des villes voisines.

À quand une plus grande ouverture ? « Cela dépendra **de** l'évolution des mœurs. »

Chapter 18 Reinforcement, p. 116

A Une période d'adaptation

L'usine où René travaillait s'est vue obligée de licencier, il y a dix-huit mois : « Je m'**y** (18.9) attendais, on **en** (18.9) parlait depuis un certain temps. Mais tout de même, ça fait un choc ! » La préretraite était préférable au licenciement et, à son âge, René a pu **en** (18.4) profiter. Juliette, sa femme, tire un bilan positif de leur situation : « La vie est faite d'étapes successives. La retraite **en** (18.4) est une. »

Les premières difficultés ont été financières. Ils **en** (18.4) ont beaucoup discuté ensemble. « Je ne l' (18.6) aurais jamais cru mais, en fait, cette période de crise n'a fait que resserrer les liens entre nous », explique René. Ensuite il a fallu trouver un autre mode de vie : « Avoir mon mari à la maison à temps complet a bouleversé mes habitudes, reprend Juliette. Au début, j'ai eu de la difficulté à m'y (18.9) habituer. Quoi que je fasse, il fallait toujours qu'il s'**en** (18.9) mêle ! »

Se retrouver en tête à tête 24 heures sur 24 peut devenir un enfer et tourner à la catastrophe. René et Juliette semblent pourtant **y** (18.9) avoir échappé.

B

1. Bien que René s'y (18.1, 18.3) soit attendu, le licenciement a été un choc.
2. « Comme je vous l' (18.1, 18.7) ai dit, cette période de crise a resserré les liens entre nous. »
3. « Elle nous a beaucoup rapprochés, même si on ne s'en (18.1, 18.9) est pas aperçus au début. »
4. Comme Juliette s'en (18.9) doutait, les débuts ont été difficiles.
5. Elle n'était pas patiente avec René, mais elle l' (18.5) est devenue.
6. En fait, se retrouver en tête à tête 24 heures sur 24 s'est avéré beaucoup plus agréable qu'ils ne l' (18.8) avaient imaginé.

C *Thème*

1. Dans les années 1970, les femmes, pour qui la liberté sexuelle était une conquête récente, étaient d'autant plus décidées à s'en (18.1, 18.4) servir et certains magazines féminins ne manquaient pas de les y (18.1, 18.9) encourager [*or* de les encourager à le faire]. La situation est sensiblement différente aujourd'hui. Comme l' (18.7) indiquent certaines études récentes, la plupart d'entre elles se rendent compte que la liberté sexuelle ne fait pas le bonheur même si elle y (18.3) contribue.
2. L'homosexualité, longtemps considérée comme une anomalie, voire une maladie, est en train d'obtenir droit de cité. Il en résulte que les homosexuels ont moins tendance à cacher aux (18.10) autres la nature de leurs relations et les magazines qui leur (18.3) sont destinés [*or* publiés à leur intention] sont en vente libre.
3. L'adolescence commence souvent plus tôt que les parents ne l' (18.8) imaginent et les expériences sexuelles des adolescents d'aujourd'hui sont plus complexes qu'elles ne l' (18.8) étaient il y a 30 ans. Cela devrait leur (18.3) permettre d'atteindre dans leur vie adulte un équilibre que les générations précédentes n'ont pas connu.

Revision 16–18 p. 117

A L'entreprise et le client

Ce sont les Américains qui ont développé la notion de « service » dans les affaires. Le service consiste à procurer au client l'objet dont il a besoin, **au meilleur** (16.6, 16.12) prix et dans **la meilleure** (16.6, 16.12) qualité, tout en se mettant à sa disposition pour lui faciliter son achat. **Le plus souvent** (16.10), c'est l'étude du marché qui permet de connaître les besoins du client. La technique **la plus en faveur** (16.4 note) pour l'étude du marché a été pendant longtemps celle du sondage d'opinion.

Une fois que l'on connaît les caractéristiques et les qualités de l'objet que le client recherche **le plus** (16.11) et que l'on sait dans quelles conditions cet objet se vend et s'achète **le plus couramment** (16.10), il est possible de fabriquer un objet conforme au goût de la clientèle, de le lui offrir dans les conditions **les plus favorables** (16.4) et d'utiliser les arguments publicitaires qui retiennent **le mieux** (16.11, 16.12) l'attention et qui sont **les plus efficaces** (16.4).

B (See 16.8 note)
L'enfant et la télévision : quelques constatations
1. Plus l'enfant est jeune, moins il est sensible au contenu réel des émissions.
2. Plus les enfants grandissent, plus ils sont nombreux à dire que la télévision leur permet de s'ouvrir au monde extérieur.
3. Moins leurs parents s'occupent d'eux, plus les enfants regardent la télévision.
4. Plus leurs parents parlent avec eux de ce qu'ils ont vu, plus ils deviennent des spectateurs intelligents.

C Embauche : les méthodes de recrutement des cadres
Vous venez de répondre à une annonce et vous avez envoyé, comme on vous le demandait, « curriculum vitae, lettre manuscrite et photo ». Il est certain que la première sélection **se fera** (14.11) sur la base de votre CV, mais il se peut que la seconde **soit** (17.9) réalisée par un graphologue bien que les psychologues **contestent** [*subjunctive*] (17.4) la validité des conclusions tirées de l'analyse de l'écriture. Quant à la photo, il est possible qu'elle **soit** (17.9) adressée à un morphopsychologue pour qu'il **définisse** (17.4) votre caractère à partir des traits de votre visage.

Les psychologues s'accordent pour dire qu'un entretien **peut** (14.11) largement suffire a choisir le meilleur candidat, pourvu qu'il **soit** (17.4) mené par une personne compétente connaissant bien l'entreprise. Dans ces conditions, pourquoi faire appel à des méthodes contestées ? Parce que pour le patron l'embauche **est** (17.6) un risque. S'il s'adresse à des spécialistes de l'extérieur c'est de manière à leur **faire** (14.2) endosser la responsabilité en cas d'erreur.

D (See 17.1)
Arts et spectacles : quelques commentaires
1. Cette représentation est bien la plus belle à laquelle j'**aie jamais assisté**.
2. C'est le seul spectacle de la saison qui **ait remporté** un tel succès.
3. Il n'est pas surprenant que la prestation d'Auteuil lui **ait valu** un prix.
4. Je ne crois pas que nous **ayons déjà vu** ce groupe en si bonne forme.
5. Il est dommage que le public **ne se soit pas montré** plus enthousiaste.
6. C'est un miracle que l'exposition **n'ait pas été** annulée.
7. Bien que **je n'aie pas pu** assister à ce concert, j'en ai entendu le plus grand bien.

E (See Appendix 4, p. 172 and Appendix 5, p. 179)
Les plaisirs du célibat
Nombreux sont les célibataires qui ont choisi **de** conjuguer leur vie au singulier. Ils tiennent **à** leur indépendance et refusent **de** la perdre.

Solène, 36 ans, est une de ces célibataires pour qui célibat n'est pas synonyme de solitude. Son désir d'indépendance résiste **au** temps et **à** l'amour. Pourtant, Michel, son amant depuis deux ans, est très désireux **de** bâtir un couple avec elle : « Il essaie **de** me convaincre **d'**habiter chez lui, explique-t-elle, mais je ne peux me résoudre **à** le faire ». Pour Solène, le célibat se résume **à** la possibilité **de** se retirer seule dans son appartement où elle n'est obligée **de** penser **à** personne d'autre, ni **de** s'habituer **aux** manies de quelqu'un d'autre.

L'indépendance est un luxe. Vivre seul coûte cher, et la possibilité **de** choisir ce mode de vie dépend en quelque sorte **du** salaire dont on dispose. Autre difficulté : la maladie. On ne peut pas demander **à** son amant **de** venir jouer les gardes-malades pendant une semaine. Ressource inestimable pour les vrais célibataires : les amis. Dans les moments de crise, c'est **à** eux que l'on s'adresse. Il faut bien avoir quelqu'un **à** qui se confier.

F *Thème*

1. Il vaut mieux créer (17.10) une entreprise sans trop emprunter à la (18.10) banque pour ne pas avoir (14.2) de lourds remboursements au début [*or* afin de ne pas avoir des remboursements élevés pour commencer].
2. Sa famille a offert de lui (18.2) prêter de l'argent, sans qu'il le demande [*subjunctive*] (17.4), pour qu'il n'ait (17.4) pas à s'adresser à une banque [*or* faire appel à une banque].
3. Comme elle nous l' (18.7) a expliqué, plus (16.8) elle ouvre de magasins, plus son chiffre d'affaires augmente, sans que ses bénéfices diminuent [*subjunctive*] (17.4) [*or* soient en baisse].

Chapter 19 Diagnostic, p. 119

A En bref ...

Proche-Orient
Israël et la Syrie viennent de reprendre leurs négociations. **Celles-ci** avaient été suspendues à la suite de l'attentat de Tel-Aviv.

Amérique du Sud
Le récent effondrement de la bourse de Buenos Aires en Argentine inquiète l'Uruguay. L'avenir de **celui-ci** dépend, en effet, de la santé économique de son puissant voisin.

Asie du Sud-Est
La crise qui bouleverse actuellement l'équilibre de toute la région est d'autant plus grave que **celle-ci** n'y était nullement préparée.

Commerce international
Le contentieux entre les États-Unis et les pays européens s'aggrave bien que **ceux-ci** aient accepté certains compromis.

B Le général de Gaulle : une certaine conception de la défense

se fit : se faire ; *essaya* : essayer ; *se heurta* : se heurter ; *fut* : être ; *revint* : revenir ; *détermina* : déterminer ; *annonça* : annoncer ; *remirent* : remettre

General de Gaulle became known in the thirties by his writings on political history and military strategy. He tried to make his contemporaries aware of the pressing need to modernize the army, but for over fifteen years he was faced with the lack of understanding of the military leaders of the time. When he was finally appointed Under-Secretary for National Defence by Paul Reynaud on 6 June 1940, it was unfortunately too late to mechanize the army and resist the enemy.

There is no doubt that when he returned to power in 1958, it was the memory of the 1940 disaster that induced General de Gaulle to equip the defence forces with the most advanced techniques. On 2 November 1959, he announced the setting up of a national deterrent, capable of safeguarding national independence. Successive governments did not question the necessity for strategic nuclear arms in the following years.

Chapter 19 Reinforcement, p. 122

A (See 19.6 for use of past historic and 4.11 for use of imperfect)
Les projets de tunnels sous la Manche au XIXᵉ siècle

C'est à Albert Mathieu que l'on attribue généralement le projet le plus ancien d'un tunnel sous la Manche. **C'était** en 1802. La reprise des guerres napoléoniennes **mit** bientôt fin à son projet et **jeta** une ombre permanente sur les implications de l'entreprise. Albert Mathieu avait du moins ouvert la voie à des générations de visionnaires qui **allaient** poursuivre son idée.

Les projets **se succédèrent** au cours du XIXᵉ siècle. Le plus près d'aboutir **fut** celui de Sir Edward Watkins, qui **fit** entreprendre le forage de puits et de galeries près de Douvres. L'on aurait pu croire que l'heure du tunnel avait sonné. A tort. Il **était** encore trop tôt, semble-t-il. Le risque d'invasion, en cas de conflit armé avec la France, **devint** l'un des thèmes majeurs d'une violente campagne de presse contre la construction d'un tunnel au début des années 80. Alors qu'il avait déjà fait creuser une longue galerie, Watkins **dut** abandonner son projet sous la pression des militaires et des isolationnistes.

B

1. Nombreux sont **ceux que** (19.2) l'idée d'un tunnel a fascinés.
2. Le projet le plus ancien d'un tunnel sous la Manche est **celui de** (19.3) Mathieu.
3. Ni le projet de Mathieu, ni **celui de** (19.3) Watkins ne purent être réalisés.
4. L'entreprise de Watkins est **celle qui** (19.2) fut le plus près d'aboutir.
5. Les objections des militaires ainsi que **celles des** (19.3) isolationnistes firent échouer le projet de Watkins.

C *Thème*

L'Organisation des Nations unies fut créée en 1945. Elle a pour mission de sauvegarder la paix et la sécurité internationales et de promouvoir la coopération entre les peuples. Il importe de ne pas confondre (17.10) les divers organismes.
• L'Assemblée générale, qui réunit tous les États membres des Nations unies, formule des recommandations bien que celles-ci (19.4) ne soient pas (17.4) obligatoires.
• Le Conseil de sécurité est un organe exécutif, responsable du maintien de la sécurité internationale. Pour tout ce qui (19.5 note) relève de sa compétence, les

décisions sont prises à la majorité. Celles qui (19.2) ne bénéficient pas du soutien de *tous* les membres permanents du Conseil ne peuvent entrer en vigueur.

• Le Conseil économique et social, dont les membres sont élus par l'Assemblée générale, assiste celle-ci [*or* cette dernière] (19.4) dans les domaines économique, social, culturel et humanitaire.

• La Cour internationale de justice juge les différends entre les États membres de l'Organisation des Nations unies. Lorsque ceux-ci (19.4) y font appel, le jugement rendu par la Cour est obligatoire.

Chapter 20 Diagnostic, p. 123

A La technologie fille de la guerre

1. **C'est à la suite de l'humiliation de Pearl Harbour en 1943 que** l'Amérique s'est intéressée aux recherches sur l'atome.
2. De même, **c'est la mise au point des bombes volantes V1 et V2 en Allemagne qui** a ouvert la voie à la conquête de l'espace.
3. **C'est pour calculer la trajectoire des premiers missiles balistiques intercontinentaux que** le premier calculateur électronique fut construit.
4. Plus récemment, **ce sont les crédits militaires qui** ont permis à l'informatique, et plus généralement à l'électronique, de se développer à une allure stupéfiante.

B Pesticides

1. De tout temps, **il a été impératif** pour l'homme **de se protéger** contre tous les animaux nuisibles qui déciment les cultures et provoquent des famines.
2. **Il est particulièrement difficile de** contrôler la prolifération des insectes ravageurs.
3. **Il s'est avéré dangereux** pour les insectes utiles et la santé de l'homme **de** recourir à des armes chimiques « lourdes » comme le DDT.
4. **Il est maintenant possible de** contrecarrer le « boom démographique » de certains insectes grâce aux progrès réalisés en chimie organique et en biologie.
5. **Il est néanmoins malaisé de prévoir** les conséquences à long terme pour la santé humaine et l'environnement de la culture des plantes transgéniques.

C

1. **Lorsqu'on parle** de technologie avancée, on pense surtout à l'informatique et aux biotechniques.
2. **Tant qu'on ne connaîtra pas** [*or* **Tant que l'on ne connaîtra pas** (24.5)] précisément les effets à long terme des produits transgéniques, il faudra faire preuve de prudence.
3. **À mesure qu'on règlera** [*or* **À mesure que l'on règlera** (24.5)] les problèmes, d'autres se présenteront.
4. **Dès que** les Américains et les Européens **seront parvenus** à un accord, la mise en place de systèmes multimédias par satellite s'accélèrera.

Chapter 20 Reinforcement, p. 128

A Sciences et techniques : quelques définitions

1. *Les biotechnologies.* **C'** (20.2) est un mot qui désigne l'utilisation des propriétés de la matière vivante dans l'industrie. Les biotechnologies touchent des domaines extrêmement variés mais **c'** (20.7) est dans les secteurs de la santé, de l'agriculture et de l'alimentation qu'**elles** sont les plus performantes.

2. *Les matières plastiques.* **Elles** symbolisent la civilisation du XXe siècle. **Ce** (20.2) sont des polymères essentiellement produits à partir du pétrole. **Ils** remplacent les produits plus traditionnels (acier, bois, verre, etc.) et disposent d'un potentiel encore largement inexploité. **Cela** (20.5) explique pourquoi certains chercheurs prétendent que l'histoire des matières plastiques n'en est qu'à ses débuts.

3. *Les matériaux composites.* La construction automobile et l'industrie aérospatiale font largement appel à de nouveaux matériaux : les composites. **Ce** (20.2) sont, comme leur nom l'indique, des matériaux dans lesquels plusieurs constituants sont associés et qui possèdent un ensemble original de propriétés. **Ils** permettent, entre autres, de réaliser de grandes structures à la fois rigides, résistantes et légères. Ainsi, **c'** (20.7) est grâce à eux, que les véhicules automobiles sont beaucoup plus performants aujourd'hui.

4. *Le laser.* **Il** (20.4.1) est de plus en plus rare d'imprimer une lettre, d'écouter un disque ou même de passer un coup de téléphone sans recourir à la technologie du laser. Des supermarchés aux boîtes de nuit, des hôpitaux aux chantiers navals, **elle** occupe une place essentielle dans la vie quotidienne et **cela** (20.5) ne fera que s'accentuer dans les années à venir.

B *Thème*

Perfect tense

C'est (20.6, 20.9) Roland Dumas, alors ministre français des Relations extérieures, qui (20.6) a lancé l'idée d'un grand programme européen de recherche vers le milieu des années 80 [*or* vers 1985]. Il était convaincu qu'une fois que les gouvernements européens auraient réussi (20.12–13) à encourager un échange intensif d'informations entre [les] entreprises et [les] instituts de recherche, la productivité et la compétitivité de l'industrie européenne s'amélioreraient considérablement. Certains de ses critiques affirmaient [*or* soutenaient] qu'en règle générale il (20.4.1) est extrêmement difficile de demander à des concurrents de partager leurs secrets et que c'est (20.7) une erreur de croire que (20.7) les programmes de coopération dus à l'initiative des gouvernements ont plus de chances de réussir que la coopération spontanée. Aussi surprenant que cela (20.5) puisse paraître, étant donné leur position sur ce point [*or* à ce sujet] à l'époque, ce sont (20.6) les Britanniques qui (20.6) ont soutenu (20.9) le plus vigoureusement le projet.

Past historic

Ce fut Roland Dumas qui lança l'idée d'un grand programme européen de recherche vers le milieu des années 80. Il était convaincu qu'une fois que les gouvernements européens auraient réussi à encourager un échange intensif d'informations entre entreprises et instituts de recherche, la productivité et la compétitivité de l'industrie européenne s'amélioreraient considérablement. Certains de ses critiques affirmaient qu'en règle générale il est extrêmement difficile de demander à des concurrents de partager leurs secrets et que ce serait une erreur de croire que les programmes de coopération dus à l'initiative des gouvernements ont plus de chances de réussir que la coopération spontanée. Aussi surprenant que cela puisse paraître, étant donné leur position sur ce point à l'époque, ce furent les Britanniques qui soutinrent le plus vigoureusement le projet.

Chapter 21 Diagnostic, p. 129

A

1. Si vous suivez un traitement médical, consultez votre médecin **avant de prendre le chemin des stations**.
2. Une mise en condition physique s'impose **avant que vous vous lanciez sur les pistes** [*or* **avant de vous lancer sur les pistes**], si vous êtes un sportif occasionnel.
3. Respectez une progression dans la difficulté des exercices **jusqu'à ce que vous vous sentiez en pleine possession de vos moyens**.
4. **Après avoir passé une journée sur les pistes**, donnez-vous le temps du repos.
5. Et enfin, en cas de mauvais, n'hésitez pas à remettre votre sortie **jusqu'au lendemain**.

B Version

Extract from the data protection law ('loi Informatique et Liberté')
Article 1: 'Information technology must be to the benefit of every citizen. It must not undermine a person's identity, human rights, the right to privacy, or individual or public freedom.'

What you need to know about computer file
– Hundreds of thousands of files exist in France. Personal information on each of us is stored on several hundred files.
– It is often useful: thanks to this information, for example, a patient can receive, in the shortest time possible, a kidney transplant from a motorist killed in a car accident.
– But it can cause concern: information that is out of date, false or malicious may be used against you; files may be used for illicit purposes by a third party.

What you need to know about your right of access and your right to correct these files
– The National Commission on Information Technology and Civil Liberties can help you find out if your name appears on any files since all personal files must be registered with them.

– You may, if you so wish, consult your file. In order to do so you must get in touch with the organisation concerned.
– You can have the information about you changed if it is inaccurate. Point out the mistakes. The person responsible for the file will have to make the necessary corrections.

Chapter 21 Reinforcement, p. 134

A Au restaurant : vos droits (See 21.1–5)

• *Dernièrement, j'ai trouvé une erreur dans ma note de restaurant. Si le propriétaire n'avait pas accepté de la rectifier, quelle attitude **aurais-je dû** adopter ?*
RÉPONSE Vous **auriez pu** lui payer ce que vous estimiez lui devoir. S'il avait refusé votre argent, **il aurait** alors **fallu** prévenir la Direction départementale de la concurrence et de la consommation.
• *Le nom du plat que j'avais commandé ne correspondait pas du tout à ce que l'on m'a servi. **Fallait-il** refuser de le payer ?*
RÉPONSE On **aurait dû** vous servir autre chose à la place. La prochaine fois, **il faudrait** insister et prendre les autres clients à témoin.

B Accession à la propriété (See 21.1–5)

L'achat d'un logement compte parmi les gestes les plus importants de la vie. Si on **veut** le réussir, **il faut** mettre toutes les chances de son côté.

Pour ne pas finir au contentieux, **il faut** être capable de faire un budget et de s'y tenir. Le coût de l'installation **doit** être examiné avec soin. Un couple qui dispose de solides revenus **peut** parfaitement s'en tirer moins bien qu'un ménage plus modeste qui, lui, **sait** épargner. Non seulement il n'est pas drôle de finir au contentieux, mais les conséquences psychologiques **peuvent** être désastreuses.

Aujourd'hui encore, on achète trop sur un coup de cœur. Si l'on ne **veut** pas s'empoisonner la vie, la première question qu'**il faut** se poser, c'est « j'achète où ? » et non pas « j'achète quoi ? ». Y a-t-il des commerces, des transports en commun, des espaces verts ? On **doit** ensuite se demander si ce dont on a envie correspond à ce dont on a besoin. Et enfin, méfiez-vous des modèles témoins « non contractuels », ce qui **veut dire** que la maison que vous achetez ne ressemble pas à celle qu'on vous montre.

C *Thème*

Ce qu'il faut (21.4) savoir avant de projeter des vacances à l'étranger.
– *Passeports.* Chaque membre de la famille devrait (21.1) avoir son propre passeport. Les enfants peuvent (21.2) figurer sur le passeport d'un de leurs parents, mais ils ne peuvent (21.2) pas s'en servir quand ils sont seuls.
– *Visas.* Vous pouvez (21.2) avoir besoin d'un visa [*or* … Il se peut que (17.9) vous ayez besoin d'un visa] Adressez-vous au consulat du pays concerné longtemps à l'avance. N'attendez pas qu'il soit (21.11) trop tard pour faire votre demande.
– *Assurance personnelle.* Il est recommandé de prendre [*or* de contracter] une assurance personnelle. Si vous avez une demande de remboursement à faire, attendez d' (21.11) être rentré [*or* attendez votre retour (21.11)].

KEY TO EXERCISES

– *Devises*. Si vous vous munissez d'une carte bancaire appropriée, vous pourrez (21.2) retirer de l'argent dans des distributeurs de billets pendant (21.8) votre séjour à l'étranger [*or* ... vous pourrez (21.2) retirer de l'argent dans des distributeurs de billets à l'étranger].

Revision 19–21, p. 135

A La pub : information ou piège?

On dit que la publicité informe. **C'** (20.4.2) est faux. Au sens propre, le mot publicité a le sens de faire connaître **ce** (15.8) qui est d'intérêt public. Mais en réalité à quoi sert la publicité sinon à vendre ? **Elle** n'éclaire pas le public ; **elle** le manipule.

On prétend aussi que la publicité favorise la vie économique. **C'** (20.4.2) est faux. **Il** (20.4.1) est prouvé que l'augmentation du pouvoir d'achat aide davantage la consommation que toutes les publicités réunies. En vérité, **ce** (20.7) que la publicité favorise, **c'** (20.7) est la surconsommation de **ceux** (19.2) qui ont déjà les moyens de consommer.

Enfin, faire croire que le bonheur est dans la consommation, **c'** (20.4.2) est répandre une illusion nocive. Bien des jeunes restent esclaves des modèles publicitaires parce que **ceux-ci** (19.4) les empêchent de découvrir leur idéal de vie authentique. Tout **cela** (20.5) est bien inquiétant.

B Hiroshima et Nagasaki, 6 et 9 août 1945 (See Appendix 2, p. 160)

Le temps **est** clair et la journée **s'annonce** belle. Il **est** huit heures et les habitants d'Hiroshima **sont** au travail. La radio **annonce** l'approche de trois bombardiers américains puis, à 8h 15 exactement, une lumière aveuglante **déchire** l'horizon. La bombe **vient** d'éclater. Tout de suite après, des ondes de chaleur insupportables **s'abattent** sur la ville qui **se met** à brûler. Ensuite une gigantesque montagne de nuages **fait** son apparition dans le ciel. Enfin, dix minutes plus tard une espèce de pluie noire **tombe** sur la ville.

Les habitants d'Hiroshima **ignorent** sur le moment qu'ils **viennent** d'être victimes de la première bombe atomique. Quelque 70 000 personnes **périssent** immédiatement et le nombre de victimes **double** au cours des mois suivants.

Trois jours après le bombardement d'Hiroshima, la ville de Nagasaki **est** la cible du second bombardement nucléaire de l'histoire. Quelque 20 000 personnes **meurent** le jour même et 50 000 autres au cours de l'année 1945.

C (See 20.6–9)

1. **Ce sont des bombardiers américains qui** ont lâché la première bombe atomique.
2. **C'est à 8h 15 exactement qu**'a éclaté la bombe.
3. **C'est une espèce de pluie noire qui** s'est abattue sur la ville dix minutes plus tard.
4. **C'est la ville de Nagasaki que** les Américains ont ensuite **prise** pour cible.
5. **C'est trois jours après Hiroshima qu'a été bombardée** la ville de Nagasaki.

D Un acteur répond à nos questions

• *Pour quelles raisons avez-vous tourné le film qui sort cette semaine ?*

– J'ai accepté par estime pour le réalisateur. Et en raison, aussi, de la qualité des autres participants. **Il** (20.4.1) est rare qu'un film réunisse les meilleurs comédiens d'un pays.

• *Vous avez souvent déclaré choisir vos films en fonction du réalisateur. J'ai l'impression que c'est une constante chez vous.*

– **Cela** (20.5) m'a toujours paru essentiel. **Cela** (20.5) correspond, chez moi, à une certaine idée du cinéma. **Il** (20.4.1) est important de travailler avec des gens intègres qui ne font pas n'importe quoi sous prétexte de remplir les salles.

• *Est-ce pour des raisons semblables que vous êtes passé de l'autre côté de la caméra pour devenir vous-même réalisateur ?*

– C'était une progression naturelle. Et puis j'aime voir travailler les acteurs. Je trouve **cela** (20.5) absolument fascinant.

E *Thème*

1. Bien qu'on n'en ait guère parlé jusqu'à (21.9) récemment, le bruit est en passe de devenir le fléau majeur de la société actuelle. Comme c'est (20.2) souvent le cas, on a attendu que le nombre de mal entendants ait (21.11) considérablement augmenté pour mesurer l'ampleur du problème. La pollution sonore touche en premier lieu les citadins et ceux qui (19.2) vivent [*or* habitent] à proximité d'un aéroport ou d'une autoroute, mais elle nous concerne **tous**. Notre santé sera en danger tant que les pouvoirs publics ne prendront (20.12–14) pas des mesures radicales.

2. L'introduction de nouvelles variétés de céréales a peut-être aidé à lutter contre la faim dans le tiers monde, mais on ne devrait (21.1) pas oublier qu'elle a également causé une profonde transformation de l'environnement [*or* … il ne faudrait (21.4) pas oublier qu'elle a aussi profondément modifié l'environnement]. Celle des (19.3) plantes transgéniques pourrait avoir des conséquences semblables.

3. De nombreux écologistes craignent que les gouvernements ne continuent [*subjunctive*] (14.8) à exploiter les combustibles fossiles jusqu'à ce que toutes les ressources soient (21.9) épuisées, sans suffisamment investir [*or* sans investir assez] dans des sources alternatives d'énergie. Tant que cette attitude prévaudra (20.12–14), il y aura de quoi s'inquiéter.

Chapter 22 Diagnostic, p. 137

A Sécurité : les contrôles d'identité se multiplient

Les contrôles d'identité **déclenchés** en octobre par le ministre de l'Intérieur ont entraîné une augmentation sensible de la présence policière dans la rue. [...] De nombreuses bavures ont été **signalées** depuis quelques mois.

[...] À Marseille, deux jeunes Maghrébins sont **contrôlés** : ils montrent leurs papiers mais refusent de se laisser fouiller. [...] Autre anecdote : cinq mineurs **interpellés** à Paris en fin de journée ont passé la nuit au poste de police sans que leurs parents soient **alertés**.

Le ministre délégué à la sécurité affirme que tout ceci n'est qu'une campagne politique **dirigée** contre le gouvernement. [...] Certains considèrent qu'une poignée de bavures ont été **montées** en épingle et qu'il leur arrive souvent d'être eux-mêmes **insultés** ou **agressés**. D'autres estiment que leurs collègues sont **poussés** à faire des interpellations et s'en inquiètent.

B Expulsion

Necmettin Erim, his wife and his three children, who did not have valid residence permits, were deported from France last Monday. It is believed that they had been denounced by their landlord. Necmettin Erim arrived in France in 1997 and was refused refugee status which had, however, been granted to his brother on similar grounds.

His request was finally turned down last autumn and on 13 April the authorities signed his deportation order. On that very day, Mrs Erim and her children were arrested at their home in the absence of the head of the family. On his return, he rushed to his lawyer, who refused to hand him over to the police who had come in the meantime to arrest him. It took more than three hours of negotiations to get the authorities to soften their attitude. If Mr Erim agreed to give himself up he would not be handcuffed and would be granted a few hours to sell his possessions.

In this case, as in many others, the law was implemented with all due firmness but the methods used were, to say the least, hasty.

Chapter 22 Reinforcement, p. 140

A (See 22.1–5)
Deux évadés retrouvés

Deux évadés de la prison des Baumettes **ont été retrouvés** dimanche matin dans un village de l'Hérault. Les deux hommes **ont été localisés** grâce à un commerçant qui avait vu leur photo au journal télévisé de vingt heures et a reconnu l'un d'entre eux. Ils **ont été interpellés** alors qu'ils s'apprêtaient à reprendre la route. Ils **n'étaient pas armés** et n'ont opposé aucune résistance.

La camionnette qui avait servi à leur évasion **avait été retrouvée** la veille près de Montélimar. Les deux détenus **avaient été condamnés** pour attaques à main armée, en juin dernier.

B Vos papiers ! (See 22.1–5)

1. Depuis quelques mois, les dispositifs de contrôle des conditions d'entrée et de séjour en France des non ressortissants européens **ont été renforcés**.
2. Plusieurs exemples récents montrent que ces dispositions **sont appliquées** avec la plus grande sévérité.
3. De nombreux ressortissants algériens **ont été refoulés** au cours du mois dernier.
4. Ainsi une vieille dame algérienne, venue rendre visite à ses enfants, **a été rapatriée** de façon expéditive.
5. Dans certaines capitales arabes, ces dispositions **sont** très mal **ressenties**.

C *Thème*

Explosion dans une usine chimique. Une personne a été tuée (22.4–5) et une douzaine légèrement blessées (22.2 note) vendredi soir, à la suite de l'explosion d'un réservoir dans une usine chimique. Trois autres réservoirs ont également été endommagés (22.4–5). Selon la gendarmerie, le nuage de fumée qui s'est dégagé (22.7.3) n'est pas toxique. Une enquête sur les causes de l'accident vient d'être ouverte (22.3–4).

Terrorisme. A la suite de l'attentat [à la bombe] de la semaine dernière à Paris, on (22.6–7) a fait appel à quelque 1 000 soldats pour patrouiller les gares et les aéroports français ; toutes les consignes ont été fermées (22.4–5) et les poubelles supprimées (22.2 note) [*or* ... on a fermé toutes les consignes et supprimé les poubelles]. En outre, on a vivement conseillé (22.6–7) aux directeurs de grandes surfaces de coopérer avec la police pour améliorer les procédures d'évacuation.

Chapter 23 Diagnostic, p. 141

A

1. Nous avons eu quelque **deux mille huit cents** visiteurs cette année.
2. Les ventes ont atteint un chiffre record : **sept millions cinq cent quatre-vingt-dix mille** francs.
3. Le bilan des accidents de la route a été de **trois cent quatre-vingts** morts en juillet.
4. Le nombre des victimes s'élève à **cinquante et un**.
5. Notre club compte **cent cinquante-cinq** membres.
6. Ce jeu-concours a suscité près de **mille** réponses.

B

1. 74 % des moins de 35 ans, **contre** 61 % des plus de 35 ans, déclarent avoir accompli au moins une tâche domestique dans les dernières 24 heures.
2. Le nombre de réfugiés recensés par le Haut Commissariat des Nations unies pour les réfugiés atteint 4 563 600, **dont** 700 000 au Liban.
3. En raison de la grève des contrôleurs aériens, Air France a annulé six vols **sur** les 290 prévus aujourd'hui.
4. A la fin du mois dernier, cette entreprise comptait 3 000 salariés, **soit** 800 de moins que l'an dernier.
5. Le prix du cuivre a augmenté de **quelque** 20 % tandis que le plomb progressait de 17.5 %.

C *Version*

1. The birth rate has dropped on average by 40 % since 1962, from 2.7 children per couple to 1.7.
2. Those over 65 made up less than 5 % of the population in around 1850. Now they constitute nearly 15 %. By 2020, it is thought that they will make up over 20 % and that, among them, those over 85 will number over 2 million.
3. Out of 800,000 people old enough to get married, 600,000 do. 200,000 get

divorced within five years, that is 33 %. 16.6 % of divorcees remarry, 50 % of them choose a single person.

4. The number of couples living together is still rising. The number of illegitimate births rose to over 30 % of all births.

5. According to population experts, the working population (those who have a job and those who are looking for one) is likely to increase by 1.5 million by 2015, reaching a total of 28 million (compared with to 26.5 million today).

6. Whereas before the Second World War, two out of ten French people lived in towns, now eight out of ten do so.

Chapter 23 Reinforcement, p. 146

A Activité professionnelle des femmes dans la région d'Aix

1. Parmi les femmes sans enfants le taux d'activité est **supérieur à** 74 %, mais parmi celles qui ont un ou deux enfants il est **inférieur à** 70 %. (23.10–12)
    or Parmi les femmes sans enfants le taux d'activité est **de plus de** 74 %, mais parmi celles qui ont un ou deux enfants il est **de moins de** 70 %.

2. Quand les femmes ont trois enfants ou plus, leur taux d'activité **tombe à** 38,1 %. (23.18)
    or ... **chute à** 38,1 %.

3. Les femmes **représentaient** 28 % des OS en 1988. (23.24)
    or Les femmes **constituaient** 28 % des OS en 1988.

4. La part des femmes parmi les OS est en **augmentation** (23.21) : 31 % en 1998, **contre** (23.19) 28 % en 1988.
    or ... est **en hausse** : 31 % en 1998, **contre** 28 % en 1988.
    or .... est en **progression** : 31 % en 1998, **contre** 28 % en 1988.

5. Quant à la part des femmes parmi les ouvriers qualifiés, elle **est passée** (23.18) **de** 14 % à 11 % entre 1988 et 1998, soit une **réduction** (23.17) de 3 %.
    or ... elle **est tombée de** 14 % à 11 % entre 1988 et 1998, soit une **diminution de** 3 %.
    or ... elle **a chuté de** 14 % à 11 % entre 1988 et 1998, soit une **baisse de** 3 %.

B

1. L'âge de la retraite **a été abaissé** (23.18) de 65 à 60 ans dans certains pays.

2. Le nombre de touristes qui se rendent en Chine **s'est considérablement accru** (23.16) [*or* ... **a considérablement augmenté**].

3. Selon les estimations, la TVA devrait **augmenter** (23.18 note) de 1 à 2 %.

4. Le pourcentage de réussite **est passé** (23.18) **de** 51 % à 67 % en moins de cinq ans.

5. Depuis longtemps déjà, le taux d'échec **a baissé** (23.17) cette année : 5 % contre 7 % l'an dernier.

C *Thème*

1. De 1975 à 1987, le taux de natalité dans les pays développés a diminué (23.17) [*or* baissé] en moyenne de 28,6 %.

2. En l'an 2020, les moins de 25 ans constitueraient (23.24) 27,5 % de la population active.
   or En 2020, les moins de 25 ans représenteraient 27,5 % [du nombre] des actifs.
3. Aujourd'hui de mille à (23.5, 23.13) quinze cents (23.3) réfugiés par mois arrivent en Europe [*or* arrivent chaque mois en Europe].
4. Sur (23.19) une population salariée de 15,5 millions, seuls quelque (23.8 note) 10 % sont syndiqués.
5. On vient de leur accorder une augmentation de (23.16, 23.21) 5 %.
   or Une augmentation de 5 % vient de leur être accordée.
6. Le nombre des jeunes chômeurs atteindra (23.15) quelque (23.8 note) 900.000 [*or* ... s'élèvera à quelque (23.15) neuf cent mille (23.3–4)].
7. La croissance économique était de 3 à 4 % (23.13) en moyenne par an vers 1995.
8. Le taux d'inflation avait été ramené (23.18) de 4,2 % en 1996 à 3,5 % en 1997, mais en 1998 il est de nouveau passé à (23.18) plus de 4 %.
   or Le taux d'inflation était passé de 4,2 % en 1996 à 3,5 % en 1997, mais en 1998 il était de nouveau à (23.14) plus de 4 %.
   or ... il a de nouveau franchi le seuil des 4 %.
   or ... il a de nouveau passé le cap des 4 %.
9. L'an dernier, le commerce extérieur de la France a enregistré un déficit de 27,3 milliards de (23.6) francs.

Chapter 24 Practice, p. 151

A Voisins ? Connais pas ! (See 24.1–5)

Ce sont les femmes qui voisinent le plus [...]. Et davantage encore dans les régions ensoleillées où **l'on vit** beaucoup plus dehors. **On voisine** bien aussi à la campagne [...].

En ville surtout, **on reste** chez **soi**, en souvenir sans doute d'épouvantables histoires de voisinage comme **on en voyait** autrefois. En partant du principe qu'à l'instar de la famille on subit bien plus **ses** voisins qu'**on ne les choisit, on ne cherche pas** à en faire des amis. [...] Que dire de plus que « bonjour, bonsoir » à une personne que **l'on croise** dans l'ascenseur aussi pressée que **vous** [...] ? Et dans les quartiers aisés, **on ne fréquente pas** les gens auxquels **on n'a pas été** présenté.

Alors **doit-on** se plaindre de cet excès de discrétion que **l'on observe** vis-à-vis de **ses** voisins ? À trop vouloir éviter les problèmes de voisinage, **on se prive** de bien des facilités et des ressources de la solidarité.

B (See 24.6–7)

Les livres pour enfants. Naguère, **il suffisait d'**un unique livre de contes pour exciter l'imagination des enfants. Ce n'est plus le cas aujourd'hui : les enfants lisent de moins en moins et sont, de surcroît, des consommateurs exigeants. Pour les encourager à lire, **il s'agit** donc **de** les motiver. Heureusement pour les parents que nous sommes, le marché du livre pour enfants s'est considérablement élargi et diversifié : bandes dessinées, aventure, mythologie, fantastique, il y en a pour tous les goûts. **Il suffit de** choisir.

KEY TO PRACTICE

L'éducation civique des enfants. Il importe de plus en plus d'apprendre aux jeunes à devenir de bons citoyens. **Il ne suffit pas**, en effet, **de** connaître les règles de la vie collective pour les appliquer. **Il s'agit** aussi **de** comprendre et **d'**admettre leur utilité. Pour cela, il faut prendre conscience que la vie d'une collectivité s'appuie sur des règles qu'il convient de respecter sous peine d'en être exclu.

C Les parents de divorcés (See 24.8–9)

« Je sais bien que **quoi qu'**il arrive, j'aurai du mal à m'habituer à la nouvelle compagne de mon fils », raconte Christian, un père effondré à l'idée de ne pas revoir sa belle-fille. On oublie trop souvent que, lorsqu'un couple se sépare, les parents qui ont établi des liens d'affection avec leur gendre ou leur belle-fille en souffrent. **Quelles que soient** les raisons de la rupture, ils éprouvent un sentiment de frustration, doublé d'un sentiment d'échec. Certains réussissent mieux que d'autres à faire face à la situation mais ils en ressentent tous douloureusement la blessure **quelles que soient** leurs facultés d'adaptation.

D (See 24.11)

Le travail des enfants. D'après certaines études, le nombre d'enfants au travail dans le monde **pourrait** atteindre 200 millions. La grande majorité d'entre eux **se trouveraient** dans le tiers monde, même si le travail clandestin des enfants n'est pas inconnu en Europe. Ils **seraient** pour la plupart âgés de cinq à quatorze ans.

Populations à la dérive. Selon les estimations des associations caritatives, quelque 1,4 millions de personnes **composeraient** la population « en grande difficulté sociale » qui, en dépit de toutes les politiques sociales mises en œuvre, **ne parviendrait pas** à se réinsérer dans la société française. Cette population **recouvrirait**, entre autres, 300 000 jeunes âgés de moins de 25 ans, 250 000 sans domicile fixe et 300 000 chômeurs de longue durée.

Translation
Child labour

According to some studies, the number of working children could be as high as 200 million. The vast majority of them are in the Third World, although illicit child labour is not unheard of in Europe. They are mostly aged between five and fourteen.

Population going downhill

Charities estimate that some 1.4 million people suffer from 'extreme social deprivation' and, despite all of the social policies implemented, fail to become part of French society. These people include 300,000 young people under the age of 25, 250,000 homeless people and 300,000 long-term unemployed.

E (See 24.10)

En général, je cherche des gens qui **sachent** faire preuve d'enthousiasme et **soient** vraiment qualifiés pour prendre des responsabilités. C'est souvent difficile à trouver. La dernière fois que nous **avons passé** une annonce, la première candidature que nous **ayons reçue** s'est avérée la bonne. Mais parfois il faut des mois pour trouver quelqu'un qui **corresponde** au profil recherché.

F *Thème*

1. Quels que soient (24.9) l'âge et les centres d'intérêt de vos enfants, vous devez choisir leurs livres [*or* il faut choisir leurs livres *or* il s'agit de choisir leurs livres] en fonction de la qualité du texte (24.15) et des illustrations.

2. Aujourd'hui [*or* À l'époque actuelle *or* De nos jours], il n'est pas très difficile de trouver des livres qui plaisent [*subjunctive*] (24.10.2) aux jeunes.

3. On se demande pourquoi nombre de gens n'échangent jamais plus de quelques mots avec leurs voisins [*or* On se demande pourquoi beaucoup de gens n'échangent jamais plus de quelques mots avec leur voisin (24.15)] surtout lorsque leur maison (24.15) est attenante.

4. Les parents de divorcés ont souvent beaucoup de mal à accepter le nouveau partenaire (24.15) de leur enfant (24.15 *meaning that they have one child*).
or Les parents de couples divorcés ont souvent beaucoup de peine à accepter le nouveau partenaire (24.15) de leurs enfants (*meaning that they have several children who got divorced*).

5. De tous ceux qui se sont présentés à cet emploi, c'est le seul qui ait (24.10.1) les diplômes requis.

6. Les chômeurs de longue durée se plaignent qu'ils n'ont pas de quoi vivre (24.14).

7. Peut-être les pays occidentaux devraient-ils (24.13) arrêter d'importer des marchandises en provenance des pays où les enfants sont forcés à travailler.
or Peut-être que (24.13) les pays occidentaux devraient stopper les importations en provenance des pays où les enfants sont forcés à travailler.

8. Il a suffi d' (24.6) un seul attentat pour compromettre le processus de paix.
or Un seul attentat a suffi à [*or* pour] compromettre le processus de paix.

9. « Quoi qu'il arrive (24.8), il s'agit de (24.7 note) poursuivre les négociations », a déclaré (24.12) le président.
or « Quoi qu'il arrive, il faut poursuivre les négociations », a déclaré le président.

Revision 22–24, p. 153

A (See 22.1–4)
Télévision : la grille de la rentrée

1. Le film du dimanche soir ne sera pas supprimé.
2. La soirée du mardi sera entièrement consacrée au cinéma.
3. Les grands sujets d'actualité seront abordés deux fois par mois, le jeudi soir, dans une émission à très gros moyens.
4. Le grand show en direct du vendredi soir sera maintenu.
5. Près de 350 millions de francs seront investis dans la production de fictions françaises.

B Les plaisirs de la table : ce qui se fait (See 22.7.2–3)

1. Ce plat se voit souvent au menu des restaurants.
2. C'est un soufflé qui se sert généralement en hors-d'œuvre.
3. Ce dessert se prépare au dernier moment.

4. Les fruits exotiques s'apprécient beaucoup.
5. C'est un vin qui se boit très frais.

C See 24.15

1 La drogue progresse

Face au fléau de la drogue, les polices du monde entier semblent impuissantes. **Leurs techniques sont** de plus en plus sophistiqu**ées** mais souvent inadapt**ées** car les trafiquants, eux aussi, affinent **leurs méthodes. Leur virtuosité** et **leur audace** sont sans limites. La liste des astuces est sans fin : on a trouvé de la drogue jusque dans **l'estomac** de cadavres rapatriés vers **leur pays d'origine**. Une autre technique répandue consiste à acheter une société de location de voitures. Les clients, en réalité des acheteurs de drogue, passent sans difficulté les frontières avec **leur cargaison**. Qui aurait l'idée de vérifier et de démonter **la carrosserie** et **le moteur** de toutes les voitures de location ?

2 Témoignage

Dans un livre intitulé « La Drogue : ses effets, ses dangers », Eric Fantin et Claude Deschamps expliquent, à partir de **leur propre expérience**, les effets des différents types de stupéfiants et **les dangers** qu'ils font courir. Ils parlent **de la vie** que mènent les toxicomanes et montrent **quel rôle peut** jouer **la famille** de ceux qui ont « plongé » dans la drogue et en sont devenus dépendants. Il leur semble essentiel que les parents soient informés des vrais problèmes, et capables de comprendre la logique **du comportement** des drogués. Ils soulignent que bien souvent les parents commencent à s'intéresser à **leur enfant** le jour où ils découvrent qu'**il se drogue**. Or il semble que certains sujets soient plus prédisposés à la drogue que d'autres et que **leurs fréquentations** ne **jouent** pas le rôle déterminant qu'on **leur** attribue d'ordinaire. La prévention, c'est donc aussi **une affaire** de famille.

D *Thème*

1. Quatre-vingt-quatre (23.3) personnes ont été victimes d'inondations, au cours de la semaine dernière, dans le nord-est de l'Inde. Plus de deux millions d' (23.6) habitants de l'État d'Assam ont été sinistrés. Les inondations dues à (22.2 note) de fortes pluies de mousson ont détruit des centaines (23.7) de maisons et dévasté deux cent mille (23.4) hectares de cultures.
2. Dans moins de (23.10) dix ans, la majorité des habitants de la planète vivra dans les villes. Il y a deux siècles à peine, 90 % d'entre eux habitaient la campagne. Dans 30 ans, la population urbaine qui croît au (23.22) rythme de 2,5 % par an, pourrait atteindre cinq milliards (23.6) d'individus [*or* de personnes]. Un citadin sur (23.16) dix vivra dans une « mégacité » de plus de (23.10) dix millions (23.6) d'habitants.
3. Il serait irresponsable d'affirmer que certains individus deviendront toxicomanes quoi qu'il arrive (24.8), quelles que soient (24.9) leurs fréquentations et la législation du pays où [*or* dans lequel] ils vivent. Il est illusoire de croire qu'il suffira de (24.6) punir les jeunes toxicomanes pour les guérir de l'envie d'utiliser des drogues illicites.

4. Dans la lutte contre le trafic de stupéfiants, les banques se sont trouvées obligées (22.7.3) de coopérer avec la police pour rendre le blanchiment de l'argent plus difficile. Aujourd'hui les trafiquants peuvent se voir refuser (22.7.2) certains services qu'ils utilisaient librement, sans qu'on leur demande (22.6–7) quoi que ce soit (24.8), il y a une dizaine d' (23.7) années.

Final practice, p. 155

A Les peines de substitution

Depuis de nombreuses années déjà, les tribunaux s'efforcent de substituer à l'emprisonnement des peines de travail d'utilité publique. **Ainsi** deux jeunes délinquants de Grenoble viennent-ils d'être condamnés à 100 heures de travail pour une tentative de cambriolage.

Ces dispositions ont l'approbation de nombreux magistrats. La majorité d'entre eux considèrent, **en effet**, que condamner un petit voleur à quelques semaines de prison n'a rien de rédempteur. Éviter aux petits délinquants le contact avec l'univers carcéral peut, **par contre**, avoir quelque chose de salutaire, **d'autant plus que** les prisons françaises sont surpeuplées. **Mais** encore faut-il que les prévenus soient consentants **car** la loi précise que l'on peut refuser cette forme de condamnation et « préférer » être privé de sa liberté.

B Les femmes et la dépression

Les statistiques révèlent que les femmes souffrent de dépression deux fois plus souvent que les hommes. Y seraient-elles génétiquement prédisposées ? Non, d'après certains spécialistes.

En examinant les données, ils ont **d'abord** découvert une vérité d'évidence, à savoir **qu'**une femme soigne son mari souffrant à domicile **alors qu'elle** [*or* **tandis qu'**elle] se voit hospitalisée si elle est elle-même atteinte. **De plus** [*or* **En outre**], les femmes font plus souvent appel au médecin et au psychologue que les hommes.

Ils ont **ensuite** analysé le rôle de l'environnement professionnel ou familial. Les conclusions sont frappantes : les femmes seules ne sont pas plus atteintes par la dépression que les hommes. Les femmes mariées, elles, le sont, **tandis que** [*or* **alors que**] les hommes mariés ont des dépressions moins fréquentes que les célibataires. **En outre** [*or* **De plus**], les dépressions sont moins fréquentes chez les épouses qui travaillent que chez les femmes au foyer.

En somme, dans ce domaine comme dans bien d'autres, on aurait tort de négliger les facteurs économiques et sociaux.